Keith Le Vake

Experiential Groups
in Theory and Practice

Experiential Groups
in Theory and Practice

Kjell Erik Rudestam
York University, Toronto

Brooks/Cole Publishing Company

Monterey, California

Brooks/Cole Publishing Company
A Division of Wadsworth, Inc.

Printed in the United States of America

10 9 8 7 6 5 4 3 2 1

Library of Congress Cataloging in Publication Data

Rudestam, Kjell Erik.
  Experiential groups in theory and practice.

  Bibliography: p.
  Includes index.
  1. Small groups. I. Title.
HM133.R82   302.3'4   81-38555
ISBN 0-8185-0470-6   AACR2

Subject Editor: *Claire Verduin*
Manuscript Editor: *Dan Brekke*
Production Editor: *John Bergez*
Interior and Cover Design: *Vicki Van Deventer*
Cover Photo: *Stan Rice*
Illustrations: *Christine Puffer, Brenda Booth, and Kathleen Kusy*
Typesetting: *Instant Type, Monterey, California*

For Edvin and Britt Rudestam

Kjell Rudestam is currently Professor of Psychology at York University in Toronto. Since receiving his Ph.D. in clinical psychology from the University of Oregon in 1969, he has maintained interests in teaching, research, and clinical practice. A practicing psychotherapist and international consultant, Dr. Rudestam is a member of the American Psychological Association and of the American Academy of Psychotherapists. He is a Diplomate in Clinical Psychology of the American Board of Examiners in Professional Psychology.

Dr. Rudestam has published numerous research reports and journal articles in the areas of self-destructive behavior, psychotherapy, and the process of change. A previous book, *Methods of Self-Change*, was published by Brooks/Cole in 1980. Kjell enjoys tennis, skiing, traveling, reading, and spending time with his wife, Jan, and their twin daughters, Monica and Kirsten.

Preface

Like many textbook authors, I set out to write *Experiential Groups in Theory and Practice* because I could never find just the right book for the courses I was teaching. My style in these courses—variously entitled "Psychology of Small Groups," "Small Group Processes," or "Group Psychotherapy"—is to integrate conceptual learning with learning by doing. Thus, I try to provide students with a cognitive understanding of group behavior by exposing them to the theories and techniques of a number of different approaches. At the same time, I typically offer them firsthand experience in being members of a group. What I wanted was a book that would combine both kinds of learning for a large number of contemporary models of group process and therapy.

The title of the resulting text reflects this aim of achieving a mesh of theory with practice. The word "experiential" is used broadly to refer to group models that emphasize the creation of an immediate, live experience for learning and growth. The book begins by addressing issues germane to all such experiential groups—concerns about group membership, leadership, goals, content, process, and ethics. Subsequent chapters introduce specific group models: T-groups and encounter groups, popular approaches such as Gestalt, psychodrama, and transactional analysis, and lesser-known, emerging approaches such as body therapies, theme-centered interaction, dance therapy, art therapy, and behavioral, skill-training groups.

Each of these chapters sets out the fundamental concepts of an approach, discusses its basic techniques with the aid of case examples, and concludes with an evaluation. To give students experience in group membership, Chapter 12 offers detailed descriptions of tested exercises that can be used or adapted to illustrate each of the group methods discussed in the text. Chapter 13 summarizes the individual models and offers some perspectives and comparisons.

Experiential Groups in Theory and Practice is intended for undergraduate or graduate level courses in clinical psychology, social psychology, human development, or education that deal with the study of small groups for counseling or psychotherapy. It should also be appropriate for practitioners who wish to sharpen their professional knowledge and skills—

including psychologists, psychiatric nurses, social workers, clergy, and mental-health paraprofessionals. Finally, the book is for anyone who is curious about what happens when people congregate in small groups to study their relationships with one another and with themselves.

Many people contributed to the preparation of this book. I give special thanks to the hundreds of students and clients who have taught me so much about the phenomenon of groups and about myself. I also thank the following individuals for their expertise and assistance at various points along the way: Noreen Nisker, Honey Rosenbaum, Brenda Gayle, Howard Fromkin, Ruth Cohn, Evelyn Challis, Christine Puffer, Martin Rappeport, Vello Sermat, and Heather White.

A number of reviewers provided thoughtful comments on the manuscript. They include: Robert W. Cash, California State University at Long Beach; Robert K. Conyne, University of Cincinatti; Dennis J. Haubrich, Ryerson Polytechnical Institute; José George Iglesias, Pima Community College; and Marva J. Larrabee, University of South Carolina.

I also appreciate the support of the Brooks/Cole publishing staff—in particular, Claire Verduin's trust in my work and the helpful suggestions of Dan Brekke and John Bergez. I am indebted to my typists, Maxine Wasserman and Dulcis Prendergast, for a job well done and for their patience in enduring my impatience. Finally, I owe a special debt to my wife and best friend, Janice Rubin, for her editing skill and her nurturance in times of stress and panic.

Kjell Erik Rudestam

Contents

13

Summary and Perspectives   294

Experiential Groups
in Theory and Practice

1

The Psychology of Groups

For just as a new friend enriches our spirit, not so much by what he gives us of himself, as by what he causes us to discover in our own selves, something which, if we had never known him, would have lain in us undeveloped . . .

MIGUEL DE UNAMUNO

From the earliest moments in human history people have gathered in groups to carve out the means to their survival and development. Primitive tribes worshipped and celebrated together in dance and ritual; many Greek philosophers used the Socratic method, a group format, to test ideas about the universe and humanity; medieval monks congregated in religious orders to cleanse the soul and follow the path to heaven. These early groups contain the seeds of the modern group movement in psychology. Despite the pervasiveness of such groups throughout history, the connections between them and the deliberate use of group processes to foster personality change in the 20th century have not been made explicit.

An indirect connection between present and past is colorfully illustrated by the infamous Marquis de Sade (1740–1814). When de Sade was incarcerated in the asylum of Charenton, he passed the time writing and directing plays that were performed before the public by his fellow inmates. De Sade's lively and perverse imagination was apparently responsible for some gut-wrenching moments in live theater as the actors/inmates peeled away layers of themselves to share their psyches with the director and the audience. The evidence indicating that de Sade's early experiment in live theater had a therapeutic effect on the prisoners has led writers in the area to cite it as one of the earliest antecedents of contemporary group psychotherapy (Corsini, 1973). However, the systematic application of dramatic techniques to personality exploration and change did not take place until the early 20th century with Jacob Moreno and psychodrama.

A second historical example of the power of the group to have a positive impact on mental health is found in the work of Anton Mesmer in the late 18th century. Mesmer (1734–1815) was an Austrian physician who acquired an international reputation in Paris for curing people suffering from a variety of somatic and psychological conditions. Mesmer believed that an invisible, magnetic fluid in the atmosphere, emanating from the stars, influences our health and that any imbalance in the fluid causes illness. Mesmer maintained that he could correct each imbalance by touching the patient with a magnetic wand and, later, through the healing power of his own hands. He gathered groups of patients around a *baquet*, or wooden tub, filled with water. He would dramatically enter the room, dressed in flowing robes and carrying his magic wand. He touched and stroked individuals as they held on to each other and to iron bars protruding from the tub. The group readily got caught up in the emotional spirit of the event, laughing, crying, even hallucinating and convulsing as they became overpowered by the "magic spell" cast by Mesmer and the "animal magnetism" supposedly generated by the water flowing around the iron rods. The result was that some people literally gave up their symptoms. An international commission of scientists headed by Benjamin Franklin was less gullible. They claimed that patients were being cured of psychological (hysterical) conditions by the power of suggestion and castigated Mesmer as a charlatan. Thus accused, Mesmer faded from the limelight, and the cult he started soon withered. Lost was the powerful truth that people in groups behave according to predictable psychological laws and that the group itself may have healing properties.

It was not until the 19th and 20th centuries that the behavior of individuals in groups and the power of groups to promote change in normal and clinical populations were systematically investigated. The development and use of groups for therapeutic purposes was, to a great extent, a function of timing and need. In the United States the earliest orientation to group therapy has been called "repressive-inspirational" and was dominant in the first 30 years of this century (Appley & Winder, 1973).

The principal practitioner of this approach was Joseph Pratt, an internist in Boston who treated patients suffering from tuberculosis who couldn't afford hospital treatment. In 1905, Pratt, to save time, began to gather the patients in groups of about 20 in their homes to instruct them in basic hygiene and the need for rest, fresh air, and good food. Pratt was a supportive and inspirational teacher who viewed his indigent patients as having a common bond in their disease. His patients kept diaries, testified to their progress, and developed a degree of cohesiveness and mutual concern. Pratt at first viewed the group format as economically advantageous but did not really value the group for its therapeutic potential. It was not until years later, long after his "class method" virtually disappeared, that Pratt became more sophisticated about the therapeutic use of group interaction. By 1930 he became convinced that psychotherapy ultimately consisted of the beneficial influence of one person on another and planned group therapy sessions for people without specific physical problems. In this endeavor Pratt apparently was stimulated by the writings of Joseph Jules Dejerline, a French physician who used persuasion and reeducation to treat neurotics (Mullan & Rosenbaum, 1962). Pratt went on to have a long professional career pioneering in group techniques.

Although Pratt's work is acknowledged today as an important forerunner of group psychotherapy in the United States, at the time his contribution was pushed to the background by the emerging psychoanalytic movement of Sigmund Freud. Freud was interested in groups, but mainly in the sense of studying mass psychology and noting that members of a group tend to follow and identify with strong, powerful leaders. Though Freud was not particularly sympathetic to group psychotherapy, a member of his inner circle, Alfred Adler, tried to adapt the methods of individual therapy to reach large numbers of people (Dreikers, 1959). While the psychoanalytic movement in Europe was individually oriented and quite elitist, Adler developed a commitment to treating working-class people and set up guidance centers that used group concepts to fulfill this interest. By and large, however, the early history of group psychotherapy is regarded as an American phenomenon (Mullan & Rosenbaum, 1962).

A number of Freud's followers developed a psychoanalytic model of group psychotherapy that focused on treating the individual patient within the group. Louis Wender in 1929 and Paul Schilder in 1934 were early group practitioners in the psychoanalytic tradition. Another leading figure in the early psychoanalytic movement, Trigant Burrow, coined the term "group analysis" as early as 1925. After years of individual analytic practice, Burrow became disenchanted with the emphasis psychoanalysis placed on the individual and became more and more convinced that in order to understand people, one must study the social group to which they belong. Once he began working with groups, Burrow lost stature in the psychiatric community. His story is a good example of how creative and original thinking can remain unappreciated if the time and setting are not ripe to receive it.

By World War II there was a shortage of trained therapists and a pragmatic need to treat large numbers of disabled veterans. Thus, the psychiatric climate was more open to experimentation. Among the well-known names who developed psychoanalytically oriented group psychotherapy practices were Samuel Slavson and Alexander Wolf. Slavson combined group work, progressive education, and psychoanalysis into "activity groups" that encouraged children to act out their conflicts and impulses in a group setting. Wolf applied traditional psychoanalytic techniques such as dream interpretation, free association, and the study of early life histories into the group setting. The psychoanalytic group model, however, will not be explored in this book because it is restricted to treating patient populations and demands considerable training in orthodox psychoanalytic theory and technique. As we shall see, experiential groups assume a broader application and different set of goals from those of traditional Freudian group psychotherapy.

Finally, one cannot document the important early contributors to the contemporary group literature without emphasizing the role of Jacob Moreno. Moreno is best known as the originator of psychodrama. His action techniques occupy a central place in the experiential group movement and will be considered in Chapter 5. Moreno was very prolific, and his work spanned several eras in the history of group therapy. He claimed to have used the method as early as 1910 and is generally credited with coining the term "group psychotherapy" in 1932 (Corsini, 1955). Although the term is used today to denote a wide range of approaches, it was intended by Moreno to refer to a method of relocating people in a community into new groups based on personal preference and sociometric evaluations. Moreno also introduced the first professional journal on group therapy in 1931, called *Impromptu*. The name has been changed a few times over the years, culminating in the current *Group Psychotherapy*, a leading journal in the group field. Finally, Moreno also claimed credit for creating the first professional organization of group therapists in 1942.

If the first major impetus to group psychotherapy in the United States was characterized by Pratt's inspirational approach and the second was dominated by the application of Freudian tenets, the third is the humanistic-experiential orientation that began in the 1960s (Appley & Winder, 1973). The name "experiential groups" has been chosen to denote the groups to be discussed in this book. In the experiential group clients are active participants who are encouraged to experience themselves as their own agents of change. Various other labels, such as group therapy, encounter, human relations training, and laboratory training have shades of meaning that will become clearer. Most experiential groups have been hatched in the self-expressive climate of the last two decades. Their focus is predominantly on growth and development rather than sickness and cure. With the exception of T-groups, which are designed exclusively for the normal population, experiential groups do not discriminate very much in the clientele that are being served.

Therapists such as Carl Rogers helped forge a shift in attitudes in a humanistic-experiential direction by reacting strongly against dogmatic psychoanalysis (as well as radical behaviorism) and by sympathizing with an anti-authoritarian counterculture focusing on free expression and self-discovery. Rogers brought his client-centered approach to groups during the experimental period that followed World War II. Client-centered therapy or counseling deals largely with present-centered, situational conflicts rather than unconscious, historical material. The therapist or group leader is nondirective, and permissive and steers attention toward interactions among the group members rather than toward intrapsychic insight as conceptualized by psychoanalysis. Rogers saw the group leader as less of an expert treating a client than as an equal forming a spontaneous I-thou relationship with someone else, unencumbered by the traditional rules and strictures of legitimate therapist behavior. The freeing of therapists to be intuitive and to share their personhood with clients helped usher in the new group approaches (Shaffer & Galinsky, 1974). Rogers' method of working with groups will be highlighted in Chapter 3.

The contribution of Carl Rogers is illustrative of the increased concern for the total involvement of the therapist in the group in the 1950s and 1960s. More "humanistic" approaches to working with groups emphasize the expression of feelings as more important than the use of intellect (see Whitaker & Malone, 1953). In addition, contemporary group practitioners have adapted more traditional learnings to suit current needs, clients, and situations. Today, for instance, body therapy groups draw from the teachings of Wilhelm Reich, theme-centered groups use much of psychoanalytic thinking combined with more humanistic values, and skill-training groups bring behavioristic psychology in contact with the experiential group movement.

Another stream of group work in psychology that group psychotherapists, striving to solve the problems of people with emotional difficulties, have not fully recognized or appreciated is the study of group dynamics by academic psychologists and sociologists. Modern sociology developed in the 19th century as a social science to study the interdependent working and living relationships brought on by increasing industrialization (Cohen & Smith, 1976). Early sociologists such as Emile Durkheim and Georg Simmel focused their observations on group processes rather than on society as a whole. They and subsequent researchers in group dynamics have been interested in formulating the laws of development and functioning that apply to a range of groups, including work groups, recreation groups, and family groups. Triplett (1897) is credited with having performed the first social psychological experiment when he measured how much bicycle riders increased their speed in the presence of other riders. He dubbed this phenomenon "social facilitation." The social facilitation effect is an example of a social psychological principle which may be applied to the understanding of the experiential group. To take a second example, researchers in the 1960s discovered that individuals are more conservative in the decisions they make alone than in the decisions they make following group discussion. This tendency to take greater chances with group-centered decisions has been called the "risky shift" phenomenon.

There is still considerable disagreement regarding the relevance of experimental studies on so-called "normal" groups to group psychotherapy. The practice of group psychotherapy has been derived largely independently from laboratory studies of group function and group dynamics, and we really do not know to what extent the processes that occur within a therapy group parallel the findings of social psychological research. George Bach (1954), a pioneer of the group psychotherapy movement, asserted, largely on the basis of faith and clinical experience, that the development of norms, cohesiveness, and communication patterns that operate in known ways in problem-solving groups have their counterparts in therapy groups. Although some of these extrapolations have more empirical support now, most are still unproven. It is simply more difficult to conduct quality research with actual psychotherapy groups in the field than with college students in the laboratory.

Psychoanalytically-trained practitioners who do individual therapy within a group setting largely dismiss the impact of the group and the relevance of the group dynamics research literature. They insist that a psychotherapy group is not a laboratory problem-solving group. On the other hand, therapists such as S. H. Foulkes, W. W. Bion, and H. Ezriel in Great Britain have maintained that the group has a life of its own and have adopted the findings of experimental studies in group dynamics into their own Freudian framework. In these applications the therapist attends to the group interaction or the development of a group theme rather than the pathology of a given participant. These therapists are important figures in the history of experiential groups, in part because they are among the few European contributors who have had an impact on the current group practice in North America. Bion's work will be examined more closely in Chapter 2.

Group dynamics proponents recognize the central place of Kurt Lewin in the history of experiential groups and accept his "field theory" as a theoretical core. Lewin, a social psychologist, had a greater impact on contemporary small group research than anyone else. Lewin suggested almost four decades ago that it is "usually easier to change individuals formed into a group than to change any one of them separately" (Rosenbaum & Berger, 1975, p. 16). Lewin and his colleagues lent credibility and legitimacy to the study of small-group behavior by behavioral scientists. How this interest accidentally led to the creation of the first T-group is a story to be told in the next chapter.

ADVANTAGES OF GROUPS

Although it is obvious that any single participant receives less personal attention in a group than he or she would in individual therapy, there are a number of reasons for the emergence and success of group therapy. Life is primarily a social event. During work, play, and moments of intimacy, we tend to relate to others or at least to share common experiences. A few years ago David Riesman dubbed an entire generation the "lonely crowd" to signify that, while we often find ourselves in the presence of others, we still may feel cut off, isolated, and alone. The bureaucratic maze of our organizational systems can leave us feeling confused, mistrustful, and powerless. Thus, a deliberately constituted group experience offers an antidote to the problem of alienation by paying specific attention to interpersonal issues in an interpersonal context. The group becomes a microcosm, or miniature society, reflecting the world beyond, adding an ingredient of realism to an artificial interaction. Factors such as peer group pressure, social influence, and conformity, which operate in everyday family, work, and interest groups, become apparent within the experiential group and affect individual attitude and behavior change. As a result, the affective experiences that occur within this learning environment are usually transferable to the outside world.

A second potential advantage of the group setting is the opportunity to receive feedback and support from others who may share a common problem or experience or who may provide helpful input. Through the process of group interaction comes the recognition of the value of and need for others. Within the group the individual feels accepted and accepting, trusted and trusting, cared about and caring, helped and helping. The reactions of others to oneself and of oneself to others within the group can facilitate the resolution of interpersonal conflicts outside the group. Within a supportive and controlled environment, the individual is able to learn new skills, experiment with different styles of relating, and experience "reality testing" with a representative collection of peers. There is a certain safety in being with peers rather than facing a therapist alone. Those who are more hesitant may not feel pressured to reveal themselves immediately. When they do reveal themselves, they feel more comfortable knowing there are others with similar problems and feelings in a supportive environment.

Third, the individual is also a spectator in the group. By observing interactions, group members can identify with others' struggles and use them as a yardstick to measure their own feelings and behaviors. Multiple feedback provides a many-faceted mirror image of the self from which to assess attitudes and behaviors. The introduction of one or more persons to a therapeutic dyad brings problems and stresses not ordinarily present in two-person relationships. These stresses can be advantageous because they highlight the psychological issues of each group member.

Fourth, the group can help facilitate the individual growth process. The individual in the group is placed in the inescapable role of self-exploration and introspection. Often people know what they want but need the sharing and acceptance of a group to ask for it. Each significant self-disclosure or effort to change earns the esteem and respect of others and, consequently, enhances self-confidence.

Finally, there are also economic advantages to the group format. It is generally less expensive for both the therapist/leader and the patient/participant to meet together with six, ten, or more people simultaneously than to see each other alone.

Other advantages of the group format are a function of a specific approach or theory. The flexibility of group therapy, as will be seen in the core of this book, makes it adaptive to a wide range of helping environments and programs and to diverse populations.

THE EXPERIENTIAL GROUP

Experiential groups have been viewed as small, temporary collections of people meeting within a specified time limit, generally using a designated leader, with the general goal of interpersonal inquiry and personal learning, growth, or discovery (Barrett-Lennard, 1975). There is considerable disagreement, however, about what happens in an experiential group. Many would argue that experiential groups are unstructured, here-and-now interactions in which the group members study their own process and share progressively deeper life experiences with one another. This format is certainly common, but some of the groups I will be discussing are very structured (for example, skill-training groups) and some deal with past experiences in addition to here-and-now feelings (for example, psychodrama).

Lakin (1972) has summarized six processes he believes to be common to experiential groups: (1) the facilitation of emotional expressiveness; (2) the generation of feelings of belonging; (3) a commitment to self-disclosure; (4) the sampling of personal behaviors; (5) the making of interpersonal comparisons as sanctioned group behavior; and (6) the sharing of responsibility for leadership and direction with the appointed leader of the group. In our context, these processes are generally applicable with the possible exception of the last one; some experiential groups retain a strong leader who does not democratically share leadership functions with the group members. The experiential group will be considered as a broad concept, reflecting the kinds of groups that are popular today and that were shaped by figures such as Freud, Reich, Moreno, Bion, and Lewin.

Experiential groups may be categorized into four clusters (Cohen & Smith, 1976): groups designed to encourage organizational development or problem solving; groups for learning interpersonal and leadership skills; growth groups; and therapy groups. These four types of groups overlap in practice, so that, for example, many learning groups are also therapeutic in effect. Within each of these clusters, the focus has a broad range: from information- or task-oriented to person- or insight-oriented; from leader-centered to member-centered; from rational thinking to affective spontaneity; from highly structured to unstructured; from short-term to ongoing; from healthy individuals to the severely emotionally ill.

Two of the most critical dimensions relevant to the types of groups described in the following chapters are the extent to which the group leader maintains a dominant role in structuring and directing the group and the extent to which there is a focus on emotional stimulation as opposed to rational thinking. The ten categories of groups presented in the book may be categorized on these dimensions as in Table 1-1. Note that there is considerable diversity with regard to how specific leaders apply the basic concepts and methods of the approach. T-groups and theme-centered groups, in particular, may be either rational or affective in orientation, depending upon the particular task or theme. Encounter groups may be leader- or member-centered, depending upon the particular leader.

SOULS, GOALS, AND ROLES

Souls: The composition of groups

Depending upon the orientation and function of the group, participants range from relatively well adjusted, emotionally stable college stu-

TABLE 1-1.   Categorization of experiential groups according
to executive function and emotional stimulation

	Leader-centered	Member-centered
Rational	Transactional analysis	T-groups
	Skill-training groups	Theme-centered interaction
Affective	Encounter groups	T-groups
	Gestalt groups	Theme-centered interaction
	Body-therapy groups	
	Psychodrama	Encounter groups
	Dance-therapy groups	
	Art-therapy groups	

dents seeking to know themselves better and grow psychologically to persons in need of help to correct incapacitating emotional or behavioral disorders. Many group leaders screen prospective candidates before admitting them into the group. However, research offers little guidance in gauging who is most apt to be a successful group participant. To generalize from individual studies to all group experiences is especially misleading, because the particular leader or therapist and the type of group are crucial determinants of outcome.

One way of assessing who may benefit most is to study early terminators, or drop-outs, from an ongoing group experience. Individuals may drop out of a group for a variety of reasons, including practical considerations such as a geographical move, time conflicts, or a change of interest. More compelling reasons were cited by Yalom (1966) in his study of nine groups in a university outpatient clinic in which 35 of 97 participants terminated prematurely. One reason given by the drop-outs was external stress—that is, a concern for issues outside the group to the extent that the group itself seemed less compelling or relevant. These external concerns were sometimes seen by the investigator as flight in the face of feeling threatened within the group, or as rationalizations used to avoid fears of aggression, self-disclosure, or intimacy. A second reason was group deviancy: the drop-outs' style of interpersonal behavior was antithetical to the behavior of other participants. These participants showed little psychological sophistication, interpersonal sensitivity, or personal insight. A third category included problems of intimacy manifested in withdrawal, inappropriate self-disclosure, or unrealistic expectations. Ironically, people who fear interpersonal intimacy are in great need of a good group experience. A fourth reason was the fear of emotional contagion: some group members were adversely affected by the problems of others in the group, which too easily spilled over into stimulating upsetting issues of their own.

It is tempting to isolate diagnostic categories or personality attributes that correlate with difficulties such as those mentioned above to select suitable group candidates. In fact, research suggests that diagnosis is not so important (Grunebaum, 1975). In most psychotherapies, including group therapy, the healthiest people make the best clients. Those whose defenses are lowest and are most capable of learning from others tend to be the most successful group participants. Practically speaking, a group of motivated persons with average intelligence should be suitable.

Although a group leader might turn away psychotics, acutely depressed individuals, and homicidal sociopaths as unlikely to profit from a shared group experience, behavior is a better prognostic indicator than is diagnostic category. People who are not appropriate for experiential groups include those who under stress of criticism predictably become either too anxious or too angry to hear what others have to say; those who, when stressed, project such strong feelings onto other group members that they feel victimized; and those who have such low self-esteem that they insatiably seek reassurance (Lakin, 1972).

The implementation of these criteria may have to be adjusted depending upon the type and purpose of the group. Furthermore, people who paralyze group interaction over a long period of time, who can't be reached by other group members because of their own chaotic behavior, who act in destructive, antisocial ways and validly frighten other group members, or who are in such constant anxiety that their behavior makes them a persistent burden to the group would not be good candidates (Leopold, 1957). Although most selection criteria are designed to protect the individual, one must also consider what a significantly disturbed person does to the group process. Those who are overly immature, grossly insensitive to others, or unable to control their impulses are impediments to the flow of the group.

The best diagnostic indicator of successful participation in a group is probably actual behavior in early group sessions. In this regard, a skilled group therapist can use this early group information and lead the group accordingly. Finally, Yalom, Houts, Zimerberg, and Rand (1967) reported that a person's eventual popularity in a group is one of the few predictors of a successful group experience. Those who do become popular, it has been found, are curious about relationships and behavior, and are high in personal self-disclosure and activity in the group.

A group should be large enough to allow opportunity for interaction and small enough for everyone to be involved and feel a part. As groups become larger, there is a tendency for the more dominant and verbal to usurp the group's time and the likelihood that subgroups and cliques will form (Hare, 1976). When a group is too small, it ceases to operate as a group, and the participants find themselves involved in individual counseling or psychotherapy within a group setting. Four members are regarded as constituting the barest minimum for a viable group.

Generally, the depth of therapy decreases as the size of the group increases (Geller, 1951). Thus, psychoanalytic group therapy, in which the therapist probes deeply into an individual's psyche, usually insists on relatively small groups, from about six to ten members. The "rule of eight" (Kellerman, 1979) suggests that eight is a good number for a therapy group—small enough to promote intimacy and allow all participants the opportunity to form direct relationships with all others, and large enough to be dynamic and offer a variety of interactive experiences. The length of each session is a relevant factor as well. It has been suggested that a 90-minute session hypothetically allows each member of an eight-person group (plus a leader) an optimal ten minutes of group time (Foulkes & Anthony, 1957).

In contrast to therapy groups, typical growth groups are somewhat larger and have from eight to fifteen members. Longer sessions, of course, allow for a greater number of participants to speak up and meet their individual needs. At the extreme, group inspirational approaches, team-building or group-orientation techniques can be used with more than 50 persons.

Another issue is whether a group ought to be heterogeneous or homogeneous in make-up. When group practitioners talk about similarities and differences among members they generally refer to demographic variables such as age, sex, and education; identified problems, such as symptoms, diagnoses, and complaints; and personality styles and behavior patterns. The blending of these components of membership will inevitably depend upon the purpose and time frame of the group. Groups that will have a short lifetime or that function to give emotional support to disturbed people tend to seek similarities among the members; groups that will meet for a longer time and that engage in interpersonal insight work may benefit from greater heterogeneity.

There is an inherent trade-off in choosing to emphasize similarities or differences among the participants. Similarity usually leads to a high degree of attraction and support; diversity may offer a better possibility of confrontation and change (Levine, 1979). Most experts favor a relatively heterogeneous mix of complaints and interpersonal styles. Whitaker and Lieberman (1964), for instance, stress striving for heterogeneity among participants with regard to conflict areas and styles of coping. Diversity, which occurs when people with different types of personalities and ways of acting are included in the group, leads to tension and confrontation; working through such issues culminates in optimal learning and growth. An individual with an emotional, expressive style, for example, can benefit from relating to others with more rational, restrained approaches, and vice versa. Kellerman (1979) argues that the ideal group needs to encourage the potential expression of the full range of human emotions, including guilt, depression, hope, sexuality, hate, and anger. Further, in order to achieve the ideal underlying emotional structure, Kellerman recommends striving for heterogeneity in terms of the problems expressed by the members and of the functions the people fill within the group.

The most commonly mentioned rationale for heterogeneity is the desire to create a representative model of society within the group. As Bennis and Shepard (1974) put it, "The more heterogeneous the membership, the more accurately does the group become for each member a microcosm of the rest of his interpersonal experience" (p. 128). However, it is important to keep in mind that group members may require considerable time to grapple with the challenge of encountering very different people who may not immediately fulfill their interpersonal needs. Likewise, the cost of heterogeneity may be too dear if it creates a group isolate. The presence of a solitary individual with an extreme personality characteristic may sap the group's energy away from more useful work. Moreover, token mixes of sex, occupation, or race may be worse than no variety at all. One elderly person in a group of college students can easily get tagged as the "old man"; one Black in a White group may become the target for fantasies and projections of the whole group (Lakin, 1972).

A group with a shorter time frame or a fixed focus, such as helping people overcome agoraphobia, may necessitate a more homogeneous membership. The format of the group is a critical factor. A collection of depressives may work in a programmed, structured format but be deadly dull in an unstructured T-group. The main drawback of homogeneous groups is that they can be self-limiting because of their restricted scope: they may not be challenging enough. On the other hand, Yalom (1975) argues in favor of similarity by stressing that homogeneous groups develop an identity more quickly, are more cohesive, offer more support and less conflict, and have better attendance than heterogeneous groups. Yalom cites research indicating that similarly task-oriented individuals can do very well together in human relationship groups (Greening & Coffey, 1966) and that compatibility in interpersonal styles correlates significantly positively with group cohesiveness. Cohesiveness, as we shall see, is an important determinant of group success. Most group leaders agree, for example, that members ought to be reasonably similar in ego strength, the ability to handle stress. Likewise, Levine (1979), who leans toward diversity in personality types, suggests first organizing groups according to common life problems and ages to encourage cohesion. Real homogeneity, however, is almost impossible to achieve in organizing a group, since people who share common problems and coping styles will still develop conflicts over intimacy, authority, and other relevant group issues.

Goals

In psychology, a small group usually refers to a few people getting together with a specific agenda such as wrestling with a problem, trying to feel better, or having a good time (Phillips & Erickson, 1970). Each person has, during the process, the opportunity to develop a relationship with the other people. Each person can take on behaviors that are either helpful or harmful to the achievement of group goals. Depending upon the type of group, members typically decide upon their own specific goals for the group experience.

When the group function is slanted in a problem-solving direction, the task is of paramount importance and the mental health of the individual is less crucial; when the group is a growth group or a therapy group, the welfare of the individual is preeminent. In growth groups, participants may seek joy and self-fulfillment. In psychotherapy groups, goals are generally concerned with increased self-awareness and self-exploration toward the remediation or prevention of serious emotional problems in an effort to provide psychological and behavioral change and direction. Such groups assume that participants are not functioning well in life and seek to overcome disability and suffering. Often, the initial goals of relief from anxiety or depression convert, as the group progresses, to interpersonal goals of wanting to communicate with others, to be more trusting, honest, and loving toward them (Yalom, 1975). Apparently the goal of building increasingly effective interpersonal interactions comes out of developing recognition of our needs as social beings. In a flexible group, individual goals can be modified and changed during the course of the group experience.

Roles and norms

The study of social behavior has been defined by Gordon Allport (1968, p. 5) as "an attempt to understand how the *thoughts, feelings* and *behavior* of an individual are influenced by the *actual, imagined* or *implied* presence of others." We are social beings largely as a result of our various affiliations and interactions with groups of relatives, friends, acquaintances, and strangers. The processes that occur in social groups or family units occur in concentrated form in the artificially constructed group. Members enter an unfamiliar group situation with a leader who may or may not give them assistance. As a result of their unique perceptions and past experiences, they arrive with certain expectations of the group and the role they will play. A *role* is the set of behaviors or functions that are seen as appropriate and acted upon within a social context. The need for role flexibility is illustrated by individuals who are expected to assume a role within the group different from that expected of them outside the group. A manager who has defined herself in terms of her abilities to direct and give orders, for example, may be disconcerted to discover that her ability to take charge is not appreciated in the group situation. Moreover, a person who adopts the role of harmonizer by offering sympathy and reassurance in early stages of the group may have difficulty confronting others as it becomes necessary later on in the life of the group.

Various group roles emerge naturally as the group progresses. Most researchers believe that roles are likely to be similar across groups and develop early in the life of a group (see Bales & Slater, 1955). Others maintain that specific roles lie latent within the group until they are elicited by specific group needs during various phases of the group (Stock & Thelen, 1958). Bogdanoff and Elbaum (1978) have concluded that basic roles evolve to help resolve predictable conflict issues faced by the group. For example, a "basic mistruster" may emerge to help group members cope with the issue of how much to self-disclose and how much to conceal from one another.

There is a long list of stereotypic roles used to describe interpersonal behavior in experiential groups. Many carry colorful names, such as self-righteous moralist, help-rejecting complainer, time keeper, and guardian of democracy. A circumplex (Figure 1-1) helps to organize roles or personality traits by locating them around the circle according to how similar or dissimilar they are from one another.

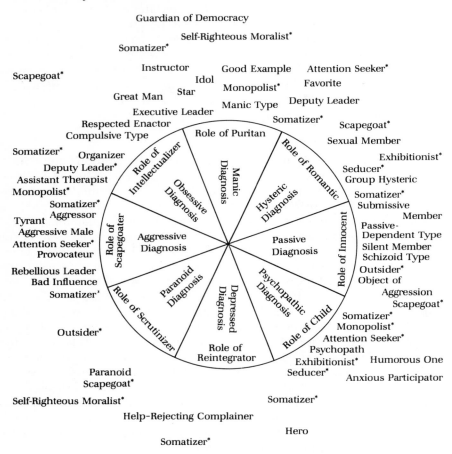

Figure 1-1. A similarity structure of 50 role types sampled from the group therapy literature and listed outside the circle. These are related to the basic role types expressing emotions and diagnostic dispositions, which are listed inside the circle. Role types listed with an asterisk are duplicated at another point on the circle. *(From* Group Psychotherapy and Personality, *by H. Kellerman. Copyright 1979 by Grune & Stratton. Reprinted by permission.)*

Factor analysis has been a favorite tool to reduce a large number of roles or group behaviors into a few primary dimensions. Most common, perhaps, are the two dimensions of anger/love and strength/weakness discerned by Leary (1957). Leary based his findings on the theories of Harry

Stack Sullivan, observations of psychotherapy and discussion groups, and verbal descriptions and inventories that subjects provided of themselves and other people. These descriptions and observations seemed to reflect four kinds of interactive behavior aligned on two bipolar dimensions. One dimension consists of the variable of dominance at one end and the variable of submission at the other end. The other consists of the extreme ends of hostility and affection. Leary constructed a circumplex for describing personality types around these two axes. More recently, Kellerman (1979) has delineated eight basic role types distributed into four pairs of polar opposites: the romantic versus the scrutinizer; the innocent versus the scapegoater; the intellectualizer versus the child; the puritan versus the reintegrator.

One of the most useful systems for understanding member (as well as leader) roles is Robert Bales' (1960, 1970) Interaction Process Analysis, which has been widely applied to both laboratory groups and psychotherapy groups. Observational studies of verbal and nonverbal communication in experiential groups have revealed two categories of functional behaviors that are necessary to the successful survival of the group: *task functions* and *maintenance functions.* Task functions are instrumental, problem-solving processes. They mobilize the group to achieve its defined goals. Task behaviors include giving and receiving suggestions, opinions, or information (Bales, 1970). Maintenance functions deal with the social and emotional climate of the group. They promote interpersonal affiliation and cohesiveness that serve to facilitate the achievement of group goals. Maintenance behaviors include acting friendly or unfriendly, agreeing or disagreeing, dramatizing, and showing tension (Bales, 1970). Bales' interaction categories for conducting a process analysis of a group by describing *how* members communicate are summarized in Figure 1-2. Note that Bales' categories were derived by observing groups of normal individuals and classifying their interactions act by act, whereas Leary's model originated in part from self-reports by psychiatric patients interacting with one another.

When members engage in particular task or maintenance roles, their behavior can either facilitate or retard group progress. For instance, excessive dependency is a negative task behavior putting a great deal of power in the hands of a few members and often breeding resentment in others. A dependent group member might continually seek advice from the leader or other members instead of stating his or her own position. Excessive tension is a negative maintenance behavior leading to communication difficulties and irrelevant chatter. Within the flow of the group, task and maintenance variables continuously interact. Task decisions will affect members' impressions and feelings about one another; feelings of jealousy or the need to control can block progress on the simplest tasks.

An effective group needs a balance of positive task and maintenance behaviors. When the group is working hard on a task, someone may engage in maintenance behavior to reduce the level of tension; when the group is

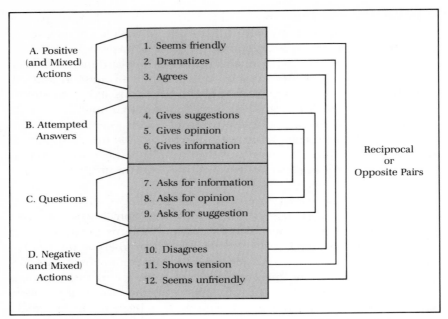

Figure 1–2. Categories for interaction process analysis. *(From* Personality and Interpersonal Behavior *by Robert Freed Bales. Copyright 1970 by Holt, Rinehart and Winston, Inc. Reprinted by permission of Holt, Rinehart and Winston.)*

complacently having a good time, someone else may move to orient the members toward the task. The more flexible members can be in their roles, the more successful the group will be in reaching its ultimate goal.

Typically, some group members will play important task roles while others take charge of keeping interpersonal relationships harmonious. Social/emotional leaders usually end up being the most-liked members of the group. In most experiential groups, of course, the primary focus is social/emotional, so that attention to feelings and attitudes is by definition task-oriented. Table 1-2 describes a number of task and maintenance roles observable in a group over time. These descriptions, adapted from the early days of T-groups (Benne & Sheats, 1948), can be used to help determine which group functions are being adequately performed and which are being overlooked or inadequately performed.

The flexibility of role behavior will depend upon the group norms. A norm has been defined as "an idea in the minds of the members of a group, an idea that can be put in the form of a statement specifying what the members or other people should do, ought to do, are expected to do, under given circumstances" (Homans, 1950, p. 123). Thus, norms are unwritten rules of behavior that guide member actions and that carry sanctions, in the form of group criticism or rejection, for violation. A sterling example of norms in small groups comes from Sherif and Sherif's (1964) work with adolescent gangs in the southwestern United States. The gangs held pow-

TABLE 1–2.   Task and maintenance roles

Group task roles	Group maintenance roles
The initiator-contributor: Suggests new ideas or a changed way of viewing the group problem or goal. Suggests ways of handling difficulties and tasks.	*The encourager:* Reinforces and supports the contributions of others. Shows understanding of others' ideas and opinions.
The elaborator: Elaborates and develops more fully the ideas or suggestions initiated by other members.	*The harmonizer:* Mediates the differences between members and diverse points of view. Relieves tension during conflicts.
The coordinator: Pulls together ideas and suggestions or tries to coordinate the activities of various group members.	*The compromiser:* Yields somewhat on his or her own views to accommodate the opinions of others and maintain group harmony.
The orienter: Points the group in the direction of its goals by summarizing what has taken place and identifying departures from the agenda.	*The gate-keeper and expediter:* Keeps lines of communication open by encouraging or facilitating the participation of others or regulating the flow of communication.
The evaluator-critic: Looks critically at group accomplishments and the suggestions of the members by comparing them to some standard of task functioning.	*The standard setter:* Expresses or applies standards for the group in regard to evaluating the quality of the group process.
The energizer: Pushes and stimulates the group to take action, make decisions, or do more.	*The follower:* Passively goes along with the ideas of the group. Serves as an audience in group discussion and decision making.

Adapted from Benne & Sheats, 1948.

erful shared expectations that members should never criticize another's performance during competitions and that it was okay to foul if one could get away with it during competitions but that it was not okay to foul during practice with other gang members, unless the violator was the gang leader.

Norms, of course, exist in any group. Sometimes the official rules and the informal group norms are discrepant. A problem-solving group, for example, may have an explicit expectation for cooperating in the sharing of ideas, yet operate with considerable backstabbing and competition. Norms help people to resolve questions such as whether and how to express feelings, how involved to become with one another, or whether to respond to someone on the basis of personal qualities or role status. In task groups the entire group can be severely disrupted by members not acting according to the norms. Picture, for instance, a person selling insurance in church.

Each experiential group establishes its own explicit and implicit norms. Typically, the encouragement of emotional expressiveness, warmth, and openness become standards. Norms of behavior should be consistent with the aims of the group. Paramount in importance is that norms for therapeutic communication be established. In most experiential groups, this means that high levels of self-disclosure, the expression of conflict and affection, and the acceptance of one's own feelings are group norms. This includes honest feedback about other members' behavior. The precise style or mode for offering and receiving this feedback may vary, so that in some groups the norms stipulate that suggestions be positive and gentle, while others support raw confrontation. Norms can also change with the life of the group. For example, high disclosure in the beginning may be discomforting to members who are just beginning to feel a part of the group, but as the group progresses, the same behavior may become second nature.

The establishment of helpful communication norms is often hindered by personal needs or concerns. The hidden goals and defenses of participants to protect themselves from anxiety, embarrassment, or potential abuse may run counter to the group's goals. Most group members care about their own images and take on certain role behaviors to insure that this image is preserved. Concern with being accepted as a member of the group may affect one's willingness to take intellectual and emotional risks. The facilitative goals of the group, when successfully implemented and maintained, act in large measure as a basis for furthering effective communication norms.

In experiential groups, it is expected that all members will at some point take on blocking roles that hinder the individual's and the group's progress. This is behavior that perpetuates the individual's hidden goals and maintains the defense and protection of the self either through resistance or manipulation. Such behavior includes withdrawing from the group, criticizing others, interrupting conversations, seeking personal recognition, or interjecting irrelevant ideas. The successful group teaches members to become aware of their blocking behaviors and enlarge their role repertoire. The group attempts to pull the blocked participant out of this nonproductive, static role by using and encouraging more group-oriented behaviors. In interaction-oriented groups, a leader may allow members to use their own caring abilities and instrumental roles to help the problem client.

Even if a leader advises against it, special friendships or subgroups often develop within the group. When these subgroups help attain the goals of the group as a whole, they may be helpful. Two inhibited people may encourage each other by their sensitivity to each other and can, initially, protect each other against pressure to behave in ways they are not yet ready to accept.

Friendships usually develop among people who share common values or experiences. These subgroups may appear more gratifying than the group to the clique and arm them with a sense of security or superiority. Those with a great need for intimacy, dependency, or dominance may be unable to perform their preferred roles with the whole group but be successful within the subgroup. These friendships, when continued outside the group, can inhibit intragroup communication because of mixed loyalties and the hesitancy to betray private knowledge. In the group, the allies tend to agree with each other, send knowing glances in each other's direction, and rally to one another's defense. The honest expression of feelings is stifled, the norms of therapeutic communication are thwarted, and the process toward growth or change is resisted. Those not included in the subgroup feel part of an "out" group, and the cohesive atmosphere of the membership is undermined.

Conformity to norms is not inevitable in groups, but is tied to certain other group variables. For instance, conformity to group norms has been found to relate to status. Low-status members tend to have low conformity rates and medium-status members tend to have high conformity rates. High-status members tend to conform to group norms as they establish a leadership position and then, once granted leadership status, may deviate on less important norms without receiving negative feedback (Crosbie, 1975). In other words, participants who are highly regarded in a group earn a certain "idiosyncrasy credit," which enables them to act independently of minor group norms. Of course, some conformity to norms is necessary to maintain order in the group and achieve group goals, since norms serve as guidelines for group interaction. Thus, some groups deliberately build in ways to reward conformity and punish deviance. The structure of the group will also affect a member's loyalty to group norms. For instance, there is more conformity to norms when groups are relatively homogeneous (Crosbie, 1975) than when their composition is heterogeneous.

Members of cohesive, harmonious groups are most apt to have internalized the group's norms. Kurt Lewin (1947) defined cohesion as "the total field of forces which act on members to remain in the group" (p. 30). Cohesion is the key concept of Lewin's group dynamics theory. Basically, the more effective a group is in meeting needs that attract people, the more cohesive it will be. The more cohesive a group is, the more group control there is over the attitudes and actions of its members, the more conformity and commitment to group norms, and the greater acceptance of group values. When a group is cohesive, there is an atmosphere of acceptance, support, and a sense of belonging. Cohesiveness binds members emotionally to the common task and to one another, assures greater stability of the group even in frustrating circumstances, and helps the group develop a shared frame of reference allowing for more tolerance for diverse individual aims (Lakin & Costanzo, 1975).

Certain findings from social psychological research have implications for cohesiveness and experiential groups. In highly cohesive groups, for instance, members communicate more with one another (Shaw, 1976) than in less cohesive groups. They are more open to influence from one another, are more accepting of hostility in the group, place a greater value on the group's goals, are more active in discussion, are less susceptible to disruption if a member leaves the group, remain in the group longer, and experience a greater reduction in anxiety (Goldstein, Heller, & Sechrest, 1966).

No research directly validates the consequences of cohesiveness in psychotherapy groups, but reports from clients and leaders as well as from laboratory work on groups indicate that within such an environment, the mechanism of cohesiveness works like an "adaptive spiral" (Yalom, 1975). By adhering to the norms of a cohesive group, members become more popular, and this helps raise their self-esteem. They are encouraged to use social skills that will further aid them in dealing with interpersonal relationships inside and outside the group. Because they feel pressured to adhere to the norms and are influenced by other members, they listen more attentively, express themselves more openly, explore themselves more deeply, and continue to do so because of reinforcement received in the form of valued peer acceptance. Cohesiveness seems to permit greater expression of hostility and conflict as well. When group members are more attracted to and accepting of one another, they are willing to bear the discomfort of negative emotions and are able to work their conflicts through to a more therapeutic end. The more attracted members are to the group, the more regularly they will attend meetings, the higher the chances they will remain in the group, and the greater their chances for a successful outcome. Since the most unique feature of therapy in a group is the presence and influence of peers, it makes a difference how involved and cohesive these relationships are.

On the negative side, in an overly cohesive group there may be a reluctance among members to think critically and make high-quality decisions. The tightly knit, friendly qualities of the group may induce a naive, overoptimistic decision-making climate, a phenomenon that Janis (1972) has labeled "groupthink." Janis believes that groupthink can have devastating effects in problem-solving groups because of the tendency for members to quickly converge on a solution and blithely agree with one another despite the possibly misguided quality of the decision.

Despite these reservations, cohesiveness is generally desirable. How can it be increased? One suggestion for increasing the attractiveness of a group to a potential member is to describe positively what can be anticipated from the experience (Goldstein et al., 1966). Members entering a therapy group with fearful and ambivalent feelings can be helped by a preparation interview in which they learn whether their motivations and expectations are congruent with the realities of the group process outlined by the leader. One approach is to provide a clear description of what "good" participant behaviors are prior to meeting with the group (Bednar, Melnick, & Kaul, 1974). This establishes group norms and behavior patterns early; once established, they are not easily changed (Yalom, 1975). Moreover, getting off to a good start is important, because most drop-outs from group therapy occur in the first few sessions.

Tasks that demand interdependent linking and cooperation among all members also help to build cohesiveness and overcome competitive and splintering subgrouping (Goldstein et al., 1966). In a classic social psychological field study, Sherif and Sherif (1953) acted as counselors to 11- and 12-year-old boys in summer camp. Competitive games such as football and tug-of-war and the natural flow of events resulted in separate subgroups of boys with considerable antagonism, bickering, and name-calling among them. Thereafter, the counselors/experimenters contrived a number of events in the boys' camp life to try to foster a cooperative climate. They arranged a breakdown in the camp's water supply; they planned to show a movie with a large rental fee; they arranged for a truck that was to pick up the boys from a hike to break down. In each case it was necessary for the boys to work together to overcome their dilemma. To deal with the broken truck, "the boys got a rope—the same rope they had used in their acrimonious tug-of-war—and all pulled together to start the truck" (p. 137). The experimenters' manipulations were, over time, effective in increasing group cohesiveness. Shared tasks and regrouping strategies may push an experiential group toward its goals as well.

LEADERSHIP

The term "leader" implies that one person is in charge of the group and has been given authority to exert influence within it (Johnson & Johnson, 1975). Particularly in therapy groups, the leader is presumed to have qualifications, training, and experience above and beyond those of the other members. A designated leader is tremendously influential in the group. How tightly or loosely the reins of leadership are held can vary greatly across groups, but leaders rarely let go of their grip completely. While striving for each member's individual responsibility and autonomy, leaders have a professional commitment to guarantee the members' personal well-being. As with all role relationships, leadership behavior is interactional in that the influence exerted is dependent upon the members' willingness or ability to accept or follow that influence (Newcomb, Turner, & Converse, 1965).

In any effective interactional group, the designated leader is not the only person to engage in leadership behavior. Other participants can lead whenever they influence another in aiding the group's goals or a member's personal goals. When leaders emerge from among a group's participants, members surrender some of their personal autonomy and decision-making prerogative to allow others to make decisions for them.

Some types of groups are self-directed or leaderless from the start. Alcoholics Anonymous is an example of a leaderless group based on a strong, ritualized tradition. Many encounter groups have been instituted without the physical presence of a leader, sometimes substituting taped exercises and instructions (Berzon & Solomon, 1966).

In most groups that do not begin with a designated leader, one or more leaders emerge as the group progresses. Those who assume leadership are determined by the role needs of the group, their individual attributes, and the members' perception of them as filling the group's role requirements. Leaders tend to be those who participate more than other members of the group. First impressions of them and their ability to contribute to the group are important determinants of their rise to power.

No single personality trait seems to guarantee a good leader, though enthusiasm, dominance, self-confidence, and intelligence are frequently mentioned characteristics. Slavson (1962), a Freudian group psychotherapist, suggests the personal qualities of poise, judgment, maturity, ego strength, freedom from excessive anxiety, perceptiveness, intuition, empathy, imaginativeness, ability to avoid self-preoccupation, desire to help people, and tolerance of frustration and ambiguity. Certainly a personal awareness of one's own conflict areas, needs, motives, and values seems essential. The Rogerian conditions of genuineness, empathy, and warmth, to be discussed later, are also mentioned frequently. Hare (1976) suggests that leaders have the same variety of traits that other group members do, but they usually rate higher on traits regarded as positive.

Group leaders may be influenced through training in a particular psychological theory. Training programs deliberately and unconsciously mold leaders according to certain theoretical and philosophical biases. Conversely, the personality of leaders may also influence their choice of theory, so that they select one that most approximates their individual attitudes about human nature and views about responsibility.

The classic studies of leadership styles in small groups were conducted by Lewin, Lippitt, and White (1939). They identified authoritarian, democratic, and laissez faire leadership styles and linked them with group task productivity and member satisfaction with group experiences. When leaders are authoritarian, they determine and direct group policy; with a democratic leader, group policy is arrived at through group discussion; a laissez faire leader yields all power to group members and participates minimally. (These distinctions are further clarified in Table 1-3.) Studies have consistently shown that democratic leaders are favored over authoritarian leaders, who may bully and dominate the group, and laissez faire leaders, who offer no structure or limits. Democratic leadership (together with authoritarian leadership) is also associated with the highest task achievement in working groups (Nixon, 1979). Leadership in therapy groups may also be viewed on a continuum from laissez faire, member-centered, and unstructured to autocratic, leader-centered, and highly structured. A leader-centered orientation usually goes hand-in-hand with a more structured group approach.

Underlying leadership styles is a set of assumptions about human nature. McGregor (1960) has postulated Theory X and Theory Y. Theory X regards humans as having little self-motivation and a desire to avoid responsibility. Theory Y assumes that people control and direct themselves toward achieving their valued objectives creatively and responsibly. (Interestingly, these same distinctions turn up in contexts as diverse as politics, law, and group dynamics.) In a highly structured, very leader-centered group, members are viewed as incapable of helping themselves, so that the leader directs and runs the group and controls its interactions.

How much a leader should participate is a focal conflict in group psychotherapy today. Bach (1954) maintains that the structured approach enhances early cooperation, decreases the leader's and the members'

TABLE 1–3.   Primary leadership styles

Authoritarian	Democratic	Laissez faire
All policies are determined by the leader.	Policies are determined by group discussion and decision, assisted by the leader.	Complete freedom of individual or group decision, with minimal leader participation.
Each step in an activity is dictated by the leader one at a time.	General steps toward a group goal are outlined during the discussion. Two or more alternative procedures are often suggested by the leader.	Materials are supplied by the leader while information is offered only when requested.
Individual work tasks and work companions are dictated by the leader.	Task division and choice of work companions are left up to the group.	No participation by the leader.
"Personal" praise and criticism of individual members are offered by the leader who remains aloof from group participation other than to demonstrate.	"Objective" praise and criticism are offered by the leader, who attempts to be a regular group member without doing too much of the work.	Member activities are rarely commented upon by the leader, who does not attempt to appraise or regulate the course of events.

Adapted from Verba, 1972, pp. 208–209.

anxiety and resistance, and concretizes the group's expectations so that they can concentrate on individual personal problems and group goals. Social psychological research suggests that in the early stages of a group, clients will be more attracted to a leader-centered therapist orientation than they will be to less leader-centered groups (Goldstein et al., 1966). Structured groups with directive leadership styles will be seen in several of the following chapters.

Gibb (1961) counters that once a leader-centered atmosphere is established, the leader must exert a high degree of control to contain the members, who incorporate an underlying resistance and sense of mistrust into the group. The risk is that these types of groups will become dependent upon their leaders, granting them total responsibility for activation. Thus, each member's autonomy needs can be met only to the extent that leaders are able and willing to expand their knowledge and skills to include them. Lakin and Costanzo (1975) stress that it is important for leaders to frustrate the dependency wishes of their groups and communicate confidence in their ability to regulate themselves. When people are viewed as capable and resourceful, leaders trust group members to do what is best for their own growth. This point of view suggests that members learn, through the distress and anxiety of an unstructured situation, the need for and the nature of positive structure. They learn the meaning of responsible freedom to act constructively on their own behalf. When successful, as in a good, unstructured T-group, there develops a positive therapeutic milieu with high morale and strong cohesiveness.

However, a leader's abdication of guidance may lead a group to mistake freedom for license. More dominant members may use strong-arm tactics, while more timid members may withdraw and stop participating. With the lack of clear expectations, members may become anxious or confused and lose a sense of direction. In this kind of freewheeling atmosphere, a leader's failure to facilitate group development can perpetuate unproductive personal distortions and fears and lay the foundation for psychological damage (Bednar, Melnick, & Kaul, 1974).

Most group leaders are somewhere in the middle of the authoritarian/ laissez faire continuum. Moreover, the ideological schools to which group leaders belong may have little bearing on their style and behavior in the group. In a study comparing several group approaches on a large scale, Lieberman, Yalom, and Miles (1973) found that both leader-controlled, highly structured groups *and* very unstructured groups were minimally effective in terms of measured outcome. The structure issue is really what kind of structuring, and how much, to provide—not *whether* to provide structure. Properly timed, structured intervention clarifies group processes, moves the group into the here-and-now, and creates a therapeutic, cohesive group atmosphere (Yalom, 1975). The challenge for the leader becomes one of providing a safe, productive atmosphere in which independence and autonomy can be promoted, while recognizing that group processes are developmental and need time to mature. Hopefully, a responsible leader, in developing a personal style, will use techniques thoughtfully and with regard to a consistent theoretical framework rather than act as a carefree social director.

The approach used by individual leaders may be subtly influenced by their personal needs. For example, a leader who can tolerate ambiguity and has the strength to risk initial member dissatisfaction and negative feedback may be comfortable with an unstructured, laissez faire group style.

Flexible, effective group leaders will recognize that they may have to vary their leadership style on the continuum in accord with situational factors or group needs. Directive leadership may be more necessary when the task itself is highly structured (Shaw & Blum, 1966), when members are under severe stress (Rosenbaum & Rosenbaum, 1971), or when the dynamics of the group are too opaque and intense for the involved members to fully and accurately perceive what's going on (Lakin & Costanzo, 1975). Basically, the more effective the behavior of the members, the less active the leader. Leaders must evaluate the group's composition, knowledge, and skills; the time available; the urgency of the task; and their own responsibility according to the needs of the particular situation. Leaders must also be sensitive to changing situations during the life of a group. Structured exercises, for instance, may have a real place in workshops or classrooms to speed the group past initial hesitations and traditionally socialized behavior so that members may experience as much as possible the developmental sequence of the small group in the limited time available (Yalom, 1975).

What are the functions of leadership? Four ongoing roles that leaders typically play in experiential groups are the expert, the catalyst, the orchestrator, and the model/participant.

The role of resident *expert* is probably the most traditional function of the therapist. In almost every group interaction, at virtually every moment, there are opportunities for the leader to comment on one of many simultaneously occurring processes on an individual, interactional, or group level. The leader's function in clarifying the relationship implications of interactional transactions (called "process") can range from comments upon single behavioral acts to observations about several acts and their consequences over a period of time, to more complex speculation about intentions and motivations, and inferences about patterns of similarity between here-and-now behaviors and those occurring in the outside world of the participants (Yalom, 1975). These comments help members understand what their behavior is like, how it affects others, and ultimately how it influences their opinions of themselves and their present circumstances. If the leader overindulges in conveying information, answering questions, and playing the expert, however, the group comes to resemble a classroom. Timing and restraint are important considerations in this context.

As *catalysts*, group leaders help make things happen by their presence. They stimulate the group to take action and channel the group's attention to the ongoing feelings and concerns of the members. As Fiebert (1968) puts it, the catalyst "holds up a mirror to the group so that they can view their behavior, chides members for their superficiality, and urges them towards bonds of intimacy" (p. 835). As catalysts, leaders use their skills to help members observe and understand what has happened in the group. Interpersonal skills such as acting in genuine, warm, and empathic ways, giving helpful feedback, and demonstrating the ability to focus immediately on what is happening in a situation are needed. The leader tries to release the group's and the individual's therapeutic potential as agents for change.

The group leader is also an *orchestrator* of group behavior (Fiebert, 1968). In this role, a leader attempts to facilitate the transmission of issues, feelings, and information among members and help the group solve problems and meet goals. When a group fails to deal effectively with a difficult situation, the leader may intervene to turn the group in a therapeutic direction. Orchestration skills include preventing inappropriate behavior by members, defining the boundaries of acceptable behavior, supporting members in appropriate but awkward attempts at exploring problems and sharing ideas and feelings, protecting members from unwarranted and harmful group behavior, and equalizing the contributions of members to the group interaction (Trotzer, 1977). Without any cues from the leader, the group situation may remain quite ambiguous and the level of anxiety high. Since a moderate amount of anxiety seems to be helpful for learning (Shapiro, 1978), the leader can orchestrate the anxiety gradient in the group by providing or withholding structure and support and by using specific techniques and interventions to point out individual behavior or to confront members.

Fourth, the group leader acts as a *model/participant* (Shapiro, 1978). Depending upon the group format, group leaders mark a fine line between being a member of the group and being an outsider. Their active participation and sharing can help members feel they are respected and cared about. In their conspicuous position, leaders cannot help but have their behavior modeled by group members. In some groups the modeling is deliberate, as in demonstrating how to deal with a passive-aggressive acquaintance, but in most experiential groups leaders do not deliberately act as ideal or exemplary group members. On the contrary, when their interventions or self-disclosures are most spontaneous and authentic, they can represent a high level of interpersonal functioning for members to observe and learn from vicariously. Particularly in unstructured groups, participants will often follow the leader's cues to reduce their own anxiety. A leader's abilities to be clear, open, caring, and effective are conveyed as skills.

By disclosing too much, though, the leader risks setting artificial standards for group members that they cannot easily live up to. In many kinds of group psychotherapy, intimate self-disclosures by the leader are prohibited because they interfere with the therapeutic process of transference, to be discussed in Chapter 9. At the same time, it is often important for leaders to disclose their motives for intervention and to share their feelings if such feelings interfere with their ability to function effectively in the group.

To be a group leader in a growth or therapy group is to be part artist and part scientist, blending feeling and intuition with the knowledge of procedures and concepts. Feelings and intuition can be a good source of information, but they are often susceptible to personal bias and distortion. With greater self-awareness and greater experience with and knowledge of group and individual dynamics comes the increased likelihood that one's intuitions will be correct. A conceptual framework, a way of making sense of the disparate pieces of behavior one observes, can guide a leader to verify feelings and hunches. However, a conceptual framework and its methods used without regard for intuition and feelings can result in a rigid, inflexible style. Effective group leadership involves timing, choice, and a wide range of creative skills.

GROUP PROCESS

The reasons group members actually improve are not presently understood with any degree of certainty. Some suggestions have already been noted regarding qualities of successful participants, the composition of the group, the type of leadership, and the multidetermined aspects of personality. There are also certain factors within the group experience that aid in fulfilling the goals of therapy or change. Virtually all groups seek to recreate clients' emotional conflicts in the group setting and to increase the accessibility of new experience (Parloff, 1970). Leaders introduce procedures that they believe will be helpful in this pursuit, and their way of doing so will depend upon their theoretical orientation. Thus, in encounter groups the leader is apt to use a host of verbal and nonverbal exercises on the path to increasing interpersonal sensitivity and relating skills. Psychotherapy groups may use some of the same experiential techniques, but go further toward relieving members' discomfort and helping them function more effectively. While the content of sessions may vary from group to group, there is considerable similarity in the process.

One of the most intriguing ways of conceptualizing the group process comes from Kelman (1963), who views therapy as a "social influence situation." Within this framework, three processes stand out as critical to every experiential group: *compliance, identification,* and *internalization.* First, group members are compliant in accepting the influence of the leader and other group members and joining in the therapeutic work. Second, group members identify with each other and the group leader. Identification occurs as the members strive to maintain desired relationships within the group. Third, members internalize group lessons. Internalization is accomplished through "corrective emotional experiences," which result from working with and resolving feeling-drenched issues within the group.

In a successful group, the changes induced will generalize to the outside environment. Kelman holds that in order for changes to generalize, simple compliance to group rules and norms is insufficient: internalization of what has been learned is necessary. Moreover, group members must actually experiment with new actions (compliance), adopt the leader's or group's vantage point for viewing themselves and their relationships (identification), and generalize therapeutic insights to specific real-life situations (internalization). In these latter stages the therapist serves as a role model, norm setter, and guide, while the group members support the process and constitute a representative microcosm of society.

The experiential group moves consistently through certain stages of development as members struggle to meet individual and group goals. Several researchers have presented their own versions of this developmental sequence. Most incorporate a group process that begins with dependency and testing behaviors and moves through periods of intragroup conflict toward cohesiveness and effective problem solving (Tuckman, 1965). One prominent and representative description of this process derives from William Schutz' (1958) FIRO (Fundamental Interpersonal Relations Orientation) theory of interpersonal behavior. In the early stages of the group, members reflect a need for *inclusion,* a need to belong in the group and relate satisfactorily to other participants. Later on the need for *control* emerges, when feelings of competitiveness and power surface and members vie for leadership and dominance. Finally, in the mature stages of the group members have become more emotionally involved with one another, and issues of attraction, pairing, and intimacy emerge. At this point the individual's need for *affection* predominates.

In most experiential groups members learn that, although the leaders are present to give guidance and direction and to function as a resource, they cannot be relied upon to do their work for them. Thus, group participants have to work out ways to relate to authority figures and other group members. Some members learn to be very dependent upon the leader and on emerging group leaders. Others, at the opposite extreme, handle their dependence through "counterdependent" behavior such as direct challenges and rebellions. Some "overpersonal" members readily sacrifice their own identity by moving toward their peers and merging their interests with those of others, while more "counterpersonal" members have a difficult time with intimacy and are cautious about yielding their individuality by joining with others.

Bennis and Shepard (1974) have elaborated on the progress of the experiential group in terms of the way group development is influenced by the internal uncertainty experienced by the participants. At the earliest stage members tend to be anxious and try to define the rules of the group in order to feel more secure. Members may test leaders' power, seek their approval, or look to them for cues regarding how to behave. Insecurity and dependency are especially evident in unstructured groups, where the leader does not provide a clear definition of goals and norms. The group may soon become more unpleasant and stressful as individuals disagree about procedure, structure, and, perhaps, the need for leadership. This phase may be resolved by assumption of leadership by members who are least conflicted in their authority relations. Those having fewer difficulties with dependency issues are most responsible for positive group movement, since only they have the objectivity to create some harmony from the group's fragmentation and to push for shared responsibility in the group.

Shortly thereafter a period of enchantment develops that may give the group a party-like atmosphere. The joviality covers the reality that legitimate problems and disagreements have not been adequately resolved. At this stage the intimacy needs of members are most important. Some members push for greater closeness to achieve understanding and meet group goals, while others pull back from such interpersonal commitment. The group has divided into subgroups again, but this time on the issue of interdependence.

Those with the least conflict on the overpersonal/counterpersonal dimension are best suited to help the group resolve this fresh dilemma. Groups that transcend this final stage are those in which members are close but can accept one another's differences, in which relationships are meaningful but not overwhelming, and in which conflicts are settled and agreements made on substantive, rational grounds. The group has become a mature social system.

Groups will vary in how they move through their life cycles, and there is no reason to believe that members are actually aware of an underlying order to the group's progression. Members inevitably realize, however, that communication processes and personality variables cannot be avoided as they strive cooperatively to meet their goals. Throughout the cycle the individual member is concerned with issues of identity, power and influence, goals and needs, and acceptance and intimacy. The success of the group experience will depend upon the ability of members to meet the challenge of these issues.

By way of summary, Yalom (1975) has isolated ten curative factors that are representative of most groups:

1. *Cohesiveness.* This factor has been described previously as a facilitative condition that encourages a successful outcome.
2. *Instillation of hope.* The belief or hope that change is possible is in itself therapeutic.
3. *Universalization.* People enter a group feeling uniquely troubled, but they soon realize that others share similar difficulties, feelings of inadequacy, and interpersonal alienation.
4. *Altruism.* The feeling of being needed and the realization that one can be helpful to others in the group can be curative.
5. *Imparting of information/intellectualization.* Some groups make use of didactic instruction and advice giving.
6. *Multiple transference.* Any distorted perceptions or maladaptive relationships still retained from early sources, especially the family, emerge in the group, which, according to psychodynamic theory, itself becomes like a family. Members' emotional attachments to the leader, to other members, or to the group as a whole are challenged, tested, and when necessary, more rationally and realistically appraised.
7. *Interpersonal learning.* The group is a proving ground for testing positive and negative emotional reactions and exploring new behaviors. Members learn that they can openly ask for help or support from others and express strong affects that lead to corrective emotional experiences.
8. *Development of interpersonal skills.* Whether implicitly or explicitly, members improve their socializing skills. Various techniques, such as feedback and role-playing, are used to assist in the mastery of interpersonal skills.
9. *Imitative behaviors.* People learn how to behave in part by observing others. At first the behavior of the leader or of other popular participants may be imitated to gain approval. Gradually, members begin to experiment, using the many models available to them in the group.
10. *Catharsis.* When bottled-up or repressed guilt, hostility, or "unacceptable" drives are strongly ventilated in the group, they bring a

sense of relief and freedom. The real benefit of catharsis, however, may lie in the strengthened cohesive bonds that result from intensive interaction in a safe, accepting environment.

According to Yalom, these ten mechanisms are interdependent, flowing together and between one another. There is no clear consensus as to which mechanisms are the vital ones and, as we shall see in succeeding chapters, different group theorists choose to emphasize some and disregard others.

ETHICS

No introduction to experiential groups is complete without a consideration of ethics. The principle and ultimate responsibility for what occurs in groups is centered on the leader. In accepting this responsibility, leaders cannot rely solely on intuition: their training and experience become the ethical foundations of group practice. The minimum requirements for group leaders can be summarized in two sets of guidelines: training and preparation, and in-group procedures.

Training and preparation

The preparation of competent group leaders generally consists of four ingredients (Shapiro 1978): (1) theory and skill learning; (2) supervised practice as a group leader; (3) observations of professional group leaders; and (4) personal membership in a group experience. The suggested movement in academic learning is from the general to the specific. A basic knowledge and understanding in the behavioral sciences would include courses in developmental psychology, personality theory, psychopathology, and, probably, social psychology. Such courses point out to would-be leaders the wide range of possible individual behaviors in certain situations, help develop a theoretical framework, and test attitudes and beliefs about human nature. Studying the many theories and practices of individual and group counseling and therapy enables the prospective leader to grasp the rationale for certain strategies and integrate theory and applied techniques in search of an individual style.

Ideally, didactic instruction and supervised training occur simultaneously and allow the opportunity to integrate content with experience. Many guidelines suggest an initial period of ongoing observation of an experienced leader. The prospective leader's experiential training typically begins with a more experienced coleader, allowing the would-be leader to taste the responsibility of leadership and providing a model and source of support to draw on. Supervision should be close and involve post-meeting discussions with the neophyte leader to offer concrete feedback and promote an increased awareness of group processes. Once prospective leaders have developed a sound base of didactic instruction and experien-

tial training, they are placed in a field setting where a variety of professionals can provide ongoing supervision and assessments of personal qualities,
competence, and technical facility.

All guidelines suggest some personal experience as a group member.
One excellent learning device is a training group for group leaders, wherein
members have an opportunity to assess their own skills and observe the
characteristics of others' leadership styles. The designated leader can be
rotated, or the group can be run by an experienced professional using
feedback and discussion sessions following the meeting. Participants gain
insight not only into how it feels to be a leader but into how it feels to be a
member experiencing the difficulties and fears of self-disclosure. Although
the function of this experience is training, most guidelines strongly suggest
involvement in personal therapy as well. Most potential leaders pursue
intensive self-exploration in both individual and group therapy to learn
more about personal strengths and weaknesses, beliefs and attitudes,
motivations and needs, and distortions and blind spots as part of the task
of becoming a detached, caring, and effective leader.

Usually, the end step of this training process is certification by a
professional organization or affiliation with some higher organization,
institution, or agency that will confirm the person's status. A degree from
an accredited graduate training program is not a guarantee of ethical and
competent leadership, but the lack of such a degree may be suspect. It is
assumed that the person will then practice the standards and codes of
ethical behavior of the affiliated organization. It is also assumed that group
leaders will continue to update and augment their knowledge and skills by
attending advanced training seminars and workshops and that they will be
aware of, and apply, current research analyses on the effectiveness of
various group procedures.

In-group ethics

In addition to negotiating a training program in group leadership,
there are specific ethical issues that relate to the ongoing group experience. The most common issues include informed consent, freedom of
choice, and the establishment of safeguards for psychological and physical
injury (Parloff, 1970).

In recent years experiential groups have become so popular that many
unsophisticated people are lining up to participate, and the number of
undertrained leaders is astounding. It is especially important, therefore,
that participants understand the nature and implications of their potential
experiences. This means that a leader ought to provide as much information as possible about the goals, techniques, cost, duration, and leadership
of the group. Obviously there is a limit to how much one can validly
describe an experience that has not yet occurred. Yet members should
have a clear notion of what they are committing themselves to. Grandiose
claims of success and promises for dramatic life changes should be

regarded with suspicion. Professional group leaders are expected to advertise modestly and openly describe the limitations of their own competence and experience.

The second guideline involves freedom of choice throughout the experience. Every member has the right not to participate in a given activity. Leaders may encourage participation but must protect the member's rights by not allowing themselves or the group to unduly pressure any member. One would hope, of course, that members will choose to extend their personal limits by engaging in activities that may be anxiety-arousing, but that the leader advocates an activity or the group members agree upon it does not justify its use. Generally, physical assaults, sexual behavior, and the use of drugs are not considered appropriate or ethical group behaviors. Even in groups where participation is involuntary (a requirement of an institution, for example) the leader should provide support for members to deal with their possible resistance and allow them the same choice of participation as a member of any other group, except for the choice of termination.

A third ethical guideline is the establishment of adequate safeguards to prevent psychological or physical injury. One safeguard is the use of adequate screening procedures to weed out prospective members who would not be apt to benefit from, or would be harmed by, the experience. To the limited extent that personal difficulties are predictable, the leader tries to insure that prospective members and the group are reciprocally suited to one another.

A second aspect of establishing safeguards is the group leader's espousal of the standard of confidentiality. With regard to client contacts, therapists are mandated to confidentiality and protection of the integrity and welfare of the individuals. An anecdote may be relevant to underline this point.

A parish priest retired after many years of service, and a banquet was held in his honor. Since the guest speaker was late, the priest made his speech first. Later, when the guest speaker arrived and after he had made his presentation, someone was promptly arrested for murder. Who was arrested and why?

The priest, in his speech, reminisced about his arrival many years before in the parish and, in particular, about the very first time he had heard confession, which, as it happened, was from a parishioner who confessed to having committed a murder. The guest speaker, a long-standing and respected member of the community, not having been present for the priest's remarks, praised the priest and proudly remarked that he had been the very first person in the parish to make a confession to the fledgling priest!

Actually, there are certain limitations with regard to privileged communication, such as when people are likely to be dangerous to themselves or others. But, with few exceptions, the element of trust is essential to enhance the facilitative environment of the group. Leaders can only vouch for their own respect for confidentiality and share any limits to that confidentiality with group members. However, they can stress the importance of not revealing information that can be tied to specific people in the group.

Finally, the leader's responsibility is not limited to actual group meetings. The possible effects of the group on the members' outside world need to be explored. The leader's responsibility extends to being available afterwards to offer assistance or referrals, and a conscientious leader will follow up terminations of all kinds to evaluate the effect of the group experience on the former member.

Limitations of groups and psychological risks

Members' group experiences are real and valid, but some group members develop a naive belief about the all-inclusive applicability of group teachings to everyday living. Thus, there may be a tendency for them to apply in-group behavior, such as self-disclosure, too quickly and indiscriminately in the real world. This leaves them feeling vulnerable and their families and associates feeling threatened. Also, the desire for the comfort and support necessary for growth in the group setting can become misguided when participants view the group environment as a substitute for a desired social group, as an end in itself. These short-sighted participants may hide in the group and never confront their problems. Others may use the group to ventilate their feelings but never move toward constructive change.

The group experience can backfire in other ways. For instance, some groups adhere to a particular philosophy and expect each member to blindly incorporate their values and beliefs. Members who are seen as deviant may be severely chastised or psychologically abused. The powerful factors of peer pressure, group norms, feedback, and confrontation can be destructive to the individual who is easily coerced or influenced, especially if other group members are unrealistic in their proposals. Psychological growth is often a painful and slow process; along the way, individuals may become depressed or hostile, or they may indulge in rash, self-defeating behavior. If adequate resources are unavailable during and after the group experience, the process may lead only to an increasingly confused state.

All groups and all leaders have not been created equal. The broad field of experiential groups includes many leaders improperly trained as well as groups lacking in sound theory and ethics. Under the proper conditions, however, limitations and risks can be minimized or controlled, and the group experience can be both potent and enjoyable.

SUMMARY

The history of group psychotherapy in North America includes the inspirational approach of Joseph Pratt, the psychodramatic techniques of Jacob Moreno, the psychodynamic principles of Sigmund Freud, and the humanistic orientation of Carl Rogers. From this background, supplemented by experimental studies in group dynamics, emerged the contemporary experiential group. The term *experiential groups* is used broadly, to describe small, temporary collections of active participants meeting to focus on interpersonal and intrapersonal learning, growth, and discovery. The groups described in the following chapters vary along dimensions such as *structured versus unstructured, leader-centered versus member-centered,* and *cognitive versus affective.*

The size of a group depends on its primary purpose. Psychotherapy groups are generally smaller than growth groups. Proponents of heterogeneous groups argue that progress is facilitated by mixing diverse complaints and interpersonal styles, whereas supporters of homogeneous groups argue that similarity encourages cohesion and reduces conflict.

Roles are behaviors adopted by group members and are seen as fulfilling group needs of the group. Typical roles found in experiential groups are the task and maintenance functions introduced by Robert Bales and behaviors located along the dimensions of anger/love and strength/weakness suggested by Timothy Leary.

Norms are unwritten rules of behavior that guide member actions and carry sanctions when violated. Self-disclosure and honesty are typical norms in experiential groups. Conformity to group norms relates to a person's status and the cohesiveness of the group.

Leadership roles are determined by the needs of the group as well as by individual attributes, such as a person's level of participation. A classic study by Lewin, Lippitt, and White (1939) classified leadership styles as *authoritarian, democratic,* and *laissez faire.* An effective group leader uses a thoughtful application of techniques within a consistent theoretical framework. The leader may function as *expert, catalyst, orchestrator,* and *model/participant* within the group. While a leader-centered, structured approach may reduce anxiety and aid initial task performance, a member-centered, less structured approach generally elicits less dependency and more autonomy among participants.

Experiential groups move through a series of stages. One conceptualization of group process, cited by William Schutz, includes the stages of *inclusion, control,* and *affection.* Another is Kelman's view of the group as a *social influence situation,* characterized by the processes of *compliance, identification,* and *internalization.*

Finally, ethical considerations are important both in the training of the group leader and the conduct of the group. Informed consent and freedom of choice, and safeguards such as confidentiality and screening are recommended as guidelines to minimize the risk of psychological and physical injury.

REFERENCES

Allport, G. The historical background of modern social psychology. In G. Lindzey & E. Aronson (Eds.), *Handbook of social psychology* (Vol. 1, 2nd ed.). Reading, Mass.: Addison-Wesley, 1968.

Appley, D. G., & Winder, A. E. *T-groups and therapy groups in a changing society*. San Francisco: Jossey-Bass, 1973.

Bach, G. *Intensive group psychotherapy*. New York: Ronald Press, 1954.

Bales, R. F. *Interaction process analysis: A method for the study of small groups*. Reading, Mass.: Addison-Wesley, 1960.

Bales, R. F. *Personality and interpersonal behavior*. New York: Holt, Rinehart & Winston, 1970.

Bales, R. F., & Slater, P. Role differentiation in small decision-making groups. In T. Parsons et al. (Eds.), *Family socialization and interaction process*. Glencoe, Ill.: Free Press, 1955.

Barrett-Lennard, G. T. Process, effects and structure in intensive groups: A theoretical-descriptive analysis. In C. L. Cooper (Ed.), *Theories of group process*. London: John Wiley, 1975.

Bednar, R. L., Melnick, J., & Kaul, T. J. Risk, responsibility and structure: A conceptual framework for initiating group counseling and psychotherapy. *Journal of Counseling Psychology*, 1974, *21*, 31–37.

Benne, K. D., & Sheats, P. Functional roles of group members. *Journal of Social Issues*, 1948, *4*, 41–60.

Bennis, W. G., & Shepard, H. A theory of group development. In Gibbard, G. S., Hartman, J. J., & Mann, R. D. (Eds.), *Analysis of groups*. San Francisco: Jossey-Bass, 1974.

Berzon, B., & Solomon, L. The self-directed therapeutic group: Three studies. *Journal of Counseling Psychology*, 1966, *13*, 491–497.

Bogdanoff, M., & Elbaum, P. L. Role lock: Dealing with monopolizers, mistrusters, isolates, helpful Hannahs, and other assorted characters in group psychotherapy. *International Journal of Group Psychotherapy*, 1978, *28*, 247–261.

Cohen, A. M., & Smith, R. D. *The critical incident in growth groups: Theory and technique*. La Jolla, Calif.: University Associates, 1976.

Corsini, R. (Ed.), *Current psychotherapies*. Itasca, Ill.: F. E. Peacock, 1973.

Corsini, R. J. Historic background of group psychotherapy: A critique. *Group Psychotherapy*, 1955, *8*, 219–225.

Crosbie, P. V. (Ed.), *Interaction in small groups*. New York: Macmillan, 1975.

Dreikers, R. Early experiments with group psychotherapy. *American Journal of Psychotherapy*, 1959, *13*, 882–891.

Fiebert, M. S. Sensitivity training: An analysis of trainer interventions and group process. *Psychological Reports*, 1968, *22*, 829–838.

Foulkes, S. H. *Group analytic psychotherapy*. London: Gordon & Breach, 1975.

Foulkes, S. H., & Anthony, E. J. *Group psychotherapy*. London: Penguin, 1957.

Geller, J. J. Concerning the size of therapy groups. *International Journal of Group Psychotherapy*, 1951, *1*, 118–120.

Gibb, J. Defensive communication. *Journal of Communication*, 1961, *11*, 141–148.

Goldstein, A. P., Heller, K., & Sechrest, L. B. *Psychotherapy and the psychology of behavior change*. New York: Wiley, 1966.

Greening, T. C., & Coffey, H. Working with an "Impersonal" T-group. *Journal of Applied Behavioral Science*, 1966, *2*, 401–411.

Grunebaum, H. A soft-hearted review of hard-nosed research on groups. *International Journal of Group Psychotherapy*, 1975, *25*, 185–198.

Hare, A. P. *Handbook of small group research* (2nd ed.). New York: Free Press, 1976.

Homans, G. C. *The human group*. New York: Harcourt, 1950.

Janis, I. L. *Victims of groupthink*. Boston: Houghton Mifflin, 1972.

Johnson, D., & Johnson, F. *Joining together: Group theory and group skills*. New York: Prentice-Hall, 1975.

Kellerman, H. *Group psychotherapy and personality*. New York: Grune & Stratton, 1979.

Kelman, H. C. The role of the group in the induction of therapeutic change. *International Journal of Group Psychotherapy*, 1963, *13*, 399–432.

Lakin, M. *Interpersonal encounter: Theory and practice in sensitivity training*. New York: McGraw-Hill, 1972.

Lakin, M., & Costanzo, P. The leader and the experiential groups. In C. L. Cooper (Ed.), *Theories of group process*. London: John Wiley, 1975.

Leary, T. *Interpersonal diagnosis of personality*. New York: Ronald Press, 1957.

Leopold, H. Selection of patients for group psychotherapy. *American Journal of Psychotherapy*, 1957, *11*, 634–637.

Levine, B. *Group psychotherapy: Practice and development*. New York: Prentice-Hall, 1979.

Lewin, K. Group decisions and social change. In T. M. Newcomb & E. L. Hartley (Eds.), *Readings in social psychology*. New York: Henry Holt, 1947.

Lewin, K., Lippitt, R., & White, R. K. Patterns of aggressive behavior in an experimentally created social climate. *Journal of Social Psychology*, 1939, *10*, 271–299.

Lieberman, M. A., Yalom, I. D., & Miles, M. *Encounter groups: First facts*. New York: Basic Books, 1973.

McGregor, D. *The human side of enterprise*. New York: McGraw-Hill, 1960.

Mullan, H., & Rosenbaum, M. *Group psychotherapy*. New York: Free Press, 1962.

Newcomb, T., Turner, R., & Converse, P. *Social psychology*. New York: Holt, Rinehart & Winston, 1965.

Nixon, H. L., II. *The small group*. New York: Prentice-Hall, 1979.

Parloff, M. B. Group therapy and the small-group field: An encounter. *International Journal of Group Psychotherapy*, 1970, *20*, 267–304.

Phillips, G. M., & Erickson, E. C. *Interpersonal dynamics in the small group*. New York: Random House, 1970.

Rosenbaum, L., & Rosenbaum, W. Morale and productivity consequences of group leadership style, stress, and type of task. *Journal of Applied Psychology*, 1971, *55*, 343–348.

Rosenbaum, M., & Berger, M. (Eds.), *Group psychotherapy and group function*. New York: Basic Books, 1975.

Schutz, W. C. *FIRO: A three-dimensional theory of interpersonal behavior*. New York: Holt, Rinehart & Winston, 1958.

Shaffer, J. B. P., & Galinsky, M. D. *Models of group therapy and sensitivity training*. New York: Prentice-Hall, 1974.

Shapiro, J. L. *Methods of group psychotherapy and encounter*. Itasca, Ill.: F. E. Peacock, 1978.

Shaw, M. E. *Group dynamics*. New York: McGraw-Hill, 1976.

Shaw, M. E., & Blum, J. Effects of leadership style upon group performance as a function of task structure. *Journal of Personality and Social Psychology*, 1966, *3*, 238–241.

Sherif, M., & Sherif, C. W. *Groups in harmony and tension: An introduction to studies on intergroup relations*. New York: Harper & Row, 1953.

Sherif, M., & Sherif, C. W. *Exploration into conformity and deviation of adolescents*. New York: Harper & Row, 1964.

Slavson, S. Personality qualifications of a group psychotherapist. *International Journal of Group Psychotherapy*, 1962, *12*, 411–420.

Stock, D., & Thelen, H. A. *Emotional dynamics and group culture*. New York: New York University Press, 1958.

Triplett, N. The dynamogenic factors in pacemaking and competition. *American Journal of Psychology*, 1897, *9*, 507–533.

Trotzer, J. *The counselor and the group*. Monterey, Calif.: Brooks/Cole, 1977.

Tuckman, B. Developmental sequence in small groups. *Psychological Bulletin*, 1965, *63*, 384–399.

Verba, S. *Small groups and political behavior: A study of leadership.* Princeton, N.J.: Princeton University Press, 1972.

Whitaker, C., & Malone, T. P. *The roots of psychotherapy.* New York: Blakiston, 1953.

Whitaker, D. S., & Lieberman, M. A. *Psychotherapy through the group process.* New York: Atherton, 1964.

Yalom, I. D. A study of group therapy dropouts. *Archives of General Psychiatry,* 1966, *14,* 393–414.

Yalom, I. D. *Theory and practice of group psychotherapy* (2nd ed.). New York: Basic Books, 1975.

Yalom, I. D., Houts, P. S., Zimerberg, S. M., & Rand, K. H. Prediction of improvement in group therapy. *Archives of General Psychiatry,* 1967, *17,* 159–168.

2

T-Groups

HISTORY AND DEVELOPMENT

To those who have not participated in a T-group (training group), the excitement and controversy generated by the group movement may be something of a mystery. Returning members, when queried about their experiences, often say something like, "It really worked, but I can't explain it exactly. You have to find out for yourself." To understand why T-groups have drawn supporters like fireflies attracted to a light bulb, a brief look at their history may be illuminating.

Kurt Lewin, a prominent social psychologist in the 1930s, is generally regarded as the father of the T-group movement. Lewin was influenced by the theories of Georg Simmel, a sociologist. Simmel (1950) saw society as a pattern of functional relationships uniting individuals into a collective whole. Simmel noted that all people belong to groups, simply by being members of society, and that group leaders and members continually influence each other. Lewin adopted the dynamic concepts of Simmel as he moved psychological research from the laboratory into the field—into society at large. Lewin believed strongly that the most effective changes in personal attitudes occur in group, not individual, contexts. He maintained that individuals must learn to see themselves as others see them in order to discover and change maladaptive attitudes and behaviors. Lewin's writings (1948, 1951) remain classics in the field of group dynamics. His commitment to collecting and acting upon scientifically validated data became a cornerstone of the T-group movement. Thus his approach to studying groups has been called "action research."

The founding of the first T-group was a fortuitous event. In 1946 a number of social scientists, led by Leland Bradford, Ronald Lippitt, and Lewin, participated in an intergroup relations workshop called the Connecticut Workshop Project, which was designed to help business and community leaders implement and assure the success of the recently legislated Fair Employees Practices Act. After one working session, the staff met in the evening to discuss their observations. A number of group participants asked to attend these discussions. It soon became apparent that the staff's observations did not always agree with the conference members' perceptions. Moreover, these evening meetings were so fascinating in themselves that they became a dramatic educative method. This was an early example of group members analyzing their own experience by employing feedback from other group members.

The success of this new method of examining group dynamics was followed up by the establishment of the National Training Laboratory for Group Development (NTL) the following year in Bethel, Maine. At Bethel, the "basic skills training group," a predecessor to the T-group, was formed. The group's purpose was twofold: to develop strategies of change in social systems and to learn about small group dynamics and interpersonal styles of functioning. At various times the T-group was involved in such diverse tasks as teaching participants about interpersonal behavior, clarifying a theory of group dynamics, discussing the problems participants brought from their home organizations, aiding them in developing leadership skills, and giving them ways to apply group learning to the outside world (Yalom, 1975). The T-group with a strong interpersonal orientation became by far the most popular format. Yet the T-group did not become the center of the training laboratory until 1956. This was due in part to differences between the original founding group, consisting largely of social psychologists devoted to Lewin's model of action research to cultivate social and organizational change, and newer staff members, who tended to be more clinically oriented (Freudian or Rogerian) and interested in group dynamics and individual behavioral change.

It will become evident that the term *training laboratory* refers to a range of experiential learning activities, only one of which is the T-group, or "training" group. The term *T-group* may now refer to a variety of purposes as well. Some T-groups continue to focus on the development of skills for more effective organizational functioning. More commonly, however, T-groups focus on interpersonal skills or the study of small group processes. Within the latter approach, attention is drawn to each person's contribution, through his or her interactive style, to the emotional climate and decision-making processes of the entire group.

A final variation on the T-group theme, influenced by simultaneous developments in personality theory and clinical psychology, emphasizes the total enhancement of the individual. Within this orientation, the improvement of group functioning or the development of personal skills are secondary to the clarification of the individual's life values and personal identity. These groups are sometimes called *sensitivity groups*, a term coined in 1954 by the more clinically oriented wing of NTL. For some group leaders, training shortly became "encountering." Their approach will be more fully clarified in Chapter 3. In any case, although it is not the only institution to conduct T-groups today, NTL remains a vibrant organization dedicated to training group leaders and furthering the development of the laboratory method.

It is fair to say that, even when the T-group is intended to foster individual growth and awareness, this always occurs in the context of understanding the group process. *Process* is distinguished from the *content* of interactions and refers to the feelings and perceptions that underlie behavior in the group. Process issues are always present in regard to what participants are saying and doing to each other. They transcend the individual problems of group members. For instance, one ongoing process centers on control and manifests itself in how norms are established and power is distributed in the group. Another process issue concerns intimacy and may be reflected in themes of becoming acquainted or becoming deeply involved with fellow participants. Such processes are present in varying degrees throughout the life of the group and serve to provoke the expression of substantive topics (Cohen & Smith, 1976).

In T-groups, as opposed to most therapy groups, content is the vehicle used to understand process. The study of group processes and group dynamics is seen as a means of shedding light on the development of interpersonal relationships and behavior in the home environment. The development of interpersonal skills and interpersonal competence implies obtaining an understanding of group processes that encourages self-acceptance (Argyris, 1967). Thus, T-groups emphasize conceptualizing the raw experiences of group members. More than other experiential groups, they comfortably draw upon the tradition of social psychology and group dynamics research.

Schein and Bennis (1965) have noted that the goals of laboratory training may vary somewhat from group to group, but they generally encompass the following dimensions: (1) the development of self-insight, such as reducing defensiveness and dishonesty at the personal level; (2) understanding conditions that inhibit or facilitate group functioning, such as group size or membership; (3) understanding interpersonal operations in groups—for example, improving communication skills and working more effectively with others; (4) developing skills for diagnosing individual, group, and organizational problems—for instance, resolving group stumbling blocks or building group cohesiveness.

In practice, the learning goals of T-groups are moderated by the group's focus and largely determined by the members themselves. Levels of group concern can include individual participants, relationships between and among group members, the organizational role of the individual, the group as a whole, relationships between groups, or issues within the organization the members represent. When the group focuses on the individual member, relevant goals might include increased awareness, attitude change, or behavioral competence. When focusing on role functions, the group might explore attitudes toward various group roles and skills in relating to superiors, peers, or subordinates. At the organizational level, the group could deal with specific organizational problems and methods for improving the organization (Schein & Bennis, 1965).

The originators of the T-group movement were committed to three sets of shared values (Bradford, Gibb, & Benne, 1964). First, the early experimenters in T-group methodology were concerned about the under-utilization of the social and behavioral sciences in the real world, and consequently, were committed to making use of scientific procedures. They taught members of groups and organizations to objectively approach a problem, look at all the facts, collaborate with other investigators, and make rational decisions based on the available data. Second, they favored a democratically functioning group and a sharing of the decision-making process. This runs counter to the authoritarian and bureaucratic way in which many organizations function. However, there is empirical evidence supporting the power of cooperation and collaboration to improve organizational productivity (White & Lippitt, 1962). Finally, the T-group movement was influenced by its founders' concern for the value of the helping relationship. Sensitivity to others' feelings and a willingness to help with and involve oneself in another's problems were ideals brought from the field of psychology to be applied to the functioning of large, impersonal organizations.

BASIC CONCEPTS

Learning laboratory

The T-group is first and foremost a *learning laboratory*. It is not a laboratory in the sense of a number of detached scientists in white coats performing complex experiments. Rather, the laboratory has been defined as "a temporary residential community shaped to the learning requirements of all its members" (Bradford et al., 1964, pp. 2–3). To be sure, the T-group can stand apart from a residential setting and still serve as a "learning laboratory." In this context the term "laboratory" refers to the accent on experimentation and the testing of new behaviors. It suggests that a group member is both a participant who can experiment with making behavioral changes and an observer who can check out their effects. The members themselves are centrally involved in setting group goals, observing behavior, planning activities, and analyzing data. The group is a microcosm of the real world in that the same kinds of tasks and interpersonal conflicts that besiege us in our lives develop within it. The difference is that the T-group provides an opportunity to solve nagging problems that are not equally solvable in other contexts. In most cases the laboratory meets in a setting quite removed from everyday concerns and schedules. Its meetings might take place over several days or even several weeks. The T-group itself is apt to constitute only one part of a residential laboratory. The rest of the schedule might include lectures to provide a cognitive understanding of group skills and group processes, and meetings of the larger community.

The T-group, however, is the core of the learning experience and, in some cases, the only item on the agenda. The entire learning community might consist of two or three T-groups of ten to 15 members each. The leader of a T-group, called a trainer or facilitator, might open the group in the following way:

> This group will meet for many hours and will serve as a kind of laboratory where each individual can increase his understanding of the forces which influence individual behavior and the performance of groups and organizations. The data for learning will be our own behavior, feelings, and reactions. We begin with no definite structure or organization, no agreed-upon procedures, and no specific agenda. It will be up to us to fill the vacuum created by the lack of these familiar elements and to study our group as we evolve. My role will be to help the group to learn from its own experience, but not to act as a traditional chairman nor to suggest how we should organize, what our procedures should be or exactly what our agenda will include. With these few comments, I think we are ready to begin in whatever way you feel will be most helpful [Seashore, 1968].[1]

The task, then, is for a group of individuals to create and maintain a social organization within a limited time period. The goals are rather general and vague. The lack of structure and agenda deliberately forces participants to "fall in on themselves" and develop their own resources. In T-groups the focus is on learning about group processes; in sensitivity groups the emphasis is on personal and interpersonal issues. In the latter case, the facilitator's opening might express a need for group members to communicate openly and share reactions in order to develop a deeper understanding of how individuals relate. When emotional issues are the paramount focus and interpersonal growth and self-actualization become the goal, the group might be called an *encounter group.*

Learning how to learn

The initial emphasis in the training laboratory is on developing a new and different approach to problems, on *learning how to learn.* Warren Bennis (1977) captures the values underlying this idea in specifying four T-group "metagoals" that characterize laboratory training in general.

First, T-groups aim to expand the awareness of individual members. The group works toward a wider recognition of the choices available for meeting the challenges and problems of life. Second, T-groups encourage a spirit of inquiry. "What is happening and why?" are questions that continually confront group members. Such self-analysis is not common in everyday encounters. Third, T-groups emphasize authenticity in interpersonal relationships. Because of the ambiguity about goals and process, a variety of feelings are aroused and expressed. An effort is made to understand these feelings, to share them, and to be receptive to authentic, disclosing communication in return. Finally, T-groups provide a model of a collabora-

---

[1]Reproduced by special permission from *NTL Institute News and Reports,* "What is Sensitivity Training?" by Charles Seashore, Volume 2, Number 2, copyright 1968, NTL Institute.

tive concept of authority. In keeping with the value of democracy, authority in T-groups is not oriented toward power politics and coercive control. Since one's peers are the basic source for learning, members come to rely upon one another rather than on teachers or leaders for input. Thus, authority is based on legitimate expertise and humanistic concern.

The built-in ambiguity of the T-group means that routine behavior will not necessarily be effective. The trainer provides so few cues and the articulated goals are so general that members have a "perception of goal-lessness" (Benne, 1964). Learning thus occurs by experiencing rather than by listening to authorities. Learning how to learn refers to a cycle of experiences consisting of *presentation-feedback-experimentation.*

Presentation of self. Throughout the life of the group individuals reveal their perceptions and actions, a concept called *presentation of self* (Blumberg & Golembiewski, 1976). One way to describe the self-presentation and sharing that occurs in a T-group is to use a simple model of disclosure called a Johari Window (Figure 2-1), named after its inventors, Joseph Luft and Harry Ingram (Luft, 1970).

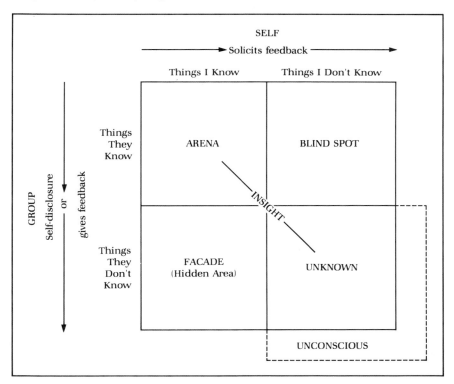

Figure 2–1. Johari Window. *(Reprinted from: J. E. Jones and J. W. Pfeiffer (Eds.),* The 1973 Annual Handbook for Group Facilitators. *San Diego, CA: University Associates, 1973. Used with permission.)*

Individuals' experiences of themselves are dissected into four compartments. The Arena refers to common knowledge, aspects of ourselves about which we and others are aware. The Facade contains things we are aware of but others are not, such as a secret love affair or the unexpressed fear experienced in confronting authority figures, as well as things we have not had the opportunity to share, such as a good mark on an exam. The Blind Spot consists of things that others know about us but of which we are not aware, such as bad breath or a tendency to interrupt speakers in midsentence. The Unknown is the space for things that are hidden from ourselves as well as others, including our hidden potential and areas in which there is room for growth.

The Johari Window suggests that an open, communicative climate increases the potential for group and individual problem solving, and that the means to increase communication is to enlarge the Arena. When group members first meet, the Arena tends to be small and superficial; as a helping relationship with others develops, more intimate communication increases and people can be more fully themselves in interactions with others. The amount of disclosure the group affords is in part a function of the degree of trust present in the group.

The variable of trust is crucial in any learning environment (Gibb, 1978). Fear causes defensiveness and stymies progress in all social systems, from the family to the community. Defensive group climates occur when members are preoccupied with issues of membership and acceptance. When the group climate is not supportive, members are less able to accurately perceive other members' motives, values, and emotions. Such members erect polite facades, rely on rigid role structures, use cautious decision-making strategies, and adopt dependent or counterdependent behavioral patterns. In the early stages of a group, prior to the establishment of an atmosphere of psychological safety, it is common for group members to defend their public images, avoid the expression of feelings and conflict, seek approval from others, or attempt to give advice to and make decisions for others. Gibb (1973) specifies two ways to create a supportive, trusting group: by replacing evaluative, judgmental communications with descriptive ones; and by replacing controlling behaviors with a joint problem-solving orientation.

Feedback.   The second element in the learning cycle is to make use of *feedback* from the group. The term "feedback" has been appropriated by group theorists from the electrical engineering literature, where it refers to messages about deviations from a desired goal. A rocket launched into space, for example, sends signals back to Earth which enable a steering mechanism here to correct the rocket's course when necessary. In group terminology, feedback occurs when group members communicate their reactions to others' behavior with the purpose of assisting them to correct their "course" toward their goals. Those who wish to increase self-awareness, for example, might get feedback that their tendency to interrupt makes it difficult for other group members to be heard. While it is true that feedback occurs naturally in all interpersonal relationships, in T-groups it is a skill that can be deliberately cultivated.

Feedback is probably the foremost contribution of the T-group, as well as the most dramatic experience for group members. Feedback, provided in an atmosphere of mutual concern and trust, allows individuals to monitor and adjust inappropriate behaviors and develop more effective ones. It is also a way of providing information about blind areas. For example, some members may believe that by jumping in to solve group problems they are being helpful, while the rest of the group may see them as trying to dominate the group or show off. Effective feedback requires group participants to inform each other about the impact of their behavior. This process helps members to accurately hear and comprehend such information and choose whether and how to act on it.

Feedback in T-groups is also used to get participants to look at the group process. Consider a session in which the group is ganging up on a member for appearing phony and hiding her true feelings. The leader might very well offer process-oriented feedback by asking members to look at how they are "helping" the closed member become more open and genuine. Alternatively, the leader might wonder aloud if the members' need to chip away at her is alleviating their own anxiety about something.

Several guidelines help to distinguish effective from noneffective feedback within the group. It is important that the person providing the feedback do so when a behavior is observed rather than waiting until the person in question is less vulnerable and the information less relevant. Useful feedback requires revealing the emotional reaction to a member's behavior rather than being critical or judgmental about the behavior. ("When you interrupt me I feel angry.") In other words, members providing feedback offer their own angry or upset feelings rather than labeling the other member's behavior as malicious or aggressive. Feedback that is behavior-specific ("You interrupted me three times") is more effective, meaningful, and acceptable than feedback that labels traits ("You're an interrupter") or personalities ("You can't stand for someone else to be right"). Obviously, one member's reactions may not be a sufficient basis on which to consider modifying behavior. When feedback is offered by several other group members, however, it can have a greater impact and is usually more valid. In general, feedback is most useful when it is representative, complete, and given by a majority of the group.

Feedback can be received optimally by members who listen closely and are subsequently able to restate the message in their own words (paraphrasing). They can learn more by checking the perceptions of others to see how they have reacted to an issue, while realizing that they do not have to change simply because someone else would like them to.

Experimentation.   The third important element of the learning cycle is a norm of *experimentation* in the group, the implicit permission to try out new behaviors and strategies. Individuals do not learn by feedback alone. They learn by inquiring, exploring, and experiencing in situations where they can receive clear and accurate feedback about the relevance and effectiveness of their behavior. Practice is equally important because it insures that the participant will become increasingly comfortable in the use of newly acquired skills. The final stage in the learning process is to apply these new skills to the environment outside of the group. Hence, T-groups try to help the individual carry learning back to his or her role in industry, education, or family.

Here-and-now

A final concept critical to the operation of the T-group is a *here-and-now* focus. Since optimal learning is thought to occur through actual experience, it is important that the group remain as live and relevant as possible. This means that digressions into storytelling and personal histories are generally not appreciated, unless accompanied by current feelings and made relevant to the ongoing interactions of the group members. Even if a member were to write principles of leadership on a blackboard, there would be an attempt to illustrate the principles with reference to current group activity. Observing and engaging in immediate experience is the fuel that heats the group and keeps it simmering. The here-and-now focus is a dominant theme in most contemporary psychological groups and will recur as an instrumental concept in succeeding chapters.

BASIC PROCEDURES

Leader behaviors

The ideal T-group trainer has been described as a combination "Jewish mother, model father, a prophet-saint, and a Mephistophelean devil" (Bogart, 1966, p. 360). In reality, the leader's behavior depends upon individual personality and style as well as upon the group's specific goals and structure. For Jack Gibb (1964, p. 305), "The primary methodological contribution that the trainer can make to the group is to express the norms of the group or how he sees them." That is, trainers orient participants to the idea of designing the training experience for themselves. Beyond that, they trust in the group's wisdom and assume that members will be able to dig themselves out of most of the pits they create. The role of the leader is to invite the participants to work together to examine their own behavior and relationships, and then to judiciously withdraw.

When the leader does withdraw, two things characteristically occur: (1) participants realize that novel approaches are needed to solve the dilemma of having to create an agenda without guidance or apparent rules; and (2) participants begin to unwittingly reveal aspects of their personalities and interpersonal styles in the face of an ambiguous situation (Lakin, 1972). Some members think that, despite the leaders' enforced abstention from the group process, the leaders are mischievously in charge of the group in a manipulative capacity. They are not. What you see is what you get.

A common failing of T-group leaders is a tendency to jump in and rescue a group when it flounders. In so doing, the leader actually prevents the group from discovering and relying on its own inherent talents and developing its own skills. It is not unusual for the members of a successful T-group to tell trainers, at an early stage, that they are neither needed nor wanted. The group, in effect, mutinies. Each member begins to accept a share of responsibility for what happens in the meetings. On the other hand, an insensitive leader might mistake indefinite floundering and frustration for learning when it is actually a stage the group needs to pass through, perhaps with a helpful nudge from the trainer (Blumberg & Golembiewski, 1976). Skillful leaders can discriminate between "creative dilemmas" that the group might solve on its own and hopeless situations that require their intervention.

The T-group leader nurtures the group and helps it understand its own processes, perhaps by stopping the flow of action occasionally or suggesting that the group try something different. The leader's most frequent interventions are invitations to members to look at their own behavior, such as "What is going on here?" "What do you want to do right now?" or "I wonder why Jack hasn't said anything." Thus, the effective T-group leader intervenes at a level just deep enough to help the group produce a solution to the problem at hand. In some ways, the leader is equivalent to a dynamic therapist who provides interpretations deep enough to be challenging but not too deep for the person to understand and use.

One leader's style is illustrated in the following excerpt from an early group session in which members are struggling to define themselves:

> (Lengthy silence)
>
> *Andy:*   I'm always the first one to talk, but not this time.
>
> *Karen:*   You just did!
>
> *Andy:*   Well, I get impatient with all of you just sitting there like bumps on the log.
>
> *Curt:*   So what do you want us to do?
>
> *Andy:*   I don't know, but I feel like some of you aren't contributing anything to this group.
>
> *Nancy:*   Just who are you referring to, Andy?
>
> *Andy:*   Well...Sue, for example...and Charlie looks like he can't wait for the session to end.
>
> *Charlie:*   Screw you, Andy! I'm as involved as you are. Just because you have a case of verbal diarrhea!
>
> *Andy:*   *(angrily)* What's that supposed to mean?
>
> *Gus:*   Hey, guys, settle down. I don't think shouting is at all helpful.
>
> *Faye:*   I know *I* don't want to be here if there's a bunch of

fighting going on. We're supposed to be rational adults, you know.

(Pause)

Trainer: It sounds like some of you are uncomfortable with what just happened between Andy and Charlie. I wonder how the rest of you feel about it.

Sue: Well, I was pretty aggravated that Andy lumped me with Charlie as not being involved in the group.

Harold: I agree with Faye that that kind of shouting isn't very productive.

Trainer: Harold, how did you feel at the time?

Harold: I guess I was afraid that Andy and Charlie would start fighting or something.

Charlie: I wasn't going to fight. I was just upset that Andy singled me out. I know I tend to pull back and not talk. I've always assumed that I didn't have much of anything to contribute. I was just upset that Andy called me on it.

Karen: So one thing Andy did was to open you up a little!

Doreen: I'm really pleased that you said that, Charlie. I feel a little closer to you because I have that problem too, and I was just relieved that Andy didn't name me.

Andy: *(laughs)* I was going to. I just didn't get a chance to when Charlie interrupted me!

Gus: Boy I'm sure glad it wasn't serious and that everything is okay again.

(Long silence)

Nancy: It seems like we always rely on Andy to start us off and if he doesn't initiate with some provocative comment, we sort of flounder. . . . So . . . I just want to say that I wish I had your nerve, Andy . . . uh . . . .

Trainer: Was there something else you wanted to say to Andy also, Nancy?

Nancy: What do you mean?

Trainer: The way you paused led me to think you had more to say.

Nancy: *(embarrassed)* I guess so. I like you, Andy. I think you're great!

Ruth: Nancy, you're always getting turned on to some guy just because he looks at you. You don't even know Andy.

Nancy: That's not true!

Ruth: Oh, sure it is. Remember that guy we met at Jerry's birthday party last weekend?

Karen: Hey, this seems really out of place to bring in a bunch of stuff from outside just because you two know each other.

Gus:	I agree.
Nancy:	Well, I'm really embarrassed now. She makes me sound like a real flirt.
Doreen:	I don't think you're a flirt, Nancy; at least you haven't been in here.
Trainer:	What just happened here?
Curt:	Well, I saw Ruth as pretty uncomfortable with Nancy's feelings about Andy . . . maybe jealous.
Sue:	I'll admit I was uncomfortable too. It's not that I'm so attracted to Andy. . . . *(Laughs.)* I don't mean that, you're okay, Andy. . . . It's just that I'm not used to hearing people state their feelings so openly.
Ruth:	Okay. I plead guilty, too. It's just that you're so damn beautiful, Nancy, and I wish I could be as confident with men as you are.
Nancy:	Confident, you think I'm confident?! I was shaking in my boots when I said that to Andy!

According to the most prevalent view, a T-group trainer avoids becoming too personally involved with the people in the group or the issues with which they are grappling. Emotional involvements with group members are accompanied by a loss of objectivity. Trainers must retain their objectivity. It is also easy for T-group leaders to forget their power, especially since they may experience the role as being indirect and tangential. Nevertheless, group members do imbue their leader with a tremendous amount of strength and potency. Effective leaders will not deliberately encourage that fantasy, but will retain a certain modesty about their role in the group.

Trainers, like most people, may have a strong need to be liked and appreciated. If not controlled, this need can have negative consequences in a T-group. For example, the leader might be threatened by any expression of group hostility and so structure the group experience to avoid it. In one study (O'Day, 1974), the most effective group trainers were those who were least active in early group sessions and were able to ignore episodes of member helplessness and dependency. They were able to deal comfortably with any resentment and rebellion that was channeled toward them by group members. Far from discouraging such a stage of group development, they facilitated it by their early passivity and subsequent ability to help members examine their actions and reflect on their motives.

The relatively passive role of the leader is especially apparent in the "small study group" that is part of the Tavistock approach to training in group dynamics. The Tavistock model was originated by Wilfred Bion (1959), whose work with groups was heavily influenced by psychoanalysis as well as by the field theory of Kurt Lewin. The name of the approach derives from the Tavistock Clinic and the Tavistock Institute of Human Relations in London, where Bion did much of his seminal work with small study groups. Other leading figures in the Tavistock movement include

A. K. Rice (1965) and Margaret Rioch (1970). While the T-group movement in the United States blossomed into a commitment to personal growth and the study of interpersonal dynamics in the 1960s, experiential group work in Great Britain became synonymous with the Tavistock group relations method (Banet & Hayden, 1979).

Some group approaches, such as Gestalt and encounter, stress the individual development and uniqueness of each person; the Tavistock group, even more than the T-group, deals with individuals only to the extent they exhibit something on behalf of the group as a whole. When people come together to form a group and share a common task, the group behaves as an interdependent system in which the whole is regarded as greater than the sum of its parts. The underlying assumption of the Tavistock group is that an individual's comments and behavior in the group mirror concerns shared by other members. The group's basic structure determines the predominant emotion and interaction evident at any given time. Moreover, the most dynamic issue facing any group is to resolve its relationship with the leader, a task that invokes all the members' early experiences with reactions to authority figures.

The group's consultant remains outside the group itself, acting in a formal and rather aloof manner as the members grapple with the task of studying their own behavior. The consultant's only role is to facilitate the group's task. In this function he or she offers observations for the group's consideration. These interventions are directed at the group-as-a-whole rather than at individuals. The consultant does not give advice or direction, offer support, or socialize with the group. The consultant will "confront the group, without affronting its members, . . . draw attention to group behavior and not to individual behavior, [and] point out how the group uses individuals to express its own emotions" (Rice, 1965, p. 102).

The consultant recognizes that while members are motivated to learn and understand, and the group is overtly working on completing a task, the members also have hidden agendas and unspoken attitudes that reflect other needs. The group makes certain basic assumptions about the kinds of behaviors necessary for its survival. According to Bion (1959), these "assumption cultures" include issues of dependency, pairing, and "fight or flight." They are designed to help members avoid anxiety and become reflected in the group process. One assumption group, for example, reflects the fantasized need of members to be dependent on and protected by someone functioning in a leadership role. Consultants may simply describe what they see or comment on how the group pursues its task in order to increase the members' awareness of the group's functioning. For example, consultants might remark that the group seems to be ignoring their presence, or cryptically ask if a particular member's angry outburst was not a reflection of the entire group's anger or frustration about some issue. As in individual psychoanalysis, the Tavistock consultant typically points out the group's avoidance of emotionally charged issues and current feelings. The focus on the group's common dilemma, together with the leader's reluctance to offer approval or structure, encourages members to take responsibility for their own progress.

Communication skills

All T-groups aim for the individual's personal growth through increased awareness of self, others, and how groups operate. T-groups can also be used as a laboratory for the development and refinement of inter-personal skills. Participants can explore their interpersonal styles and experiment with changes by forming relationships with other group members who provide ongoing feedback. Leaders may also play an active role in disseminating information, modeling skills, and giving their own feedback to the group. Communication skills fostered within the T-group include behavior description, communication of feelings, active listening, feedback, and confrontation. The successful adoption of these skills by group members minimizes confusion and alienation within the group and enhances cooperation and the fulfillment of other group goals.

Behavior description means reporting others' specific, observable actions without evaluating them or ascribing motives, attitudes, or traits to them. For instance, saying "Stuart, you're always trying to impress us" is mind reading, whereas saying "Stuart, I notice that whenever someone else does well, you tend to talk about your own accomplishments" is behavior description. "Helen, you're a slob!" is name calling, whereas, "Helen, you spilled the coffee and didn't clean it up" is behavior description. The first step in developing a talent for behavior description is to improve skills of observation and to withhold judgments. In general, feedback that is based on observable behaviors elicits the least hostile defensiveness and the greatest willingness to understand and change.

Communication of feelings is another valuable skill. It involves record-ing one's inner state as clearly as possible. Since feelings can express themselves in bodily changes, actions, and words, it is easy to be confused about someone else's feelings. For example, a tight mouth might signal anger to one person, but it may actually reflect fear in the sender. Group members need to help other participants understand how they feel in order to elicit meaningful responses from them. A person who communi-cates feelings clearly makes reference to "I" or "me" and specifies some kind of feeling by name or metaphor ("I feel embarrassed" or "I feel like I've just been caught with my hand in the cookie jar").

Many times we couch our feelings in terms that do not describe them at all. For example, to say "This has been an awful meeting" is to attribute feelings to a meeting and deny them in oneself. To say "I felt disgusted by this meeting" is more honest and direct. People also confuse thoughts with feelings. Thoughts are cognitive observations or conclusions rather than descriptions of bodily states. Statements like "I feel that Linda is not very helpful" or "I feel that we should not be doing this" are really judgments or conclusions in which the word "think" should replace the word "feel."

Active listening involves taking responsibility for what one hears by accepting, clarifying, and checking the meaning and intent of what the other person is saying. Active listening is sometimes taught in the context of learning the basic ingredients of a helping relationship as defined by Carl Rogers and his colleagues (Carkhuff, 1969). Chief among these helping skills is *accurate empathic understanding* (empathy), which combines good listening behavior with the ability to communicate what one has heard to the other person. Use of accurate empathy, together with the primary helping skills of "genuineness" and "respect," has been found to facilitate positive therapeutic outcomes in many studies (Rogers, Gendlin, Kiesler, & Truax, 1967; Truax & Wargo, 1969). In recent years, teaching of skills has become less conceptual and more action-oriented. The focus today is less on understanding accurate empathy, for example, as a therapeutic *condition* than as a set of specific, observable behaviors (Cash & Vellema, 1979; Egan, 1975).

Achieving accurate empathic understanding consists of a process of *discrimination* and a process of *communication.* To discriminate accurately means to adopt the perspective of someone else's experience, going beyond identifying the content of a verbal message to grasp its meaning and significance. It consists of being sufficiently involved with other people to see the world through their eyes, and yet to be clear enough to differentiate their experiences from one's own. Accurate and perceptive discrimination is a necessary condition for good communication, but it is not itself sufficient. To communicate empathetically means to convince others that the listener understands both their feelings and the behavior and experience underlying these feelings (Egan, 1975).

Minimal empathic understanding consists of accurately reflecting another person's meaning and affect. The helper shows that he or she understands the *explicit* meaning of a communication. For example:

> *John:* Whenever I stand up in front of a group to speak, I lose track of what I want to say because of all the faces out there.
>
> *Mary:* You freeze up and get tongue-tied looking at all those people.

With more advanced levels of empathic understanding, the content and feeling of people's expressions are heard and commented upon so that their most personal moments are shared. The helper goes beyond surface feelings and meanings to reflect those hidden from the client's awareness. For example:

> *Jill:* My father really bugs me. He expects me to spend all my time studying and get perfect grades.
>
> *Jack:* You're pretty angry at him for being so unreasonable and demanding, and maybe you feel a little sad about disappointing him.

The following guidelines are instrumental in learning accurate empathic understanding (Carkhuff, 1969):

1. Concentrate intensely upon the other person's verbal and nonverbal messages and expressions.
2. In the early stages of learning empathy, try to discover words or expressions that are interchangeable with those the person uses in terms of their meaning and emotional loading. This is also called paraphrasing.
3. Formulate responses in language that is most attuned to the other person.
4. Use a feeling tone similar to that communicated by the other person.
5. Move toward deeper levels of empathy by clarifying and expanding on the other person's communications. This helps the person reach previously unexpressible feelings.
6. Look for feelings or thoughts that are not being expressed directly by the other person, but appear to be intended in the message. Try filling in what is missing from the communication rather than merely feeding back the expressed content.

There is extensive empirical evidence indicating that accurate empathic understanding can be taught to uninitiated people in a relatively short time (Cash & Vellema, 1979; Truax & Carkhuff, 1967).

Confrontation is a particularly potent form of communication that has the potential for both growth and harm. Confrontation is said to occur whenever one person does something that causes others to reflect on, question, or change their behavior (Egan, 1975). When confrontation is used skillfully, it helps people examine their behavior more closely and change it in a direction consistent with their goals and development. Confrontations are apt to be more productive if the confronter:

1. has established a positive relationship with the persons being confronted and is willing to become further involved with them
2. phrases confrontations as suggestions or requests rather than demands
3. specifies concrete behaviors rather than assuming or ascribing hidden motives
4. makes the confrontation positive and constructive rather than negative
5. states the confrontation directly, representing facts as facts, hypotheses as hypotheses, and feelings as feelings (Pfeiffer & Jones, 1973).

The receiver will benefit from a confrontation by being open to feedback from others and viewing it as an invitation to explore oneself, an invitation that may involve some temporary conflict or disorganization. However, confrontation will probably be met defensively unless the group atmosphere is trusting and accepting. The nature of the confrontation should be consistent with the group's goals; thus, intimately personal confrontations would be out of place in task-oriented T-groups. Skilled confrontation requires a sensitivity to the vulnerabilities and psychological state of the recipient and a keen awareness of one's own motives. Much supposedly "therapeutic" confrontation may really express a need to punish, dominate, or be provocative rather than a willingness to help and become more involved with another individual.

Structured interventions

Many T-groups today do not have the luxury of an extended period of time in which to create their own social organizations and struggle with clarifying goals and setting agendas. Consequently, the leader may be more active in telescoping time for short-term groups, functioning in many ways as a member, confronting and providing feedback throughout the duration of the group. The "structured" laboratory learning session provides a specific goal for each meeting and a task, activity, or exercise intended to achieve that goal. The activity typically involves focused observation on a process that is conceptually important to T-groups, such as levels of participation and influence, norms and group atmosphere, or decision-making procedures. The leader creates the tone for the session by giving the group the task. The group then tries to solve the task in its own way. Planned activities may be designed to stimulate individual participation or to highlight behaviors in areas such as conflict resolution, competition, and leadership. For instance, the group might be directed to create a simulated company or an ideal society. Throughout the process and at the end group members give each other interpersonal feedback, and the leader takes the opportunity to provide input. The experiential exercises described at the beginning of Chapter 12 are structured T-group experiences.

Organizational applications

Through the years, the T-group has expanded greatly from the unstructured, basic skills training group format. In the late 1960s and early 1970s, T-groups and sensitivity groups were widely used in organizational settings. They were a frequent intervention of external consultants called in to troubleshoot with existing work groups to improve the job experiences of employees. The results of some of these interventions were disappointing. Sensitivity training was oversold, employees were often not told what to expect and, hence, felt coerced to participate, and the groups were not always beneficial to the needs of the organization. Currently T-groups are used less frequently and more selectively in business settings. They usually constitute part of an approach to planned organizational change called Organization Development, or OD (French & Bell, 1973). Organization Development consists of planned intervention strategies to help organizations use their personnel resources more fully and function more effectively. A specific OD goal might be to reduce interdepartmental conflict, develop shared leadership methods, or improve decision-making procedures.

Central to OD efforts is a reliance on experience-based learning and the action-research model of intervention (Sherwood, 1977). The action-research approach consists of gathering data from individuals and groups, feeding the data back to group members, and jointly planning action based on the feedback. The basic strategy is to intercede in the organization's ongoing activities and employ such specific OD procedures as environmental assessment, process consultation, strategic planning, intergroup problem solving, confrontation meetings, and planned renegotiation. Within this context, the traditional T-group has largely been supplanted by a more directed application of laboratory training methods called "team building." The idea is to improve work relationships by focusing on the organization itself or the team within the organization, as opposed to encouraging individuals to become more successful organization members. This thrust, incidentally, is consistent with Kurt Lewin's original commitment to effect change in social systems rather than in individuals.

APPRAISAL

Leonard Blank (1969) describes a cartoon in which two women sitting under hairdryers are comparing notes about their group experiences. One remarks to the other, "I don't know what I'm getting out of my group but I certainly have got the goods on a lot of people." In some T-groups this comment may accurately reflect the extent to which learning has occurred. Most T-groups, however, create the opportunity for valuable personal changes or growth in their members in several general ways (Hampden-Turner, 1966). First, the group can improve an individual's communication skills and conceptual understanding. This leads to an increased sensitivity to one's own and others' needs, and to the development of a greater number of alternative behaviors to meet problems in living. Second, the T-group can help people clarify their personal identity and suggest directions for future development. Finally, the group can aid a person in increasing self-esteem and feelings of personal worth.

Research on T-groups

Exactly how T-groups create these changes is not clear. Hampden-Turner (1966) offers an existential model of human learning and personality development that, he believes, adequately describes the changes that take place in a T-group. The quality of group members' cognition, the clarity of their identity, and the extent of their self-esteem blend to form a measure of overall competence. Competence influences the extent to which one reaches out to others in the group to seek self-confirmation while striving to integrate the feedback group members provide. Early research found that T-groups do have a positive influence on these variables. For example, the quality of a person's cognitions does, in part, involve a sensitivity to the needs of others. Bunker (1965), who evaluated a number of conferences at National Training Laboratories, found that T-group participants become significantly more sensitive to the feelings of other group members. Self-awareness is one path toward strengthening one's own identity. Studies by Bunker (1965) and Valiquet (1964) discovered that T-group members become more aware of their own behavior and develop greater self-insight. With regard to self-esteem, research by Argyris (1964, 1965) found that experiences of personal adequacy and interpersonal competence increase for T-group participants.

In recent years, research on T-groups has shifted from a concern with group dynamics and group processes to applied studies of the outcomes of T-group experiences (Golembiewski & Blumberg, 1977). There is still reluctance among some T-group trainers to welcome objective, scientific evaluation of their work, since such procedures tend to be seen as interfering with the process of the group and incompatible with its humanistic bias. However, some early empirical generalizations appear to retain their validity today (Luke & Seashore, 1977). For instance, it appears that members who come to the group with behavioral styles that are quite different from the values of the T-group milieu often benefit more than those whose styles are more congruent with the group culture. Moreover, members' willingness to involve themselves in the group process is apt to be a better predictor of change than any particular personality variables. When Campbell and Dunnette reviewed the T-group literature in 1968 they were forced to rely on studies that did not always adhere to sound methodological principles, such as the inclusion of control groups, the use of a repeated-measures design, and a reasonable time duration. A few years later Smith (1975) was able to review more carefully designed studies. Smith concluded that on self-ratings and psychometric instruments participants have better self-concepts at the close of the group, become more open to others and to new experiences, and score higher on positively valued traits. Frequent measures of these changes include Schutz' FIRO-B, Shostrom's Personal Orientation Inventory (POI), and Jourard's self-disclosure questionnaire. In addition, T-group graduates are perceived by nonparticipants as behaviorally changed for the better and regarded as possessing improved communication skills. Sensitivity training in programs for organizational development has also shown a variety of positive effects, though the data base for these results rests on more weakly designed studies.

Outcomes of T-group experiences are affected by variations in leader behavior and the personalities and motivations of the group members. One of the nagging problems of research in this area is to demonstrate long-term changes. Few studies have used follow-up measures and related group changes to actual performance criteria in the specific home or job setting. The successful transfer of learning from the training experience to the home environment seems to be facilitated by (1) an acknowledgement by participants of some personal interaction problem, such as a difficulty in giving and receiving compliments, and (2) their perception that some commonality exists between the group and everyday life experiences (Lakin, 1972). T-groups that emphasize back-home applications of the group interactions have demonstrated greater post-group behavior changes than those that do not (Bunker & Knowles, 1967). The highest rate of follow-up change is found among organizational groups that meet together for training and remain intact thereafter (Smith, 1975).

From another point of view, the most critical determinant of transfer of learning is the acquisition of the basic skills necessary to diagnose new situations accurately and to be able to cooperate with others to achieve behavior appropriate to the situation (Argyris, 1973). In short, group partici- pants must learn to (1) communicate accurately with one another; (2) give and receive beneficial feedback; (3) perform these skills in a manner where- by trust and self-acceptance increase; and (4) set up groups in which problem solving can occur—that is, groups that effectively use the abilities of the members and show respect for their individuality.

Implications and extensions

It is clear that laboratory learning processes have had a remarkable impact on society at large. One effect has been to expand the segment of society that is comfortable talking and thinking in psychological terms. This is demonstrated in the tendency among some to believe that people are not really alive or worthwhile if they don't make a periodic pilgrimage to an experiential group. More people are developing a better understanding of psychological processes in everyday life. Related to this, laboratory education has helped us discover that we do have more control over our lives than we ever believed (Steele, 1968). In times of social catastrophe or environmental crisis, such as the power blackout in the northeastern United States in 1965, it is amazing how social interaction patterns change and instant friendships are formed. The T-group experience teaches members that there is no need to wait for a fortuitous crisis in order to create exciting new situations or to make more meaningful choices.

As the helping professions have become increasingly influenced by the T-group movement, heavier emphasis has been placed on encouraging individual growth and authenticity. The popularity of the term "sensitivity training" reflected this shift from a group focus to an individual fulfillment model. Today sensitivity groups and T-groups in their pure forms are not as prominent as they were a few years ago. Rather, the principles and methods of laboratory education have shifted in at least two directions. On one hand, there has been a move toward groups that stress conceptual understanding and skill building. Program brochures from NTL and other centers for T-group training are filled with descriptions of groups on specific themes such as family relationships, the needs of men or women, and the training of teachers or administrators. The second development has been the incorporation of methods from other group approaches into traditional T-groups.

There are distinctions between T-groups and psychotherapy groups that will be explored in the following chapter. It is enough to say at this point that the T-group is not equivalent to intensive group psychotherapy. However, the open and honest feedback participants typically receive in the T-group may encourage some to seek out more intensive and personalized group experiences.

SUMMARY

Training groups (T-groups) were developed by Kurt Lewin and his colleagues in 1946 when they noted that group members benefited from analyzing their own group experiences. Training laboratories offer a range of experiential learning activities, focusing on the development of interpersonal skills and the study of small group processes. Some T-groups, called *sensitivity groups*, may push for the total enhancement of the individual participants.

The underlying values of the T-group movement include *a commitment to the behavioral and social sciences, democratic* as opposed to authoritarian processes, and the power of *helping relationships*. The basic concepts associated with T-groups include the *learning laboratory, learning how to learn*, and an emphasis on the *here-and-now*. A learning laboratory stresses the testing of new behaviors in a non-threatening environment. Learning how to learn involves a cycle of *presentation of self, feedback*, and *experimentation*. Feedback, exemplified by the *Johari Window*, is the most important concept in T-group methodology.

The T-group leader (trainer) trusts the group members to work together to examine their own behavior and relationships. A distant cousin of the T-group, the Tavistock small study group, operates on the principle that individual behavior reflects concerns of the whole group. The Tavistock leader assumes an even more passive and indirect role than the T-group leader. T-groups also help participants to develop specific communication skills such as *behavior description, communication of feelings, active listening*, and *confrontation*. Some T-groups utilize structured interventions to meet group members' specific goals.

Research on T-groups can be divided into two areas: research on group process and evaluations of outcome effectiveness. There is a need for more long-term follow-up studies, particularly to examine transfer of effects from the group experience to home situations. T-groups have helped promote the popularity of groups in general and have increased familiarity with psychological concepts. They have been part of an ongoing public interest in individual growth and authenticity. Recently, T-groups have begun to focus on specific skill building and have started to incorporate group techniques from other orientations.

REFERENCES

Argyris, C. T-groups for organizational effectiveness. *Harvard Business Review,* 1964, *42,* 60–74.

Argyris, C. Explorations in interpersonal competence. *Journal of Applied Behavioral Science,* 1965, *1,* 58–83.

Argyris, C. On the future of laboratory education. *Journal of Applied Behavioral Science,* 1967, *3,* 153–183.

Argyris, C. The nature of competence-acquisition activities and their relationship to therapy. In W. G. Bennis, D. E. Berlew, E. H. Schein, & F. I. Steele (Eds.), *Interpersonal dynamics.* Homewood, Ill.: Dorsey Press, 1973.

Banet, A. G. Jr., & Hayden, C. A Tavistock primer. In J. W. Pfeiffer & J. E. Jones (Eds.), *Small-group training, theory and practice* (2nd ed.). La Jolla, Calif.: University Associates, 1979.

Benne, K. D. History of the T-group in the laboratory setting. In L. P. Bradford, J. R. Gibb, & K. D. Benne (Eds.), *T-group theory and the laboratory method.* New York: Wiley, 1964.

Bennis, W. G. Goals and meta-goals of laboratory training. In R. T. Golembiewski & A. Blumberg (Eds.), *Sensitivity training and the laboratory approach.* Itasca, Ill.: F. E. Peacock, 1977.

Bion, W. R. *Experiences in groups.* New York: Basic Books, 1959.

Blank, L. *The use and misuse of sensitivity and other groups.* Paper presented at the American Psychological Association convention, Washington, D.C., Aug. 31–Sept. 4, 1969.

Blumberg, A., & Golembiewski, R. T. *Learning and change in groups.* Baltimore, Md.: Penguin, 1976.

Bogart, D. The complete trainer. *Journal of Applied Behavioral Science,* 1966, *2,* 360–361.

Bradford, L. P., Gibb, J. R., & Benne, K. D. (Eds.). *T-group theory and the laboratory method.* New York: Wiley, 1964.

Bunker, D. R. Individual applications of laboratory training. *Journal of Applied Behavioral Science,* 1965, *1,* 131–147.

Bunker, D. R., & Knowles, E. S. Comparison of behavioral changes resulting from human relations training laboratories of different lengths. *Journal of Applied Behavioral Science,* 1967, *3,* 505–523.

Campbell, J. P., & Dunnette, M. D. Effectiveness of T-group experiences in managerial training and development. *Psychological Bulletin,* 1968, *70,* 73–104.

Carkhuff, R. R. *Helping and human relations* (Vols. 1 and 2). New York: Holt, Rinehart & Winston, 1969.

Cash, R. W., & Vellema, C. K. Conceptual versus competency approach in human relations training programs. *The Personnel and Guidance Journal,* 1979, *58,* 91–96.

Cohen, A. M., & Smith, R. D. *The critical incident in growth groups: Theory and technique.* La Jolla, Calif.: University Associates, 1976.

Egan, G. *The skilled helper.* Monterey, Calif.: Brooks/Cole, 1975.

French, W. L., & Bell, C. H. *Organization development: Behavioral science interventions for organization improvement.* New York: Prentice-Hall, 1973.

Gibb, J. R. Climate for trust formation. In L. P. Bradford, J. R. Gibb, & K. D. Benne (Eds.), *T-group theory and laboratory method.* New York: Wiley, 1964.

Gibb, J. R. Defensive communication. In W. G. Bennis, D. F. Berlew, E. H. Schein, & F. I. Steele (Eds.), *Interpersonal dynamics.* Homewood, Ill.: Dorsey Press, 1973.

Gibb, J. R. *Trust: A new view of personal and organizational development.* Los Angeles: Guild of Tutors Press, 1978.

Golembiewski, R. T., & Blumberg, A. (Eds.). *Sensitivity training and the laboratory approach.* Itasca, Ill.: F. E. Peacock, 1977.

Hampden-Turner, C. M. An existential "Learning theory" and the integration of T-group research. *Journal of Applied Behavioral Science*, 1966, 2, 367–386.

Lakin, M. *Interpersonal encounter: Theory and practice in sensitivity training.* New York: McGraw-Hill, 1972.

Lewin, K. *Resolving social conflict.* New York: Harper, 1948.

Lewin, K. *Field theory in social science: Selected theoretical papers* (D. Cartwright, Ed.). New York: Harper & Row, 1951.

Luft, J. *Group processes: An introduction to group dynamics.* Palo Alto, Calif.: National Press, 1970.

Luke, R. A., & Seashore, C. Generalizations on research and speculations from experience related to laboratory training design. In R. T. Golembiewski & A. Blumberg (Eds.), *Sensitivity training and the laboratory approach.* Itasca, Ill.: F. E. Peacock, 1977.

O'Day, R. The T-group trainer: A study of conflict in the exercise of authority. In G. S. Gibbard, J. J. Hubbard, & R. E. Mann (Eds.), *Analysis of groups.* San Francisco: Jossey-Bass, 1974.

Pfeiffer, J. W. & Jones, J. E. (Eds.), *Small-group training, theory and practice* (2nd ed.). La Jolla, Calif.: University Associates, 1979.

Pfeiffer, J. W., & Jones, J. E. The Johari Window: A model for soliciting and giving feedback. In J. E. Jones & J. W. Pfeiffer (Eds.), *The 1973 annual handbook for group facilitators.* La Jolla, Calif.: University Associates, 1973.

Rice, A. K. *Learning for leadership.* New York: Humanities Press, 1965.

Rioch, M. J. The work of Wilfred Bion on groups. *Psychiatry*, 1970, 33, 56–66.

Rogers, C. R., Gendlin, E. T., Kiesler, D., & Truax, C. B. *The therapeutic relationship and its impact.* Madison, Wis.: University of Wisconsin Press, 1967.

Schein, E. H., & Bennis, W. G. *Personal and organizational change through group methods.* New York: Wiley, 1965.

Seashore, C. What is sensitivity training? *NTL Institute News and Reports*, April, 1968.

Sherwood, J. J. *An introduction to organization development.* In J. W. Pfeiffer & J. E. Jones (Eds.), *Organization development: Selected readings.* La Jolla, Calif.: University Associates, 1977.

Simmel, G. *The sociology of George Simmel.* Glencoe, Ill.: Free Press, 1950.

Smith, P. B. Controlled studies of the outcome of sensitivity training. *Psychological Bulletin*, 1975, 82, 597–622.

Steele, F. I. *The T-group movement: Its past and future, or, the socket-wrench saga.* Paper presented at a symposium on T-group training at the Midwestern Psychological Association Convention, Chicago, May 1968.

Truax, C. B., & Carkhuff, R. R. *Toward effective counseling and psychotherapy.* Chicago: Aldine, 1967.

Truax, C. B., & Wargo, D. G. Antecedents to outcome in group psychotherapy with outpatients: Effects of therapeutic conditions, alternate sessions, vicarious therapy pre-training and patient self-exploration. *Journal of Consulting and Clinical Psychology*, 1969, 33, 440–447.

Valiquet, M. I. *Contribution to the evaluation of a management training program.* Unpublished doctoral dissertation, Massachusetts Institute of Technology, 1964.

White, R., & Lippitt, R. Leader behavior and member reaction in three "social climates." In D. Cartwright & A. Zander (Eds.), *Group dynamics: Research and theory.* New York: Row, Peterson, 1962.

Yalom, I. D. *The theory and practice of group psychotherapy.* New York: Basic Books, 1975.

3

Encounter Groups

What began as an adventurous experiment in group process at the National Training Laboratories in Bethel, Maine, has since mushroomed in countless directions. There are now a host of experiential groups around the world. Most are labeled "encounter groups," a gentle term that somehow elicits devotion among supporters and fear or hostility among critics. Unfortunately, however, the term does not refer to a single, clearly articulated approach to groups. In fact, it is challenging to try to define encounter groups by theoretical construct or technique because of the wide variety of group experiences within this category.

The first use of the term "encounter" is attributed to Jacob Moreno, the founder of psychodrama (see Chapter 5). A contemporary definition is provided by William Schutz (1971): "Encounter is a method of human relating based on openness and honesty, self-awareness, self-responsibility, awareness of the body, attention to feelings and an emphasis on the here and now" (p. 3). This is the definition we will use for the type of encounter group examined in this chapter.

HISTORY AND DEVELOPMENT

It has been said that there is an East Coast–West Coast distinction within the sensitivity group movement. The East Coast growth centers spawned groups that were task-oriented, exploring issues such as communication, problem solving, and leadership. The West Coast group is the more "communion-oriented," developing the capacity of members for closer and more intimate relations (Kaplan & Sadock, 1972). It is no accident that much of the impetus for spawning the encounter group movement originated on the West Coast. The lifestyle and climate of California seem to encourage social experimentation. Moreover, Carl Rogers and

William Schutz, two powerful forces behind the movement, were residing there.

Carl Rogers' greatest claim to fame is in laying the groundwork for a client-centered therapy that has come to dominate counseling centers throughout North America. Rogers referred to the encounter group movement as the greatest social invention of the 1960s. Reflecting on the overly rational and bureaucratic aspects of contemporary culture that alienate us from one another and from ourselves, Rogers (1968, pp. 268–269) predicted "there will be possibilities for the rapid development of closeness between and among persons, a closeness which is not artificial but is real and deep, and which will be well-suited to our increasing mobility in living. Temporary relationships will be able to achieve the richness and meaning which heretofore have been associated only with lifelong attachments." For Rogers, one such vehicle for change, perfectly coordinated with a counterculture social movement, is the encounter group. His legacy to the encounter movement is the "Basic Encounter," conceptualized while serving on the faculties of both the Western Behavioral Science Institute and the Center for the Study of the Person, in La Jolla, California. This contribution to the encounter movement remains perfectly consistent with the humanistic orientation to individual counseling that Rogers developed in the 1940s and 1950s.

Rogers' approach stresses a phenomenological position. Counselors attend closely to the client's communication, empathizing with the client without imposing their own value judgments and trusting clients' inherent growth potential to reach their own productive conclusions. In much the same way, Rogers' (1970) Basic Encounter maintains a faith in individual growth as group members express and accept their own feelings and the feelings of others. Unlike T-groups, the focus of Basic Encounter is not on understanding the group process or on developing interpersonal skills, but on finding authenticity in relating to others. The leader tries to create and facilitate an atmosphere of safety and trust in order to encourage members to share their innermost thoughts and feelings. Rogers minimizes the need for active techniques and group exercises and relies on his unusually accepting personality to draw out and involve participants.

The source of the dramatic change and explosion in the encounter group movement was the Esalen Institute in Big Sur, California, an idyllic expanse of land on cliffs overlooking the Pacific Ocean. Esalen was established in 1962 as a center for the study of human potential by Michael Murphy, a Stanford University graduate who owned the land, and his friend Richard Price. While on the East Coast NTL was restricting itself to studying group processes, Esalen opened itself to a variety of therapeutic and pseudotherapeutic experiences. Included was the exploration of non-Western philosophy and religious thought, inspired by Murphy's sojourn to India. The Esalen-type group, unlike the traditional T-group, did not train people in the processes of group activity, but instead offered a smorgasbord of psychological, therapeutic, and spiritual experiences that encouraged the expansion of human potential, using the key concept of encounter. Within a few years Esalen became the inspiration for like-minded growth centers around the country. It offered workshops on topics from Zen Buddhism to meditation to bioenergetics to encounter, led by a permanent residential staff and stimulated by new methods introduced by visiting experts.

If Esalen was the amphitheatre of the encounter group movement, then Bill Schutz was the performer at center stage. A former social psychologist from Harvard, Schutz' academic credentials rested on a book called *FIRO* (1958), which attempted to relate psychoanalytic theory to group dynamics. By the time Schutz arrived on the scene at Esalen, he had a versatile background, including training in psychodynamic theory, bioenergetic analysis (see Chapter 6), and NTL group leadership. Pulling together these strands of experience, Schutz emerged as the leading "guru" of the encounter movement, labeling his unique blend open encounter. Utilizing contributions from Wilhelm Reich, Alexander Lowen, Moshe Feldenkrais, and Ida Rolf, all of whom are discussed in Chapter 6, Schutz made the unity of body and mind the critical concept in open encounter. His theoretical stance assumed that emotional conflicts reside and are expressed in specific areas of the body through muscular tension, and that any psychological treatment that ignored the body was incomplete. Consequently, Schutz began to deal with emotionally blocked areas by studying problems in posture and movement within the group, then suggesting vigorous body exercises, as well as verbal confrontation techniques, to reawaken long-suppressed emotions.

Although current Esalen-type groups may incorporate methods and concepts from a wide array of sources, there seem to be at least two identifiable trends in contemporary group work: those approaches that are primarily somatic or body-oriented, such as sensory awakening, bioenergetics, and structural reintegration; and those approaches oriented more toward interpersonal and intrapersonal awareness, such as encounter, Gestalt, and psychodrama. The somatic approaches will be discussed in Chapter 6. Gestalt (Chapter 4) and psychodrama (Chapter 5), which are themselves popular group approaches, are also logical antecedents of encounter. Many encounter group leaders are influenced by their own experiences with Gestalt and psychodrama, which facilitate affective expression in nonverbal ways.

BASIC CONCEPTS

Schutz' definition of the encounter group refers to the principles of openness and honesty, self-awareness and awareness of the body, self-responsibility, attending to feelings, and staying in the here-and-now.

Self-disclosure

The concepts of openness and honest are manifest in the group value of *self-disclosure*. Encounter groups encourage self-revelation as a way to foster intimate or close relationships among group members. Participants are encouraged to disclose their feelings and thoughts, particularly as they relate to other group members or to the group's experiences at any given time. These expressions are in contrast to historical personal disclosures that are unrelated to the group process. It would be relevant, for instance, to reveal that another group member reminds you of an older brother who always left you feeling scared and intimidated. It would be inappropriate to disclose the relationship with your brother without relating it to the here-and-now group context.

It is ironic that we may need a group experience in order to share ourselves intimately with others. But in society it is often more adaptive to conceal our true feelings, our deepest needs and doubts. Self-disclosure makes us vulnerable, and tends to make us seem weak. People who engage in a lot of self-disclosure may be viewed as pathetic and needy or as exhibitionistic and inappropriate. Sidney Jourard (1964) was especially insistent that the potentially terrifying experience of fully disclosing one-self to another human being is actually a mark of a strong and healthy personality. When we try to avoid becoming known by others, we make an active effort to construct a false public self. Although playing social roles may be inevitable in some situations, such as work or school, people who overemphasize roleplaying may feel cut off from others, lonely, estranged, and alienated from themselves. One reason that counseling and psycho-therapy involve self-disclosure may be the opportunity to reveal oneself fully to a sympathetic listener, which can be therapeutic regardless of the listener's response or feedback.

Although the risk of disclosing oneself may seem overwhelming, there is a price for hiding our real thoughts and feelings from others. We can avoid admitting any unpleasant facts about ourselves, but in so doing we avoid intimacy. In fleeing from self-disclosure, we may present a whole-some, perfect image to others at the cost of building any meaningful relationships. There is also reason to believe that suppression or repres-sion of significant inner experiences can lead to a host of psychosomatic disorders, including ulcers, hypertension, asthma, and migraine head-aches. O. H. Mowrer (1964) maintains that many psychological symptoms, such as withdrawal, excessive eating or drinking, taking drugs, or develop-ing stomach aches or headaches, may be attempts to escape the pain of admitting uncomfortable things about oneself. According to Mowrer, lone-liness, guilt, and depression are accompaniments to self-concealment. He suggests that the power of the Catholic confessional may come from disclosing difficult truths about oneself (Mowrer, 1970). "Sinners" can absolve themselves of the burden of guilt regarding some real or imagined misdeed by self-disclosing. Mowrer has taken the confessional directly into the encounter session. In his "integrity groups," participants are encour-aged to assume responsibility for their problems by revealing unconfessed, irresponsible behavior as the group progresses.

In many ways, the encounter group gives us permission to reveal ourselves to peers beyond those ritualized listeners—ministers, physicians, counselors, and therapists—to whom we are encouraged to communicate intimately about ourselves in times of stress (Egan, 1970). To be sure, indiscriminate self-disclosure may not be appropriate either. Although most people learn in encounter groups that they are habitually more closed off from friends and acquaintances than they need to be, premature disclosure has a way of overwhelming others and making people appear to be inappropriate in their demands. Luft (1970) suggests that self-disclosure is more appropriate when it is a function of an ongoing relationship; when both people in the relationship share themselves reciprocally; when the timing of disclosures is tuned to what is happening in the relationship; when disclosures come gradually rather than in an avalanche; and when the person is sensitive to the effect the disclosure is apt to have on the listener.

Perhaps the existential concept of authenticity comes closest to describing the open and honest relating that is central to the successful encounter group. Authenticity implies living in accordance with how things really are in the world. According to Maddi (1967, p. 315), an alienated person lacks a solid sense of self or personal identity and tends to consider himself or herself as nothing more than "a player of social roles and an embodiment of biological needs." As such, the individual might satisfy biological needs, such as food and sex, and present a socially acceptable and admirable facade without considering his or her deeper psychological and human needs. Authentic persons express themselves spontaneously and nondefensively, openly sharing what they think and feel in the group. In short, they are "genuine" (Carkhuff & Berenson, 1977).

Of course, one can only risk being genuine and authentic in a trusting environment. According to Rogers (1970), the disclosure of immediate interpersonal feelings in the group does not generally occur until members go through a series of experiences: feeling frustrated by the lack of structure; resisting personal expression or exploration; describing past and, consequently, relatively safe incidents and feelings; expressing negative attitudes to test the group's trustworthiness; and beginning to explore personally meaningful material. For members to explore unknown feelings, feelings that have previously been denied awareness, they must have a sense of being accepted unconditionally by the group's other members.

Self-awareness

The second element of Schutz' definition of encounter refers to the development of *self-awareness*. As participants disclose personal thoughts and feelings and receive feedback from other members, they are in a position to examine themselves from an enriched perspective. Self-awareness develops as one begins to understand one's own strengths and weaknesses. People become more conscious of self-destructive patterns and the way they affect and are affected by others in the group. A group member might explore, for example, a pattern of unsatisfactory relationships with members of the opposite sex. Growth in self-awareness leads members to become more comfortable with themselves and more able to change in an ideal direction.

One way the encounter group encourages the development of self-awareness is through the use of confrontation, which forces individuals to reflect on, consider, examine, or question their behavior. Usually, the confrontation points out a discrepancy between the way group members experience themselves and the way someone else experiences them. Ideally, confrontation is not used simply to tell people off or dump hostility. It is only appropriate to confront someone if you intend to involve yourself with that person (Egan, 1975). A group member's confrontations should express a concern and interest for other people that will lead them to examine their own behavior. Used appropriately, confrontation invites self-examination and is not a forceful pressure to change.

To be effective, confrontation must be sensitive to the needs and vulnerabilities of the person confronted. Some topics, such as sexuality, may require particularly delicate confrontation. There are encounter groups, though, where confrontation is intentionally rugged and vehement.

One controversial example is Synanon, another West Coast application of the encounter method. Synanon was started in 1958 by Charles Dederich, a nonprofessional ex-alcoholic who was concerned about developing a workable method for treating drug addicts. Dederich set up a self-help community in Santa Monica, California, that requires motivated addicts to live at Synanon and immerse themselves in a comprehensive treatment program. House rules are numerous and firm, and include abstaining from all drugs, including alcohol; carrying out household chores; and attending leaderless small-group sessions. Although membership in these groups, called "synanons," shift as members come and go, attention is focused on each member for a rather prolonged period of time. The nucleus of this focus is a strong confrontation that attempts to cut through the excuses, rationalizations, and game-playing of the hard-core addict. Experienced, nonprofessional ex-addicts may have an advantage over most trained professionals with this group, since they have similar experiences to share and can self-disclose relevant aspects of themselves with group members.

To the uninitiated observer, the Synanon confrontation technique may appear to subject members to unwarranted and humiliating attacks. The seasoned participant, however, sees the relentless verbal cross-examination as the most effective way to push the addict through emotional blocks and change from a generally self-destructive lifestyle. Addicts gradually learn that the Synanon community will not feed their dependency but rather will recognize their potential strength and try to teach assertive alternatives to acting out stress and anxiety through the use of drugs or alcohol. Synanon groups have not always been restricted to addict populations (see Casriel, 1963) and the focus on verbal, as well as physical, confrontation has found its way into the general encounter format.

Another aspect of self-awareness that Schutz includes in his definition of encounter is awareness of the body. Many encounter group leaders strike a balance between verbal and physical exercises. Body awareness and the use of body work in therapy is based on the assumption that an individual's earliest feelings are encoded and expressed in body language long before verbal skills are developed to express them. The sensations accompanying feelings of calm or upset, or happiness or anger, are very primitive and basic. Group members who feel "trapped" by their life situation may gain more insight and feel more exhilarated by expressing their conflict in physical terms—by literally breaking away from people who are holding on rather than by verbally describing, explaining, rationalizing, or obsessing about their feelings of being trapped. I am not suggesting that verbal consolidation of a cathartic emotional experience is not helpful, but rather that a physical exercise or intervention may be a particularly powerful starting point. The focus on body awareness is consistent with Schutz' disillusionment with the traditional "talk" therapies as a basis for lasting change.

Responsibility

The third element in Schutz' definition is *responsibility*. Humanistic therapies generally maintain a fundamental respect for clients, viewing them as capable of change and able to participate actively in the change process. Group members are expected to take responsibility for behavior in the group and, more broadly, for their own lives. Schutz begins an encounter group by laying the ground rule that participants are responsible for everything they choose to do or not to do in the group, including going crazy. He insists that the group should not parentally protect individuals but encourage them to use their own resources and decision-making capacities. In Schutz' view, symptomatic and limiting behaviors are themselves evidence of a refusal to take responsibility for our lives.

Most encounter group leaders take a less radical position on the responsibility issue. All agree that one goal of any therapeutic system is to help clients expand the range of options they experience as available to them in their lives. As leaders guide group members toward developing a sense of responsibility, they refuse to "rescue" members from the anxiety that is inevitably part of the process of becoming aware. They may, however, set limits to the kinds of behaviors that are to be tolerated in the group. Physical fighting may be forbidden, or there may be an insistence on a policy of confidentiality.

The emphasis on clients' responsibility aside, one cannot totally deny the group leader's responsibility in the therapy process. Helmut Kaiser (1955), a psychoanalytically trained psychotherapist who was at the vanguard of the existential therapy movement, remarked that once a client is diagnosed as treatable, the therapist is responsible for developing the client's sense of responsibility. Simply put, once a leader decides that a person is eligible to participate in a group, that leader is responsible for therapist-initiated outcomes. Group leaders who refuse to accept responsibility for what happens to their clients, emphasizing instead group members' responsibility to resist pressure, are denying their role in the interaction process. The group leader is usually the most powerful individual with whom the members interact in the group.

This point is illustrated in a fable concerning three boys. The first is named Therapist, the second Awareness, and the third Client (Peterson, 1977). As the boys are walking down the street, Therapist gives Awareness a shove so that he falls into the third boy, throwing Client to the ground. Client accuses Therapist of knocking him over, but Therapist denies that he was responsible and blames Awareness. The moral is that it is the irresponsible therapist who claims that any negative outcomes result from the client's own inability to grow.

Attention to feelings

Schutz also includes *attention to feelings* in his encounter definition. Central to all encounter is the goal of a richer awareness of our affective potential. The strong feelings that the group generates have been amply documented in such first-person accounts as Jane Howard's (1970) *Please Touch* and Rasa Gustaitis' (1969) *Turning On.* According to Warkentin (1969), the most significant shortcoming in many therapies is a lack of emotional intensity and inadequate participant involvement. In contrast, many encounter group leaders make use of the expressive, awareness-oriented techniques of Gestalt and psychodrama to facilitate intense and meaningful affective experiences.

Before people can act responsibly, they must be aware of their feelings at all times. By attending to sensation and feelings, encounter groups attempt to balance the scales against what many see as an overly cognitive, intellectualized cosmology of Western technocracy. In promoting awareness and acceptance of inner experiences and feelings—whether joy, sadness, fear, anger, or sexuality—the encounter group upholds the basic value of emotional expressiveness as the most genuine form of human relating. The means to this goal is to minimize intellectual defensiveness as a barrier to emotional insight. At its best, encounter helps one deepen personal awareness and learn to recognize and validate the personal experiences of others. Encounter group participants often leave the group feeling a strong sense of compassion, closeness, and warmth toward fellow members and the world in general.

Here-and-now

The last element Schutz uses to define encounter groups is an emphasis on the *here-and-now.* The focus on the present is a legacy from sensitivity and T-groups. This perspective, discussed in Chapter 2, contrasts with that of groups that deal chiefly with personal histories and incidents that have occurred outside the group setting. Rogers' Basic Encounter model is a partial exception to the exclusive preoccupation with present feelings.

Although Rogers prefers group members to express their here-and-now reactions, he does allow participants to bring in statements about past events (Rogers, 1970).

Psychotherapy versus growth

A final encounter concept to consider is the distinction between psychotherapy and personal growth. Originally, encounter groups were considered to be distinct from traditional psychotherapy groups in both methods and goals. For example, whereas therapy has always been aimed at rectifying the symptomatic behavior of the neurotic or psychotic individual, encounter was seen as encouraging the psychological growth and self-realization of the well-functioning person. Strupp (1973) maintains that encounter groups are fundamentally opposed to the values implicit in traditional psychotherapy. He regards encounter's focus on immediate, affective experience at the expense of long-range personal goals as reflecting the American *Zeitgeist* ("spirit of the times") of the late 1960s and early 1970s. People were disenchanted with the tedious procedures of traditional psychotherapy and attracted to the instant happiness and inexpensive cures seemingly promised by encounter groups.

However, the bonds between therapy and encounter are fuzzier than one might expect. Many psychotherapy groups make use of encounter methods. It is also true that psychotherapy is no longer intended exclusively for the "sick" population. A lack of joy in one's life is a symptom sufficient to seek therapy. Since symptoms imply limitations in behavior potential no matter how they are conceptualized (that is, as attempts to cope with antisocial, intrapsychic impulses or as maladaptive reactions to environmental stimuli), it is difficult to distinguish group experiences that try to remove symptoms from those that aim to disinhibit the potential for enjoyment and productivity (Mintz, 1971).

There are still many differences between the encounter group and the traditional psychotherapy group (Goldberg, 1970). For instance, traditional therapy is long-term and continuous. Encounter and most other new group approaches tend to be much shorter, often lasting a single day or weekend. In the encounter group, therefore, if individual participant goals are identified at all, they are formulated very early. Traditional group psychotherapy tends to rely on historical material and to recognize the limitations of individual constitutions and life situations. Because encounter is here-and-now oriented, there is an emphasis on group members' immediate choice and responsibility for their predicaments.

Also, whereas traditional group therapies attempt to help patients adapt to society, encounter theory sees each person as having the right and opportunity to seek pleasure and fulfillment, to become "actualized," rather than adapt to the possibly arbitrary and stifling demands of society. Self-actualization is a concept created by Abraham Maslow (1968), who believed that healthy people, having met their basic needs for safety, belonging, love, respect, and self-esteem, turn to developing their talents and potentials. The cult movie *Harold and Maude*, in which a zany old woman teaches a suicidal young man how to live life to the fullest, nicely illustrates the value of personal actualization and its interaction with social realities.

Encounter group leaders act as models of self-disclosure and confrontation. This contrasts strongly with traditional therapy, where the leader remains virtually anonymous, striving to be a "blank screen" on which group members can project their own needs and expectations. The model of the disclosing therapist probably originates from Carl Rogers' research demonstrating that empathic, transparent therapists are particularly successful (1967). Rogers maintains that a genuine, caring therapist can create a climate of unconditional acceptance in which clients will bloom on their own. The tendency for group leaders to feel free to share of themselves in the group takes its extreme form in existential group psychotherapy, where the leader is seen as being the "most experienced patient" (Warkentin, 1969). As such, leaders may exaggerate their own experience of the group in order to promote an authentic "happening."

Finally, traditional therapy approaches are more or less intellectually oriented, preferring to deal with "mind" rather than body. Encounter stresses the importance of the body and of gut feelings. (It is ironic that psychiatric training, which begins with studying the physiology of the human organism, tends to be particularly antisomatic and antierotic.)

BASIC PROCEDURES

There are many kinds of activities common to encounter groups. Although there are differences between individual group leaders, the basic principles of encounter discussed previously guide their actions. The leader tries to create a meaningful emotional experience for members by drawing from a pool of techniques and exercises.

Since fear can impede productive movement in the group, leaders typically attempt to create a close and trusting atmosphere by demonstrating their own ability to trust and take risks. Very little conceptualizing or didactic input is provided by leaders. Being skilled professionals versed in group dynamics, they look for areas of conflict, ambivalence, or vulnerability and focus on them to encourage participants to explore such feelings further. The experienced group leader knows when to push and confront and when to withdraw in order to preserve individual integrity and boundaries. A leader's interventions work either to promote interpersonal communication directly or to explore individual resistances.

Participants are generally asked to observe some universal ground rules: to engage in open and honest communication, to pay close attention to feelings generated in their bodies, to concentrate on feelings rather than ideas, and to stay in the here-and-now as much as possible without drifting into past history or intellectualized discourse (Schutz, 1967). Participants are usually reminded that they are responsible for themselves, and that their group experience will be what they choose to have it become. Tension relievers such as coffee, cigarettes, and wristwatches are often discouraged to embolden members to deal with their discomfort in more direct and therapeutic ways.

Most of the techniques or exercises introduced by the leader lead to emotional self-exploration, or even to an emotional catharsis, followed by an opportunity for cognitive integration and understanding. The kind of exercise used depends both on the group's make-up and the stage of the group process.

Making contact

In the early stages of the group, members are most concerned about making contact, fitting in, and reducing tension and uncertainty. They have what Schutz (1958) calls a need for *inclusion*, a need to belong in the group and relate satisfactorily to other participants.[1] During the initial meeting, members might be asked to introduce themselves with pseudonyms that communicate something more revealing than their given names. In another opener, participants are encouraged to get to know one another, in pairs or in mini-groups, by exchanging first impressions and feelings. Some exercises involve maintaining eye contact without exchanging words. Others use touch, encouraging partners to explore one another's hands or faces. Although these techniques scare most people initially, they break the ice by overcoming normal social conventions and thus creating instant involvement.

Often physical exercise is used at the beginning of a group to help energize participants and break down barriers. Members can be instructed to take several deep breaths in unison, jump up and down, or shout.

Building trust

Feeling left out of a group may be a normal experience for participants who find it difficult to trust others or who feel anxious about sharing themselves with others. As members begin to trust and disclose themselves, they start to become aware of their underlying similarities, whereas earlier they may have noted only their differences. There are numerous interventions for dealing with the trust variable. Although the spontaneous sharing of feelings and experiences helps build an underlying communality, it is sometimes more powerful to translate feelings of distrust or exclusion into physical activity. One common exercise is "breaking into the circle." Group members stand and form a circle by interlocking arms. The participant who feels left out is instructed to try to break through the circle and penetrate to the center. Those forming the circle are encouraged not to yield easily so that the excluded participant will realize that she must make a determined effort if she is to become, at least in symbol, a fully participat-

---

[1]Needs for inclusion, control, and affection are part of Schutz' FIRO (Fundamental Interpersonal Relations Orientation) theory of interpersonal behavior. The FIRO is a questionnaire used to measure an individual's standing along these three interpersonal dimensions.

ing group member. As a physical experience, breaking into the circle is generally more meaningful for the individual than simply talking about feeling left out. A member who feels trapped in the group could likewise be encouraged to break out of the circle to deal with feelings of dependency or weakness.

A well-known technique for exploring the issue of trust is to instruct members to do a "trust fall" in pairs. In this exercise one person stands with closed eyes and then falls backwards, trusting that his partner will catch him. The partner assumes a crouching or kneeling position and catches the faller before he touches the floor. The faller is encouraged to be aware of his feelings prior to and during the fall. Observers also note whether the faller cheats by taking a couple of stutter steps prior to letting go. Although some participants will trust virtually any group member to catch them, others will find it difficult to trust anyone. For those people, this exercise can be a traumatic experience generating many feelings on trust issues.

Exploring conflicts

Conflict in groups is likely whenever members share their impressions and feelings. One type of conflict relates to leadership or dominance and has been called the control dimension (Schutz, 1958). At this stage of the group, competitiveness and power struggles surface. Conflicts can sometimes be explored verbally, and the leader may intervene to facilitate a discussion by encouraging members to listen carefully or speak honestly. At other times, conflict can be explored on a physical level. Wrestling can provide a clean discharge for competitive or hostile feelings between group members or between any two people who tend to verbalize exhaustively and avoid physical contact (some couples can also benefit greatly from this kind of intervention). The leader, of course, must take some precautions before encouraging the physical expression of aggression by stripping the room of dangerous objects and perhaps setting some minimal safeguards such as prohibiting the use of fists.

Elizabeth Mintz (1971), a psychotherapist who blends encounter techniques with psychoanalytic theory, has noted that physical games in encounter groups very rarely result in injury. As an encounter therapist, Mintz uses a conflict technique called "hand pressing." This exercise can be very helpful for agitated members who have repressed strong feelings toward some figure in their past. Mintz instructs members to close their eyes and place their hands over her clasped hands. She then plays the role of the historical figure, often a client's mother, talking to the client and imitating the figure's speech. The client is encouraged to say to the figure whatever thoughts come to mind and to simultaneously express feelings by exerting pressure on Mintz' hands. As the client combines physical and verbal expression, the repressed emotion tends to build up and then be released. Often the client experiences tremendous feelings of anger followed by a strong sense of relief. After the clients have regressed and relived the childhood event, they may talk about their experience and feelings to help cognitively integrate new information. The presence of other group members provides a supportive environment adding nurturance and reinforcement to the process of resolution. A sensitive therapist learns when to terminate exercises that stimulate the emotions and when to continue them, discriminating between the predictable anxiety and pain of someone exploring new ground and the reality-based message that someone has reached the limit of tolerance and needs to stop.

Exploring resistance

Sometimes in an encounter group, members may resist continuing or defend themselves in habitual, limiting ways. At such times, the group leader may use some indirect method for exploring the resistance and gently inviting the person to risk going further. One such approach is a secret-sharing exercise, where a member is asked to think of something personal that would be difficult to share with the group. At this point the person is asked to imagine disclosing the secrets to particular members and imagine their responses to the disclosure. The resistant individual is encouraged to share hypotheses regarding how others would react rather than to share the secret itself. This information may be useful feedback for other group members, as well as the first step toward greater openness for the resistant member.

Fantasy approaches can also be useful. In some ways, they serve as doors to the unconscious, bypassing the resistance generated by conscious ego functioning. For example, a client may be totally unable to recall a memory or to answer the group leader's questions. However, by framing the request in the form of a fantasy in which the client is approached by a wise old man who asks him the same question, the participant often finds that a response is more accessible.

One of Schutz' (1967) favorite fantasy techniques is the "guided daydream." In this exercise, the leader suggests a particular starting image and instructs the participants to continue, with eyes closed, to form a fantasy around it. One kind of guided daydream is the body fantasy, in which group members lie on their backs with their eyes closed and take a make-believe trip through their bodies, entering wherever they choose, exploring what they see, and remaining in close contact with their feelings and reactions. If the travelers become frightened or resistant, or if they are impeded along the way, the leader provides reassurance or makes suggestions to help move the fantasy along. The body fantasy is a provocative way of expressing an emotional conflict in symbolic form when unconscious material is sought and resistance limits the utility of a more direct approach. People with persistent stomach cramps, for instance, might go into their stomachs and discover repressed feelings of loneliness and barriers to reaching out to others. Time may be needed at the conclusion of the exercise for some debriefing and cognitive clarification.

Fantasy techniques can be either structured or unstructured. In an unstructured group fantasy, several members might lie down like spokes in a wheel and spontaneously share a visual fantasy, interrupting one another to carry the narrative along. In structured fantasies, members might be asked to choose an animal with which to identify, or to imagine looking in the window of an antique store and choosing one item to treasure.

Nurturance and support

Some encounter techniques are intended for nurturance and support. In the group's last stages the affection dimension becomes more relevant (Schutz, 1958). Members have become more emotionally involved with each other so that issues of attraction, pairing, and intimacy emerge. Typically, members are encouraged to refrain from protecting one another from risky self-exploration of new feelings and experiences. The need to reach out to stroke or hold or verbally reassure a group member who appears to be in pain or conflict may reflect the helper's anxiety more than the other's need for support. After clients have been confronted and their issue has been processed, however, they may indeed need some reinforcement from the group. Some members have a great deal of trouble asking for or receiving nurturance. Many people are socialized to blush at compliments and to reject outside support ("Aw, shucks, it was nothing, ma'am!"). At times the entire group, with or without initiative from the leader, can spontaneously bombard a member with positive feedback.

The leader may also initiate physical exercises to act out support. For example, the group might be asked to stand in a closed circle around the chosen member, who has his eyes closed, and to rock him from one side of the circle to another, letting him relax and rely on the group for physical support. As a variation, a member might lie on the floor with her eyes closed and allow the group as a whole to gently pick her up, raise her, and rock her back and forth before carefully lowering her to the ground.

Exercises involving touch can occur at any time during the group process. However, when exercises that insist on considerable physical exploration are prescribed early in the group, the physical contact may be a substitute for genuine intimacy.

The following excerpt from an extended encounter group illustrates a group member taking a risk by requesting feedback and nurturance from the group. Sarah is a 39-year-old woman distressed about her loneliness and struggling with how to include others in her life. "M" is the group leader.

> M: Suppose you just close your eyes and start to tell us what you feel like doing, and then let your body do whatever it wants to do. And if you get a notion that you want somebody to do something to you, or with you, tell us about it.
>
> Sarah: (eyes closed) Well...uh...one thing that I thought earlier was that I would really like to be rocked. Uh...that was one thing I thought of...

(The group lifts Sarah up and rocks her for three minutes, humming the syllable "OM." Then they lower her to the floor, where she continues to lie.)

Sarah: I feel at peace...I feel relaxed, relaxed. And I feel good that so many people are touching me....

M: What would you like right now? How would you like us to involve ourselves now?

Sarah: Well, I'd like to be asked something.

M: Who do you want to ask you something?

Sarah: You.

M: What could I do to make you feel stupendous?

Sarah: I'm not sure...

M: (after a pause) What could I do that would please you the most right now?

Sarah: You could hold my hand.

(M takes Sarah's hand in his and holds it.)

Sarah: (continuing) What I'd really like to know from everybody is what it is they think I do that keeps them at such a distance, and leaves me in such a...(her voice trails off again).

Kari: A frailty, I feel a frailty.

Sarah: You mean that I'd be hurt?

Kari: Yeah. Fall apart, maybe, so there might even be little pieces missing.

Jane: I feel a little helpless with you. Like your being strong, like your being self-contained...so that nobody has anything you'd want of them.

M: That's what I think too—so solid and beyond that nobody has anything you'd want of them.

Shershonsky: The same words went through my head. Self-contained. I had a feeling like, you know, that I would have nothing to give you, that you seem, well, you know, self-contained.

Bernard: I feel a little different. I felt that you did want something from us. I, uh, didn't feel adequate to give it to you. Uh...I suppose that when I relate to women, I, uh... have to have more polarity. And I feel, relating to you, that I'm not sure I could, uh...not sure I would really be strong enough to give you what you wanted.

Sarah: You mean that I would want so much that you couldn't satisfy it? Or just that you wouldn't know what it is?

Bernard: Um...you give the impression of an enormous amount of assurance, and, uh...I don't know...I'd feel very hesitant about asking you to go out into the other room and roll on the floor with me...um...whereas I can do it with some of the other girls here. And while I feel that

you would probably like it, I feel that I would...um...
not feel, uh, quite up to it with you because you might
feel that I was, uh, a little bit ridiculous, and I couldn't
quite put it over as I might with some of the others.

Sarah: Hhhmmnn.

Little Prince: I'd like to give you something, but, uh, I wouldn't know
what to give you.

Sarah: As you can see, I'm not awfully good at saying what the
hell it is I really want.

Little Prince: That's what I thought.

M: Are you getting what you want now?

Sarah: Yes.[2]

Later in the session Sarah continues to involve the group members in her
life and begins to explore her difficulty in asking for what she wants in her
relationships with men.

Alternative formats

Encounter groups can vary widely in basic format. Whereas some
groups meet on a regular basis, there are also "marathon" groups that meet
once for a single, continuous period lasting from 12–48 hours, with short
periods for rest or sleep. The marathon is an extreme type of encounter
originated by Fred Stoller (1972) and George Bach (1966), psychoanalytically
oriented group therapists experimenting with alternatives to the traditional treatment paradigm. Although basic encounter concepts are adhered to,
the extended format readily encourages the growth of a trusting and open
climate. It also enables each group member to receive some attention, so
that even participants who tend to passively withdraw in a shorter group
will be confronted and become involved. It is difficult to hide when you are
constantly bumping noses with a group of people for two or more days!
Moreover, the extended session allows sufficient time for working through
feelings so that members have an opportunity to deal fully with proble-
matic issues. The fatigue that inevitably results from lack of sleep and
prolonged emotional contact may also lower defenses and elicit greater
risk-taking behavior. However, it is doubtful that exhausted group
members can generalize from the group experience to make effective
change in their everyday lives. Although lowered defenses can help break
rigid behavior patterns and expose vulnerabilities, some cognitive alert-
ness may be necessary to assimilate and integrate the experience.
Moreover, some defenses may serve a useful purpose in that fatigued
members, for example, may make poor judgments by not being fully in
touch with their needs. Most contemporary marathons recognize this and
allow for periods of rest and recreation rather than pushing ahead
nonstop.

[2]Reprinted by permission of G. P. Putnam's Sons from *Marathon 16* by Martin Shepard &
Marjorie Lee. Copyright 1970 by Martin Shepard & Marjorie Lee.

Perhaps the most controversial application of the encounter group is nude encounter, a format initially developed by Paul Bindrim. Nude encounters actually constitute only a very small percentage of encounter groups. The group typically meets in a warm swimming pool, and sensory awareness exercises are used along with interpersonal sharing to reduce any anxiety the participants may have about their bodies. Bindrim (1968) has suggested that voluntary excursions into group nudity increase interpersonal transparency and promote "nakedly" honest interactions and a sense of freedom and belonging.

APPRAISAL

Although encounter groups can be dynamic and powerful motivators toward growth, they are not without their detractors. Kurt Back (1972), one of encounter's most forceful critics, warns that the encounter movement's discovery of the power of group processes to elicit intense emotional experiences is not necessarily a virtue. When self-expression becomes an end in itself, symbolic statements and abstract conceptualizations tend to be devalued or dismissed. Although encounter groups attempt to increase contact and intimacy, the strong emotions generated by interpersonal encounter, according to Back, are not at all intimate and not particularly meaningful. He claims that each participant is used as a tool or object to create an experience for other group members, and that group relationships are neither personal nor genuine. Consequently, when the encounter group ends, participants rarely care about one another nearly as much as they have been led to believe.

Because encounter groups endorse a unique, intimate style of relating that dispenses with social conventions, participants sometimes experience reentry problems in conventional social situations. This painful transition was illustrated in the movie *Bob and Carol and Ted and Alice*, in which a couple returns from a workshop at Esalen with little patience for their less "open," more "insecure" friends back home.

Although not didactic, the encounter group sanctions values uncommon in daily social contexts. Thus, there is disappointment with the realization that others do not share this newly developed belief system, and that strangers are not prepared to relate to returning participants as if they are instant kin. This reentry phenomenon is probably most difficult to deal with when one partner of a couple returns from a growth group to find his or her spouse unchanged and not a little threatened by the richness of the returning mate's experiences. Seasoned encounter group participants learn to temper their expectations for maintaining the instant highs they receive in the group.

Because it is difficult to retain encounter values in most social contexts, some people become encounter-group addicts. Many encounter-group "junkies" move from group to group, seeking more intense and meaningful experiences. Although much is to be gained from group interactions, these junkies may be unable to change or adapt to the real world, feeling safe and comfortable only within the group's narrow confines. If growth groups fail to encourage a transfer of learning to nongroup contexts, they may become a secure haven for the regressive and dependent individual.

Since encounter's overriding concern is with change in almost any direction, it may hold a greater risk of psychological damage than most other group experiences. Encounter's disadvantages have remained unspecified partly because of the lack of any consistent, guiding theory (Burton, 1969). Because encounter's philosophical basis challenges much of the fabric of conventional social values, there is no real ethic that has been consistently endorsed either by encounter advocates or by critics.

The group leader is one of the most important factors in determining the outcome of the encounter experience. It has been noted that charismatic leaders are most influential in stressful situations and that fearful and anxious followers may imbue them with superhuman attributes (Tucker, 1968). Such leaders can, for better or worse, have a tremendous impact on members' thinking in the emotionally charged atmosphere of an encounter group.

Moreover, many encounter groups do little if anything to screen participants in terms of suitability or risk. Although this avoids creating an arbitrary model distinguishing between healthy and sick potential members, there are great differences among people in ability to handle interpersonal stress and intense feelings. Most often, the group's wisdom, if not the group leader's, prevails, and vulnerable participants are treated with gentleness and understanding. However, there is also the possibility for ignorant, if not psychopathic, members (and leaders) to cause harm. Groups that utilize strong emotional confrontation are safest when the leader makes use of screening procedures that weed out those who cannot benefit from, and may be harmed by, the group.

A final criticism of encounter is its relative lack of follow-up data. Encounter may be singled out unfairly in this respect, since very few recent group techniques have been adequately researched for follow-up effectiveness. One difficulty inherent in encounter, however, is clearly identifying relevant outcome variables. Unlike traditional psychotherapy, where change is indicated by the elimination of a specific symptom, encounter's goal tends to be growth or change in general. Testimonials to the validity of the experience are certainly numerous and overwhelmingly positive. Gibb (1971) and Rogers (1970) cite studies in which the encounter group experience has been shown to increase interpersonal sensitivity, management of feelings, self-esteem, and self-acceptance. Bebout (1973) adds that encounter invariably reduces alienation and lessens individual problems, and clients' self-concepts change in many positive directions.

The capacity of the group experience to generate long-term behavior change is more suspect. However, encounter's proponents argue that even temporary changes are worthwhile, since they include an awareness of the possibility of change. A college student illustrates this point as she recounts how her encounter group experience has given her an awareness that she could again get close to feelings of personal growth if she desired:

> As time passes the more valuable my "breakdown" with the group becomes. It was one of the very few times where I was verbally completely honest with myself and exposed it to others. And you people showed such compassion and warmth. I was really in touch with myself, the very gut of my soul was out in the open. What a feeling! I walked around in wonderment for a while, savoring the moment until I backslid and closed up again. But that's okay because it will happen again to me and to others whom I can share with and feel with. That moment was community [Keyes, 1973, p. 164].

Are there casualties? There are undoubtedly individuals who are stripped of their normal defense mechanisms without developing any adequate substitute methods of coping. The most detailed study exploring outcomes of experiential groups was conducted by Lieberman, Yalom, and Miles (1973) with Stanford University undergraduates. The authors identified ten types of experiential groups. The distinctions among them are rather arbitrary and a number might qualify as "encounter" groups. The authors defined a casualty as "an individual who, as a direct result of his experience in the encounter group became more psychologically distressed or employed more maladaptive mechanisms of defense, or both; further, this negative change was not transient but an enduring one, as judged eight months after the group experience" (Yalom & Lieberman, 1971, pp. 17–18). According to this criterion, about 9% of the undergraduates who completed the study were considered to have been psychologically damaged by the group. This figure is considerably higher than other estimates. Gibb (1970), Ross, Klingfeld, & Whitman (1971), and Hartley, Roback, & Abramowitz (1976) all have reported casualty rates of less than 1%. The Lieberman, et al. study has also come under methodological attack (Rowan, 1975, Russell, 1978; Schutz, 1974).

Particularly provocative was Lieberman, et al.'s conclusion that aggressive, stimulating, charismatic leaders had a disproportionately large number of casualties, although Russell (1978) has asserted that very few group leaders in the study were rated high in emotional stimulation, presumably a major characteristic of encounter group leaders. Another factor clearly related to hazardous outcomes was the psychological make-up of the participants. Students who became casualties were fragile prior to the group, had lower self-esteem, had unrealistic expectations of the group experience, and were more escapist than assertive when stressed. In other words, group members who are psychologically fragile yet have strong needs for change and growth, who are relatively inadequate in relating interpersonally and so cannot capitalize on the group experience, constitute the gravest risks. The naive expectation that encounter is an inevitable and miraculous source of permanent change is a much greater problem than the small and unavoidable risk of a negative outcome.

Finally, in order to arrive at a fair appraisal of encounter, one must understand that during its heyday in the 1970s, detractors and defenders became polarized into armed camps, either roundly condemning encounter or unequivocally praising it. A balanced evaluation would consider the phenomenon's complexity and the fact there is almost as much diversity among encounter group practitioners as there is similarity. Personal experiences and a selective perusal of the literature can significantly alter or bias one's judgment. Thus, Strupp (1973) and Hogan (1976) are able to look at the same issues and draw completely different conclusions; Arbuckle (1973) can respond to Koch's (1971) scathing criticism of the encounter group movement by saying "His reading material has obviously been somewhat different than mine. By using a similarly skewed and biased reading list, I could conclude that religion consists of meetings where (for a price) psychotic evangelists deliver a group of fearful, ignorant people from the clutches of the devil" (pp. 49–50).

North America furnished fertile soil for encounter partly because its value system meshes with an individualistic, frontier spirit and the pursuit of happiness in this lifetime. Some view the encounter movement as a secular substitute for the healing functions previously performed by traditional churches (Sampson, 1971; Steinberg, 1975). As such, the concepts of encounter parallel those of the Christian mystical belief system, emphasizing disclosure, honesty, communion, conversion, and rebirth. Certainly peripatetic encounter group leaders have appeared, seeming at times like circuit riders holding revivalistic tent meetings. Perhaps one of encounter's initial strengths has become one of its limitations: the capitalistic, marketing orientation of America, which heartily sold encounter through many well publicized growth centers, may also lead to its increased mechanization and dilution (Steinberg, 1975). Although encounter can offer a genuine growing experience, the skills learned in an encounter group may be used for manipulative as well as humanitarian purposes. Encounter has promoted greater openness among people, but some participants do learn to "produce" feelings and play phony roles.

Encounter's active, risk-taking orientation has made a visible dent in current group practice, a fact that will become clearer in the following chapters. Many people originally turned to encounter when traditional therapy failed to meet their needs for socialization and intimacy. In many ways encounter can be regarded as a progression in formal psychotherapy, broadening therapy to include people who wish to expand their awareness or improve their interpersonal communication. Encounter has also found its way into more traditional structures, such as church groups, education, and community organizations. The encounter movement gave people a taste of "community," so that groups with very different names, goals, and functions have adopted encounter styles and methods as their own (Coulson, 1973). Some of the guiding philosophy of encounter may not be as relevant to students today as it was a few years ago, however. The fight for personal freedom and honesty has been fought and replaced, to some extent, by a return to more established values and a pragmatic concern for material success and achievement. But as long as alienation, estrangement, and the restricted development of human potentials exist, there will be some need for encounter-type groups.

SUMMARY

Encounter groups developed out of the T-group movement. One distinction in encounter groups is between the *task-orientation* of East Coast groups and the *communion-orientation* of West Coast groups. The best known formats for encounter are Carl Rogers' *basic encounter* and William Schutz' *open encounter*. Rogers' approach grew out of his theory of client-centered counseling and focuses on finding authenticity in relating to others. Schutz' approach derived from his experiences at Esalen Institute and focuses more on the integration of body and mind.

Basic concepts identified with encounter are *self-disclosure, self-awareness, responsibility, attention to feelings,* and the *here-and-now.* Self-awareness includes acknowledging personal strengths and weaknesses, as well as awareness of the body. Encounter groups routinely place a strong emphasis on a group member's responsibility for his own behavior. The limits of the group leader's responsibility are more controversial. Focusing on the here-and-now implies an emphasis on the present-centered experiences of group members and a deemphasis on their life histories.

A final conceptual issue concerns the distinction between psychotherapy and growth. Encounter is oriented toward the growth of well-functioning individuals, adopts a shorter time frame, and encourages self-disclosure from the leader. Although this differs from traditional psychotherapy, the distinction between psychotherapy and growth is not clear-cut. Self-awareness, joy, and the development of affective potential can be seen as legitimate goals for both patients and relatively healthy individuals.

Encounter group leaders draw upon active techniques to encourage participants to make contact with each other, to build trust, to explore conflicts and resistance, and to provide nurturance and support. Several alternative formats of encounter are available, including marathons and nude encounter. Perhaps the most controversial aspect of encounter is the extent to which self-expression is a valid goal in and of itself. The encounter movement has been immensely popular, but critics point to its lack of guiding theory, its failure to screen participants, and its lack of adequate follow-up data. It seems clear that the personality and approach of the group leader is a critical determinant of outcome, and that fragile, interpersonally inadequate, yet needy, group members are the most vulnerable to negative outcomes.

REFERENCES

Arbuckle, D. Koch's distortions of encounter group theory. *Journal of Humanistic Psychology*, 1973, *13*, 47–52.

Bach, G. R. The marathon group: Intensive practice in intimate interaction. *Psychological Reports*, 1966, *18*, 995–1002.

Back, K. W. *Beyond words: The study of sensitivity training and the encounter movement.* New York: Russell Sage Foundation, 1972.

Bebout, J. A. A study of group encounter in higher education. *Educational Technology*, 1973, *13*, 63–67.

Bindrim, P. A report on a nude marathon. *Psychotherapy: Theory, Research, and Practice*, 1968, *5*, 180–188.

Burton, A. Encounter, existence, and psychotherapy. In A. Burton (Ed.), *Encounter: Theory and practice of encounter groups.* San Francisco: Jossey-Bass, 1969.

Carkhuff, R. R., & Berenson, B. G. *Beyond counseling and psychotherapy* (2nd ed.). New York: Holt, Rinehart & Winston, 1977.

Casriel, D. *So fair a house: The story of Synanon.* Englewood Cliffs, N.J.: Prentice-Hall, 1963.

Coulson, W. R. *A sense of community.* Columbus, Ohio: Charles E. Merrill, 1973.

Egan, G. *Encounter: Group processes for interpersonal growth.* Monterey, Calif.: Brooks/Cole, 1970.

Egan, G. *The skilled helper.* Monterey, Calif.: Brooks/Cole, 1975.

Gibb, J. R. Sensitivity training as a medium for personal growth and improved interpersonal relationships. *Interpersonal Development*, 1970, *1*, 6–31.

Gibb, J. R. Effects of human relations training. In A. E. Bergin & S. L. Garfield (Eds.), *Handbook of psychotherapy and behavior change.* New York: Wiley, 1971.

Goldberg, C. *Encounter: Group sensitivity training experience.* New York: Science House, 1970.

Gustaitis, R. *Turning on.* New York: Macmillan, 1969.

Hartley, D., Roback, H. B., & Abramowitz, S. I. Deterioration effects in encounter groups. *American Psychologist*, 1976, *31*, 247–255.

Hogan, D. B. The experiential group and the psychotherapeutic enterprise revisited: A response to Strupp. *International Journal of Group Psychotherapy*, 1976, *26*, 321–333.

Howard, J. *Please touch.* New York: McGraw-Hill, 1970.

Jourard, S. M. *The transparent self: Self disclosure and well-being.* Princeton, N.J.: Van Nostrand, 1964.

Kaiser, H. The problem of responsibility in psychotherapy. *Psychiatry*, 1955, *18*, 205–211.

Kaplan, H. I., & Sadock, B. J. (Eds.). *Sensitivity through encounter and marathon.* New York: Jason Aronson, 1972.

Keyes, R. *We the lonely people, searching for community.* New York: Harper & Row, 1973.

Koch, S. The image of man implicit in encounter group theory. *Journal of Humanistic Psychology*, 1971, *11*, 109–128.

Lieberman, M. A., Yalom, I. D., & Miles, M. S. *Encounter groups: First facts.* New York: Basic Books, 1973.

Luft, J. *Group processes: An introduction to group dynamics.* Palo Alto, Calif.: National Press, 1970.

Maddi, S. The existential neurosis. *Journal of Abnormal Psychology*, 1967, *72*, 311–325.

Maslow, A. H. *Toward a psychology of being* (2nd ed.). New York: D. Van Nostrand, 1968.

Mintz, E. E. *Marathon groups: Reality and symbol.* New York: Appleton-Century-Crofts, 1971.

Mowrer, O. H. *The new group therapy.* New York: D. Van Nostrand, 1964.

Mowrer, O. H. Peer groups and medication, the best "therapy" for professionals and laymen alike. In *Where do therapists turn for help?* Symposium presented at American Psychological Association, Division 29, Miami, September, 1970.

Peterson, R. L. Choice, responsibility, and psychotherapy. *Psychotherapy: Theory, Research, and Practice*, 1977, *14*, 106–119.

Rogers, C. R. (Ed.). *The therapeutic relationship and its impact.* Madison: University of Wisconsin Press, 1967.

Rogers, C. R. Interpersonal relationships USA 2000. *Journal of Applied Behavioral Science*, 1968, *4*, 208–269.

Rogers, C. R. *Carl Rogers on encounter groups.* New York: Harper & Row, 1970.

Ross, W. D., Klingfeld, M., & Whitman, R. W. Psychiatrists, patients and sensitivity groups. *Archives of General Psychiatry*, 1971, *25*, 178–180.

Rowan, J. Encounter group research: No joy? *Journal of Humanistic Psychology*, 1975, *15*, 19–28.

Russell, E. W. The facts about "Encounter groups: First facts." *Journal of Clinical Psychology*, 1978, *34*, 130–137.

Sampson, E. Social psychology and contemporary society. New York: Wiley, 1971.

Schutz, W. C. *FIRO: A three-dimensional theory of interpersonal behavior.* New York: Holt, Rinehart & Winston, 1958.

Schutz, W. C. *Joy: Expanding human awareness.* New York: Grove Press, 1967.

Schutz, W. C. *Here comes everybody: Bodymind and encounter culture.* New York: Harper & Row, 1971.

Schutz, W. C. Not encounter and certainly not facts. In J. W. Pfeiffer & J. E. Jones (Eds.), *The 1974 handbook for group facilitators.* La Jolla, Calif.: University Associates, 1974.

Shepard, M., & Lee, M. *Marathon 16.* New York: Putnam's, 1970.

Steinberg, R. *The encounter group movement and tradition of Christian enthusiasm and mysticism.* Unpublished doctoral dissertation, York University, 1975.

Stoller, F. H. Marathon groups: Toward a conceptual model. In L. N. Solomon & B. Berzon (Eds.), *New perspectives on encounter groups.* San Francisco: Jossey-Bass, 1972.

Strupp, H. H. The experiential group and the psychotherapeutic enterprise. *International Journal of Group Psychotherapy*, 1973, *23*, 115–124.

Tucker, R. C. The theory of charismatic leadership. *Daedalus*, 1968, *97*(3), 731–756.

Warkentin, J. Intensity in group encounter. In A. Burton (Ed.), *Encounter: Theory and practice of encounter groups.* San Francisco: Jossey-Bass, 1969.

Yalom, I. D., & Lieberman, M. A. A study of encounter group casualties. *Archives of General Psychiatry*, 1971, *25*, 16–30.

4

Gestalt Groups

HISTORY AND DEVELOPMENT

The history of the Gestalt approach to group work is in many ways the history of its founder, Fritz (Frederick S.) Perls. Trained in neuropsychiatry at the University of Berlin, Perls entered psychoanalysis with Karen Horney in 1926 and began his own practice adhering to Freudian principles. Perls emigrated from Germany to South Africa when Hitler took power in 1933. By then, Perls had explored and been influenced by existential philosophy, the Gestalt school of theoretical psychology, and Wilhelm Reich's theory of the physiological manifestations of psychological problems.

The popularity of existentialism in the 20th century has been in part a reaction to the disillusionment of two world wars, a severe economic depression, and the dehumanization associated with mushrooming technology and bureaucracy. Existentialism lent psychology the belief that humans must take responsibility for shaping their own world (Cohen & Smith, 1976). Existential philosophy helped to shift Perls' concept of humanity from his original psychoanalytic focus, which stressed the importance of the individual's developmental history. Instead of looking to the past to understand a client's problems, Perls began to look to the present and the way people adapted to and lived in their world. With this new focus, therapy was no longer a system of retrieving important or insightful information from memory. For Perls, the information essential for therapeutic change was available in the way his client engaged and encountered him.

From the Gestalt school of theoretical psychology, Perls acquired an emphasis on phenomonology, the importance of immediate experience. He became wary of interpreting the unconscious and instead focused on visible cues to a patient's problems (Perls, 1969a). Whereas existentialism is concerned with how people *experience* their immediate existence, academic Gestalt psychology was concerned with how they *perceive* their immediate existence (Kempler, 1973). The founders of pre-clinical Gestalt psychology, Kohler (1947), Koffka (1935), and Wertheimer (1945), emphasized the perceiver as an active participant who can impose pattern and meaning on discrete events. They were reacting to earlier theories of perception that studied mental processes by reducing them to their component elements and that viewed the perceiver as a passive recipient of the qualities of form. One of Perls' teachers, Kurt Goldstein, had applied Gestalt concepts to the field of motivation. Perls extended Gestalt perceptual theory to personality functioning. He retained the "figure-ground" concepts of Gestalt theory and applied them to the perception of feelings, emotions, and bodily sensations. Kurt Lewin, the original force behind the T-group movement and a contemporary of Perls, took Goldstein's holistic concepts and applied them to the social environment and social change.

Wilhelm Reich influenced Perls' conceptualization of therapeutic resistance. *Resistance* is the term used to describe the blocks people experience to changing their behavior or gaining insight about themselves. Resistance can be thought of as protection from the stress of growing and changing. Reich, a past disciple of Freud, suggested that resistance eventually becomes part of a person's body armor, or physical defenses. He believed that resistance to change can be overcome by working directly on the body. Reich's approach will be described more fully in Chapter 6. From Reich, Perls adopted the concept that resistance is manifest in nonverbal behavior or body language. Gestures, mannerisms, facial expressions, and posture are considered to contain messages of which the client is not immediately aware.

By the time Perls immigrated to the United States in 1946, he had developed most of his startling and original theories of personality development and therapeutic change. In 1952, he opened the Institute for Gestalt Therapy in New York City, the beginning of what was to become, during the late 1960s, a large and powerful psychotherapy movement. Perls settled at the Esalen Institute in Big Sur, California, from 1964 to 1969, conducting Gestalt seminars, workshops, and therapy groups. In 1969, he moved to Cowichan, British Columbia, to establish the Gestalt Institute of Canada. He died that winter.

Throughout his life, Perls dabbled in such diverse areas as Kurt Lewin's field theory, theater, bioenergetics, and the Alexander Technique of body awareness. From each source he extracted aspects that he considered to have great value for his own developing therapeutic model. Like Lewin, he rejected causality, the search for the "why" of behavior, where the person is seen as a passive pawn vulnerable to environmental forces. Instead, Perls focused on the interaction between active individuals and their environment and the "what" and "how" of behavior. From psychodrama, bioenergetics, and Alexander, he borrowed exercises and techniques for use in therapy, adapting them to his own theoretical constructs.

Although Gestalt is used as an individual therapy approach, the group format predominates. In the mid-1960s Perls actually announced his intent to give up individual sessions as outdated, in favor of group workshops (Perls, 1967). However, the traditional Gestalt group is unlike most other group approaches. Whereas encounter and T-groups engage all group members and encourage interaction, Gestalt therapy in its purest form, as taught by Perls and practiced by most of his followers (Simkin, 1968), is typically a contracted engagement between the group leader and a single participant who volunteers to become the patient by sitting in the "hot seat," a chair next to the therapist. The rest of the group watches, without commenting on the therapy process between therapist and client. Although the whole group may participate in some Gestalt exercises, it more often assumes the role of audience and provides a sense of community support. The group's value, according to Perls (Stevens, 1977), is that self-recognition occurs as the audience observes other clients' behavior. Group members can identify with the therapeutic work of the participant in the hot seat. At the same time, as one participant becomes emotionally expressive, a chain reaction of intense feelings can affect each group member. Thus, it is suggested that observation alone can facilitate self-change.

Not all Gestalt therapists make so little use of group interaction and support. At East Coast institutes, in particular, therapeutic work is not restricted to an exchange between the group leader and a single participant but is expanded to include other members as well. The hot seat becomes a "floating hot seat," which moves from person to person (Polster & Polster, 1973). One person works at a time, but others may spontaneously join the fray whenever they choose. There is an understanding, in fact, that whatever happens in the group on a moment-to-moment basis is potentially relevant to the others and needs consideration. In this way, group members become directly involved in and touched by an individual's therapy.

There is a growing recognition that Gestalt therapy is compatible with the study of group process and group dynamics. In those Gestalt groups that honor the importance of the group process, the social interactional nature of a person's individual work is fully explored (Zinker, 1977). For instance, if one group member is seen to whine and beg, it can be assumed that there are group members present who will refuse to respond and others who will give too much. In this model, interpersonal implications of individual behaviors are acknowledged and actively encouraged. Groups at the Cleveland Gestalt Institute have been at the forefront of attending to the intrapersonal, interpersonal, and group levels of functioning (Kepner, 1980). Thus, if a woman expresses anger toward a man in her group, the leader might intervene to work on her anger toward men in general, focus on the relationship between the two individuals involved, or explore the outburst (as in a Tavistock group) as reflecting a group issue.

The Gestalt method generally emphasizes the presence of strong, active leadership to encourage individual autonomy and independence. In groups that are not designated as Gestalt, the group leader may encourage spontaneous interaction, using an encounter or T-group model and applying Gestalt techniques when they appear most appropriate and beneficial. Since the 1960s, when it emerged as a popular group model, Gestalt's techniques have been adopted into the mainstream of group counseling and therapy.

BASIC CONCEPTS

Although Perls (1969a) decried theory as "elephant shit," his therapeutic approach is based on five key theoretical concepts: the relationship between figure and ground; awareness and present-centeredness; polarities; safety functions; and maturity and responsibility. Although Gestalt techniques have been popularized since Perls' death, an understanding of their conceptual basis provides a meaningful rationale for their use.

Figure and ground

The first basic concept is the relationship between *figure* and *ground*. Gestalt researchers in perception have found that people organize incoming information so that events that are immediately important or meaningful take a central position in awareness, while less relevant information recedes into the background. Perls adopted this formula to describe personality functioning as a rhythm of figure formation and dissolution, where figure is a need, for example, to receive support or to express anger.

Gestalt theory states that all organisms function on the basis of self-regulation. In our natural state, therefore, we maintain our dynamic balance, or homeostasis, by being alert to needs both within ourselves and in our environment, and by satisfying them as they occur. When a need arises, we focus most of our attention on satisfying it while any unrelated objects or events recede into the background. Consider, for example, a person who has been studying for an important exam for several hours without a break. Suddenly she realizes the need to go to the bathroom and relieve herself. The pressure on her bladder receives more attention than her studying. In fact, she finds that she is less and less able to concentrate on studying. Finally, her studying recedes into the background, her bladder becomes figural, and she races to the bathroom in the nick of time.

The relationship between figure and ground is an important concept in Gestalt theory. The organismic process of self-regulation is one of figure, or gestalt, formation. A gestalt is a pattern or configuration that cannot be broken down without destroying it (Latner, 1973). Gestalt formation always occurs in the context of a field or background. We select from the field what is important or meaningful to us; thus, what is important or interesting to us becomes a gestalt. In a perceptual exercise, such as Figure 4-1, the figure can be perceived as either a vase or two faces. In groups, the figure is usually a feeling that needs to be expressed. Certainly, feelings of anger, disappointment, fear, joy, sexuality, or love easily become figural, while other aspects of our experience slip into the background.

Figure 4–1. In this perceptual exercise, we may perceive either the vase or the faces as figure.

Once a need has been satisfied, the gestalt is no longer important. It recedes into the background, allowing a new gestalt to be created. Once the person has gone to the bathroom and relieved herself, the exam may become figural once again and she returns to studying. This rhythm of creating and dissolving clear gestalts is the natural rhythm of the organism.

Sometimes, needs cannot be satisfied and the gestalt cannot be dissolved. When group members become angry at the group leader but fail to express that feeling, their need to express themselves has not been satisfied. They may continue to feel angry at the group leader even after the group has ended. Or they may renew their grudge each time they see the leader. When a need does not become a clear figure, it cannot be satisfied and the gestalt cannot be dissolved. This is "unfinished business." These unacknowledged or unexpressed feelings are unresolved issues from the past that continue to interfere in the present. Group members who haven't expressed their anger may become reluctant to work with the leader or may show the anger in more subtle ways. Unfinished business may also be brought to the group from the participant's past. Members who have difficulty relating to men in the group may have unexpressed feelings for important men in their lives. The gestalt approach helps the group member clarify the figure so that feelings can finally be expressed, the gestalt can be destroyed, and other salient issues can be worked on.

Awareness and present-centeredness

In order to be able to clearly create and dissolve gestalts, we must be fully aware of ourselves in the present. *Awareness* and *present-centeredness* are key Gestalt concepts. In order to satisfy our needs, we must be constantly in touch with both our inner and outer zones. The inner zone is the site of processes and events that occur within our bodies. We respond to our inner zone needs when we put on a sweater because we feel cold or when we crawl into bed because we feel fatigue. The outer zone is the locus of external events that come to our awareness as raw sensory data, such as loud noises. Information from the inner and outer zones is unprocessed, uninterpreted data.

Besides the inner and outer zones, we also have a middle or fantasy zone. The middle zone consists of thoughts, fantasies, beliefs, attitudes, and other intellectualized or conceptualized events. Perls (1969a) believed that neurosis is the result of a tendency to focus on the middle zone to the exclusion of inner and outer events. This tendency interferes with the natural pattern of organismic processes. Certainly we have received most of our training, socially and culturally, in perfecting our middle zone processes: we learn to conceptualize our thoughts, support our beliefs, defend our attitudes, and make immediate judgments about others. However, Perls maintained that pathology was rooted in the interruption of awareness by our tendency to fantasize and intellectualize. When we live in the middle zone, we concern ourselves chiefly with the past and the future. We reminisce, make plans, regret, and hope. We do not live in the present and consequently do not focus our awareness on inner- and outer-zone events. Organismic self-regulation depends on *present-centered awareness*, the ability to live fully in the here-and-now.

The pressure on members of Gestalt groups to stay in the present and avoid excursions into past experiences and projections into future plans has received its fullest support in Perls' assertion "*Nothing exists except the here and now. The now is the present . . . . The past is no more. The future is not yet*" (Perls, 1969a, p. 44). Some Gestalt therapists are more tolerant in their willingness to include the inevitability of other time perspectives into the group. For instance, Polster and Polster (1973, pp. 7–8) offer the following caveat:

> As many have realized, a rigid view of the present—one which permits none but literally present experiences to enter into any engagement—is stultifying. . . . The dimensions of past and future give recognition to that which once was and that which some day may be, thus forming psychological boundaries for present experience and a psychological context which provides the figural present a background upon which to exist.

Polarities

A *polarity* is a single evaluative construct or continuum. For example, good and bad are poles of such a continuum. According to Gestalt theory, we organize our perceptions of the external world according to polarities. Perls suggested that the personality is organized along the same principles. Each of us experiences polarities within ourselves: we both love and hate our parents, we become both happy and depressed when we complete a major project that has occupied much of our time, we are both grateful and resentful to someone who has helped us solve our problems. It is important to realize that polarities are not irreconcilable differences, but distinctions that can be integrated by gestalt formation and dissolution. Once we can fully experience each part of a polarity, instead of denying the less savory half, we become more aware of ourselves and our needs. By becoming cognizant of previously undifferentiated aspects of ourselves, we can form a clear gestalt, identify our need, and satisfy it.

The topdog-underdog polarity is the most common in Gestalt therapy. The topdog, like the Freudian superego or conscience, is authoritarian, self-righteous, and demanding. The underdog is defensive, apologetic, and powerless. "Like every parent and child, they strive with each other for control" (Perls, 1969a, p. 19). The struggle between these polar opposites within the self is often worked on by group members and is known in therapy as the self-torture game. A group member who feels guilty when she imagines telling her mother she plans to move to her own apartment is probably struggling with a self-torture game. One voice within her, the topdog, tells her "You should stay at home where you belong. You know how much mother needs you. How can you desert her at a time like this, you ungrateful wretch!" A second voice whines "But I want to have my own place. I can't live my life for her. Besides I'll visit her all the time and make sure she's OK." When topdog and underdog engage each other in battle, we become immobile, unable to make decisions, and depressed, guilty, or frustrated.

The concept of polarities bears on personality functioning as well. Personality is described as a unitary construct, a seamless whole, operating out of two modalities, the *ego* and the *id.* When individuals act from the ego mode, they are able to distinguish between what is the self and what is not the self. A rigid experiential barrier, the ego boundary, is created to help the person keep the self separate from the rest of the world. When people function in the id mode, they are in contact with the environment, the ego boundary is vague and flexible, and there may be a feeling of oneness with the external world. Id-mode functioning is known as *identification.* These complementary aspects of personality functioning are responsible for the creation and destruction of gestalts. The ego mode clearly differentiates the figure from the ground; the id mode dissolves the gestalt and returns the figure to the field (Latner, 1973).

Safety functions

Most problems in living can be described in terms of faulty transactions at the ego boundary. We respond to threats or stress by withdrawing, running away, desensitizing ourselves to pain, and even by hallucinating or becoming delusional (Latner, 1973). These responses are known as *safety functions.* They are defensive tactics: they distort or terminate our contact with the threatening situation at the ego boundary. We suspend our awareness until the emergency has passed. This is highly adaptive in some circumstances—for example, delaying gratification when it is inappropriate or when our needs are in conflict. However, if the emergency persists, or if we are bombarded by a variety of emergencies for a prolonged period of time, we become afraid to sniff the air without the protection of our safety functions. We learn that contact with others or with parts of ourselves is never safe, so we maintain our safety functions even after the emergency has passed. When the id- and ego-mode functions become impaired, we lose our ability to contact our bodies and our environment.

The Gestalt idea of contact and contact boundaries forms a natural transition to group process, because it is a statement about individuals in an environmental field and their interactions with others (Kepner, 1980). In Gestalt, there are four major defensive styles of contact at the ego boundary: confluence, retroflection, introjection, and projection (Perls, 1973; Perls, Hefferline, & Goodman, 1951).

Whereas identification is the healthy aspect of id-mode functioning, confluence is a neurotic mechanism for avoiding contact. Confluence occurs when no boundary is experienced between self and other. Because people are unaware of the difference between themselves and others, they cannot discriminate between where they end and the other begins. Confluence may be recognizable by the use of the pronoun "we" rather than "I" when referring to oneself. Group members who assume that other group members feel the way they do are using confluence. They may feel rejected or reject others when they discover that there are differences between individuals, because they do not expect and cannot tolerate differences. The loss of boundary for these people is such that they cannot easily distinguish their own thoughts, feelings, or needs from those of others. As a result, they can neither make good contact with others nor withdraw from them.

Retroflection, introjection, and projection are faulty ego-mode transactions. The ego boundary separating self from other is inappropriately placed, either disposing of true aspects of the personality or incorporating aspects that are not of the self into the personality.

Literally, retroflection means "turning back sharply against" (Perls, 1973, p. 40). In retroflection, the ego boundary between the personality and the environment is drawn down the center of the self. Thus, individuals treat themselves the way they originally wanted to treat other persons or objects. Historically, an individual's original attempt to satisfy his needs was met with strong opposition. However, instead of continuing to direct energies outward to change the environment, he redirects energies inward and substitutes himself as a target. In effect, the person treats himself as an object. The original conflict between self and other becomes a conflict within the self.

Grammatically, the use of the reflexive pronoun is indicative of retroflection. The retroflector says "I must control myself," "I must force myself to do this job," or "I am ashamed of myself," clearly distinguishing between self as agent and self as object. The retroflector is the participant who is sitting on the hot seat saying "I'm so angry at myself I could scream!" According to Gestalt principles, the person is really angry at someone else, but has learned that it is dangerous to direct anger at the real target. The leader may ask retroflectors to find various reasons for being angry at other group members and to confront them angrily. In this way, the anger is appropriately expressed outward.

Introjection is a tendency to adopt others' beliefs and attitudes uncritically, without mastering and assimilating them to make them congruent with the self. Introjects are alien beliefs, attitudes, thoughts, or feelings that have not been destructured, analyzed, and restructured so that they are truly part of the individual. As a result, the boundary between the self and the world is buried deep within the self, and there may in fact be little of the self apparent. Individuals who introject may be so busy maintaining alien beliefs that they fail to develop their own personalities. They may also direct their energies toward reconciling incompatible foreign concepts and ultimately tear themselves apart.

The earliest introjects are parental messages, which are unselectively maintained by the self without a critical evaluation of their worth. With time it becomes difficult to distinguish between introjects and authentic beliefs. The introjector may be the sensitive man who tries to prevent himself from crying in front of the rest of the group because he believes that grown men should not cry in public. Is this belief an old parental dictum swallowed whole by the participant? Does the group member really want to cry but stop himself by setting up this introjected barrier? It is important in the Gestalt group to question beliefs and attitudes to determine whether they represent the member's true position or the undigested beliefs of others.

Projection is the reverse of introjection. Whereas introjection is the tendency to own parts of the environment that are not part of the self, projection is the tendency to make the environment responsible for what originates in the self. An example of the projection mechanism is the man who continually complains that the world is cold and uncaring. Instead of experiencing feelings of alienation within himself, he experiences them as being directed toward him by the environment. As Perls put it, "We sit in a house lined with mirrors and think that we are looking out" (Perls, 1969b, p. 158).

Whereas the introjector makes the self a battleground for conflicting and unassimilated ideas, the projector makes the world a battleground for intrapsychic conflicts. The projector is the group member who confronts another participant for enjoying the discomfort of the participant in the hot seat. Unless the confronted member admits to this feeling, it is a good guess that the confrontative member has actually been enjoying the incident, but has attributed this behavior to another because of its unacceptability. In projection, the ego boundary clearly differentiates between self and environment, but is positioned so that unacceptable fragments of the self can be placed on the non-self side of the boundary. As Perls (1973) sums up the neurotic defense mechanisms:

The introjector does as others would like him to do, the projector does unto others what he accuses them of doing to him, the man in pathological confluence doesn't know who is doing what to whom, and the retroflector does to himself what he would like to do to others [p. 40].

The Gestalt group's thrust is to unblock awareness by relaxing retro-flected energies, assimilating introjects, and changing projections into direct expression (Enright, 1975).

Maturity

In Gestalt theory, optimal health is defined as *maturity*. In order to mature, individuals must transcend their need for environmental support and discover their own supportive resources. This is somewhat similar to the young adult leaving home, without the financial support of parents, and discovering ways to make a living. In Gestalt, maturity is not financial but emotional. If we are immature, we manipulate the environment to satisfy our needs rather than take responsibility for our distress and satisfy our own needs. Maturity comes when we mobilize our resources to over-come the frustration and fear we feel when environmental support is not forthcoming, and self-support appears to be inadequate. The impasse is the point at which we are able neither to engage the support of the environment nor to provide any on our own. Maturity requires that we take risks at the impasse. If risks are not taken, we resort to role-playing in order to manipulate others: we may play helpless to remain dependent or play dumb to receive intellectual support (Perls, 1969a).

Perls suggests that adults must sift through the layers of their neu-roses, like peeling back the skins of an onion, to achieve maturation and take responsibility for themselves. The first level is called *cliché*. When we contact others at this layer we do so in stereotypical and inauthentic ways. Beneath this skin is the *synthetic* layer, where games and roles predomi-nate. Our interactions are superficial, and pretense defends our true feel-ings. It is at this level that we manipulate others to provide us with the support we believe we require. Beneath the synthetic layer is the *impasse*, the layer where environmental support is withdrawn and self-support is inadequate. We tend to avoid this level in the same way that we tend to avoid pain of any kind. The experience at the impasse is one of feeling lost, stuck, and frustrated. Beneath the impasse is the *implosive* or death layer. Once we make contact with this layer, we touch our authentic selves, the personality that has been buried beneath our defenses. Perls maintains that contact with the implosive layer creates an explosion into authenticity.

Many Gestalt exercises focus on the impasse experience. The thera-peutic encounter creates a safe emergency and the group setting provides an atmosphere of *safe risk-taking*. The emergency is in the process of frustration; the safety factor is that there is no real-life danger. By refusing to indulge group members, the leader forces them to discover their own resources. As Laura Perls puts it, the leader should "give as much support as necessary and as little as possible" (Feder, 1980, p. 45). Another safety element is that the participant is always free to refuse to do an exercise or to terminate it at any time.

BASIC PROCEDURES

The goal in the Gestalt group is to reawaken the organismic process in each participant. Although the group's long-term goal is the achievement of maturity through the letting go of obsolete behaviors and the introduction of new ones, each technique used by a group leader is chosen to encourage group members along the road to full functioning and authenticity. Each time the group leader focuses the group on awareness of inner and outer zone processes, members' ability to contact themselves and their environment increases. As awareness grows, group members become better able to attend to the natural processes of making contact with and withdrawing from the environment. This makes it possible to identify and effectively deal with unfinished business. The Gestalt approach is itself a gestalt: each experiment is intended to stimulate the organismic process and to increase the potential for maturity.

Group leaders are responsible for setting the group's pace. They may begin by introducing a series of group exercises that focus on awareness or on contact and withdrawal. Later, they may ask for a volunteer to work in the hot seat. The group leader may begin by asking volunteers to stay in the here-and-now and to report on their awareness (Fagan, 1971). The leader does not offer interpretations or direct members toward a particular issue, but follows their narrative to ensure that the members are aware of their feelings and nonverbal communications. Together, they stay in present-centered awareness.

In order to succeed, group leaders themselves must be capable of remaining aware in the here-and-now and of contacting group members authentically. To accomplish this task, a group leader must have a minimal need for support and admiration from the group. To be maximally effective, the group leader must be able to make creative use of the experiments in Gestalt and to choose exercises congruent with group members' needs. Kaplan (1978) describes five ways in which Gestalt leaders use the group. Because of the diversity of leadership styles, these "modes" are not equally applicable to all Gestalt groups:

• The group as a supportive base for experience. Incoming members of Gestalt groups, as with all experiential groups, are apt to feel alone, uncertain, and vulnerable. Shortly they discover the requirements of the "worker" role, which means accepting the leader's guidance in seeking self-awareness and engaging in behavioral "experiments"; and the observer or "witness" role, which means listening to, empathizing with, and vicariously becoming involved with a worker. Although some Gestalt leaders wait for support and cohesiveness to emerge spontaneously in the group, others use exercises to foster it. Feder (1980), for example, notes that Gestalt groups are often short on support and believes that a primary task of the leader is to create a nurturing group climate. He frequently asks group members to report their current level of "safety" on a scale from zero to ten. When member feedback indicates low safety levels, the leader has an invitation to explore material prohibiting group progress.

• The group as an opportunity for awareness of here-and-now experience. A leader may ostensibly work with one participant and concurrently use the group members to elicit a meaningful experience for that person. Those who feel self-conscious in the group, for example, might be asked to attend to their experience of the group setting and other people in the room. The group is made meaningful for the individual by lending support or by joining in live interaction.

• The group as a basis of current experience. In this mode, group action is viewed as an instigator of a member's here-and-now experience. Participants' hot-seat work, for instance, may stimulate others to identify with them and ask themselves, "Am I like that?" Gestalt leaders differ considerably in their recognition of group-level issues and their willingness to deal with them.

• The group as dramatic participant in an individual's work. Group members can be included in a person's work by adopting or being assigned roles to help accomplish a here-and-now experience of a memory, dream, or fantasy as part of a guided or a spontaneous experiment. Although members will project their own issues into the role, an individual is free to accept as much of their contribution as he or she wishes.

• The group as a kinetic, everpresent process. As we have seen, the Gestalt group generally functions as background to the individual's work. At times, group issues may move to the foreground when members focus on their experience within the group. Joseph Zinker (1977) is one of an increasing number of Gestalt therapists to make use of group forces that continually affect members. Zinker recognizes that members can learn to ask one another for what they want or need, obtain feedback, resolve interpersonal conflicts, and support, energize, and help one another to grow without exclusive dependence on the leader.

Procedures used in Gestalt groups can be divided into six functional categories. There are procedures for increasing awareness, integrating polarities, increasing access to feelings, working with dreams, taking responsibility, and dealing with resistance. Gestalt techniques are extremely powerful. They can take persons deep within themselves very quickly, so that some exciting yet frightening aspects of self are discovered. Consequently, it is a good idea for the group leader to be experienced. Although this admonition applies to all group approaches, it is especially relevant when Gestalt methods are used, since they require a careful blend of frustration and support.

Increasing awareness

Exercises that direct awareness to the inner and outer zones are commonly used in Gestalt groups to encourage participants to become more present-centered and to help them function more completely in the here-and-now. The leader might instruct group members to close their eyes and concentrate fully on inner processes. These processes include breathing and the physical sensations of the skin, joints, muscles, stomach, and genitals. To themselves, participants complete the sentence "Now I am aware of..." (Stevens, 1971). They are then directed to open their eyes and focus their awareness on the outer zone. Participants complete the same statement with sensations from the external world, such as sounds, smells, and sights. Members may also be asked to shuttle between the inner and outer zones, steering their awareness to each area in turn. Initially, these exercises may strike some group members as superficial or silly, but they are effective in increasing the possibility of receiving and tolerating new experiences (Polster, 1975). Eventually, the participants may become open to dealing, without resistance, to crucial emotional experiences unfinished in their history.

A variation on this opening procedure is for each group member to use a few minutes of the group's time to complete the statement "Now I am aware of..." aloud (Enright, 1971). The group leader offers no further instructions, but probes the hesitant group member by asking "What are you experiencing right now?" There is an important distinction between the content and the process of awareness. Group members may not wish to reveal certain information about themselves in the group's early stages, and yet find that that information dominates their awareness during the exercise. The information is the content of awareness. In Gestalt, it is important to be in touch with the process of awareness. In this case, group members may be aware of nagging thoughts at the back of their minds or of censoring self-disclosure. There is little pressure in the Gestalt group to reveal all about oneself. Instead, the leader attempts to teach group members to attend to their organismic processes.

In awareness exercises, group members are encouraged to note data coming from their bodies and from the external world without interpreting, judging, appreciating, enjoying, or storing the experience for future use. There is some similarity between meditation and Gestalt awareness exercises. Meditators are passive observers of the thoughts that float through their minds. They neither stop the thoughts from coming nor linger on any single thought. In Gestalt, participants note the muscle aching in the back, the hair tickling the ear, the pressure of a crossed leg on the leg beneath it. However, they do not hold on to any of these impressions to determine if a feeling is unpleasant or if it would disappear by a change in posture.

It is a curiously demanding task to keep oneself from interpreting and judging awarenesses, thoughts, and experiences. This difficulty is due to interference from the middle zone. One exercise that is often initiated in a Gestalt group is for participants to divide into pairs and share awareness about each other. Middle-zone processes can easily intrude. A sentence such as "Now I am aware of your warm smile," does not really express awareness. The word "warm" is interpretive, a product of middle-zone fantasies. One way to help differentiate between true awareness of internal or external events in the present and middle-zone fantasies is to complete two statements each time: "Now I am aware ... And I imagine that ..." The statements in the previous example might become "Now I am aware of your smile. I imagine that it means that you feel warmly toward me." Through practice, group members learn to differentiate accurately between what is really happening and what they imagine.

Awareness is crucial in hot-seat work. Typically, when participants begin interaction with the group leader, they are asked to attend to breathing, posture, facial expression, or unconscious motor activity. These directives bring members into the here-and-now, reducing middle-zone distractions so that the work becomes spontaneous and present-centered. Many people are anxious working in front of an audience for the first time. This anxiety or embarrassment can be a resistance to change. By focusing on the inner zone, members become aware of their clenched stomachs, jaws, or other tense areas. The group leader may direct participants to attend to various important nonverbal behaviors such as smiles, postures, or voice qualities by asking "Are you aware that you're smiling?", "Can you experience how you are holding your body?", or "How does your voice sound to you?"

The following exchange illustrates how one group member responded to this kind of intervention:

Therapist:	What are you doing with your hand?
Participant:	*(slightly startled)* Uh, making a cross.
Therapist:	A cross?
Participant:	Yes. *(Pause)*
Therapist:	What might you do with a cross?
Participant:	Well, I certainly hung myself on one this weekend, didn't I? [Enright, 1975, p. 16.]

The group member's attitude of martyrdom and its contribution to his current status is now open to discussion.

When the nonverbal behavior involves another group member, the participant may be instructed to directly address that individual. A participant might, for example, express positive feelings verbally while leaning away from someone. Awareness of body position might lead to an understanding of a complex mix of feelings of fear and attraction. Here the group leader is attending to group members' blocks by enhancing their awareness of how they prevent themselves from changing. The goal of awareness, in short, is to promote self-understanding (Perls, 1973).

In the following example, the group leader works to promote aware-ness and change in a 35-year-old woman who, by her own admission, feels uncomfortable around people, closed to her sensual feelings, and stuck in her expressive abilities (Zinker, 1977). The therapist shares his thought processes as he searches for an experiment that will be maximally helpful. The interaction also illustrates that Gestalt experiments are typically cre-ative occurrences growing out of the group's experience rather than pat exercises prepared beforehand.

> As I talk with Sadie in the group, I begin to formulate a range of experiments which may be useful for the exploration of her social-sexual behavior. I think of the simple act of walking across the room and feeling sen-sual as one walks. I have a fantasy of the variety of walkers I see at the local shopping mall. Some people, I think to myself, really luxuriate in their bodies when they move through space. Sadie looks stiff and wooden when she walks into the room. I think to myself, it would be nice to get her out of her words and into some concrete actions.

Joseph (therapist): Sadie, how would it be for you to walk across the room as if you were feeling really sensuous?

Sadie: That's kind of scary to me. I don't want to do that. I feel a little shaky in my voice just telling you that.

> *(Inside my head)* Boy, I really overstepped in suggesting that experiment. She seems to be comfortable and more in contact with her voice.

Joseph: How do you feel about your voice now?

Sadie: It's kind of pitched high and jittery. *(Pause)* I used to sing as a kid. I like my voice ordinarily.

> *(Inside my head)* I'll go with her voice and work into her sexual feelings later.

Joseph: Would it be more comfortable experimenting with your voice?

Sadie: I guess.

Joseph: Okay, then how about telling me what you feel in your voice now.

> *(Inside my head)* I'm going to start exactly where she's at.

Sadie: It's a bit less jittery now. Seems like my voice is getting a little deeper as I am talking to you.

Joseph: Sounds very different now, almost a bit hoarse.

Member of group: Sadie, you are blushing around your neck as you talk with Joseph. You look pretty with that color in your face, too.

Sadie: Really?

Joseph: Sadie, are you aware of your face?

Sadie: *(to group)* I am feeling shy and excited all at once.

Joseph: I experience the sensuousness of your voice now.

Sadie: Yes, I feel that a little.

Joseph: Could you continue talking with us with that sensuous quality in your voice?

Sadie: Yeah, sure. *(After a pause she turns to another member of the group.)* You know, John, I have always found you good-looking. *(Everyone laughs. There is excitement in the room.)* [Zinker, 1977, pp. 133–135.][1]

Integrating polarities

Gestalt formation and dissolution depends upon our ability to identify our needs and to make contact with the environment to satisfy them. Contact can refer to two different phenomena. The first is the ability to clearly differentiate between the self and the environment. In the case of introjects, for example, it becomes important to be able to distinguish between ourselves and our parents. The second is the ability to segregate and clarify different aspects of the self. We organize our environment and ourselves into polarities. Sometimes the extreme points of a polarity coexist peacefully. At other times they make war and struggle to dominate each other. In Gestalt theory, the battles we experience between ourselves and others usually represent two sides of a conflict within ourselves.

Empty-chair or two-chair work is the hot-seat exercise that most effectively deals with the contact functions. There is some similarity between two-chair work in Gestalt and the use of auxiliaries in psychodrama. However, whereas the psychodrama exercise is an opportunity to reenact a painful event, the Gestalt technique directs the participant to create both sides of an internal conflict and establish a dialogue between them. Thus participants fully experience two fragments of themselves, including the noxious aspect that is typically denied or rejected. Once both sides of the polarity are experientially understood, they can be more easily integrated within the personality. As an example, many people have internalized conflicts between being passive, appeasing pushovers and aggressive, overbearing steamrollers. The adaptive integration of this polarity might be represented by an assertive yet sensitive position, or by drawing upon the extremes in appropriate situations. Other common polarities include being dependent/alienated, rational/emotional, and self-centered/selfless.

Neurotic mechanisms are processes in which aspects of a person's personality may be enmeshed, as in confluence and introjection, or fragmented and denied, as in projection and retroflection. As mentioned

[1]From *Creative Process in Gestalt Therapy*, by J. Zinker. Copyright 1977 by Brunner/Mazel, Inc. Reprinted by permission.

previously, the most common polarity tackled in the Gestalt group is the topdog-underdog conflict. The bullying topdog contains introjected parental wishes and expectations. It dictates what the person "should" do. The apologetic underdog constantly sabotages the forceful manipulations of the topdog by whining "I try my best. I can't help it." When the topdog dominates, the group member may complain about feeling driven to achieve perfection in all things. When the underdog dominates, the person may never seem to be able to accomplish or finish a task.

The empty-chair technique strengthens the weaker or overwhelmed side of the conflict, so that the two poles can engage in a dialogue between equals. For example, a group member who is always late for his appointments may set up a two-chair dialogue between his topdog and his underdog. While sitting in the first chair, he would speak from his underdog to his imaginary topdog in the second chair. He might whine, confess, and rationalize his chronic lateness. After a minute or so, he would shift to the other chair and take on the topdog's traits and lecture the underdog. From this position he might argue, bully, and demand that he should always be on time. After a short interval, the person would shift again to the underdog chair and continue to switch chairs and roles until the extremes are fully experienced and the dialogue reaches closure. The group member is not encouraged to choose one set of impulses and reject the other. The purpose of the two-chair dialogue is to revive the processes of gestalt formation and dissolution. Resolution of the conflict might require a compromise between the two impulses or merely the peaceful acceptance of a noxious aspect of the self. Gestalt's paradoxical theory of change advises that "change occurs when one becomes what one is, not when he tries to become what he is not" (Fagan & Shepherd, 1971, p. 77).

The following empty chair dialogue occurred in a Gestalt group with a woman who wanted an intimate relationship with a man, but kept ruining relationships shortly after they showed promise.

Underdog:	I'm so lonely, I wish I had someone to come home to at the end of the day.
Topdog:	You have the children; that should certainly be enough for you.
Underdog:	I'm all right during the day as long as I'm busy and at night I'm all right if I'm tired enough, but . . .
Topdog:	Don't be such a baby; you should certainly be more self-sufficient than that!
Underdog:	But I don't want to be self-sufficient! I want a man to take care of me, and make some decisions for me, and . . .
Topdog:	Decisions, ha! What man is really strong enough to make your decisions? They're all weak—you'll end up taking care of him!

Underdog: I won't! Paul was wonderful about decisions, he made everything so easy for me, I really loved him until...

Topdog: Yeah, until! Until he couldn't make a move without you; until you could do nothing except worry about his falling apart. You aren't any good for a man.

Underdog: But I want to be! I hate myself when I turn on men this way, when I can't give them the time of day after they've been so wonderful.

Topdog: Forget it baby; go it alone. You can do it; there's something wrong with all of them! [Fantz, 1975, pp. 91–92.][2]

The dialogue revealed to the woman that her topdog reminded her of her father, a loving man who had died some years ago. By engaging in a further dialogue between her "father" and herself, she was able to see him as having sabotaged all her relationships with men. Finally, the group leader asked another member to play her father, and the woman was able to express her love to him and at the same time let go of a need to carry him inside of her. This type of experiment illustrates how two parts of the personality can vividly come to life and how an introject can be discovered and dealt with.

Some polarities are first experienced as conflicts between self and others. For example, the group member who feels guilty when she imagines telling her mother that she plans to move away is probably projecting her own ambivalence onto her mother. Because she has never candidly confronted her mother on the issue, her guilt may be based on the fantasy that mother will become depressed, physically ill, or rejecting should she reveal her plans. In Gestalt, guilt is always assumed to represent projected resentments, behind which lie various unexpressed demands and appreciations (Perls, 1969a). Theoretically then, the group member may feel guilty because she has made neither her demands nor her appreciations known to her mother.

The group leader will likely direct her in two-chair work to help her identify and clarify any polarities involved in her conflict. In the first chair, the participant acts as herself and tells her mother her plans, appreciations, and demands. In the second chair, she role-plays the way she believes her mother would respond. As the extremes engage in dialogue, the two points of view are brought into awareness and are clearly differentiated from each other. Instead of being stymied and unable to act, her confused feelings become separated and clarified. She also learns to differentiate between real events and her fantasy projections.

Although the two-chair exercise tends to be individual hot-seat work, polarities can also be explored within the group whenever interpersonal conflicts emerge between group members or when members seek to

[2]From R. Fantz, "Polarities: Differentiation and integration." In F. D. Stephenson (Ed.), *Gestalt Therapy Primer*, 1975. Courtesy of Charles C Thomas, Publisher, Springfield, Illinois.

understand their feelings. In order to explore the full range of feelings for another group member, participants might be asked to go around the group and tell each member a resentment and an appreciation. In fact, "making the rounds" can be a useful exercise anytime a group member may benefit from feedback from the rest of the group or from rehearsing a behavior or expressing a feeling or attitude.

Increasing access to feelings

One goal of awareness exercises is to help group members contact their feelings. None of us wants to feel the deep personal pain we may carry with us. Yet by denying this pain, we remain fettered by unfinished business. The woman who is constantly afraid of being abandoned by her mate, even though she has received maximal assurance of fidelity, may be haunted by unfinished business. She may be responding to her lover as she would to a rejecting or punishing parent. Her present fear and distrust may be related to her persistent denial of old pains that have not been fully experienced. The process required is one of gestalt formation and dissolution so that the power of the past can recede and she can relate more appropriately in the present.

To complete the gestalt, old feelings must be fully experienced. This is important for at least two reasons. First, the energy required to keep the roof on painful feelings can be liberated for productive use when the emotions attendant on unfinished business are expressed. Second, it clarifies the polarities of any conflict so that divergent fragments can be more readily integrated. When we fully experience our feelings we realize what it is we want and need. Most of the experiments suggested by the group leader, including awareness exercises and two-chair work, will help to increase access to feelings. In addition, there are techniques that explicitly focus on this aspect of Gestalt work (Polster & Polster, 1973).

One technique for heightening the expression of feeling is the use of *enactments*. Enactments are exhibitionistic expressions in which a role is played out so that true feelings are fully experienced. As awareness elicits action, deliberate acting leads to increased awareness. The group member in the next example begins by becoming aware of his voice:

> *P:*   I would like to understand...
> *T:*   I hear a wailing in your voice. Can you hear it?
> *P:*   Yes...There is a trembling.
> *T:*   Be your voice now.
> *P:*   I am a weak, complaining voice, the voice of a child that doesn't dare to demand. He is afraid...
> *T:*   I am...
> *P:*   I am a little boy and I am afraid to ask for anything, can only ask for what I want by showing my sadness, so that mommy will have pity and take care of me...
> *T:*   Could you be your mother, now? [Naranjo, 1975, p. 39.]

Enacting mother's and child's voices led to a dialogue between them and an expanded awareness of how the participant was manipulating others by playing a helpless child. In enactment, the group member is encouraged to try on unfamiliar behaviors to discover the energy and excitement contained in them. For example, a participant may complain that nobody ever listens to her. The group leader (and group members as well) might play deaf, creating a situation in which the participant must experiment with new ways of making herself heard. She might become aggressive and angry, placating and tearful, or assertive and self-confident. According to theory, each behavior that group members choose to over-come their dilemmas are true aspects of themselves that have been denied. As they act out each role they experience the feelings associated with them and can reintegrate these parts into their conscious personalities.

The group leader may use enactments to help a group member discover a projected aspect of the self. A participant may believe that other group members are kind, but that she is fundamentally an unkind person. The leader might invite the participant to act out her meaning of the word "kindness." The enactment helps the group member experience, and perhaps rediscover, the capacity for kindness within herself. Enactments are often intentional exaggerations, so that the shy, placating group member might be invited to stand on a chair and dish out commands in an arrogant, stentorian voice. The empty-chair technique could be considered an elaboration on the enactment exercise.

Feelings are enhanced when group members are asked to *exaggerate* their nonverbal behaviors. A participant sitting in the hot seat may be quietly describing her unhappy marriage, unaware that she is striking her thigh with her fist. The group leader is on the lookout for such body language and is likely to refocus the participant from her unanimated storytelling to her active fist. Perls believed that needs are never totally repressed; nonverbal behavior, or body language, is one way in which frustrated needs are expressed. By deliberately exaggerating the movement of pounding her fist into her thigh, the group member contacts the unac-knowledged feelings that her nonverbal behavior represent. She might, for instance, contact feelings of anger, guilt, or resentment related to her marriage. Or she might discover that an exploration of conflicts in her marriage reminds her of how she rebelled against her father to marry in the first place. The leader might even ask her to "become" her fist and supply a sentence to capture the spirit of her pounding. A spontaneous dialogue between her fist and her thigh might be encouraged. This intervention could help unlock repressed feelings and unveil the internalized conflict that the pounding fist symbolizes.

Body language is not the only nonverbal behavior that can offer access to emotions. Voice quality also carries some of the message of unexpressed feelings. When the group leader detects a whining voice, the speaker might be asked to exaggerate it, to ham it up and enjoy the opportunity to whine and complain with the group's attention and permission.

Working with dreams

Some of Gestalt's most exciting hot-seat work occurs when a group member begins to unravel the meaning of a dream. Perls (1973) believed that dreams are the most spontaneous production of our existence. Dreams are nonintellectualized creations of our personalities. Theoretically, dream images are really fragments of the self that have been rejected or disowned. Therefore, they have meaning that is unique to the creator. In Gestalt, dreams do not have universal symbolic meaning as they do in psychoanalysis, where any weapon, projectile, tower, or other elongated object, for example, is apt to be interpreted as a representation of male sexuality. Consequently, the figures and objects inhabiting the dream are neither analyzed nor interpreted by the group leader. Instead, dream work in Gestalt involves two processes: bringing the dream back to life, and reowning the fragmented parts of the personality that have been projected onto the dream image.

To bring the dream back to life, the group member is directed to recount the dream in the present tense. Describing it in the past tense ("I dreamed I was being chased through a valley between two tall, snow-capped mountains.") objectifies the dream and invites intellectualization and interpretation. By describing it in the present ("I am running through a valley. There is someone after me and I'm scared. I'm surrounded by two huge snowcapped mountains, and there is no way to go but straight ahead."), the group member reenters the dream and reexperiences the original events and feelings in the group setting.

Each dream object or figure is a disowned fragment of the personality. In the dream already introduced, the fragmented parts of the dreamer's personality are hidden in the pursued, the unknown pursuer, the path, the mountains, and even the snow on the mountain peaks. In order to reown each fragment, the dreamer must first discover them by identifying with each object in the dream. A dreamer may be asked to describe himself in the first person as the mountain ("I am a mountain. I am massive and significant. I am unmoved by your puny insignificance."), the path ("I am a sure path through these mountains. I can guide you safely if you follow me."), and the unknown pursuer ("You don't know who I am, but I'm gonna get you.").

As dreamers take on the roles of each person and object in turn, they identify aspects of themselves that they have never fully experienced before. They may contact feelings of superiority or security, of insignificance or fear, of hostility or being threatened. The group leader may direct the participant to focus on one dream object that appears particularly significant, or to shift from object to object, sampling the feelings associated with each.

Another variation in the method is for the dreamer to describe the dream from the perspective of various dream objects. This can increase contact with feelings associated with each fragment. It is not necessary to use an entire dream in Gestalt dreamwork. A short dream fragment can provide copious material. Participants who have difficulty remembering dreams may prefer to explore a waking fantasy or daydream.

When the dream's nucleus is a discussion or argument with other people, the empty chair can be used to contact polarities. The dreamer can enact a dialogue between two principals in the dream, exploring the extremes of each polarity before attempting integration. It is also possible to select other group members to portray dream figures. Unlike psychodrama, in which group members are given some license to respond to the worker, group members are used in the Gestalt exercise to invoke spatial relationships, postures, and, perhaps, a retrievable statement from the dream. The dreamer takes on the role of each figure in turn, creating dialogues between them. This process gives the dreamer access to the dream's gestalt and heightens the potential for reclaiming its message.

Taking responsibility

Each neurotic mechanism is associated with an inability to take responsibility for the self. Introjectors fail to differentiate between their own feelings and beliefs and the alien faith they have adopted. Projectors experience their own impulses as belonging to others. In confluence, people cannot disassociate themselves from the larger "we"; and retroflectors objectify and disown aspects of themselves. The Gestalt approach alters these experiences by changing the group member's use of communication and language.

A value specifically encouraged by Gestalt is speaking *directly* to other people in the first person and not about them in the third person. Gossiping, advice giving, intellectualizing, psychologizing, and violating someone else's boundaries are discouraged. The group leader helps the members become sensitive to their use of pronouns and verbs. For example, a participant might say "It's awful for people to hit their children." The leader will ask the person to identify the "it" or to change the "it" to "I". When the statement has been reformulated as "I'm awful to hit my kids," responsibility is taken for the action and the feeling. Other pronouns that the leader is sensitive to are "we" and "you" when they refer to the self. By personalizing pronouns the gray state of confluence and the dissociating functions of introjection and projection can be changed to the experience of contact.

The Gestalt leader is also alert to the use of verbs, particularly *can't*, *need to*, and *have to*. By changing them to *won't*, *want to*, and *choose to*, members take responsibility for the thoughts, acts, or feelings they are relating. The action is willed. Group members gain control of their behaviors and thoughts rather than being controlled by them. The leader also encourages the member to change the use of the conjunction *but* to *and*. When two clauses are joined by *but*, the first clause is negated or qualified by the second. The statement "I want to work on this problem, but I'm afraid," can be completed by "so I won't," whereas "I want to work on this problem and I'm afraid" has a quite different meaning. *But* prevents the speaker from taking responsibility for the first clause. In the same way, questions are generally discouraged and rephrased as statements to help group members discover the resources in themselves that they sought to mobilize in others by acting helpless.

Responsibility can also be promoted by bringing to awareness the ways in which we give away power, stop ourselves, or desensitize ourselves to our sensory functioning. By giving away power, the Gestaltist means that group members believe that their feelings are created by others, and that they are victims of others' influence. A group member who believes that he feels depressed because his girlfriend "makes" him feel that way may be directed to say to her, in fantasy "I give you the power to make me feel depressed." This helps the person learn to take responsibility for displacing his power and giving control of his feelings to someone else. In time he may be able to genuinely say "I feel this way when you...," thereby increasing the responsibility he accepts for himself in the encounter (Passons, 1975).

When we assign our personal power to the environment, it often means that we have a hole in our personality. According to Perls (1969a), we project onto the environment what we cannot mobilize in ourselves. In the Gestalt group, leaders understand that they are projection screens for members' limited resources. By refusing to respond to the pleas or accusations of group members, the leader frustrates them, forcing them to rediscover those resources within themselves and consequently, to take responsibility for their own feelings.

Dealing with resistance

Resistance is a concept common to most schools of psychotherapy and counseling. Resistance is usually taken to mean that the client is obstructing the helpful therapist. It is an evaluative commentary on clients: resistant clients are bad and don't know what's good for them. In Gestalt, resistance means that the group member will not perform the experiments or exercises that the leader recommends (Latner, 1973). Rather than being a frustrated therapist's statement about the client who refuses to be helped, in Gestalt, resistance is a statement about the relationship between the group leader and the group member. Resistance demonstrates how group members interfere with their own free functioning. The Gestalt leader uses the opportunity of resistance to enlarge group members' self-awareness, including their unwillingness or felt inability to do or experience something (Latner, 1973). In short, resistances are not cumbersome blocks that must be crushed and destroyed, but interferences that can be used to increase self-awareness.

Resistance is manifest in the way group members stop themselves. Perls (1973) described the neurotic as a self-interrupter. Resistance develops as a response to the felt needs of the personality since it is used to reduce the risk of contacting negative feelings. Later it restricts free functioning. Gestalt's goal is to transform resistance into awareness. The leader can do this by asking the group member to stay with the resistance, to repeat, for instance, the statement "I won't do it!" or complete the sentence "What I am avoiding is . . ." in order to draw out fresh awareness.

Resistance can be manifest in muscular tension or in physiological self-restraint. The group leader may draw a participant's attention to the way he is choking his voice by tensing his vocal chords, or focus awareness on the way he is sitting with his arms tightly folded across his chest. The leader steers the member by asking questions such as "Can you hear your voice? How does it sound to you?" or "Can you experience how you are sitting in the chair?" or "Can you describe what you are doing with your arms?" (Enright, 1971). When group members restrain themselves bodily, they are engaged in retroflection. By becoming aware of their resistance to experiencing, feeling, or continuing with the process of Gestalt work, they become capable of transcending their own interference on the road to integration.

Group members may protect themselves by becoming desensitized to sensory functioning. That is, they may fail to hear what is said, see what they are doing, or experience their own feelings. Again, as members become aware of these resistances, they are able to take responsibility for their unwillingness to see or hear. The resistance to experiencing feelings, particularly painful ones, is also manifest in breathing. Group members may choke back tears by breathing shallowly or holding their breath. The sensitive group leader will encourage members to breathe deeply to allow the feelings to be expressed and experienced.

The physiological expression of resistance can be dealt with in an empty-chair exercise in which the group member engages the tense body part in a dialogue. For example, the man sitting with his arms tightly folded across his chest might be directed to fantasize his arms in the empty chair and ask them what they are doing. Often the tension is expressed between two body parts or even between two halves of the body. While a woman talks about her work, the leader may notice that her right hand is clutching and squeezing her left hand. The struggle between the right and left hands might signify a conflict which could be explored in a dialogue between the hands. Her left hand might say "Ouch, stop squeezing me so hard!" and the right hand might respond with "I don't mean to hurt you, but there are other things that hurt more and I'm keeping us from those feelings."

Again, Gestalt does not emphasize destroying one's resistance. One must first become aware of resistance and acknowledge that something is indeed being avoided. Frequently this awareness stimulates the group member to go further and risk experiencing the blocked feeling. At other times, the mere acknowledgement of the resistance helps the participant transcend it.

APPRAISAL

It is not always easy to dissociate the Gestalt approach from its founder, Fritz Perls. Although Perls was a uniquely insightful and sensitive therapist, his flamboyant and charismatic personality and his confrontive and challenging style, demonstrated, in the eyes of many, an extreme arrogance. Group leaders today, however, whether they practice primarily within the Gestalt mode or have borrowed only a few of its techniques, adopt the theoretical constructs and applied experiments most consistent with their own styles. As a result, it is important to differentiate between Gestalt and its founder's provocative personality.

One of the stamps of Perls' innovations is the Gestalt prayer:

I do my thing, and you do your thing.
I am not in this world to live up to your expectations.
And you are not in this world to live up to mine.
You are you, and I am I,
And if by chance, we find each other, it's beautiful.
If not, it can't be helped.

The philosophy embodied in the prayer reflects Perls' concern with issues of responsibility and self-awareness. It speaks directly to a willingness to take responsibility for one's life in satisfying personal goals, and, in particular, knowing who one is. In this spirit, it is a valid response to social and family pressures to conform to convention or to meet arbitrary expectations. As a result, the prayer often finds its way onto the dormitory walls of university students when they are getting their first tastes of the delicious fruits of freedom. Unfortunately, the Gestalt prayer is easily distorted by group members, group leaders, and the lay public alike. "I do my thing, and you do your thing" is too often used to give license to an attitude of insensitivity to the needs and feelings of others. By laying the responsibility for pain, as well as growth, at the feet of group members, egocentric group leaders absolve themselves for lack of concern. In some ways, the prayer is anti-gestalt; it focuses on our independence without considering our interdependence in serving our needs and assuring that the potential for human development is met. In this context, Greenwald (1976) has noted that some Gestalt groups become toxic because they unduly pressure participants and overemphasize strongly emotional, cathartic experiences. A warm, nourishing group leader may promote more awareness and risk-taking than a distant, autocratic one.

Perls' largely anti-intellectual position, reflected in such statements as "lose your mind and come to your senses," is also easily distorted and simplified. Perls reacted to the primarily cognitive therapy of the early psychoanalysts by espousing a total commitment to the expression of feelings. As a result, there is a tendency for group leaders adopting the Gestalt approach to ignore the valuable problem-solving skills and conceptual abilities of group members. Perls' intention was to swing the balance away from an overemphasis on the role of mind at the expense of the role of body. However, the reverse of this dualism, emphasizing feelings and the body at the expense of the intellect, may not provide the optimum therapeutic approach either.

Although Perls was a creator and an innovator, many of today's group leaders have evolved beyond following rigidly in the master's footsteps. Gestalt theory has spawned a large selection of exercises and experiments, from two-chair work to fantasy dialogues with dream figures, that are valuable in the context of therapy and growth groups. However, Gestalt is not in theory an approach that offers prepackaged techniques for group technology. Many ill-trained practitioners are guilty of relying on technique without considering theory and the individual needs of each group member. The best Gestalt leaders are those willing to experiment with technique, to create novel approaches to individual problems, and to respond with insight to needs of individual group members at specific times. Gestalt is too powerful an approach to be implemented as an endless string of marketed exercises without a guiding knowledge of its concepts.

Good research on the Gestalt approach has been meager. Prochaska (1979) reviewed several contemporary studies and concluded that though some found increased personal growth following involvement in the Gestalt group, other studies show minimal effects. In a study with 60 university students, a Gestalt workshop experience was found to generate increased self-actualizing behavior as measured by the Personal Orientation Inventory (Foulds & Hannigan, 1977). In recent, controlled investigations, Gestalt techniques have led to greater depths of experiencing and awareness (Greenberg & Clarke, 1979) and to increased empathy, feelings of being understood, self-autonomy, and cohesiveness, and less alienation between group members (Anderson, 1978).

Yet it is clear that additional empirical research is needed to support the value of this popular and potent method, which has influenced the practice of a great many group therapists and remains both a challenging and enjoyable avenue of exploration and personal change.

SUMMARY

Gestalt therapy was forged by Fritz Perls out of his early training in psychoanalysis and subsequent exposure to existential philosophy, the Gestalt school of theoretical psychology, and Wilhelm Reich's work on the physiological roots of resistance. Today Gestalt groups are known for their strong, active leadership and their orientation toward the development of autonomy and responsibility among participants.

The basic concepts of Gestalt groups are *figure and ground, awareness and present-centeredness, polarities, safety functions,* and *maturity.* Perceptual research suggests that whatever is most compelling to us at a given moment forms a figure that stands out in our awareness before a background. This figure-ground gestalt shifts over time through a process of *organismic self-regulation.* Neurotic functioning is said to occur when *inner* and *outer zones* of awareness are disrupted by the *middle zone* of thoughts and fantasies. The concept of polarities, of which the topdog-underdog split is representative, describes the struggle between two opposite and extreme sides of oneself that coexist. Safety functions are ineffectual ways of dealing with threat or stress and include *confluence, retroflection, introjection,* and *projection.* Maturity refers to the goal of discovering one's own supportive resources and taking responsibility for one's life.

The goal of Gestalt groups is to reawaken the organismic process of participants by encouraging awareness and moving toward maturity. The traditional group leader works with a single volunteer on the *hot seat.* Group members are available to offer support, identify with the person who is working, and participate in active experiments to aid the individual's work. More recently, Gestalt therapists have attended to the group process as well. The group leader initiates experiments for increasing awareness, integrating polarities, increasing access to feelings, working with dreams, taking responsibility, and dealing with resistance.

Critics accuse Gestalt therapists of encouraging self-indulgence in participants and fostering an anti-intellectual attitude. Nonetheless, Gestalt groups have a broad and popular following. One of their central contributions has been to provide an option to traditional, overly cerebral group therapies.

REFERENCES

Anderson, J. D. Growth groups and alienation: A comparative study of Rogerian encounter, self-directed encounter and Gestalt. *Group and Organizational Studies,* 1978, *3,* 85–107.

Cohen, A. M., & Smith, R. D. *The critical incident in growth groups: Theory and technique.* La Jolla, Calif.: University Associates, 1976.

Enright, J. B. An introduction to Gestalt techniques. In J. Fagan and I. L. Shepherd (Eds.), *Gestalt therapy now.* New York: Harper & Row, 1971.

Enright, J. B. An introduction to Gestalt therapy. In F. D. Stephenson (Ed.), *Gestalt therapy primer.* Springfield, Ill.: Charles C Thomas, 1975.

Fagan, J. The tasks of the therapist. In J. Fagan and I. L. Shepherd (Eds.), *Gestalt therapy now.* New York: Harper & Row, 1971.

Fagan, J., & Shepherd, I. L. *Gestalt therapy now.* New York: Harper & Row, 1971.

Fantz, R. Polarities: Differentiation and integration. In F. D. Stephenson (Ed.), *Gestalt therapy primer.* Springfield, Ill.: Charles C Thomas, 1975.

Feder, B. Safety and danger in the Gestalt group. In B. Feder and R. Ronall (Eds.), *Gestalt approaches to group.* New York: Brunner/Mazel, 1980.

Foulds, M. L., & Hannigan, P. S. Gestalt workshop and measured changes in self-actualization: Replications and refinement study. *Journal of College Student Personnel,* 1977, *18,* 200–205.

Greenberg, L. S., & Clarke, K. M. Differential effectiveness of the two-chair experiment and empathic reflections at a conflict marker. *Journal of Counseling Psychology,* 1979, *26,* 1–8.

Greenwald, J. A. The art of emotional nourishment: Nourishing and toxic encounter groups. In C. Hatcher and P. Himelstein (Eds.), *The handbook of Gestalt therapy.* New York: Jason Aronson, 1976.

Kaplan, M. L. Uses of the group in Gestalt therapy groups. *Psychotherapy: Theory, Research and Practice,* 1978, *15,* 80–89.

Kempler, W. Gestalt therapy. In R. Corsini (Ed.) *Current psychotherapies.* Itasca, Ill.: F. E. Peacock, 1973.

Kepner, E. Gestalt group processes. In B. Feder and R. Ronall (Eds.), *Gestalt approaches to group.* New York: Brunner/Mazel, 1980.

Koffka, K. *Principles of Gestalt psychology.* New York: Harcourt, Brace, 1935.

Kohler, W. *Gestalt psychology: An introduction to new concepts in modern psychology.* New York: New American Library, 1947.

Latner, J. *The Gestalt therapy book.* New York: Julian Press, 1973.

Naranjo, C., I and thou, here and now: Contributions of Gestalt therapy. In F. D. Stephenson (Ed.), *Gestalt therapy primer.* Springfield, Ill.: Charles C Thomas, 1975.

Passons, W. R. *Gestalt approaches in counseling.* Holt, Rinehart & Winston, 1975.

Perls, F. Group vs. individual therapy. *Etc. A review of general semantics,* 1967, *24,* 306–312.

Perls, F. *Gestalt therapy verbatim.* Lafayette, Calif.: Real People Press, 1969. (a)

Perls, F. S. *Ego, hunger, and aggression.* New York, Random House, 1969. (b)

Perls, F. *The Gestalt approach and eye witness to therapy.* Palo Alto: Science and Behavior Books, 1973.

Perls, F. S. Group vs. individual therapy. In J. O. Stevens (Ed.), *Gestalt is . . .* New York: Bantam Books, 1977.

Perls, F., Hefferline, R. F. & Goodman, P. *Gestalt therapy.* New York: Julian Press, 1951.

Polster, E. Techniques and experience in Gestalt therapy. In F. D. Stephenson (Ed.), *Gestalt therapy primer.* Springfield, Ill.: Charles C Thomas, 1975.

Polster, E., & Polster, M. *Gestalt therapy integrated.* New York: Brunner/Mazel, 1973.

Prochaska, J. O. *Systems of psychotherapy: A transtheoretical analysis.* Homewood, Ill.: Dorsey Press, 1979.

Simkin, J. Gestalt therapy in groups. In G. M. Gazda (Ed.), *Basic approaches to group psychotherapy and group counseling.* Springfield, Ill.: Charles C Thomas, 1968.

Stevens, J. O. *Awareness: Exploring, experimenting, experiencing.* Lafayette, Calif.: Real People Press, 1971.

Stevens, J. O. *Gestalt is . . .* New York: Bantam Books, 1977.

Wertheimer, M. *Productive thinking.* New York: Harper & Brothers, 1945.

Zinker, J. *Creative process in Gestalt therapy.* New York: Brunner/Mazel, 1977.

Zinker, J. C. The developmental process of a Gestalt therapy group. In B. Feder and R. Ronall (Eds.), *Gestalt approaches to group.* New York: Brunner/Mazel, 1980.

5

Psychodrama

Classical psychodrama is a therapeutic group process that uses the dramatic tool of improvisation to explore the client's world. Psychodrama is essentially a form of drama that reflects actual client problems instead of the imaginary creations of the playwright. In psychodrama, the fictitious character of the traditional theater is replaced by the client's spontaneous behavior.

It is important at the outset to realize that psychodrama is first and foremost an acting-out method designed for the exploration of personal problems, dreams, fears, and fantasies. Psychodrama is based on the premise that the exploration of feelings and the development of new attitudes and behaviors is enhanced through action that clearly approximates life, rather than through verbalization. In this way, psychodrama is akin to the body approaches that will be introduced in Chapter 6. Perhaps more directly than any other group method, psychodrama possesses the potential for transforming a five-minute verbal exchange into a half hour of active exploration. This expansion of experience is fostered through the use of a variety of psychodramatic techniques that facilitate the expression and clarification of feelings.

HISTORY AND DEVELOPMENT

The origins and development of psychodrama are intrinsically a part of the life history of Jacob Levy Moreno (1892–1974), founder of psychodrama, sociometry, and according to some, the group psychotherapy movement. Although legend has it that Moreno was born on a boat in the Black Sea, other documentation indicates his birthplace as Bucharest, Romania (Anderson, 1974). As a young child, Moreno moved with his family to Austria, where he eventually studied both philosophy and medicine at the University of Vienna. While still a medical student, he organized self-help groups among alienated prostitutes in Vienna, a project that he later viewed as the beginning of group psychotherapy. Moreno focused on the dynamic factors within the groups as a means of assisting the women to realize their personal goals. Moreno (1947) wrote that the meetings highlighted four basic considerations that became the cornerstone of group psychotherapy: the autonomy of the group; the presence of group structure; the problem of collectivity; and the problem of anonymity. In 1916 Moreno began his second project, working with Italian peasants who had been forced to relocate and helping them adapt to their new environment. From these two projects he developed the sociometric group-analysis techniques that form the underpinnings of his system of psychodrama and group psychotherapy.

The concept of drama as therapy evolved from a theatrical experiment Moreno launched in Vienna after World War I called the "Theatre of Spontaneity." Moreno first conceived of the acting-out technique basic to psychodrama when he observed children enacting their fantasies as they played in the parks of Vienna. As such, psychodrama grew out of the principle of play. Moreno intended the Theatre of Spontaneity simply as a new form of entertainment, so that initially his concern with fostering personality change and mental health was limited. These positive consequences were noted by Moreno only as side effects. His central idea and motivation was spiritual: to release the spontaneously creative self in a theater of life that provided an unlimited opportunity for freedom of expression. In fact, he considered his theater to be a kind of dramatic religion experienced in a "theatrical cathedral."

According to Moreno, therapeutic psychodrama had its origin when an actor shared with him some problems he was encountering with his angry fiancee. With the theatrical company's assistance, Moreno put the actor and his personal problems on stage. The experience was meaningful and successful, both for the couple and the group's other members. Consequently, Moreno began to experiment more formally with group enactments, developing various techniques that have become an intrinsic part of the psychodramatic approach.

Moreno came to the United States in 1925 and continued to develop psychodrama as he worked with children at the Plymouth Institute in Brooklyn, New York. At the same time, he further developed his sociometric-analysis technique in his work with prisoners at New York state's Sing Sing Prison and with disturbed children at the New York State Training School for Girls. A significant product of these group-interaction therapy sessions was the sociogram.[1] In 1929, Moreno began the first regular program of large-scale "open" psychodrama in the impromptu Theater Group at Carnegie Hall. In 1931 and 1932, Moreno coined the terms "group therapy" and "group psychotherapy" in connection with a specific

[1] A sociogram is a diagram portraying the forces of attraction, repulsion, and indifference in a group.

set of operations that he described in a monograph, "Application of the Group Method to Classification." The distribution of this work culminated in the Conference on Group Methods, which represented the first organized effort to bring group psychotherapy to the attention of the American Psychiatric Association.

BASIC CONCEPTS

A frequently recounted incident from Moreno's childhood highlights some of the key theoretical concepts contained in his theories of personality and psychotherapy (Anderson, 1974). Moreno, 4 years old at the time, was playing with a group of children in the basement of his parents' home. He organized the group into an impromptu play in which he took the role of God and the other children played angels. In keeping with his role as God, Moreno sat atop a number of stacked chairs. One of the children suggested that Moreno try to fly. He tried it and found himself on the floor with a broken arm. This incident was a long way from formal psychodrama, but it nevertheless illustrates most of psychodrama's basic elements: role-playing, spontaneity, tele, catharsis, and hopefully, insight.

Role-playing

Role-playing which involves acting a part in some impromptu production, is a practice frequently associated with psychodrama. Role-playing is used as a therapeutic technique in a number of theoretical orientations, most clearly in Gestalt therapy and in the behavioral school, where it is used to rehearse or refine desired behaviors.

Role-playing occupies a central position in psychodrama. Although the term may imply a contrived or artificial performance, Moreno did not view acting as necessarily contrived. In response to a compliment from talk-show host Dick Cavett on the greatness of his acting skills, Marlon Brando said "Everybody is an actor. You're doing it now. You are playing the role of an interviewer. People play the roles of parents, politicians, teachers. Everyone is a natural actor" (Yablonsky, 1976, p. 214).

Psychodrama recognizes the natural acting ability of people and provides a setting in which individuals can creatively work through personal problems and conflicts using the vehicle of role-playing. Moreno objected to the stale passivity of psychoanalysis, in which a patient would lie on a couch and verbalize free associations and dreams to a probing analyst. He believed that psychodrama can provide the opportunity to actively experiment with both realistic and unrealistic roles in life. Moreno, the humanist, liked the image of people playing God in the sense of exploring all of their dimensions and pushing themselves beyond their current level of functioning toward self-actualization. In the pursuit of exploration, there is nothing to prohibit a group member in a psychodrama from enacting the role of a brutal murderer, a seductive temptress, or something equally unrealistic or grotesque.

There is a fundamental difference between the kind of role-playing that occurs in psychodrama and the role-playing associated with legitimate theater. Professional actors are given lines to recite by writers; they are restricted by the dialogue they have been given. Even method acting, which emphasizes immersing oneself in a part by studying and becoming the people who play that role in real life, calls for perfecting the ability to adopt a role in a theatrical production, not in life itself. As a matter of fact, an acting background may be a liability in psychodrama. It is not uncommon for professional actors in encounter groups to be attacked for hiding behind false facades.

Moreno has noted that many people are as role-bound in real life as actors are in the theater. They lack spontaneity and engage in meaningless rituals and react to lines that others proffer. Take, for example, people who blandly smile their way through victory and disappointment alike in order to please others and not make waves. Psychodrama offers a means for breaking out of such scripted behavior.

Psychodrama, in contrast to legitimate theater encourages the exploration of roles that are real and meaningful to the participants. The lines and staging are the person's own and not based on a writer's ideas. Yet psychodrama can be fabulous theater. As fact is often more exciting than fiction, psychodramatic performances can be tremendously engaging for the actor and for the audience.

Spontaneity

The concept of *spontaneity*, and its sister concept, *creativity*, serve as the core of Moreno's theories of action and self. Both are rooted in his play-acting experiences with children and in the development of the adult Theatre of Spontaneity. Moreno was inspired by the psychological freedom exhibited by the children playing in the public gardens. The children seemed to be able to stay in the living moment in their use of fantasy and imagination and not be deadened by stereotyped behaviors. The Theatre of Spontaneity was formed in response to Moreno's disenchantment with legitimate theater, particularly the rigidity of scripts. Moreno also saw people becoming robot-like social machines devoid of creative vitality. In psychodrama groups, then, there is no rote script. A psychodrama session provides an endless variety of alternative paths and roles. The scene can be altered, the dialogue can be changed, actors can follow their feelings or hunches down any unknown path. This method is in sharp contrast to legitimate theater, in which the same script is repeated over and over again in search of an optimum performance.

Moreno saw the spontaneity training psychodrama offers as an antidote to the increasing rigidity of social role-playing. Psychodrama group members learn to expand their role repertoire and explore dimensions of themselves that they may have never before encountered. Participants may also discover solutions to specific personal problems as the drama unfolds. Moreno thought psychodrama could even help humans evolve into a new kind of being who is creative, uninhibited, and free from anxiety (Greenberg, 1974). Indeed, Moreno (1953) seemed to believe that as humans evolve, only the creative will survive.

Spontaneity is the key to unlocking creativity. As Moreno puts it, "Creativity is a sleeping beauty that, in order to become effective needs a catalyzer. The arch catalyzer of creativity is spontaneity" (Moreno, 1974a, p. 76). In other words, ideas are brought together through spontaneous action, and with good fortune and sufficient persistence, a creative act may result.

The end product of the creative process is the "cultural conserve" (Bischof, 1964). The cultural conserve is anything that preserves a culture's values, such as literature, art, ceremonies, or language. The conserve provides people with a tie to the past and helps them deal with situations that recur without having to begin all over again with each new problem. Although the conserve is indispensable to survival, a culture could become lazily obsessed with conserving and lose the skill of creating.

The stress on spontaneity does not imply that psychodrama consists of totally uninhibited action. Moreno's concept of spontaneity contains two important variables: *adequate response* and *novelty*. Thus, behavior must be both novel and adequate to a situation. A creative, novel response to the question "What is two plus two?" would be five, but in most mathematical systems, five would be an inappropriate response. A group member unfamiliar with the societal limitations placed on performance in a role may produce spontaneous, creative behavior that is pathological.

Therapeutic goals in group psychodrama often involve familiarizing the client with cultural and social limitations while facilitating the development of potentially creative spontaneity. Why is there so little spontaneity in the world? According to Moreno, modern humans fear it in the same way that primitive human beings feared fire until they learned to tame and control it. Moreno used the theater as a laboratory for spontaneity research. He found that spontaneity could be nurtured and controlled, and developed psychodramatic techniques specifically aimed at spontaneity training.

Through its allegiance to the concept of spontaneity, psychodrama shares with many other group approaches a focus on the here-and-now. Problems and relationships are not dissected verbally; they are experienced in action in the present. There is no past or future in a psychodramatic situation, only the present. Natural barriers of space and time are obliterated. Geographical distance between lovers is no issue, nor is a parent's death. Past problems and future fears are reenacted in the here-and-now of the psychodramatic confrontation. In a sense, psychodrama provides a participant with the opportunity to objectify a significant memory of an important event lodged in the psyche.

Unlike Gestalt's exclusive focus on current feelings and relationships, psychodrama leaders are not obligated to stay with the immediate situation. They may carry the session to the past or future, depending on the perceived needs of the participant. The here-and-now in psychodramatic terms is an expanded dimension encompassing both re-creation of past encounters and preparation for future ones. The emphasis is always on the learning that results from the reality of present experiences and reactions as opposed to the verbal rehearsing of past events or buried feelings (Shaffer &. Galinsky, 1974). The psychodramatic confrontation in the here-and-now is essential to the realization of the therapeutic goal of spontaneity in reality.

Tele

Spontaneity and creativity are dynamic concepts. Moreno also shares with the psychoanalysts a belief in the power of transference energy discussed in Chapter 10. However, he regards the concept of transference as too limited to account for the powerful feelings that take place in therapy groups. Whereas transference is a one-way flow of emotions from the client to the therapist, and countertransference is a one-way flow of emotions from the therapist to the client, *tele* refers to the two-way flow of emotions between client and therapist.

Tele consists of all the positive and negative feelings occurring between people in a psychodramatic situation. Moreno called it a "feeling of individuals into one another, the cement which holds groups together" (Moreno, 1945, p. xi) and, in another context, "flow—to and fro—of affectivity between individuals" (Moreno, 1956, p. 62). In other words, tele is the sum total of the emotional aspects of transference, countertransference, and empathy. Whereas empathy is a one-way feeling into the private world of another, tele involves a mutual exchange of empathy and appreciation. When group members reverse roles or try seeing the world through each other's eyes, they are involved in a telic relationship.

One implication of the tele concept to the study of groups is that we view others not just as they are, but as they are in relation to ourselves. Group psychodrama provides a laboratory in which to analyze our perceptions of others. Tele is especially relevant to sociodrama, a specific kind of psychodrama. In sociodrama there is a group theme. Instead of exploring personal problems, participants deal with problems that affect everyone present. Group members use role-playing to examine their own feelings about sociocultural issues such as racism, prejudice, parent-child relationships, or conflicts between police and citizens. Through creative and spontaneous action, participants explore their perceptions, responses, feelings, and behaviors and try to further group understanding.

Catharsis

The notion of *catharsis* is derived from the ancient Greek dramatists, who believed that staged tragedies relieved spectators' overpowering emotions. Drama was employed as a vehicle for expressing the dilemma of the human condition, and the resulting group catharsis was seen as assisting the audience in better understanding aspects of their own personalities.

Although Moreno employs the term in the Aristotelian sense of an emotional release (in the same way that Freud wrote about catharsis as the emotional resolution of hypnotic treatment with hysterical patients), he expanded the concept to encompass the actor as well as the audience. "It (the psychodrama) produces a healing-effect—not in the spectator (secondary catharsis) but in the producer-actors who produce the drama and, at the same time, liberate themselves from it" (Moreno, 1974b, p. 157).

In traditional theater, spectators can become emotionally caught up in the dramatic action if the script touches a respondent chord in their own personalities. Stage actors, however, rarely experience catharsis. First, they are typically not portraying significant events from their own experiences. Second, the frequent repetition of the script dilutes the material's cathartic potential. Even the actor who finds a part that accurately hooks his private emotions will soon treat the script as a cultural conserve rather than as a living experience.

Moreno believed that he went beyond Freud in developing the therapeutic value of catharsis and eliciting it through spontaneous dramatic action. In Greek drama, catharsis was secondary in importance to developing the story line; in psychoanalysis, catharsis is secondary to the task of analysis that follows it; but in psychodrama, the process of catharsis and integration is more important than the script or an analysis of the experience (Ginn, 1973). The psychodramatic situation is ripe for total emotional release. The amount of catharsis participants experience is related to the act's spontaneity. Participants who experience catharsis are both the authors of the drama, because the material is drawn from their private experience, as well as the actors who carry it out.

The psychodrama's audience may also become emotionally involved to the extent of experiencing catharsis. Initially, psychodrama spectators consisted only of those directly necessary to carrying out a person's treatment (Moreno, 1974b, p. 188). Today, audiences may consist of people who don't play active roles in a given psychodrama. Yet they still become emotionally involved in the session. The difference between the spectator in conventional theater and in psychodrama, according to Moreno, is comparable to the difference between a person viewing a film of an erupting volcano and a person watching the eruption from the foot of the mountain itself (Moreno, 1974b).

Insight

The final outcome of the psychodramatic process is a change in how participants structure their perceptual field, a change known as *insight*. Insight is a kind of configurational learning that yields an immediate solution to, or new understanding of, a problem (Greenberg, 1974). Group psychodrama aims to create a climate in which there can be a maximum of catharsis, relearning, and insight. The psychodrama provides group members with the opportunity to reexperience important events in their lives in a different way. The high emotional point in the group usually occurs during the action on the stage rather than during the information-elicitation preceding it or the group analysis following each scene. Insight, however, may take place simultaneously with catharsis or following the experience, when the group discusses the psychodramatic enactment.

BASIC PROCEDURES

Psychodrama roles

Many of the terms used in association with psychodrama are reminiscent of the theater. The group leader is known as the *director*. The director helps establish a climate for group work and helps guide group members toward an exploration of their problems. Psychodrama directors tend to be among the most active of group leaders. By taking charge and "running the show," they give permission to reticent, inhibited group members to experiment with role-playing.

Directors have three different roles: producer, therapist, and analyst (Moreno, 1945). When functioning as producers, they orchestrate the session and encourage group members to translate their thoughts into dramatic action. The producer must be acutely sensitive to the verbal and nonverbal indicators which chart the psychological state of the players and the mood of the "audience" that is observing the session. Creativity, flexibility, and the ability to keep the entire group involved in the action are key characteristics of the good producer.

In the role of therapist, the psychodrama director tries to help group members resolve disadvantageous behavioral patterns. Therapists may sit back passively and allow group members to carry the session forward. On the other hand, they may become quite aggressive, pushing and cajoling participants and shocking them into action. As very visible leaders, therapists may become the target of group commentary and criticism, and as group members, they must deal with it nondefensively and openly.

In the analyst's role, the group leader interprets and comments on group members' participation. In addition, the analyst seeks the reactions and analyses of all the group members regarding a particular enactment.

The group member who is the subject of a particular psychodramatic enactment is called the *protagonist*. Protagonists portray their own lives. When doing so, they are the leading characters in the session and the eyes of the group are on them. Protagonists have the rare opportunity of presenting their version of events and controlling the action in front of a group of involved peers. Protagonists are allowed considerable latitude in sketching their perceptions of events or individuals. If they perceive the boss as a vicious tyrant, they have the right, in fact, the obligation, to cast him that way. With the aid of the director, audience, and special production techniques, protagonists set up a here-and-now construction of their psychological reality in order to gain insight and improve functioning.

Another participant in a psychodramatic enactment of a protagonist's issue is the *auxiliary ego*. Auxiliary egos represent significant others in the protagonist's life. The characters in the protagonist's life are recreated in the psychodrama by members cast in those roles to help intensify the interpersonal experience. Thus, group members may be asked to play domineering mothers, withdrawn lovers, abusive fathers, or nurturing friends. Zerka Moreno (1978) has recently summarized five functions of the auxiliary ego:

- to take on a role required by the protagonist to conduct the psychodrama;
- to understand how the protagonist perceives relationships with absent members of the enactment;
- to clarify aspects of such relationships the protagonist is unaware of;
- to therapeutically guide the protagonist to resolve interpersonal and intrapersonal conflicts;
- to construct a bridge to facilitate the protagonist's travel between the enactment and the real world.

Good auxiliaries are able to involve themselves in a role rapidly and accurately. They must play the role as it has been described or as they intuit it and not as they would respond in the situation themselves. Some groups contain "professional auxiliaries" trained to slip into a variety of roles with great facility. Sometimes an auxiliary can take risks in embellishing a character in highly accurate and intuitive ways. A person playing the role of a guilt-inducing mother might throw out the line "Don't you ever think of what's going to happen to me when you leave?" and capture a valid but unstated fear of the protagonist. The use of diverse auxiliary egos encourages total group involvement in the session. As auxiliaries attempt to be sensitive to the protagonist's world and follow the director's coaching, they can learn about their own attitudes as well as the protagonist's problem.

The *audience* consists of group members not actively playing roles in a psychodramatic session. In the session's summary phase, they share their emotional reactions and disclose similar problems and conflicts with the group. By staying involved with the psychodrama, they stand to gain insight into their own problems, in the same way that we might learn something about ourselves by watching a gripping emotional drama on the screen or stage.

Phases of the psychodrama group

The first phase of a classic psychodrama group is the *warm-up*. The warm-up has three stages: gradually increasing the participants' physical movement; developing spontaneous behavior; and directing the group's attention to a specific task or theme (Blatner, 1973).

Warm-ups help members to overcome their fears of making fools of themselves or their anxiety about their acting ability. Directors also need warming up. They can do so by moving freely around the room, informally sharing some of their ideas, and trying to develop tele within the group (Blatner, 1973). Above all, the director uses the warm-up to create an atmosphere that encourages spontaneity and risk taking. Members need to feel trusting and safe to explore new responses. A leader's forceful authority helps participants realize that they can be playful and silly without feeling hurt or humiliated.

Warm-ups are particularly useful in psychodrama groups in which participants are resistant about moving into a theme immediately and are shy in volunteering to be the first protagonist. In such cases, warm-up techniques can get the participants into the flow of the group, allow them to get to know each other a little, and reduce their anxiety level. In addition, the director can glean information about who might be willing to participate in a psychodrama and what problem areas or themes are relevant to most members. Warm-ups may be verbal or nonverbal, borrowed from other group approaches, or originated by a creative director.

Many good warm-ups have been summarized by Weiner and Sacks (1969). In one exercise, participants are asked to sit silently and look around the group for someone they don't know well and then ask that person a question. The group often begins with rather harmless, nonthreatening questions and answers, but, with the director's encouragement, moves toward sharing feelings and more personal material.

There are warm-ups that function at a low-threat level and are intended to encourage spontaneity and build group cohesion. Others demand more self-disclosure and may generate significant emotional material. The following exercise has been described as an exceptionally supportive warm-up for slow-moving groups: "Think of a sentence you'd really like to hear (or wouldn't want to hear) from someone else in this room, or from a friend or member of your family. Be that person and say the sentence" (Leveton, 1977, p. 19). If the group is a class, social club, business organization, parent group, or other organized group, each person might be asked to share a request or complaint. This provides the director with valuable information about potential psychodrama themes.

Some warm-ups are nonverbal and can indirectly help participants push through their resistance to talk openly about feelings and issues. Movement exercises, such as getting up, moving around the room, and looking at people without talking, are energy-generating. Other forms of movement, such as those encouraged in dance therapy (see Chapter 7), may be appropriate. One of Leveton's (1977) favorite devices, a means of helping participants recall childhood experiences that can be relevant to psychodramatic conflicts, is to ask the group to write with the unaccustomed hand. Paper and crayons are distributed, and group members are asked to imagine themselves at an age when they were just beginning to write. Next, participants are instructed to concoct a little story about themselves at that age, using the unaccustomed hand. The childlike scrawl that is produced has a way of breaking through adult defenses. All nonverbal warm-up techniques, of course, require subsequent verbal sharing and discussion.

Finally, one widely used psychodramatic warm-up is the "magic shop" (Weiner & Sacks, 1969). The director has the group imagine a small shop on the stage, containing all sorts of wonderful qualities, such as love, courage, and wisdom. Volunteers are asked to come forward and barter for one or more items. One person might, for example, ask for "respect." The director, in the role of shopkeeper, asks for more specific information inquiring, perhaps, how much respect, or from whom, or about what. The shopkeeper then asks for something in return. Perhaps the volunteer offers to give up acquiescing so often to people as the purchase price for respect. With a little elaboration, volunteers begin to clarify goals and look at the consequences of their actions. A psychodramatic theme may also have been discovered in the process.

After the warm-up the group is ready for the *action phase* of psychodrama. Sometimes the director invites a participant on the basis of an established theme, previous knowledge, or the emergence of a likely candidate during the warm-up. At other times, protagonists volunteer to present personal issues or problems. The director listens as a protagonist explains the problem, obtaining enough information about the issue to translate it into action. The mention of another person is a good cue to set up an enactment. So is the mention of a particular time or place. Once a specific example has been elicited, the group member is encouraged to act out the incident rather than talk about it.

The protagonist sets the stage by improvising with the environment to recapture the event. The space used for psychodrama groups must allow considerable flexibility. The classic psychodrama setting has seats like a theater for the audience, and a multileveled, circular stage that looks like a tiered wedding cake. At the rear of the stage is a partially enclosed area and a balcony. Moreno believed that the levels of the stage contributed to the levels of action that could be performed on it. Many psychodrama group leaders today dispense with the formal stage, but they still insist that the setting be flexible.

The protagonist chooses and establishes in concrete form a representative scene. For example, a young woman who has difficulty dealing with aggressiveness in men might choose an episode in which her father reprimanded her for wanting to move away from home. If the original incident occurred in the kitchen, the stage is arranged to approximate the original scene as closely as possible. Then the roles of the relevant characters are filled by auxiliary egos. Since the protagonist typically chooses her own auxiliary egos, her perception of a group member as appropriate for a given role is more important than any physical or personality similarities the people might share in reality. Sometimes the director helps with the selection, choosing a trained auxiliary or someone in the audience who can benefit from playing that role. For instance, a man in the group who has an overbearing father is a good bet to play an overbearing father; a woman who complains about a philandering husband might benefit from playing a philandering wife. Thus, the auxiliary egos achieve a meaningful emotional experience on the coattails of the protagonist's conflict.

Psychodramatic enactments do not always represent real circumstances and situations, but loyally reflect the perspective of the protagonist. Although it may be clear to everyone in the audience that protagonists are distorting the feelings of other characters, other approaches and points of view are explored only after protagonists present their version of the conflict. Moreover, as protagonists broach unexpressed feelings and resentments, they may become threatened and resistant.

The director's skill is called on to help the protagonist explore new territory and gain fresh understanding without feeling overwhelmed. As Moreno describes the group leader's sensitivity, "We don't tear down the protagonist's walls; rather, we simply try some of the handles on the many doors, and see which one opens" (Blatner, 1973, p. 63). Through this process, the protagonist may experience very powerful emotions. A group member who is hurt and furious with her father for never being around might be asked to use a bioenergetic pillow-pounding exercise to ventilate these deep feelings (see Chapter 6). An auxiliary ego could first be used to precipitate the feelings by playing the bad father, and later on another auxiliary ego might play the good father who gives warmth and nurturance. As emotions build, the protagonist is always given the option of continuing with the enactment or terminating it. As acts are completed, and, perhaps, catharsis and insight achieved, the action is allowed to wind down and close.

The *post-discussion* or integration is the last phase of classical psychodrama. When the enactment is completed, the experience is discussed by the protagonist and entire group. At first, group members are encouraged to share their feelings and tell how the session related to them. A member of the audience might, for example, tell how a death scene played out in front of the group saddened her because it put her in touch with the death of her own mother six months earlier. After emotional responses have been shared, group members can provide concrete feedback to help the protagonist learn from the enactment. Suggestions for handling confrontations in other ways and theoretical interpretations are appropriate here, depending on the group's purpose.

In summary, one version of the psychodramatic session from beginning to end is depicted in Figure 5-1 (Blatner, 1973, p. 75).

Production techniques

Throughout the psychodrama, the director helps the protagonist move the action forward using psychodramatic techniques. Among the most common are soliloquy, doubling, role reversal, and mirroring.

A *soliloquy* is a theatrical aside or monologue in which protagonists express hidden thoughts and feelings both to themselves and to the audience. The soliloquy is a useful technique for providing protagonists

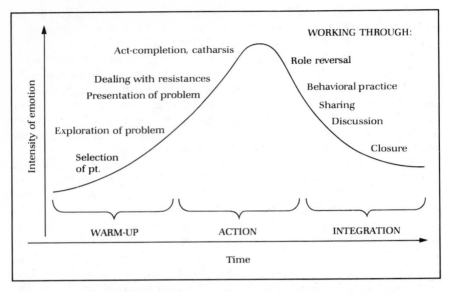

Figure 5–1. Psychodrama curve. *(From* Acting-in: Practical Applications of Psychodramatic Methods, *by H. A. Blatner. Copyright 1973 by Springer Publishing Company, Inc., New York. Reprinted by permission.)*

with an opportunity to gain some distance from their emotions and thereby to explore more successfully their reactions to the immediate situation. It is particularly effective in highlighting the disparity between their covert and overt feelings and thoughts. For instance, a male protagonist might be cordial and polite to an attractive woman in a psychodrama enactment, while covertly feeling tremendous sexual attraction. The soliloquy capitalizes on this disparity and may sound something like "Boy, I'm really turned on by her, but if I share my feelings she'll laugh at me and I'll feel silly." Thus, the technique also provides information for the audience about the protagonist's hidden thoughts and action tendencies, while furthering the psychodrama's development.

The *double,* or "alter ego," is one of the most common psychodramatic tools. Doubles deliberately attempt to *become* the protagonist. By assuming protagonists' physical postures and behavioral habits, doubles give support and help to the protagonist. They try to get under the skin of protagonists and add something significant to their performance. In many psychodramas, group members take turns acting as doubles either for the protagonist or for an auxiliary ego whenever they feel they have something to offer to the drama. For example, if the protagonist is stuck in the enactment, a double could help further the action by expressing feelings that are difficult for the protagonist to express. An alter ego might even reach for ideas and feelings that lie just outside the protagonist's range of awareness. Since doubles function as inner voices for protagonists, it is important that they try to identify with them and not share their own feelings and reactions within a scene. Since even skillful doubles can err, protagonists are encouraged to respond to their doubles by signifying either agreement or disagreement. To minimize confusion and keep the action going forward, however, auxiliary egos in enactments are urged to attend only to the words of the protagonist.

Leveton (1977) has enumerated several different types of doubling. One style is the "colorless" double, who functions to validate the protagonist's views and extend them a bit:

Sam: I really don't want to work in my dad's business, but he expects me to after I graduate.

Double: Yes, he's really counting on me.

Sam: That's right, but I can't stand him giving me orders all the time.

Double: He makes me feel like such a little kid.

Sam: Exactly! I wonder what mom thinks about me working for him. She never mentions it.

Double: I don't get much out of her either way. I wonder what she would say if I asked her?

Sam: No point in that. What dad wants, dad gets.

Another variation is the "satirical" double, who takes an exaggerated, even humorous approach to encouraging the protagonist to question his/her assumptions and look more closely into something:

Madge: Mom's always quizzing me about where I'm going and what I'm doing.

Double: I'm sure she spends all her time worrying about me.

Madge: But whenever I get angry at her and start to tell her off, she looks real hurt and I just can't do it.

Double: Yeah, she'd probably have a heart attack if I confronted her.

Madge: Well, no, but you just shouldn't have thoughts like that about people.

Double: Not me, anyway. I never have nasty thoughts about anyone.

The "passionate" double is useful in helping a protagonist to express strong feelings that are being held in check with great effort. The double does the emoting and in so doing, teaches the protagonist alternative solutions. The doubling still must reflect hidden feelings of the protagonist, however, rather than the feelings of the double:

Oscar: I want you to stop calling me and prying into my affairs.

Double: Get off my back and leave me alone!

Oscar: She means well. It's just that she doesn't have anyone else to turn to.

> *Double:*   But I'm not her father! Why do I have to take responsibility for her?
> *Oscar:*   I just want to tell her to find someone else.
> *Double:*   I want to tell her to stop calling me, but I'm afraid.

The "oppositional" double tries to expose the opposite side to feelings and thoughts that are expressed in an attempt to foment an argument with the protagonist and force him or her to look at alternatives:

> *Beth:*   I hate you! I'm intimidated by you in class!
> *Double:*   I'm excited by you and attracted to you.

This bird's-eye view of the action gives the double the opportunity to gain an understanding of the protagonist that no one else in the group has.

In *role reversal*, protagonists play the roles of other key figures in their dramas while auxiliary egos play them. One purpose for role-reversal is to help the auxiliary ego portray a role more accurately by watching the protagonist adopt that character for a few moments. At other times, it is a method for developing an empathic understanding of others' predicaments and temporarily viewing the world from their vantage points. By playing someone else, you become able to see yourself through that person's eyes. This provides a bridge to understanding and resolution of interpersonal conflict.

Sometimes it is very difficult for a protagonist to reverse roles. This difficulty in itself can demonstrate a lack of understanding of another. At other times the role might be played with considerable distortions or projections based on the protagonist's very biased perception of a significant other. This information can later be fed back to the protagonist by the audience in order to clarify distorted perceptions. When spouses fight, for example, asking them to change seats and assume each other's roles can push them through a very stale interactional pattern and stimulate new insights.

An example of role reversal in action comes from a defensive interchange between husband and wife in which the husband is proud of recent evaluations at work and the wife resents his increasing withdrawal from her into his profession:

> *Mary:*   (playing John's role) That's right. I'm a big wheel at work.
> *Director:* What kind of big wheel are you, John?
> *Mary:*   Well, I get the most commissions in the place. I know how to sell. So I get higher pay and the bosses think I'm great. (Mary laughs.) It's really different at home!
> *Director:* Is there anything you want to tell Mary, over here, about that? What's different at home?
> *Mary:*   Well, Mary, you don't ever seem to think anything I do is right. (Mary is still smiling self-consciously).
> *Director:* Go ahead, Mary, how about responding to that?

> John: *(playing Mary)* Well, all you care about is your work. That's all you care about. That's why you're gone all the time. I'm going to get a job as your secretary so I can see you every once in a while. *(John, too, is smiling as he does Mary's part of the familiar routine.)*
>
> Mary: *(more serious)* Well...you just blame me all the time. How can I show you anything? I get so mad at you! [Leveton, 1977, pp. 62–63.][2]

By reporting feelings and actions rather than counterattacking and withdrawing, this couple moves forward in the difficult negotiation of their conflict. The director would probably ask them to return to their original roles and then shift back into role-reversal periodically to develop a better way of relating.

Another example shows how role-reversal can be integrated with doubling in a psychodrama session (Yablonsky, 1976). Early in the session a young woman says she is attempting to separate from her husband and is in great pain about it.

> L.Y.:   Okay. Come on up, Jane. First introduce yourself to the group.
>
> Jane: I'm twenty-eight and I've been married to Bill for seven years. I've never been with another man sexually. Bill is like the only family I've known. But I'm just bored to death with him!
>
> L.Y.:   Let's get into the role-playing. When you talk too much about a problem, it dissipates the act-hunger.[3] Have you told him about your feelings?
>
> Jane: That's part of the problem. He doesn't listen. He's like a stone.
>
> L.Y.:   Okay. When was the last time you confronted him?
>
> Jane: He just came back from two days on a boating trip. He went alone with another guy. We had agreed to separate briefly.
>
> L.Y.:   Is there someone here who looks like Bill who could play him?
>
> Jane: Well, no one in particular.
>
> L.Y.:   Okay. Can this be Bill? *(I select a young man from the group.)*
>
> Jane: Yeah. He even looks a little like him.
>
> L.Y.:   Okay, set up the scene. Where are you? Where is he? What does the room look like? It's important for you and the group to move into the ambience of the situation.

[2]From *Psychodrama for the Timid Clinician*, by E. Leveton. Copyright 1977 by Springer Publishing Company, Inc., New York. Reprinted by permission.

[3]Act-hunger is a concept from psychodrama referring to the drive to fulfill basic impulses.

(Jane sets up the scene, in their bedroom. There's a water bed and very little furniture. It's midnight and he's just returned from a trip.)

Bill: Boy, am I tired.

Jane: Bill, I have to talk to you.

Bill: Oh, Christ! Let's not do that number again. I'm tired.

Jane: *(pleading)* Please, Bill. Just listen to me, I *hurt!*

Bill: That's not my fault.

Jane: Don't you know I'm going to leave you—if you don't talk to me. There's no communication.

Bill: Save that communication bullshit for your sociology class. I don't feel we have any problem. I'm very happy.

Jane: I'm miserable. Can't you see it? I'm twenty-eight and my goddamn eye twitches!

Bill: It's not my fault.

Jane: Nothing is! Please listen to me. You know I read books, I go to class and hear new ideas. It turns me on. I come home and want to talk to you about the things that are important to me....

Bill: I don't want to hear that shit! It's twelve o'clock. I've had a long trip. *(Pause)* Come on. Why don't we make love? *(He approaches her.)*

Jane: No, please don't do that to me. I don't feel like it. I want to talk.

Bill: Come on. Making love is communication. Come on. Everything will be fine.

Jane: Please don't. I'm not going to *submit* to you again.

(At this point, I ask Jane if the auxiliary ego "Bill" has given an accurate portrayal. She says "pretty close." I then have her reverse roles. She becomes Bill and the auxiliary ego becomes "Jane." The action continues for a few minutes in the same vein.)

L.Y.:   Hold it a minute, Bill. *(Jane is now Bill.)* We're going to ask you a few questions *(to get her more into the role of Bill)*. Tell us something about yourself. *(The following dialogue is her response to me and questions from other members of the group.)*

Jane: *(as Bill)* I'm thirty. I teach high school. I love my wife. I don't know what's happened to her. She used to be quiet and cuddly, and she did the housework without any complaints. She was my little Janey. Now she runs to these classes. I think she even has another guy she's interested in. She wants to talk about a lot of bullshit I'm not interested in. She's changing and I'm the same. I don't know what she wants from me.

Jane: *(played by the auxiliary ego)* I want you to understand. You bore me to death.

Jane: *(as Bill)* I bore you. Who needs you and takes care of you when you're sick and has supported you for seven goddamn years?

L.Y.:   Okay, reverse roles.

(Jane becomes herself again, and as the conversation continues in the same vein, I have the auxiliary ego who is playing Bill spread his arms in crucifixion style to reveal his "saintliness.")

Bill: *(played by auxiliary ego)* How can you do this to me? I've been so good. I've always been the kind of husband I promised you I would be when we got married.

Jane: *(smiles)* God, he lays guilt on top of guilt on me. He's right. He has been so good. He's perfect. I feel like a complete bitch. But he bores me every way possible. In bed. In conversation. Everywhere. I want out. I'm suffocating.

L.Y.:   How about your parents?

Jane: Oh, I knew that was coming.

(We move into a scene with her mother and father. With them she plays little Janey. She distorts the real situation to her parents and implies to them that Bill also wants out. We put in a double behind Jane who introduces the reality that she is the dissident. Jane tries to stifle her double when she blurts out the truth of her unilateral desire to leave Bill—she wants to hide this from her parents.)

Mother: You get right home. You're a spoiled child. You'll never get a boy as wonderful as Bill. I'll fix it up. I'll call him.

Jane: No, Mother, please. I want to leave him.

Father: *(to wife)* Tell your daughter to go right back to him. He's a wonderful boy. How can she even think of leaving him? It's your fault. You never raised her to be a real woman; a real woman takes care of the house, has babies.

Jane's double: Oh, God. Now I know why I'm so stuck. If I leave Bill, I'm not only leaving him, I'm leaving my mother and father. It scares me to death. These three people *are* my family. *I can't leave my only family.*

Jane: Yes, that's exactly right. There's something else I just realized. If I leave Bill, I have to give up the role of cute little Janey, the role I play with Bill and my mom and dad. It scares me. My identity as a grown woman isn't that secure.

    Bill: If you leave me, you'll really be sorry. I'm so good to you.
    Jane: Oh, fuck you, man. I can't stand you anymore. All you
            do is make me feel guilty about how *good* you are. I have
            to go. [Yablonsky, 1976, pp. 53–56.][4]

Role reversal, in which group members are encouraged to imitate nonverbal mannerisms as well as overt behaviors and hypothesized thoughts and feelings, can yield an exciting psychodramatic experience and promote considerable tele and group cohesion.

Mirroring is a close relative to role-reversal. Through mirroring, protagonists are made aware of how others perceive them. When the director thinks that this technique is required, protagonists are asked to move aside and observe while a stand-in auxiliary ego portrays them in a psychodramatic enactment. Protagonists are often very surprised at how they come across. Mirroring helps them reflect on their performance from a sufficient distance to gain some perspective and insight into their behavior.

Mirroring is also a method of choice in psychodrama groups which focus on helping group members develop behavioral skills. That is, some psychodrama groups are constituted to develop mastery in practical skills, such as dating, assertiveness, and job-seeking while enjoying group support in the process. Mirroring allows protagonists to get continual visual and verbal feedback on their behavior from auxiliaries who can exaggerate bad habits or demonstrate preferred alternatives.

Most of the time spent in a psychodrama group is taken up by the spontaneous portrayal of scenes created by the designated protagonist. Numerous production techniques, such as those described above, are selectively applied by the skillful group leader to help participants achieve a state of spontaneity and structure relevant problem situations to facilitate catharsis and insight. The range of techniques employed depends primarily on the director's experience and orientation. In addition to the four techniques just described, other common interventions include the "future projection technique," in which protagonists prepare for anticipated situations by acting them out and making adjustments in their behavior; the "candle technique," in which each member in turn assumes the spotlight and becomes the protagonist for a few minutes; and the "behind the back technique," in which the protagonist sits with his back to the group and listens as they describe their impressions of him. The choice of a given technique depends upon the readiness of group members to engage spontaneously in meeting group goals and upon the nature of the group. Some techniques are especially appropriate to warm up the group for choosing a theme or a protagonist, whereas other interventions belong more to the group's action or post-discussion phases.

[4]From *Psychodrama: Resolving Emotional Problems through Role-playing,* by L. Yablonsky. Copyright 1976 by Basic Books, Inc. Reprinted by permission.

APPRAISAL

It is possible that Jacob Moreno has had a more profound impact on the group movement than anyone else. In addition to developing psychodrama and sociodrama, Moreno originated action techniques that have subsequently become commonplace in contemporary encounter, Gestalt, and T-groups, to name a few. Moreno (1969) also insisted on crediting himself for these and other contributions. His conviction about the importance and universality of the concepts and techniques underlying psychodrama have made him a controversial as well as a charismatic figure. Moreno can also be credited with taking a broad view regarding the practice of group encounter and psychotherapy. He had a lifelong investment in criticizing discriminatory or inhumane social practices and constantly championed ways to enhance humanity's basic worth and dignity. He saw the goal of psychodrama as the treatment of all people. One problem in translating Moreno's ideas into reality, despite his reputation as an inspiring teacher, are his writings, which are often unclear and difficult to absorb.

One of the most prominent advantages of psychodrama is its reach beyond the exclusively verbal domain of psychoanalysis. Whereas Freudian psychoanalysis secures its data from the client's earliest recollections, Moreno's psychodrama investigates conflict in its immediate form. It is this combination of staying in the here-and-now and adding the role-playing dimension to group experience that makes psychodrama so vibrant and entertaining. It is a very lifelike approach. Psychodrama can help people develop a realization of themselves in all their roles in a setting where errors of judgment are not penalized. However, because psychodrama is such a potent technique, it requires competent direction; misguided directors can exploit the group members to gratify their own needs.

As with most of the group approaches described in this book, the group leader encounters participants in a warm, human relationship, rather than coolly sitting back as an impersonal, scientific observer. The director in psychodrama is, together with the Gestalt therapist, the most active of leaders. Unlike the Gestalt leader, however, the psychodrama director functions as a catalyst with status more or less equal to the group members'. Moreover, he does not typically work one-to-one with a group participant, but is forever conscious of drawing upon the resources of the whole group. One virtue of psychodrama is that group members become actively involved in the proceedings, especially if they are chosen to participate as auxiliary egos during the enactments. Group dynamics such as group norms, themes, and power struggles are important in psychodrama. Feedback from group members, as in T-groups and encounter, is treated as a substantive reality rather than as a projection that disrupts the therapeutic process.

Psychodramatic enactments have been applied to many kinds of groups and in many settings. Gestalt, encounter, transactional analysis, or behavioral groups can and do make use of the role-playing methods of psychodrama. In therapy contexts, psychodrama has been used with alcoholics (Weiner, 1965), drug users (Deeths, 1970), delinquents (Hill, 1977), inpatients (Gonen, 1971), and children (Drabkovna, 1966). In addition, psychodrama has been applied to enhance self-awareness and interpersonal skills in educational and industrial settings (see Stanford & Roark, 1975).

Research on psychodrama has been inadequate. The official organ of the American Society of Group Psychotherapy and Psychodrama is a journal entitled, *Group Psychotherapy, Psychodrama, and Sociometry.* The journal reports recent innovations in psychodrama application and technique, as well as case studies. Although the journal also reports some process-and-outcome research, one reason it is difficult to evaluate the method is the difference in behavior and style among psychodrama leaders. A recent review of 14 research studies reported generally positive results but stressed the need for a uniform definition of psychodrama to include the enactment of at least one scene and the use of at least one psychodrama technique (Kipper, 1978).

Some evidence of the significance of the individual group leader comes from the research of Lieberman, Yalom, and Miles (1973) and Yalom and Lieberman (1971) comparing the effectiveness of a number of group approaches. In their investigation, two psychodrama groups were assessed and the results indicated that the leaders were more divergent from each other than they were from several other group leaders representing different approaches. One psychodrama group leader was quite similar to a Gestalt leader, whereas the other leader had characteristics shared by Rogerian and T-group leaders.

As we sample the basic concepts and techniques associated with yet another approach to group work, a compelling theme is beginning to emerge. Namely, there is as much variability within the practice of a given group approach as there are differences between approaches that are supposedly distinct and unique. It becomes decidedly risky to label group leaders and trust that the label will predict the kind of group experience they provide.

SUMMARY

Psychodrama was developed by Jacob Moreno, one of the founders of the group psychotherapy movement, as a way of exploring personal problems, dreams, fears, and fantasies using dramatic techniques. Psychodrama emerged from Moreno's Theatre of Spontaneity in Vienna, Austria, where he discovered that drama could serve as therapy and that action had advantages over verbalization in enhancing the exploration of feelings and the development of new attitudes and behaviors.

Role-playing is the first basic concept of psychodrama. Unlike theater, the psychodrama participant acts a part in an impromptu production by actively experimenting with a meaningful role from real life. *Spontaneity*, a second concept, was noted by Moreno in the imaginative play of children. He believed it was a way to unlock the door to creativity. *Tele* is Moreno's answer to transference, a two-way flow of emotions between all participants in a psychodramatic situation. *Catharsis*, the emotional release that comes from being an actor in a psychodrama, is a very important step in reaching the final outcome of developing insight, a new understanding to a problem.

The basic roles in a psychodrama include the *director*, who serves as producer, therapist, and analyst, the *protagonist*, the *auxiliary egos*, and the *audience*. Psychodramas begin with a *warm-up phase*, move into an *action phase* in which a protagonist enacts a scene, and conclude with a *post-discussion phase* with the entire group. The director draws upon specific production techniques such as the *soliloquy, doubling, role reversal*, and *mirroring* to therapeutically develop the psychodrama.

Psychodrama adds the important dimension of here-and-now role-playing to the experiential group. The approach has enjoyed a variety of applications in both treatment and growth contexts. As with most experiential groups, there seems to be as much variability within psychodrama as between it and other approaches to groups.

REFERENCES

Anderson, W. J. L. Moreno and the origins of psychodrama: A biographical sketch. In I. A. Greenberg (Ed.), *Psychodrama: Theory and therapy*. New York: Behavioral Publications, 1974.

Bischof, L. J. *Interpreting personality theories*. New York: Harper & Row, 1964.

Blatner, H. A. *Acting-in: Practical applications of psychodramatic methods*. New York: Springer, 1973.

Deeths, A. Psychodramatic crisis intervention with delinquent drug users. *Group Psychotherapy*, 1970, *23*, 41–45.

Drabkovna, H. Experiences resulting from clinical use of psychodrama with children. *Group Psychotherapy*, 1966, *16*, 32–36.

Ginn, I. L. B. Catharsis: Its occurrence in Aristotle, psychodrama, and psychoanalysis. *Group Psychotherapy and Psychodrama*, 1973, *26*, 7–22.

Gonen, J. The use of psychodrama combined with videotape playback on an inpatient floor. *Psychiatry*, 1971, *34*, 198–213.

Greenberg, I. A. Moreno: Psychodrama and the group process. In I. A. Greenberg (Ed.), *Psychodrama: Theory and therapy*. New York: Behavioral Publications, 1974.

Hill, J. G. Reducing aggressive behavior in the institutional setting through psychodrama techniques. *Group Psychotherapy, Psychodrama, and Sociometry*, 1977, *30*, 86–96.

Kipper, D. A. Trends in the research on the effectiveness of psychodrama: Retrospect and prospect. *Group Psychotherapy, Psychodrama, and Sociometry*, 1978, *31*, 5–18.

Leveton, E. *Psychodrama for the timid clinician*. New York: Springer, 1977.

Lieberman, M. A., Yalom, I. D., & Miles, M. B. *Encounter groups: First facts*. New York: Basic Books, 1973.

Moreno, J. L. *Application of the group method to classification.* Monograph published by the National Committee on Prisons and Prison Labor, March, 1932.

Moreno, J. L. *Psychodrama: Vol. 1.* New York: Beacon House, 1945.

Moreno, J. L. *The theatre of spontaneity: An introduction to psychodrama.* New York: Beacon House, 1947.

Moreno, J. L. *Who shall survive?* New York: Beacon House, 1953.

Moreno, J. L. (Ed.), *Sociometry and the science of man.* New York: Beacon House, 1956.

Moreno, J. L. The Viennese origins of the encounter movement. *Group Psychotherapy,* 1969, *22,* 7–16.

Moreno, J. L. The creativity theory of personality: Spontaneity, creativity, and human potentialities. In I. A. Greenberg (Ed.), *Psychodrama: Theory and therapy.* New York: Behavioral Publications, 1974. (a)

Moreno, J. L. Mental catharsis and the psychodrama. In I. A. Greenberg (Ed.), *Psychodrama: Theory and therapy.* New York: Behavioral Publications, 1974. (b)

Moreno, Z. T. The function of the auxiliary ego in psychodrama with special reference to psychotic patients. *Group Psychotherapy, Psychodrama, and Sociometry,* 1978, *31,* 163–166.

Shaffer, J. B. P., & Galinsky, M. D. *Models of group therapy and sensitivity training.* Englewood Cliffs, N.J.: Prentice-Hall, 1974.

Stanford, G., & Roark, A. E. Role playing and action methods in the classroom. *Group Psychotherapy and Psychodrama,* 1975, *28,* 33–49.

Weiner, H. Treating the alcoholic with psychodrama. *Group Psychotherapy,* 1965, *18,* 27–29.

Weiner, H. B., & Sacks, J. M. Warm-up and sum-up. *Group Psychotherapy and Psychodrama,* 1969, *22,* 85–102.

Yablonsky, L. *Psychodrama: Resolving emotional problems through role-playing.* New York: Basic Books, Inc., 1976.

Yalom, I. D., & Lieberman, M. A. A study of encounter group casualties. *Archives of General Psychiatry,* 1971, *25,* 16–30.

6

Body-Therapy Groups

Some groups, such as encounter and Gestalt, focus on participants' physical processes as well as on their verbal communication. However, a number of group approaches emphasize physical variables and might be called "body therapies."

The reason for involving the body in group work is fairly straightforward. Imagine the following situation: your girlfriend or boyfriend has just informed you that she or he is leaving you for your best friend. As you dwell on the situation, note your body's reactions. You may feel a constriction in the chest or diaphragm, a shortening of breath, or a tightening in the jaw, arms, or legs. According to body-therapy proponents, even if you do not deliberately and consciously deal with a stressful incident, the incident's impact will nonetheless be recorded automatically in your body. Experiences are reflected in the way people move, breathe, and hold their muscles, and in the kinds of illnesses they suffer. Moreover, peptic ulcers, high blood pressure, and other somatic ailments are at least in part psychologically induced byproducts of enduring stress.

Body therapists maintain that most psychological methods are overly cerebral and cognitive. Whereas traditional psychoanalysis outlawed any physical contact—or even visual contact—between therapist and patient, contemporary group approaches abide by no such deprivation model. As far as Freud was concerned, humans may as well have been cut off at the neck, the head symbolizing all reason and maturity and the body representing humanity's base, animalistic nature. Body therapies attempt to transcend this barrier by crossing into the taboo territory of the human body and emphasizing the integration of body and mind. Body therapists also assume that there is an inherent wisdom in physiological functioning. They trust that there is a physical counterpart to Carl Rogers' concept of a natural organismic valuing process. As a result, they encourage people to trust the body's primitive animalistic feelings.

The idea behind body therapy is different from that underlying the physical training of a dedicated athlete. Although thorough physical conditioning is commendable and contributes to good mental health, physical fitness fanatics generally approach their bodies as objects to be tamed into submission and sculpted for adoration. In contrast, body therapies stress familiarity with the body, which implies becoming more aware of deep organismic sensations, exploring how needs, wants, and feelings are encoded in various body states, and then learning to resolve conflicts in these areas realistically.

The best-known body therapies did not originate within the context of the group movement. Thus, though body therapies are frequently used in groups, it is not always clear how they can be best employed. In this respect, body therapies and Gestalt therapy are similar. They emphasize the relationship between the group leader and individual participants, and only secondarily draw upon group members to stimulate or support one another. And like Gestalt, a number of body therapies fall somewhere between the cognitive and the physically oriented approaches. These include bioenergetics, the Feldenkrais method, the Alexander technique, structural integration (Rolfing), and primal therapy. All of these methods owe a historical debt to the theorizing and treatment model of Wilhelm Reich (1949). Consequently, this chapter is oriented around Reichian therapy and its direct descendent, Alexander Lowen's bioenergetic method.

HISTORY AND DEVELOPMENT

Not so many years ago psychologists avoided attributing any worthwhile contributions in psychotherapy to Wilhelm Reich. Although Reich began his career as a reputable member of Sigmund Freud's circle, at the end of his life he was emotionally disturbed, imprisoned on contempt-of-court charges, and generally discredited for his maverick ideas. Many of Reich's writings are contentious and controversial, particularly those that equate mental health with the ability to have orgasms, but his earlier work on character analysis is a rich lode of psychological insight that has been profitably mined by a number of contemporary practitioners. Essentially, Reich believed that the psychological defense mechanisms that inhibit healthy functioning could be confronted and modified by direct body contact. He maintained that defensive behavior, which he called "character armor," is reflected in tension in the muscles, called "body armor," and in constricted breathing, and that repressed material could most quickly and advantageously be released therapeutically by the direct manipulation of the tense areas. His techniques were designed to reduce the chronic tension stored in each set of muscle groupings, which in turn released the pent-up feelings they camouflaged. Ultimately, the kind of energy flow that Reich described and was most concerned with was sexual energy, and he would instruct his patients to disrobe and lie on a couch or bed while he directly manipulated the areas of tension.

Reich's best-known student and the originator of bioenergetic therapy is Alexander Lowen, a New York psychiatrist who studied under the master. He channeled Reich's approach away from the sexual direction, and incorporated body work into ongoing verbal therapy. Lowen has probably been more successful than any other contemporary practitioner in overcoming the standard psychoanalytic bias against physical, nonsexual contact between therapist and patient, and his bioenergetic approach has been a significant contribution toward the holistic treatment of the person in individual and group therapy.

BASIC CONCEPTS

Energy

The concept of *energy* is of critical importance in understanding body therapies. In bioenergetics the body is studied through its energetic processes and has been described as a "bio-electric ocean" of chemical and electrical energy exchanges (Keleman, 1975). For group members to relate to their bodies optimally is to develop a spontaneous energy flow that involves the entire organism from the periphery of the skin to the metabolism's innermost regions (Brown, 1973). Anything that disrupts the expression of energy in any part of the body, from the muscles to the organ systems, affects a person's sense of pleasure and connectedness. According to Lowen, neurotics cannot handle much excitement and have a minimal toleration for both pain and pleasure. They expend most of their energy in maintaining their psychological defenses to guard against threatening internal thoughts and feelings or external events. It is not only neurotics, however, who have energy problems. Breathing shallowly, for example, is a way anyone might restrict emotional excitement.

Body therapists insist that a free-flowing, natural life energy is an integral part of healthy personality functioning. Reich coined the term "orgone" energy to represent this life force. Built up by the intake of food, fluids, and oxygen, this life energy is thought to stream continuously through the body of the healthy person. An excess of energy, according to Reich, is experienced as sexual tension, and a total, bodily orgasm is needed to bring relief. Neurotic individuals invest their energy in maintaining muscular tension and thus limit their potential for sexual excitement and release. The marketing of his so-called "orgone accumulators" to help clients achieve sexual fulfillment brought Reich trouble with the law and resulted in a two-year prison sentence.

Lowen has not attempted to clarify the concept of energy other than to suggest that some kind of life energy, called "bioenergy," is involved in all life processes, including moving, thinking, and feeling. In fact, his energy model is rather vague and inconsistent. It may make more sense to regard energy as a subjective experience rather than as a substance within the body. Some people, especially those who are depressed and withdrawn, appear to have little energy. It is standard procedure with depressed individuals to try to increase their energy level by encouraging better eating and sleeping habits.

Bioenergetic techniques aim to free self-expression by mobilizing the body's energy and restoring people to their primary nature. A person's primary nature is unadulterated pleasure, as in a young child's curiosity and wonder. Pleasure is freedom of movement and freedom from tension. The capacity for achieving pleasure is compromised by the socialization process, as we deny our primary needs by accepting social conventions and acquiescing to the needs of others. According to Lowen, a commitment to the life of the body brings us closer to our primary nature and diminishes the alienation from oneself and from others that most people feel (Lowen, 1967).

Lowen is probably correct when he states that a lack of feeling (or confusion about feeling) brings people to therapy (Lowen, 1975). This is particularly true in regard to groups, where participants typically feel alienated and seek to enliven themselves and develop the capacity to form energizing relationships. Body therapies maintain that interpersonal estrangement is rooted in estrangement from one's body, since one can experience life only through the physical being. As we shall see, body therapy groups encourage the expression of strong feelings to help individuals reenergize themselves.

Muscular armoring

A second concept critical to body therapy is *muscular armoring*. As Reich developed his theories, he focused on chronic energy blockages occurring on a physical level. He described the defenses or defense mechanisms used to hide unfinished emotional business as "character armor." By armor, Reich meant the chronic muscular tensions that insulate a person from feeling unpleasant emotions. As muscles tighten, feelings become deadened. In other words, armored muscles interfere with the streaming of orgone energy up and down the body.

From the Reichian point of view, there is not only a parallel between chronic energy blockages at the physical level and repressed, emotional material on the psychological level, but the physical and mental dimensions are inextricably united:

> The armoring *is* the character structure in its physical form. Therefore if one can break down the armoring one will to the same degree change the neurotic character structure. But since the rigidity of the character is locked into the body, in the armoring, it is more effective to loosen the armoring than to try to

change neurotic character traits by forms of talking-out therapy like psychoanalysis [Mann, 1973, p. 62].

Patterns of muscular tension are created by the psychological events and traumas people experience in growing up. The process of building character and armoring is a dialectic one in which psychological factors and the body continuously interact (Lowen, 1975). The general bioenergetic model suggests that feelings and impulses that are blocked from expression through fear become altered or buried, leading to body rigidities, energy disruptions, and personality changes.

Imagine, for instance, a small boy who is trying to prevent himself from crying. He may do this by consciously and deliberately clenching his jaw, constricting his throat, holding his breath, and tightening his stomach. This is the first stage of the process of building character armor. Thereafter, similarly disturbing situations, those that prompt tears, might elicit an automatic inhibitory response to avoid the conscious awareness of the hurt and the social stigma of crying. Over time the impulse is held in check unconsciously and the muscles of the face, jaw, throat, and stomach chronically contract. This muscular armor makes the free expression of grief or sadness almost impossible.

The basic theme of bioenergetics is "you are your body" (Lowen, 1975). Lowen believes that a person's disposition toward life is reflected in posture, movements, gestures, and physique. There is good reason, says Lowen, behind the colloquial use of anatomical expressions. Group participants may indeed appear to be "shouldering responsibility," "weak-kneed," "spineless," "tight-assed," or "sticking their necks out," reflecting their particular attitudes or personality styles. Moreover, careful observation might confirm that these people do, in fact, carry their bodies in those predictable ways.

Reich posited that the tension stored in the body's skeletal muscles could be found in seven rings of muscular armor existing deep within the organism and running transversely around the body. These rings act as barriers to the spontaneous flow of life energy up and down the body. The armor rings are found at the level of the eyes, the mouth and jaw, the neck, the chest, the diaphragm, the abdomen, and the pelvis. Reich's "vegeto-therapeutic" techniques involved directly manipulating the rings to dissolve the armor. By pressing and massaging eye-level muscles that inhibit crying, people begin to sob; by working the jaw muscles that inhibit angry screaming, they begin to rage. Once people are able to cry and rage again, the old feelings associated with the build-up of armoring rise to the surface so that they can be analyzed verbally. According to Reich, the pelvis is the last bastion of defense after the other zones are freed of armoring, and only after working through feelings of anger, sadness, and longing can a person surrender totally to a loving sexual experience.

Lowen has not adopted Reich's seven rings into his bioenergetic approach. He has, however, described five character types based on the defensive posturing that occurs on the psychological and muscular levels.

The labels for the five defensive patterns reflect Lowen's psychoanalytic background. Group members usually demonstrate various combinations of the character types.

The "schizoid" character structure refers to those whose thoughts are not clearly connected to their feelings and who tend to withdraw inwardly and lose contact with social reality. As such, energy is stored in the center and withheld from the periphery of the body, blocked by chronic muscular tension from flowing freely to the face, hands, feet, and genitals. Schizoid individuals have clear difficulty acting spontaneously and their movements may have a stiff, jerky quality. They do not feel connected to their bodies. They also tend to have low self-esteem. Physically, the schizoid's body is often narrow and contracted. It may appear to be poorly connected. In some cases, the top and bottom halves, divided by the waist, or the left and right sides, seem as if they do not go together. The person's face may look more masklike than alive, and the arms may hang limply to the sides.

The "oral" character is one who needs considerable support from others and is apt to be dependent and clinging in interpersonal relationships. Energy is not frozen in the core of the organism, as in the schizoid structure. However, it flows only weakly to the body's periphery. The body tends to be tall and thin, with long arms and legs, underdeveloped musculature, and signs of physical immaturity. Psychologically, oral people have difficulty standing on their own two feet, both literally and figuratively. Moving with a low energy level, they may constantly need and seek support and help from others. They may also tend toward depression when basic needs are not being met.

The "psychopathic" character structure describes those with a need for power and control and a preoccupation with social image. A need to rise above others may be reflected in the overdevelopment of the upper half of the body with concomitant underdevelopment of the lower part. Energy is generally displaced toward the head and blocked at the waist from flowing downward. The eyes may appear watchful and suspicious because of the great concern with maintaining control over others and the environment.

The "masochistic" character type describes a person who whines and suffers while remaining helpless to actively solve problems. The masochistic character is fully charged energetically but holds on tightly to feelings. This person holds muscles in as if to avoid exploding. The result is a short, thick, muscular body. Since the throat is also choked with tension, only a whine escapes and self-assertiveness is very limited.

Finally, the "rigid" character structure refers to ambitious, reality-oriented persons who function well but exert a high degree of control over their behavior. They hold themselves stiff with defensive pride, and fear letting go totally in the pursuit of pleasure. Bioenergetically, the body is charged in the periphery for contacting the environment and it is also charged at the core. Feelings flow freely but their expression is limited.

Usually the body is alive and well-proportioned. When the rigidity is more severe, the person may be less coordinated and look less alive.

It is easy to extrapolate from the character types to the predominant behavior each pure form would likely display in a group. Schizoid characters, for example, will avoid intimate closeness with other group members; oral characters will seek closeness in childish ways, for warmth and nurturance; psychopathic characters will insist on controlling a relationship in the group and can relate only to those who need and look up to them; masochistic characters will have close relationships, but in a submissive way because of a fear of expressing negative feelings that may threaten the relationship. Finally, the rigid character will form fairly close relationships and as a result may be able to benefit most from a growth group, where the search for intimacy, commitment, and free expression of feelings can be channeled and affirmed.

Grounding

The final concept integral to the body therapies is *grounding,* a concept referred to by others as Lowen's principal contribution to the Reichian tradition (Bellis, 1976). Grounding refers not only to standing on one's own feet physically, but operates as a metaphor for the Freudian reality principle. "The more a person can feel his contact with the ground (reality), the more he can hold his ground, the more charge he can tolerate and the more feelings he can handle" (Lowen, 1975, p. 196). Lowen saw that many clients lack a sense of being solidly grounded and, correspondingly, feel out of touch with reality. Being grounded means being in energetic contact with the ground. That is, through our legs we get a sense of stability and trust as well as a means of locomotion. People "high" on alcohol, drugs, or infatuation may experience themselves as flying. Bioenergetically, their energy has left the feet and legs and moved upward. Effective functioning in the real world literally means coming back to earth.

Another bioenergetic therapist, Stanley Keleman (1975), includes in his concept of grounding being connected to our emotional needs, our organismic energy currents, and all the patterns of actions that make up our physical and psychological processes. He claims that group members may avoid grounding for fear of experiencing too much pleasure or excitement. Experiencing too much excitement implies venturing into the unknown, which brings anxiety. Exercises are used in Keleman's workshops to specifically encourage grounding and to overcome attitudes of doubt and worthlessness. For example, participants might be asked to stand on one foot and experience connection with the ground, then to massage that foot and reexperience the connection. Or to hop on one foot and then stand once more on both feet to intensify the feeling.

Reactions of various participants reflect their ungrounded psychological states. A reluctant member says "I am cautiously nibbling at life. I never feel sure of the ground. I slouch with my chest sucked in." A placating member observes "I like to excite you because I want attention. But when I get it I get scared and I close down." A rescuing member reflects "I try to help people. When I do, I stiffen my neck and legs. I hunch my back and encourage people to lean on me. I seek them out. I hold on to others because I feel empty in myself. I waddle with my head jutting forward. I like to rescue people in need even though I feel some grimness and bitterness in me when I rescue them" (Keleman, 1975).

Members of bioenergetic groups are evaluated according to how well they are in touch with the ground. Then specific exercises are prescribed to foster an increase of energy flow and solid contact with the ground, and, accordingly, a stronger sense of self. The concept of grounding is important in bioenergetics because it offers a reality orientation that balances the strong focus on the expression of primary feelings and emotional break-throughs (Olsen, 1976).

BASIC PROCEDURES

In addition to more traditional individual therapy and group encounter, bioenergetic practitioners employ a variety of stress positions, activity exercises, and verbal emotional-release techniques to mobilize the flow of metabolic energy. The techniques make participants aware of muscle tension, energy blocks, and restrictions in the breathing cycle and help them to loosen their muscular armoring (Brown, 1973). Since mental and bodily events are considered equivalent, rigidity on one level assumes rigidity on the other. Bioenergetic techniques are introduced to dissolve rigidity, a process that often sparks anxiety and emotional distress.

Breathing

Breathing is our most fundamental life-sustaining activity. It gives immediate energy to the organism for movement and functioning of the body. Thus, most bioenergetic sessions begin with breathing exercises and constant reminders to group members to consult the inhalation/exhalation cycle. In orthodox Reichian therapy, the client disrobes, lies down, and begins deep breathing. By focusing on bodily sensations, clients will often talk about material that relates meaningfully to their physical state. Reichian therapists may also physically manipulate the client's body with their hands and encourage relaxation.

Lowen also begins with breathing exercises. However, the person is usually in a stress position, such as bent over a special stool, as shown in Figure 6-1. This is in line with Lowen's emphasis on stimulating the sympathetic arousal system as opposed to Reich's focus on relaxation and the parasympathetic arm of the autonomic nervous system. The autonomic nervous system innervates the internal organs, glands, smooth muscles, heart, and lungs during emotional experiences. In general, the sympathetic branch of the autonomic nervous system prepares the body for response to stress by stimulating the release of adrenaline, increasing the heart rate, and mediating the release of sugar from the liver to the muscles. The parasympathetic nervous system, on the other hand, plays a

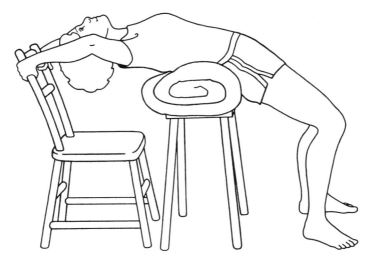

Figure 6–1.

major role in conserving and protecting bodily resources by maintaining functions such as digestion and elimination.

Inhibition of breathing is known to be an effective way to avoid deep feelings—of rage, sadness, fear, or sexuality. Body therapists have noted a direct relationship between restricted breathing and the experience of anxiety. Lowen (1975), in fact, attributes the word "anxiety" to the German root "angst," meaning literally a "choking in the narrows." On a physical level, a "narrow" might refer to any constricted passage of the body, such as the throat. Thus, tension in the neck and throat creates obstructions to breathing fully, which results in anxiety. The tension is a product of holding strong and emergent feelings in check. The anxiety is the organism's way of noting a disturbance in the normal functioning of the body. We have seen that fresh insights and new behaviors generally generate anxiety among members in the initial stages of a group. When participants experience strong feelings emerging, they may choke them off in panic. As mentioned before, the inhibition of deep and early feelings occurs automatically over time and causes areas of tension that also reduce the body's overall energy level. By relaxing the jaw muscles, opening the throat, and breathing deeply and fully, checked feelings can be completely discharged.

Body assessment and stress positions

Members of bioenergetic groups typically meet dressed in shorts or leotards. By wearing light clothing, members have full mobility in body exercises, and the leader and participants have a clear view of the body and any muscular armor. Lowen discourages total nudity in his groups because it is overly provocative and distracts members from more therapeutic goals. However, some exposure of the body within the group context helps to desensitize members to their sexual inhibitions and to remove one of the facades behind which people typically hide their doubts and vulnerabilities. People well-trained in bioenergetic analysis are able to infer a great deal about an individual's personality from the form and shape of the person's body and from its relative flexibility or rigidity. As we have seen, Lowen has, in fact, created a loose diagnostic system based solely on physical characteristics.

In a typical bioenergetic group, each member stands in front of a mirror while other members look on. Members are then asked to describe the person in front of them. One person might be described as a "reed bending in the wind," while someone else might be seen as muscular and solid in the legs but more frail and asthenic above the waist. The leader and group members might then hazard inferences from the person's physique about character armor and blocks and how these might relate to problems the person has expressed in the group. There is a continual attempt to relate body work to ongoing psychological issues.

An example of this process is provided by Mintz (1971) in an excerpt from one of her groups. A group member is discussing his growing awareness of the significance of a bulge on his upper back:

> [The group] started to ask me about the hump on my back and I said it was just poor posture and they said no, it could not just be poor posture ... I did not want to discuss it but I am aware of the association I then made. I associated the hump with both of my parents and they were always saying I should stand straight and if I did not, I would have a hump when I grew up. And their saying that if I did not they would take me to a doctor and then I would have to wear a brace. And I could never get myself to tell them that I wished they really would take me to a doctor because I wanted to be able to stand straight. I blame them very much for the fact my posture is so bad I have to walk hunchbacked [p. 151].

Muscular tension is further diagnosed through the use of bioenergetic stress positions, exercises that encourage adrenalin secretion and the experience of stress. Since chronic muscular tension affects motility, or movement, motility problems become clearer whenever a person is asked to assume stressful physical postures.

The most fundamental Lowenian position is the arch, or bow, which was derived from bioenergetic therapy and is illustrated in Figure 6-2. According to Lowen, he subsequently found the position illustrated in Taoist writings. When performed correctly, an imaginary line extends from a point midway between the shoulder blades to a point midway between the feet. Energetically speaking, this person is charged from feet to head and is perfectly grounded and balanced. Tense individuals, on the other hand, tend to be too physically rigid to make the arch successfully. Others, who are excessively flexible in the back, do not provide enough support for

Figure 6-2.

their bodies, which may reflect overly compliant, "pushover" personalities. A third type may lack symmetry and harmony because the body parts do not seem to line up and flow together. For instance, the head and neck might be angled in one direction, the trunk in the opposite direction, and the legs in the initial direction. These people may appear split (schizoid) and disjointed in their personalities as well. Again, the metaphor of the body may provide clues to interpersonal behavior: rigid people are apt to be stubborn and withholding; pliable people may be unable to assert themselves sufficiently. Lowen has such faith in the arch position as a diagnostic indicator that he claims he has never seen a profoundly disturbed person assume the position correctly (Lowen, 1975).

There are a variety of bioenergetic stress positions, each aimed at specific areas of muscular armoring. Members are encouraged to maintain each position as long as possible and to breathe fully and deeply throughout the exercise. The more chronic muscular tension, the more stressful it is to maintain the position. If the body is energetically charged and alive, there will be unintentional vibration of the stressed area, such as the muscles of the lower legs. The bioenergetic therapist encourages the individual to endure the position as long as possible. Oftentimes the participant moves beyond maintaining normal controls to discharge a tremendous amount of energy bound up with negative emotions. Regular use of the stress positions can help people get in touch with their bodies and retain feelings of harmony under stress.

Movement exercises

Stress positions are used to locate areas of tension and work directly on relaxing tense muscles. Movement exercises are more dramatic in that they tend to regress the group members to primitive feeling states.

Television personality Orson Bean recalls his first encounter with his Reichian therapist, when he was directed to breathe deeply and do a bicycle kick (Bean, 1971):

> I began to raise my legs and bring them down rhythmically, striking the bed with my calves. My thighs began to ache and I wondered when he would say that I had done it long enough, but he didn't. On and on I went, until my legs were ready to drop off. Then, gradually, it didn't hurt anymore and that same sweet fuzzy sensation of pleasure began to spread through my whole body, only much stronger. I now felt as if a rhythm had taken over my kicking which had nothing to do with any effort on my part. I felt transported and in the grip of something larger than me. I was breathing more deeply than I ever had before and I felt the sensation of each breath all the way down past my lungs and into my pelvis [p. 20].

Bioenergetic theory assumes that a chronically contracted muscle is holding back an impulse that would arise if the muscle had free movement. Therefore, encouraging free movement should release the impulse and the locked-in feelings. One of the most basic physical protest movements is kicking. By lying on the back, sticking the heels out, pumping the legs, pounding the arms on the floor, and rolling the head back and forth, a person imitates a young child's protest actions. By adding the vocal dimension, a loud "No!" or "I won't!," the person achieves access to blocked anger and rage.

The function of the other group members is to facilitate the person in letting go. They might actively stimulate the process by chiming in with verbal challenges of "yes" to the person's "no," or "you will" to "I won't." In short, the group interacts with the principal participant by encouraging a more complete expression of feeling. The leader or a fellow member might comment on disparities between clients' words and their body movements, such as the phony smile that often accompanies a hostile gesture or comment. At other times group members will "mirror" the movement of working participants by shouting or hitting along with them to accentuate the emotions. Sometimes the object of a person's anger becomes very clear, so that rage is directed at an absent parent or sibling. In bioenergetics, the root of repressed experiences is generally regarded as an introjection of negative messages and restrictive attitudes from one's parents. Clients may be asked to name the object of their anger. Sometimes the leader or another member can facilitate the emotional discharge by role-playing that identity in a transference fashion.

In addition to kicking, a straightforward expression of negative emotion can occur by hitting or pounding on a mattress or chair. A group member may use a tennis racket to pound a couch while screaming at a fantasied object of displeasure. A bataca, or foam-filled bat, works well for this purpose because it renders a satisfying sound while being virtually harmless on impact. The physical movement allows an expression of primitive anger in a relatively innocuous way and helps drain some of the client's stored-up rage. In addition, the chronic tension slowly weathers away and some of the resistance to opening up one's feelings crumbles.

Movement exercises work best when the person is already angry and seeking an outlet, rather than when it is performed as a mechanical ritual. In any case, a dangerous explosion of anger is very unlikely. The most typical negative outcome is holding back the intensity of the outburst, so that the exercise fails to accomplish its purpose. Mintz (1971) cautions that a group needs to be careful not to reject a person's expression of powerful negative feelings since rejection merely reinforces the pattern of inhibition that was begun many years earlier.

In bioenergetic groups, negative emotions are also communicated toward other members. There are occasions when wrestling and other physical contact can be helpful. Pierrakos (1978) cautions that a group maturity must exist prior to encouraging this kind of physical work. That is, members must learn to trust one another sufficiently to accept direct, negative communications. Throughout the experience, members are reminded to take responsibility for their feelings. Interpretations are sometimes used to suggest that feelings may be misguided, belonging to historical figures rather than to fellow group members.

Work with negative feelings such as anger, fear, and sadness almost inevitably precedes the expression of positive feelings. Negative feelings seem to hide deep needs for positive contact and reassurance and must be worked through before the group member is ready to accept positives. Affection, according to Lowen, cannot be trusted until repressed negative feelings have been expressed. He believes that though not all people will acknowledge unexpressed anger, anyone in a therapy group can find something to be angry about.

An example of how confrontative physical contact between two group members might facilitate the working through of anger in one individual is cited by Mintz (1971). A female group member revealed that though naturally assertive, she had been indoctrinated by family and others to submerge her strength and adhere to the cultural stereotype of the submissive, sweet woman. She particularly feared revealing her hidden strength to a man for fear of being seen as unfeminine and therefore being rejected. A suitable man in the group was chosen to arm wrestle with her. To counteract biological differences in strength the woman was allowed to use both her hands. An energetic, relatively evenly matched contest ensued. After considerable grunting and gasping, both participants collapsed in laughter and exhaustion. Symbolically, the woman had contacted a core part of herself, had experimented with expressing it, and had been warmly accepted by the group for her efforts.

In other situations a person might be held down by group members as a symbolic way of being weighted down by others. This technique can elicit tremendous anger and rage, so it should be reserved for emotionally stable members and the leader should take physical precautions to insure the safety of participants (Mintz, 1971).

Movement exercises can be initiated in the group by any member who wants to work. Pierrakos (1978) also suggests that the group as a whole can be encouraged to explore deep feelings. He favors having participants lie on the floor in a mandala position, on their backs with their feet meeting at the center and their bodies reaching outward like spokes in a wheel. He finds that the mandala configuration can generate tremendous energy for a group, especially when the members start to breathe together. It is as if the energy system of each member accelerates the energy build-up in the group as a whole. In order to encourage positive feelings Pierrakos reverses the mandala so that members lie with their heads in the center and with legs radiating outward.

The radiation of feelings and energy from one member to another has been cited as an advantage of practicing bioenergetics within the group context (Keleman, 1975). Keleman uses active techniques to energize his groups and get people to experience kicking, hitting, protesting, screaming, reaching, breathing, and pleasure, and to feel the accompanying emotions that add meaning to the behavior. He focuses on natural movements, like reaching out to someone or thrusting from the pelvis, rather than mechanical exercises. His groups work primarily on a nonverbal level and participants become involved by sharing feelings generated by the person who is working. Throughout the group's life he helps members identify barriers to feelings of excitement, and then encourages movement to aid the free expression of feeling. A strong sense of connection among members almost invariably develops.

Body therapists claim that the intense, physical release of affect can lead to personality changes (Olsen, 1976). In addition, when people get used to opening up one emotion, their potential for experiencing the full range of feelings is enhanced. In most bioenergetic groups, members go beyond emotional discharge and use the new feelings to interact with others, seek feedback, and work through their reactions verbally.

Physical contact

It has been suggested that there is a place for physical contact in most body-therapy groups. In some approaches the role of body contact is especially pronounced. Orthodox Reichian therapy relies on muscular massage to encourage the process of emotional discharge. Reich would touch, squeeze, and pinch his clients to help dissolve their character armor. He always began at the top ring of muscular armoring and worked down the body, reaching the pelvic region last. By direct manipulation of the muscular layers (called vegetotherapeutic techniques), unconscious feelings would be released in a torrent of negative emotion. A typical exercise at the top ring might have the client open the eyes wide as in fright and release a verbal expression of emotion. To deal with the thoracic chest ring, the client might be asked to breathe deeply while the therapist pushes the chest.

Lowen's bioenergetics departs considerably from Reichian technique. For instance, he does not insist that each ring must be dissolved from the head to the feet, in order, and he uses fewer direct body-contact techniques (Brown, 1973), preferring to rely on stress positions, activity exercises, and emotional-release verbal techniques to increase energy flow. Lowen recommends physical contact between group members apart from physical manipulation (Lowen, 1969). Massage-like contact between participants can help soften muscles and areas of chronic tension. In addition, it can convey support and reassurance. Holding people in distress or embracing them after hard work also conveys acceptance. In Lowen's groups, members are taught simple ways to knead tight muscles around the back of the neck and the shoulders. Deeper forms of body massage require the expertise of a trained leader.

OTHER BODY-THERAPY APPROACHES

Feldenkrais method

The Feldenkrais method is a body-therapy approach to building better body habits and increasing awareness, self-image, and potential (Feldenkrais, 1972). It is perhaps the most influential system for exploring the relationship between body posture and the force of gravity, thus suggesting the concept of grounding. Moshe Feldenkrais, an Israeli engineer and judo champion, has been a popular contributor to the group movement and has demonstrated his methods at Esalen and other growth centers during the past decade. His techniques are clever and original and usually take place in a group setting. Unlike Lowen and other body therapists, however, Feldenkrais does not deal with the emotional source of most physical tensions.

Briefly, Feldenkrais maintains that faulty early patterns of physical action become habits that operate outside awareness. Our skeletal structure is intended to counteract the pull of gravity to leave our muscles free for adaptive movement. With poor posture, however, our muscles are engaged in part of the work of the bones. Awareness is the principal lever for changing habits. By being attentive to the muscle movements involved in voluntary actions, we begin to recognize the muscular efforts that are normally concealed from awareness.

The Feldenkrais exercises are used to reduce excess effort in single acts, such as standing up, and to free muscles for their intended uses. In the same way that our lower jaws do not fall and our eyelids stay up in spite of the force of gravity, the basic equilibrium of the organism can and should be maintained by the older parts of the nervous system and not by taxing muscular effort.

Feldenkrais groups stress finding the best possible positions compatible with a member's inherited physical structure to facilitate awareness and fluidity of movement. The following exercise shows how the movement of the eyes helps organize the movement of the body. As with all Feldenkrais exercises, it should be done with conscious attention and gentle effort.

> Sit down; bend your right leg to the right and draw your left leg toward your body. Turn your body to the left and lean on your left hand, placed as far to the left as possible within the limits of comfort. Raise your right arm to eye level and move it to the left on a horizontal plane. Look at your right hand and turn your head and eyes to any point on the wall, far to the left of your hand. Then look at your hand, then at the wall, then at your hand, repeating the movement about twenty times: ten with the left eye shut, and the movement from hand to wall executed by the right eye only; and then with the left eye only. Then try to carry out the entire movement once again with both eyes open, to see if the range of the twisting movement to the left has increased. The improvement is often astonishing.
>
> Bend your left leg backward, draw the right leg inward, and try to improve the movement to the right as well. Remember to carry out the exercise with each eye alternately open and shut [Feldenkrais, 1972, p. 149].[1]

According to Feldenkrais, by engaging in these painless awareness exercises, people of all ages can become dexterous enough to succeed at such stunts as touching their big toes to their foreheads and placing a foot on top of the head, in addition to building better body habits in general.

Alexander technique

A second approach that emphasizes the functional unity of body and mind and works to build improved habits of posture and carriage is the Alexander technique (Barlow, 1973). F. Matthias Alexander was an Australian actor who in the 1890s suffered a loss of voice, a bad enough problem for most people but particularly incapacitating for a person dependent upon a forceful, resonant voice for his livelihood. Using a mirror, Alexander began observing how he was speaking. He noted that he had developed the bad habit of throwing his head back, depressing his larynx, and sucking in his breath before he spoke, in effect strangling his vocal cords. He then set about trying to unlearn these bad habits and to consciously substitute more adaptive movements. With remarkable persistence, he was able to return to the stage, but not until he discovered that his throat problem was connected to the movement of his head and torso and the misuse of his

---

[1]From *Awareness through Movement*, by M. Feldenkrais. Copyright 1972 by Harper and Row, Publishers, Inc. Reprinted by permission.

entire body. He earned a reputation as the "breathing man" and began to teach the technique that bears his name to others.

Part of Alexander's reputation was built on his direct influence on famous contemporaries such as Aldous Huxley and George Bernard Shaw. During the 1920s and 1930s it was fashionable among some intellectual circles in England and America to take lessons from Alexander. His methods were applied to diverse groups of people, including those with bad posture, those with medical problems that became worse due to faulty body use, and those who must use their bodies with maximum ease and fluidity, such as actors, dancers, singers, and athletes. Recently there has been a resurgence of interest in Alexander's reeducation methods as part of the spirit of the body therapies.

Briefly, Alexander maintained that the human being is a unified whole, and that one defective component will affect the entire body. Treatment of a single ailment often provides only temporary relief, since many physical problems arise from a system of bad habits. According to Alexander (1932), use determines functioning. Use is the characteristic way people respond in everything they do. Habit patterns are learned through use and the posture a person habitually uses may not necessarily be correct. Bad habits may first appear as behavioral inconsistencies, muscular pain, or clumsiness. Over time more pronounced problems with the body may develop and interfere with optimal performance when it is required. The Alexander technique seeks to change body alignment and create a proper relationship among the parts. The head should move from the top of the spine and lead the body. The spine should be free of abnormal curves and pressures and the muscles supporting the skeletal frame should be in dynamic balance.

In a typical demonstration, an Alexander teacher might apply very light pressure with the hands to an individual's head in such a way that the muscles in the nape of the neck lengthen (Jones, 1976). This allows the head to rotate forward a little as it lifts from the shoulders, creating a new relationship between the weight of the head and the tonus of the muscles. The teacher might continue the process with slight manipulations during everyday movements such as walking, sitting, and standing up. The result is a sensory experience of "kinesthetic lightness" in which the subject feels suddenly relaxed and at ease, the lightness affecting all subsequent movements for several hours or days. Basically, the technique acts to inhibit automatic, habitual responses, thereby releasing the reflexes that lengthen the body and facilitate movement. The key is in becoming aware of habitual movement and substituting alternatives.

In addition, the Alexander procedure involves correcting mental attitudes as well as rehabilitating physical habits. The teacher offers directive orders such as "let the head drop," and "let the arms be free," as the subject consciously rehearses new patterns of use. Each technique consists of determining what needs to be done, reflecting on the best way to do it, and doing it. The teacher guides the subject toward discovering body/mind awareness and experiencing oneself as an integrated, total person (Ruben-feld, 1978). In groups, Alexander techniques might be used to overcome habits, such as clenching fists or fidgeting, that bring a discharge of feelings as the body tension dissipates. Simple patterns of movement are practiced over and over again to bring about profound changes in body form and more graceful functioning.

Structural integration

Physical contact in the body therapies is most clearly seen in the controversial technique of *structural integration*, also called "Rolfing" after its founder, Ida Rolf. Rolfing is basically a physical intervention used to modify the psychological personality. Unlike bioenergetic approaches, Rolfing hypothesizes physical causes of tension rather than psychological stressors.

Essentially, Rolf believed that a well-functioning body remains upright and vertical against the force of gravity with a minimum of energy. However, the body sometimes becomes compromised and distorted because of stress. The most dramatic changes occur in the muscle fascia, the connective tissue that surrounds a muscle (Rolf, 1976). The fascia are typically quite resilient, but under stress they shorten and may even change chemically.

The aim of structural integration is to manipulate and loosen the muscle fascia so that the surrounded tissue can realign itself to its rightful position. The therapy process consists of a deep massage using fingers, knuckles and elbows. This massage can be very painful. The more tension, the more pain, and the greater the need for manipulation. Because of the interconnectedness of the fascia throughout the body, stress in one area may have pronounced functional, compensatory effects in another area. For instance, stress to the leg muscles may lead to a progressive tightening of the back muscles and neck muscles in an effort to maintain vertical alignment and balance in the body. A neck massage might yield temporary relief, whereas, as in acupuncture, the more critical focus could occur in the legs.

The Rolfing procedure consists of ten basic sessions in which the body is covered in ordered progression, freeing and reorganizing the joints. As the therapist manipulates the muscle fascia, the soft tissue returns to its normal position, the related joint performs its appropriate physiological movement, and the muscle moves in a more appropriate pattern. The first session includes releasing tension of the rib cage, which increases blood flow to and from the heart (Schutz, 1971). Subsequent sessions focus on the feet and ankles, which affect the pelvis and back, the side and trunk, and so on to the tenth session, which incorporates the major joints of the ankle, knee, pelvis and shoulder. As in Reichian therapy, the pelvis is primary in importance with regard to total physical well-being.

Schutz has done the most to bring Rolfing into the experiential group movement. He reports that stimulation of a particular area of the body is often connected with certain kinds of emotional problems. For example, the person who figuratively tiptoes through life or the person who stubbornly digs her heels in to resist pressure from others might also experience physical foot problems, such as pinched toes or poorly distributed body weight. In Rolfing, an emotional discharge is apt to accompany the release of tension that comes from manipulating the relevant body area. Because of the pain associated with the procedure, as well as the possibility for structural damage to the organism, Rolfing should only be carried out by trained practitioners. The method may be especially helpful once muscular armoring and tension have reached an advanced state. This alteration of body distortion can aid in the use of more psychologically based therapies later on.

Primal therapy

The rage-release techniques found in bioenergetic groups are similar in many ways to the approach of *primal therapy.* Primal therapy, attributed to Los Angeles psychologist Arthur Janov, is perhaps the best known and most controversial of the body therapies. The publicity that primal therapy has generated has been due in part to the fact that the late John Lennon and other well-known figures have undergone this type of therapy.

The closest interface between bioenergetics and primal therapy in method is Lowen's practice of asking participants to lie on their backs and get in touch with primitive feelings directed at significant others in their early development. For Janov the solitary cause of neurotic behavior is blocked, painful emotions and the single cure is to reexperience these hurtful feelings (Janov, 1972).

Briefly, the theory suggests that when one's infantile needs, such as to be fed when hungry, kept warm, stimulated, held, and allowed to develop one's potentials, are denied, the frustration and hurt become stored as "primal" pain that becomes covered by layers of physical and psychological tension. Neurosis symbolizes primal pain in the sense that people find an outlet for the tension in such a way that they are able to deny full awareness of the painful feelings. The outlets are invariably symptomatic behaviors, behaviors that are shortsighted and self-destructive and meant to minimize anxiety. The self-defeating behavior is repeated over and over in a vain attempt to be rid of the undefined pain (Harper, 1975). Unfortunately, merely discharging tension along the way is insufficient; one must live out the full extent of the original pain and connect the current experience with the early memories (Janov, 1972). Although all body therapies seek to bring clients' awareness into contact with their deepest organismic sensations and needs, only primal therapy restricts the reexperiencing to the distant past, where the most emotionally laden material exists.

Janov's most significant innovation is a set of techniques that push the client into recalling (or mimicking) early memories that are the most difficult to reexperience and hence the most significant for dealing with early pain. For the first three weeks of therapy, clients are seen individually by a therapist who is on exclusive call to them. During this period, clients are deprived of normal tension-reducing mechanisms such as cigarettes, television, books, or friends, and are repeatedly confronted by a persistent therapist who encourages the recall of past feelings. The therapist follows the patient, who provides the insights and content. When unfinished interactions are hinted at, the therapist encourages the client to speak directly and symbolically to the relevant figures and make some statement to them. At any sign of distress or anxiety, the person is instructed to breathe deeply from the lower stomach, stay with the feeling, and make sounds that help bring it forth. The person may scream, writhe, or vomit. In a direct and sometimes savage fashion, Janov might ask the client to express anger at a sibling or ask for help from a parent and thus relive key scenes from the past that represent unfinished feelings. As the feelings are totally reexperienced, the person may make mental connections between the pain and its origins. At no time, however, will Janov allow defensive rationalization, interpretation, or avoidance. Meanwhile, he guards the person's physical safety.

The primal process can be illustrated by the case of a man who has been manipulated for years by a controlling mother who has intruded in each segment of his life (Brown, 1973). The man might be placed on his back, spread-eagled, and asked to address his mother after he has recalled some early memories of her pushy tactics with him. His memories and negative emotions, coupled with bodily restraint by the therapist, build up a tremendous amount of energy from the force of suppressed and repressed feelings when his mother suffocated his yearning independence. All his anger might come barreling out in a torrent of primitive rage whereupon sheer words are not enough and body movements take over.

In summary, primal therapy combines memory associations from the distant past with the mobilization of the metabolic energy flow in the present using verbal confrontation and breathing techniques (Brown, 1973). Unlike practitioners of other body therapies, Janov does not stop with releasing bound-up energy but persists until he reaches a greater pain. This pain is the increasing awareness of the parent's lack of unconditional love for the child and the need for the person as an adult to give up the search for love that will compensate for past deprivations (Brown, 1973).

As every geyser generates a score of other wells, so too has Janov's success spawned a number of benefactors. In Holistic Primal Therapy, psychiatrist Tom Verny (1978) aims to integrate the feeling function, which is so pronounced in Janov's approach, with cognitive, sensing, and intuitive/creative functions. The sensing function in particular acknowledges the role of body sensations in generating feelings. Verny appears to use body work more individualistically than Reich, who used a set pattern of exercises, and less directively than Janov, by following the client's lead in the same way that a surfer waits for a wave before jumping aboard. The key to reliving important past events is to reconstruct the original conditions as faithfully as possible. Thus, if the client reports tightness in the neck, Verny might apply direct pressure to the neck to intensify the tightness. To enhance bodily sensations is to encourage the feelings. If the client complains of a pain in the chest, Verny might apply pressure to the chest and, in so doing, stir an early memory. The holistic primal therapist aims through these efforts to direct group members to their past, overcome resistance, and intensify feelings.

The aspect of Janov's primal therapy that is most relevant to group process is the period following the introductory three weeks of individual therapy. At that point the person is placed in a primal group that meets at least weekly. Members in the group have as their common goal to help one another reach and endure primal pain and to support one another in the process. The sheer drama of a profound emotional response leads others to empathize with a person's struggle and has a contagious effect within the group.

In many primal groups, however, there is virtually no interaction among group members, who are explicitly admonished not to interfere with the work of other participants (Verny, 1979). The group is simply a common meeting place where several clients come to work independently with a few therapists who circulate around the room to facilitate an individual's primal process. At any time, two or three members might be experiencing and expressing strong feelings, while other members might be lying silently in thought or talking to a therapist about their real-life problems.

Why meet in a group at all? Verny (1979) cites three reasons in support of the group setting. The first is financial, since the presence of a dozen participants cuts the costs for the individual. Second, a definite group energy is produced that helps members in their work. Passive members in particular are encouraged to "take feelings" from someone else and allow those feelings to move them into their own pools of memories and emotions, much like a football receiver catches a pass from the quarterback and runs with it. Finally, the presence of others stimulates certain important themes and feelings. Sibling rivalry issues, for instance, might be generated in a participant who perceives someone else getting more of a therapist's attention.

Much of the resistance among professionals to accept the evident potency of primal therapy may be due to Janov's initial, overly enthusiastic statements about it, coupled with his tendency to refuse anyone credit for influencing his thinking. Janov's writings are consistently grandiose—for instance, claiming that virtually all forms of therapy other than primal therapy are self-defeating and ineffective. Such eulogizing is done without adequate empirical evidence. One of the few studies attesting to the effectiveness of primal therapy is a series of reports by Karle, Corriere, and Hart (1973), who seemed to verify Janov's claims by finding physiological changes such as reduction in clients' pulse rates and rectal temperatures and changes in their electroencephalograms after the first three weeks of intense primal therapy. Although such changes appear impressive at first glance, one wonders about the long-term stability of the effects and the possibility that similar physiological changes occur as a result of any cathartic-type therapy (Harper, 1975). Fortunately, other primal therapists are more modest than Janov in their claims.

On a more theoretical level, Janov has been criticized for his concepts of primal pains and memories as not fitting the biological facts of developmental psychology (Brown, 1973). In the first place, there is considerable disagreement about whether young infants have the capacity to realize that their deepest primary needs, in the form of parental love and attention, are not being met (Winnicott, 1965). Second, it is hard to believe that this cognitive material would subsequently be available to the adult to recapture in intimate detail in therapeutic regression. More likely, the young child reacts automatically by means of physiological withdrawal and self-protective devices to aversive experiences before the memory system is fully formed. The experience of primal pains and memories may largely be a product of the adult's identification with and belief about childhood experience. Janov's description of the storage and location of primal pains and memories and the way they are processed has been one of his most creative ventures, but evidence to validate his theories is not yet available.

Janov's approach has also been criticized as being rather single-minded by focusing on a violent and brutal upheaval of negative emotions and neglecting any positive feelings and the healing power of human relationships. Janov describes his therapy as non-relationship-oriented in that the therapist is a "dealer in pain" and not someone with whom to engage in an interpersonal encounter. Patients can become habituated to primal, acting-out coping styles. In other words, some vulnerable people become dependent on the primal environment to deal with anxiety-arousing material of any kind rather than learn new skills and synthesize the anguish caused by the primal session.

Critics have characterized the finished product of primal therapy as a self-sufficient automaton who becomes disengaged from parents, family, and career. It is hard to discover any encouragement of people's softer sides in Janov's writings or, for that matter, to actually locate a "post-primal" character. In a world free of bacteria we would not require methods of immunization. It seems likely that one needs a little bit of armor in this world to cope with difficult life situations and reach realistic goals.

APPRAISAL

Most of us are shy about our physical selves, being relatively unaware of how our bodies function and how that functioning intersects with our personalities. Touch, in particular, is alien to many people who have grown up in most Western societies. Body therapies provide a means for including the physical dimension in the group experience and help restore a balance to approaches that emphasize the first half of the mind/body formula. As such, they have been used by themselves and as adjunctive methods to complement verbally-oriented group approaches.

Reichian therapy, bioenergetics, Rolfing, primal therapy, and other variations are powerful methods for inducing emotional release and bringing about dramatic changes in the body, feelings, and the personality. Given their inherent power and their potential for abuse, these groups are among the most speculative and controversial approaches practiced today. These groups' aims, however, are not so different from those of other group approaches, such as Gestalt, which strive to reach feeling dimensions through the phenomenological field of awareness.

Body therapies are suitable for most interested participants, with two possible exceptions: poor communicators, who may seek body-therapy groups to avoid improving communication skills; and individuals with deep-seated needs to be touched or to physically hurt others, who might use the group as a socially sanctioned outlet to act out these needs (Verny, 1979). Knowing how, when, and whom to touch is a very important consideration in conducting a group. The ethical considerations described in Chapter 1 are particularly relevant with regard to leading body therapy groups.

One controversial issue relating to body therapies is the notion of catharsis (Nichols & Zax, 1977). Most body-therapy theorists assume that emotions are stored somewhere in the body until they are eventually discharged. This makes it appear as if the emotion itself is a concrete entity, something like a genie in a bottle who dramatically pops out when the conditions are suitable. It is more likely that memories, not feelings, are stored in the nervous system, and when old memories are recalled, similar feelings are stimulated. From this point of view catharsis does not involve discharging energy; it involves remembering something with feeling and engaging in the bodily actions that are part of having that feeling. When emotions are expressed physically there is certainly some tension reduction. But more important, experiencing deeply felt emotions helps to combat a learned pattern of emotional avoidance. In the process, people expand their emotional repertoire and learn that emotional control can be compromised without horrible repercussions. The integration of the experience afterwards also provides new self-understanding.

Lowen has bought into Reich's concept of energy discharge and tends to focus too much on the sheer amount of energy that is mobilized as a measure of mental health. Reich himself adopted the unverified assumption that armoring ultimately exists solely to prevent the body from fully experiencing the orgasm reflex. Bigger and better orgasms are seen as *the* cure for anxiety and other emotional difficulties. Reich neglected to look at the many other growth-enhancing needs that psychologists like Maslow and Rogers see as part of the self-actualization process.

Lowen, on the other hand, has gone beyond Reich's single-mindedness to become the leading proponent of body therapies today. Lowen prods his patients to assume stress positions and engage in physical exercises to expel muscular tension. At its worst, the therapy may be too athletically demanding and more like a gymnasium workout than a meaningful exploration of conflicts and emotions (Brown, 1973). As such, a person's spontaneous exploration of inner experience is neglected while the therapist's expertise in diagnosing muscular rigidities and inferring their link to character problems is emphasized.

A final criticism of Lowenian bioenergetics concerns the assumption that a direct parallel exists between body functioning and psychological processes. Can one cavalierly conclude that a man is "shouldering responsibility" because he is stoop-shouldered, for instance? Lowen tends to use language symbolically and then reify the concept he is using. Thus, Lowen tends to simplify the relationship between character traits and body structure beyond the limits of reasonable evidence. It is quite possible to have a well-functioning body, good energy, and total orgasms, and still have character problems.

In summary, there is much ritual in the body therapies that may have no healing function, and it is difficult to identify the active ingredients that lead to real change. Many contemporary group therapists have moved considerably beyond Reich's seminal writings. One new direction is the integration of body techniques with verbal models of therapy. Another is the gradual replacement of excessively painful, discomforting procedures by physical interventions that are gentler, more humane, and equally effective.

SUMMARY

The body therapies include *bioenergetics,* the *Feldenkrais method,* the *Alexander technique, structural integration, primal therapy,* and other group approaches that emphasize physical variables. The body therapies owe a collective debt to Wilhelm Reich, who described how defensive behavior is reflected in muscle tension *(body armor)* and constricted breathing.

Basic concepts are derived from Reich's pupil, Alexander Lowen, the father of bioenergetics, and include *energy, muscular armoring,* and *grounding.* Chronic blockages to a spontaneous flow of energy are reflected in posture, movement, and physique. There is a close relationship between these physical variables and character structure or personality types.

Body therapy groups use *breathing exercises* to encourage an energy flow and the release of feelings. Motility problems can be identified through the application of *stress positions,* such as Lowen's arch. *Movement exercises,* such as kicking, encourage the release of primitive feelings. Many body-therapy leaders use physical contact, such as massage, to release tension.

The Feldenkrais method focuses on body posture to build better body habits and promote increased self-awareness and improved self-image. The Alexander technique explores habits of posture and carriage and promotes change by encouraging correct mental attitudes. Structural integration, also called *Rolfing,* makes use of direct manipulation to alter muscle fascia and realign the body. Primal therapy, developed by Arthur Janov, strives to discharge primitive feelings that were blocked in early childhood. Janov has been very influential, but has been criticized for his grandiose claims and his developmental theory.

The body therapies offer an alternative to overly cognitive and cerebral group methods. They are powerful methods for generating emotional release and may stimulate issues and feelings in group members who are observing or facilitating another person's work. Critics object to the harshness of some methods, their ritualistic aspects, and the underlying theory of catharsis.

REFERENCES

Alexander, F. M. *The use of the self.* New York: Dutton, 1932.

Barlow, W. *The Alexander principle.* London: Camelot Press, 1973.

Bean, O. *Me and the orgone.* New York: St. Martin's Press, 1971.

Bellis, J. M. Emotional flooding and bioenergetic analysis. In P. Olsen (Ed.), *Emotional flooding.* New York: Human Sciences Press, 1976.

Brown, M. The new body psychotherapies. *Psychotherapy: Theory, Research, and Practice,* 1973, *10,* 98–116.

Feldenkrais, M. *Awareness through movement.* New York: Harper & Row, 1972.

Harper, R. A. *The new psychotherapies.* New York: Prentice-Hall, 1975.

Janov, A. *The primal revolution.* New York: Simon & Schuster, 1972.

Jones, F. P. *Body awareness in action.* New York: Schocken Books, 1976.

Karle, W., Corriere, R., & Hart, J. Psychophysiological changes in abreactive therapy—study 1: Primal therapy. *Psychotherapy: Theory, Research, and Practice,* 1973, *10,* 117–122.

Keleman, S. *The human ground.* New York: Science & Behavior Books, 1975.

Lowen, A. *The betrayal of the body.* New York: Macmillan, 1967.

Lowen, A. Bio-energetic group therapy. In H. M. Ruitenbeek (Ed.), *Group therapy today.* New York: Atherton Press, 1969.

Lowen, A. *Bioenergetics.* New York: Coward, McCann & Geoghegan, 1975.

Mann, W. E. *Orgone, Reich, and eros.* New York: Farrar, Straus, & Giroux, 1973.

Mintz, E. E. *Marathon groups: Reality and symbol.* New York: Appleton-Century-Crofts, 1971.

Nichols, M. P., & Zax, M. *Catharsis in psychotherapy.* New York: Gardner Press, 1977.

Olsen, P. *Emotional flooding.* New York: Human Sciences Press, 1976.

Pierrakos, J. C. Core-energetic processes in group therapy. In H. Mullan & M. Rosenbaum (Eds.), *Group psychotherapy theory and practice.* New York: Free Press, 1978.

Reich, W. *Character analysis.* New York: Orgone Press, 1949.

Rolf, I. Structural integration: Counterpart of psychological integration. In P. Olsen (Ed.), *Emotional flooding.* New York: Human Sciences Press, 1976.

Rubenfeld, I. The Alexander technique and Gestalt therapy (Gestalt synergy). In H. H. Grayson & C. Loew (Eds.), *Changing approaches to the psychotherapies.* Jamaica, N.Y.: Spectrum Publications, 1978.

Schutz, W. C. *Here comes everybody.* New York: Harper & Row, 1971.

Verny, T. An introduction to holistic primal therapy. *Canadian Psychiatric Association Journal,* 1978, *23,* 381–387.

Verny, T. Personal communication, May 31, 1979.

Winnicott, D. W. *The maturational processes and the facilitating environment.* New York: International Universities Press, 1965.

7

Dance Therapy

HISTORY AND DEVELOPMENT

Just as psychodrama is an adaptation of staged drama, dance therapy is a descendant of creative dance. Early in our history, dance became a vehicle for expressing thoughts and feelings that could not easily be translated into words. The origins of dance have been traced back to the spontaneous movements and gestures that served as human communication long before the development of formal language (Langer, 1953). For thousands of years, different cultures have had ritual dances to celebrate victory in war, to bury and grieve the dead, and to cure the sick. Dance has been a powerful medium for the expression of feelings and the fulfillment of self. In religious rituals, dancers have sought to leave themselves behind and become part of the cosmos. In mimic dances, participants identified with the strength and ferocity of jungle animals or the unacceptable motives of witches and devils. In virtually every society, folk dancing developed as a popular pastime that offered relief from boredom and despair and reflected the character and traditions of the common people.

Over time, dance in Western cultures evolved from a type of social communication and self-expression into an art form, intended for the edification and amusement of an audience. By the 19th century, dance had become a formalized medium best illustrated by the emergence of classical ballet. One person who contributed to the revitalization of dance in North America in the 20th century was the flamboyant, free-spirited Isadora Duncan. She provided the energy for modern creative dance by pushing aside the formalization of traditional ballet, replacing romantic illusion in dance with realism. For Duncan, dance could be used to express people's natural reaction to their innermost feelings or "soul." In this way, modern

160

dance developed as a means of individual expression and a rejection of classical forms of movement.

Today dance is used to give expression to the full range of human emotions, ideas, and attitudes. When dance is presented as a performance, feelings are deliberately created using a series of highly structured movement forms, much as the actor draws upon a script in staged drama. When dance is used in therapy, however, the feelings are spontaneously released in free movement or improvisation, and the stylized qualities that make dance a performance or art form are not very important. What counts is communication through movement. Consequently, there is no standard dance form in dance therapy, and forms such as primitive tribal dance, folk dance, waltz, rock, and polka can all be used to encourage personal expressiveness. This focus on dance as communication has been expanded upon by expressive dancer Mary Wigman (1963):

> The dance is a living language which speaks of man—an artistic message soaring above the ground of reality in order to speak, on a higher level, in images and allegories of man's innermost emotions and need for communication. It might very well be that, above all, the dance asks for direct communication without any detours. Because its bearer and intermediary is man himself, and because his instrument of expression is the human body, whose natural movement forms that material for the dance, the only material which is his own and his own to use [p. 10].

Four events have been cited as historically instrumental in the development of dance therapy (Schmais, 1974).[1] The first was the problem posed by veterans returning from the Second World War who needed physical and emotional rehabilitation. Dance therapy became an adjunctive treatment in the rehabilitation process with hospitalized patients, many of whom did not speak and were not open to verbal forms of intervention. St. Elizabeth's Hospital in Washington, D.C., was probably the leading treatment and training center in these early stages of the dance therapy movement. Marian Chace (1953) has been called the "first lady" of dance therapy for her innovative work there. A dancer and dance teacher, she focused on the individual student, each of whom described feelings of emotional release and harmony after working with her, thereby generating interest among local psychiatrists.

A second event that contributed to interest in dance therapy was the discovery of tranquilizers in the 1950s. Availability of the drugs helped clear the closed wards of psychiatric hospitals and enabled many chronic, sometimes nonverbal patients to be either released from the hospital or transferred to open wards and more active treatment programs. Dance therapy became an alternate treatment method and a component of these programs. A third factor in the growth of dance therapy was the human-

---

[1]There is no clear distinction between dance therapy and what is known as "movement therapy," although movement therapy, which is usually practiced by those trained in dance therapy, is a more encompassing term.

relations training movement of the 1960s, which fueled the development of more experimental ways of training awareness and working with groups. Finally, research on nonverbal communication, in particular the analysis of the communicative behavior of the human body, called kinesics (Birdwhistell, 1970), has fomented interest in new programs in dance therapy. One recent thrust of this research has been an effort to educate the intuitive mind by focusing on the development of the brain's right-hemisphere functions (Bogen, 1977).

Psychoanalytic theory has also had an influence on the development of dance therapy. Wilhelm Reich (1942), Carl Jung (1961), and to a lesser extent, Harry Stack Sullivan (1953), stand out as making specific, albeit indirect, contributions to the field. Reich, as we have seen, tried to decode the language of the body and described how tension is stored and expressed physically. His emphasis on the body's role in emotional development and the work of his followers, such as Alexander Lowen, on ways of releasing stress through physical movement, have been very influential. Dance therapists today try to reduce muscular tension and increase mobility among group members. Jung promoted the therapeutic value of artistic experience or what he called "active imagination." He believed that artistic experiences, such as dance, can evoke material from the unconscious and make it available for cathartic release and analysis. Jung's focus on symbolic activity and creative expression for psychotherapy have had an impact on the dance-therapy movement. Finally, dance therapy makes use of Sullivan's theories of socialization and human interaction when it is used to resocialize disturbed and inhibited patient populations. It can be seen as a primary means of encouraging nonverbal interactions between client and therapist and among participants.

Today a number of universities offer bachelor's and advanced degree programs in dance therapy to prepare students for work in hospitals, clinics, rehabilitation centers, prisons, nursing homes, and other places where movement work can be useful. This work is primarily done in groups.

BASIC CONCEPTS

General goals

Dance therapists consider at least five goals for their work with groups. One goal is to provide group members with an awareness of body parts, their use, and capabilities. Not only does this enhance physical and emotional well-being, but, for most well-functioning people, this is also the fun of dance therapy. Early in the group's life, the dance therapist observes and evaluates the strengths and deficiencies in the movement repertoires of the participants, then decides which components to alter or refine, and determines which movements are best to do so. Most of us can use some help in strengthening muscles, becoming less rigid, coordinating movement, and increasing energy. More disturbed groups, such as those made up of psychotic or autistic children, may need intensive help with such basic motor activities as walking, running, bending, and jumping.

A second goal of dance therapy is to increase feelings of self-worth by building a more positive body image. Seriously disturbed individuals may be unable to clearly differentiate between their bodies and the environment and others in it. For this group, dance therapy is used to establish a secure body image. For most others, dance helps to develop a more likable body image, which is directly linked to a more positive self-image.

Third, dance therapy is used to improve social skills through the group experience. Again, patient populations may need rudimentary social-skill training. Psychotic patients in particular cannot meaningfully communicate their emotional needs. Dance therapy provides a relatively safe means of successfully relating to others while learning socially approved behavior. For more normal groups, dance therapy offers the opportunity to relate creatively with others by erasing the barrier and conventionality of words.

A fourth goal is to put group members in touch with their feelings by relating feelings to movement. Creative dance is expressive, allowing the release of submerged feelings and the exploration of hidden conflicts that may be the source of psychological tensions (Rosen, 1974). Here the psychodynamic notion of catharsis is extended to dance, in which movement leads to the expressive, therapeutic release of pent-up feelings. In addition to the expressive potential of dance, movement exercises, such as those which involve swinging or stretching, are physically tension-reducing.

A fifth goal of dance therapy has been described as the "magic circle" (Langer, 1953). The functions of a dance-therapy group—working, playing, and exploring together in a rhythmic activity, experimenting with gestures, postures, and movements, and communicating nonverbally with one another—all combine to promote a profound group experience. This experiential effect, operating at an unconscious level, is the magic circle.

Relationship between movement and mind

The basic concepts underlying dance therapy reflect the intimate relationship between body, and more specifically, movement, and mind. A principal assumption in dance therapy is that the way we move reflects our personalities. The kind of physical contact we enjoyed as infants, the freedom to locomote we experienced as toddlers, the friends we have acquired, the work we have done, the roles we have played, and the stresses we have confronted all make a contribution to the way we move (Schmais, 1974). We can identify people solely on the basis of how they move. It often happens that we can recognize an acquaintance without hearing the voice or seeing the face, but merely by catching a familiar gesture, posture, or body movement.

The dance therapist is especially interested in what, where, how, and with whom we move. The basic conceptual commitment and applied technology in dance-therapy groups is the generation and understanding of *spontaneous movement*. According to Schilder:

> There is so close an interrelation between the muscular sequence (involved in all expressive movements) and the psychic attitude that not only does the psychic attitude connect up with muscular states, but also every sequence of tensions and relaxations provokes a specific attitude. When there is a specific motor sequence it changes the inner situation and attitudes and even provokes a phantasy situation which fits the muscular sequence [1950, p. 208].

Dance therapy encourages free, expressive movement to promote change in physical motility and strength on both physical and psychic levels. The body and the mind are treated as a unified whole. A key belief is that *movement reflects the self*, so that as emotions change, so do our feelings about ourselves and our bodies, and so does the way we move.

BASIC PROCEDURES

Role of the therapist

The dance therapist serves as a codancer in the group session, a director of the events, and a catalyst to facilitate the members' growth through movement (Schmais, 1974). An important function of the dance therapist is to create a safe environment so that the participants can feel free to get in touch with, explore, and understand themselves and their interactions with others. The group leader attends to members' nonverbal communications and attempts to respond empathically in order to establish an effective therapeutic relationship. The elements of acceptance and empathy are derived from Carl Rogers' theories of therapeutic change. In dance therapy, empathy occurs beyond the primarily verbal mode used by most therapists by including the reflection of feelings on a physical level. The dance therapist shows empathy by mirroring the movements of the patient through dance. As Marion Chace describes the therapeutic process:

> The therapist, by dancing with the patient, says, "I feel every emotion—I know hate, sadness, and loneliness; I know all these moods that separate you from people. I can feel all these things too, and I am not repelled. By dancing with you, I accept you—and we know one another for a moment" [Rosen, 1974, p. 60].

The individual's spontaneous movements are thus reflected, developed, and extended by the therapist. In each instance, patients give outward expression to their conflicts and the therapist gives answering movement to communicate acceptance and understanding and enable patients to change their behavior patterns. As the group warms up by stretching and moving, the dance therapist makes an effort to contact members and draw them out by reflecting their movements. Dance therapist Helen Lefco describes the difficulty in reaching a strange and withdrawn 35-year-old man in her group and encouraging him to dance along with the other patients:

> For me, it is Brian who is the hardest to reach. Tall, dark, electrifyingly intense, he dances to his own music, beats his own body masochistically like a drum. His dances have no beginning, no middle, no end. They are short, angry bursts of attack. He refuses to be questioned, interpreted, or structured. When we form a circle, he will run, skip, and leap around its periphery. Sometimes I will join him in his animated leaping, fascinated as I watch his feet hit his buttocks like some woodland animal. For a moment, as our strides match and our rhythms mesh, he looks down at me with recognition and joy. But the moment passes, and he is off again in his private world [Lefco, 1974, p. 52].

A little later in the session Brian claims that he is "angry at the wall of life behind you" (p. 54), referring to the love, warmth and companionship that he imagines exists on the other side of a room divider behind the leader. As Brian dances closer to the "wall," he falls into a fetal position. Several group members follow Brian's lead, using movement to respond in their own ways to the dilemma of sanity and hope behind the curtain, and madness and despair on the group's side of the room.

Obviously, successful dance therapists need a wide movement repertoire of their own in order to freely follow a participant's lead. Because of the close relationship between movement and feelings, the leader also must have access to a broad range of personal emotions in order to pick up the threads of a person's feelings and not be inhibited by fear or anxiety. For most people, those who are uptight or mildly neurotic, spontaneous movement helps them get in touch with their childlike aspects and permits them to play a little. For patients who are fairly disturbed and just beginning to make contact with reality, spontaneous responses may be too threatening, and structured exercises may be more appropriate.

Some structured exercises emphasize swinging movements, whereas others stress placement and control; some focus on relaxation and concentration through breathing, whereas others encourage moving in space (Espenak, 1968). The first few minutes of a dance therapy session often involve a "limbering-up" period, to help members prepare their bodies for work in the same way that an orchestra tunes up for a performance. Free-form, spontaneous movement to various musical selections is one opening. Another, used by Wethered (1973) in her group-movement approach, makes use of shaking, stretching, swinging, clapping, and rubbing movements. For example, the session might begin with members shaking their hands, then moving on to their elbows, shoulders, heads, and chests. Gradually, the shaking movement is changed to a swinging or stretching movement until the group is thoroughly warmed-up. Thereafter, a group theme is developed, much as in psychodrama.

One theme might be "meeting and parting," a theme that has obvious, rich therapeutic potential for real-life application. On a movement level, different parts of the body can move to "meet" one another, then "part." Hands and elbows, for instance, experiment with meeting and parting, meeting and fighting, and meeting and caressing. To promote group inter-action, one person's hand might meet and part from another member's elbow, or a member's arm might meet and pass a partner's arm. In the final stages of the session, the group theme is explored by making total use of the space allowed to the group, by changing patterns and speeds of movement, leading and following the leader and other group members, and, perhaps, adding music to accompany the dance.

The dance therapist's techniques are not limited to encouraging struc-tured or spontaneous movement. The therapist may use play and fantasy to stimulate body awareness, which is often limited in individuals who lacked the opportunity or permission to play in childhood. For instance, Laban (Wethered, 1973) sometimes asks group members to fantasize them-selves as newly born and experiment with the very beginnings of physical movements, whereas other group leaders will encourage "rebirthing" of participants. Specific themes and the symbolic use of space and objects can also be incorporated into the dance. The person who wants to cry out for mother, for example, may use movement to express this emotion by reaching out and pulling close. The kicking and punching motions that are used in body-therapy groups can also help members play out fantasies and release built-up anxieties.

Analysis of movement

Fundamentally, dance therapy is a kind of psychotherapy in which the therapist uses movement as a primary intervention for accomplishing therapeutic goals. It is part of the therapist's task to draw upon a group member's spontaneous, or natural, movement repertoires and use his or her skills to refine and extend them.

The most famous diagnosis of movement comes from Rudolph Laban, a dancer and architect who devised a system to analyze and describe movement behavior. Laban's system, known as *effort* or *effort-shape* (Laban, 1960), uses symbols to represent the dynamic and spatial aspects of movement, diagnose client needs, and help therapists choose movement sequences for meeting treatment goals. According to Laban, the effort system describes the dynamics of movement in terms of four motion factors: space, force, time, and flow. Each factor has two dimensions, so that space can be either direct or multifocused, force (weight) can be strong or light, time can be sustained or sudden, and flow (energy) can be bound or free. Any type of movement can be measured on these scales and the combination of these elements makes up the eight basic effort actions. For instance, the effort of pressing is sustained, strong and direct, whereas the effort of punching is sudden, strong and direct. A notation system created by Laban, shown in Figure 7-1, facilitates a movement analysis.

An individual analysis of movement, based on the Laban system, can provide the groundwork for the dance therapist to help the group explore and widen the movement repertoire of its members. Preston (1980) has catalogued a number of ways in which therapists can facilitate group

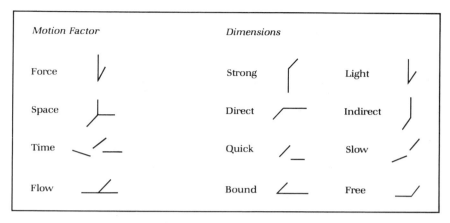

Motion Factor		Dimensions			
Force		Strong		Light	
Space		Direct		Indirect	
Time		Quick		Slow	
Flow		Bound		Free	

Figure 7-1. Notation for Laban's Effort System

members' experience of all the effort actions and help build their dancing vocabulary. Movement is improved by working through the weight, space, and time properties of an effort action. Basic movements such as jumping, turning, or locomoting, can be practiced in this way to capture their potential properties. Later on, effort may be directly approached by attending to inner feelings and attitudes. A dance therapy based on movement principles such as Laban's effort system is still in its infant stages of development though it has become very popular in the last few years. Among other applications, Laban's theories have been extensively applied in studies of schizophrenic patients (Davis, 1968) and autistic children (Kalish, 1971).

Psychodynamic approaches

Most dance therapists still conceptualize the actions of group members in terms of psychoanalytic theory. The purpose of experiencing effort actions is to bring the corresponding emotions to awareness. The *body-ego technique* of Jeri Salkin (1973) is an example of an attempt to mesh the effort system with psychoanalytic theory. The elements of space, force, time, and flow are used in special goal-directed physical movements with the object of strengthening self-identity by reexperiencing the normal developmental sequences the person passes through during the first years of life. Movements that express conscious and unconscious thoughts and feelings are encouraged and stimulated. As the group member experiments with riskier physical and emotional expressions, new feelings and actions emerge to promote personality growth.

A therapist who uses the body-ego technique knows the way that movement patterns can be related to emotions. For example, disturbed individuals often exhibit exaggerated body postures. An anxious person might rock in agitation and have twitching hands and a tense facial expression. The group leader might attempt to establish rapport with the person by sensitively mirroring these movements and guiding the person to try alternative motions. With severely disturbed participants, the goal might be to achieve a clear body image and define a boundary between self and others, and between fantasy and reality. With most people, movements are not apt to be so exaggerated or regressed. Nonetheless, fixed postures or ways of moving may reflect developmental lags, fears, or idiosyncratic personality traits. The group tries to help each member experience an emotional change through a change in physical posture and movement.

Salkin's groups are used with children of all ages, with retarded or emotionally disturbed populations, as well as with normal adults and professional dancers. Because of the need to accept the group at its level of functioning, she divides classes by age and by dancing skill.

Bernstein's (1979) dance-movement therapy is another psycho-dynamically-oriented approach that views therapy as the remediation of unfinished developmental tasks. The group environment is deliberately constructed to serve the same function as a primitive culture's rite of passage. We do not have elaborate rituals in our society, maintain Bernstein and Bernstein (1973-74), to mark a person's movement to a new developmental stage. An American Indian tribe, for example, observes an adolescent boy's passage into manhood through the ritual of sending him out to hunt his first deer entirely on his own. Modern cultures, though, tend to protect their young from crises and confrontations and thus avoid a necessary developmental process. Dance-movement therapy aims to create and resolve a controlled crisis in a safe environment to educate people who have been unable to come to terms with traumatic life events. Particular periods of developmental crisis are reenacted and worked through to integration.

The group leader in this approach acts as a facilitator/choreographer who directs and manages the crisis within therapeutic limits. The leader must be able to maintain a level of confrontation that encourages growth while keeping anxiety at a level that group members can handle. Through this process, participants learn to function without support and assistance from the group by developing their own ability to cope with interpersonal problems. Group members might open a session by improvising movements to music, programmed to begin slowly and gently and mounting to fast punching, bouncing, or pressing movements and a cathartic release.

As participants interact and begin to move with one another, they are encouraged to express hidden feelings and fantasies in a movement drama. The use of symbolic role-playing in dance-movement therapy to transcend a developmental crisis is illustrated by an adolescent girl who had difficulty dealing with irrational authority figures (Bernstein, 1972):

> The sessions often commenced with interactional movements evolving into use of strong, quick, direct patterns. Trust developed when Betsy was allowed to work through her repressed anger in psychomotor situations in which the therapist would cower in defeat as the aggressive object—an overpowering figure in her past—while being "destroyed" with punches, kicks, slashes and

angry verbiage. Betsy's voice and movements became stronger and more assured by expressing her anger at her mother's inadequacies in movement with other group members. Changes in attitude and feeling could be identified through the reclamation of her body and flow of her dance movements [p. 166].

The symbolic ritual process so evident in Bernstein's approach is even more apparent in Albert Pesso's (1969, 1973) psychomotor training, which probably provides the best bridge between the body therapies and dance therapy.[2] The goal of psychomotor training is "to provide a controllable movement arena for the clear and satisfying expression of emotions" (Pesso, 1969, p. 70). To achieve this goal, Pesso blends his experience in performing and teaching dance with his exposure to the encounter methods of William Schutz and the bioenergetic teachings of Alexander Lowen in a structured group approach.

The emphasis in psychomotor training is less on the discipline of dance and more on the release of important affective material through movement. Briefly, application of the approach consists of three stages. In the first stage, members are taught to become sensitive to their motor impulses, which can be divided into reflexive, voluntary, and emotional impulses. Reflexive impulses deal with the reality of gravity; voluntary impulses deal with the senses and the external world; and emotional impulses focus on the internal world of feelings. The first skill usually taught in a psychomotor group is the "species stance."

The stance is achieved by relaxing all the skeletal muscles, short of causing the participant to fall to the ground. Participants must expel virtually all thoughts and feelings from their minds in order to do this successfully. Although the species stance is regarded as point zero, the starting position for attempting the other exercises, there are other motility skills that also operate on the reflexive level. Work with voluntary impulses involves exploring consciously controlled movements, some of which may be goal-directed, such as canvassing the room to satisfy curiosity. To become sensitive to emotional impulses, group members work to sharpen the identification of the basic emotions (fear, anger, love, and joy) and to act on them within the safe confines of the group. For instance, participants might be asked to assume the species stance, recall a time in life when they felt very frightened, and respond as rapidly as possible to the unspoken muscular messages that the memory of the incident provokes. The memory stimulates emotional impulses which become translated into action. One group member might dive under the nearest piece of furniture. Another might curl into a ball and shake. Another might laugh loudly. At this point, group members discuss the experience. They share their thoughts about how feelings found psychomotor expression, how the

[2]An argument could be made that Judith Aston's Aston-Patterning movement education integrates dance therapy with the body therapies as impressively. Aston-Patterning teaches physical balance and the reduction of unnecessary stress by working on structural and functional "holding patterns" of the body.

expression might have been facilitated, and offer support to one another.

In the second stage the action becomes more interpersonal. Group members help process the emotional experiences of one another. According to Pesso, to process an emotion motorically, it must first be experienced, which requires a specifically recalled incident, and then the body needs to move as spontaneously as possible to express it. Direct action, which cuts through words, is the clearest form an emotional impulse can take. Finally, the environment, in the form of other group members, needs to react as if the action engendered by the emotions was effective. The emotion will not be resolved and integrated into the personality unless it is "accommodated," or expressed in relation to others. In a typical exercise at this stage, the leader might designate some group members as leaders ("controllers") and others as followers ("controllees"). Controllers use gestures to indicate how they wish controllees to move, and experiment with changes of speed, direction, and levels of movement. Other interpersonal exercises may involve physical contact among group members.

In the third stage of the psychomotor group, emotional motoric expression is processed through "structures," which are similar to psychodramatic scenes. For example, a participant might recall being hurt and frustrated by his parents in a particular situation. The leader then selects structures that permit the person to experience his old pain and anger and to allow these feelings to be expressed in action. "Negative accommodators" provoke the participant, making him feel increasingly angry and frustrated. Once the negative experience is worked through and the participant reaches catharsis, "positive accommodators" offer the wished-for comfort and nurturance. One crucial difference between psychodramatic scenes and psychomotor structures is that the structural action is primarily nonverbal. It focuses on movement.

APPRAISAL

The most sophisticated dance therapy has been conducted with severely disturbed individuals, where diagnosing movement irregularities and designing a systematic program to enhance coordinated and fluid movement is especially needed and appropriate. The use of dance therapy in experiential groups with college students and well-functioning adults has been less focused. Perhaps the overriding interest is simply in doing something together. Dancing is democratic. Everyone can dance. Some individuals may appear to be "better" dancers than others, but whenever dance is interjected into an ongoing group, comparisons in skill levels are quickly erased and each group member's concern is generally channeled into personal gratification.

Among the universal benefits of group dance are a reduction in self-consciousness and an improvement in physical health and fitness. Another benefit is the opportunity to interact and share in groups. Dance therapy promotes the experience of pleasure and, in so doing, offers participants the opportunity to try on new modes of behavior. As such, it can be a vehicle for examining issues of alienation, body image, self-assertion, and sexuality. At its best, the exploration of movement helps participants translate feelings into actions and actions into insights.

Dance therapy is a relatively new field tied to an old art form. In recent years it has spread from clinically institutional settings to independent practice, school systems, and community centers. Since most dance thera-pists were initially trained in the psychoanalytic tradition, this theoretical heritage predominates and is evident in concepts such as catharsis. One of the hazards of conducting dance therapy without some training in psycho-therapy is the possibility of stimulating very strong feelings that may not be easily resolved. Physical movement can generate surprisingly powerful emotions. Combining movement with body contact and intense interper-sonal interactions underscores this concern.

Newer approaches to dance therapy are moving beyond the psycho-analytic heritage. Today there is significant diversity in the field, as evi-denced by the methods described in this chapter. Contemporary eclectic therapists and group leaders are also finding a place for group dance and movement within the experiential group.

SUMMARY

Dance therapy is a descendant of creative dance. Dance in therapy, unlike dance as performance, uses relatively unstructured movement forms and spontaneously released feelings. Dance therapy became popu-lar after World War II, inspired by early practitioners such as Marian Chace.

The goals of dance therapy include developing *increased body aware-ness, a positive body image, social skills, the exploration of feelings, and a profound group experience.* Fundamental to dance therapy is the relation-ship between spontaneous movement and mind and the belief that move-ment reflects personality.

The leader of a dance-therapy group functions as a *codancer, a direc-tor of events,* and a *catalyst* to facilitate growth through movement. The therapist creates a safe environment for the exploration of self and others and acts to reflect and extend the group members' spontaneous move-ments. Dance therapists make use of structured exercises for relaxation, breathing, placement and control, and movement in space. Laban's *effort-shape system* is often used to diagnose movement and help members widen their movement repertoire.

Most approaches to dance therapy are influenced by psychodynamic theory. Salkins's *body-ego technique* uses goal-directed physical move-ments to strengthen self-identity. Bernstein's *dance-movement therapy* uses ritual and fantasy to explore hidden feelings and unfinished develop-mental tasks. Pesso's *psychomotor training* deemphasizes the discipline of dance and emphasizes the expression of emotions through movement.

Whereas dance therapy was formerly used almost exclusively with severely disturbed populations, dance is being used increasingly with well-functioning adults to promote fitness, pleasure, and group interaction, as well as to express and channel powerful emotions.

REFERENCES

Bernstein, P. *Theory and methods in dance-movement therapy: A manual for therapists, students, and educators.* Dubuque, Iowa: Kendall/Hunt, 1972.

Bernstein, P. *Eight theoretical approaches in dance-movement therapy.* Dubuque, Iowa: Kendall/Hunt, 1979.

Bernstein, P., & Bernstein, L. A conceptualization of group dance-movement therapy as a ritual process. *American Dance Therapy Association Proceedings Monograph No. 3,* 1973–74, 120–132.

Birdwhistell, R. L. *Kinesics and context.* Philadelphia: University of Pennsylvania Press, 1970.

Bogen, J. E. Some educational implications of hemispheric specialization. In M. C. Wittrock (Ed.), *The human brain.* Englewood Cliffs, N.J.: Prentice-Hall, 1977.

Chace, M. Dance as an adjunctive therapy with hospitalized children. *Bulletin of the Menninger Clinic,* 1953, *17,* 219–255.

Davis, M. Movement characteristics of hospitalized psychiatric patients. *American Dance Therapy Association Proceedings, Third Annual Conference,* 3, 1968.

Espenak, L. Diagnosis and treatment in psychomotor therapy. Lecture demonstration presented to the American Dance Therapy Association, Hunter College, New York, May 26, 1968.

Jung, G. C. [*Archetypes and the collective unconscious.*] In *The Collected Works* (2nd ed.). Princeton, N.J.: Princeton University Press, 1961.

Kalish, B. "Eric," ADTA writings on body movement and communication. *ADTA Monograph No. 1,* 1971.

Laban, R. *The mastery of movement* (2nd ed.). (L. Ullman, Ed.). London: MacDonald & Evans, 1960.

Langer, S. K. *Feeling and form: A theory of art.* New York: Scribner, 1953.

Lefco, H. *Dance therapy.* Chicago: Nelson Hall, 1974.

Pesso, A. *Movement in psychotherapy.* New York: New York University Press, 1969.

Pesso, A. *Experience in action.* New York: New York University Press, 1973.

Preston, V. *A handbook for modern educational dance.* (Revised ed.) Boston: Plays, 1980.

Reich, W. *Character analysis.* New York: Farrar, Straus & Giroux, 1942.

Rosen, E. *Dance in psychotherapy.* New York: Columbia University Press, 1974.

Salkin, J. *Body ego technique.* Springfield, Ill.: Charles C Thomas, 1973.

Schilder, P. *The image and appearance of the human body.* New York: International Universities Press, 1950.

Schmais, C. Dance therapy in perspective. In K. C. Mason (Ed.), *Dance therapy: Focus on dance VII.* Washington, D.C.: American Association for Health, Physical Education, and Recreation, 1974.

Sullivan, H. S. *The interpersonal theory of psychiatry.* New York: W. W. Norton & Co., 1953.

Wethered, A. *Movement and drama in therapy.* Boston: Plays, 1973.

White, E. Q. Effort-shape: Its importance to dance therapy and movement research. In K. C. Mason (Ed.), *Dance therapy: Focus on dance VII.* Washington, D.C.: American Association for Health, Physical Education, and Recreation, 1974.

Wigman, M. *Language of the dance.* Middletown, Conn.: Wesleyan University Press, 1963.

8

Art Therapy

HISTORY AND DEVELOPMENT

Although artistic achievements have given us pleasure for centuries, art therapy is a relatively recent phenomenon. The term was coined by Adrian Hill in 1938 to describe his work with sanatorium patients ill with tuberculosis. Not long thereafter the term was used to refer to all art conducted in hospitals and mental health centers, though many in the field consider such a definition too broad and imprecise. The virtue of using art in treatment contexts is that it is a method that allows one to experiment with, explore, and express a variety of experiences at the symbolic level. The use of symbolic art can be traced back to the cave paintings of primeval man. The ancients used symbolic art to identify their place in the cosmos and search out the meaning of human existence. Art reflects the culture and society from which it emanates. In our century, this is evidenced by the frequent transformation of artistic styles in response to rapid shifts in cultural mores and values.

In its beginning stages, art therapy reflected a psychoanalytic emphasis in which the patient's finished product, whether drawn, painted, sculpted, or constructed, was regarded as an expression of unconscious processes within the psyche. In the 1920s Prinzhorn (1922/1972) conducted a classic study of mental patients' art and concluded that their artistic creativity revealed the areas of their most intense conflict. Margaret Naumburg was one of the early initiators of the art-therapy movement in the United States. She began her work in 1941 at the New York State Psychiatric Institute working with children with behavior problems and later developed psychodynamically-oriented art-therapy training programs in New York State. Her work is based on the Freudian notion that since human beings' primary thoughts and feelings are derived from the unconscious, they are often expressed in images and symbols rather than words (Naumburg, 1966).

Art threrapy is used as a medium for symbolic communication between the patient and the therapist. The images found in art work represent all kinds of unconscious processes, including fears, conflicts, childhood memories, and dreams, phenomena identical to those that Freudian therapists explore with patients in analysis. Although Freud (1922/1963) did not actually use art therapy with his patients, he came very close to championing its use:

> We experience it [a dream] predominantly in visual images; feelings may be present too, and thoughts interwoven in it as well; the other senses may also experience something, but nonetheless it is predominantly a question of images. Part of the difficulty of giving an account of dreams is due to our having to translate these images into words. "I could draw it," a dreamer often says to us, "but I don't know how to say it" [p. 90].

The techniques of art therapy are founded on the belief that the inner self expresses itself in visual forms whenever a person is spontaneously painting, drawing, or sculpting. Whereas Freud was well aware of the world of the unconscious appearing in symbolic images, he did not utilize nor directly encourage his patients' drawings. Carl Jung, on the other hand, inspired his patients to express their dreams and fantasies in pictures. Jung's thoughts on personal and universal symbols and the use of imagination have deeply influenced art therapists (Garai, 1978).

Traditionally the art therapist has functioned as an adjunct to psychiatrists and psychologists on treatment teams, where the drawings and paintings of children and hospitalized adults have been used to aid in diagnosis and therapy. As we shall see, this use of art is different from projective tests, such as the Rorschach or the Thematic Apperception Test (TAT), in which subjects give immediate responses to structured inkblots or pictures, and which are used to assess personality functioning.

Art therapists are now accorded the status of independent practitioners and recognized as able to make contributions in assessment and treatment on their own. This development is not supported by everyone in the field, however. One camp, represented by Edith Kramer (1958, 1978) and many recreational and occupational therapists, view art as healing in and of itself. These art therapists emphasize art over therapy and exclude procedures in which completion of the creative process is not a primary goal. They do not see art therapy as a substitute for psychotherapy. Others, represented by Margaret Naumburg, minimize artistic goals in favor of therapeutic goals. They generally have more of a clinical background and claim that art therapy can at times be an independent technique as well as adjunctive to more traditional approaches. Both schools, of course, share an interest in using the visual arts to assist in the integration or reintegration of personality functioning (Ulman, 1975).

Art therapy is now practiced not only on hospital wards, but in many other contexts as well, both as a pure form of intervention and as a supplement to other group approaches. A large group of art therapists in North America continue to operate from either a Freudian or a Jungian position. However, many art therapists today have been influenced by the humanistic movement in groups and find that humanistic personality theories offer a more appropriate rationale for their work than traditional psychoanalytic theory (Hodnett, 1972-73).

BASIC CONCEPTS

Among the reasons cited for using art therapy are the following (McNiff, 1976):

1. to provide an outlet for expressing aggressive feelings and other conflicts in a socially acceptable manner. Drawing, painting, or sculpting are safe ways of letting off steam and discharging tension.
2. to facilitate therapeutic progress. Unconscious conflicts and inner experiences are often easier to express through visual images than with the spoken language of verbal psychotherapy. Nonverbal communication can more readily escape the censorship of conscious control.
3. to serve as the basis for interpretations and diagnostic work in therapy. The productions are lasting and can't be denied by the patient. The content and style of the art work provides a wealth of information to the therapist, and the artists can contribute to the interpretation of their own creations.
4. to work through thoughts and feelings that seem overwhelming. Sometimes a nonverbal medium is the only viable tool for expressing and then clarifying intense feelings and beliefs.
5. to help cement a therapeutic relationship. The act of sharing in an art activity can facilitate the development of empathy and positive feelings between two people.
6. to establish a sense of internal control and order. Drawing, painting, or modeling involve the need to organize forms and colors.
7. to develop increased sensory awareness. Art is a creative enterprise that offers the possibility of experimenting with and refining the visual and kinesthetic senses.
8. to improve the participant's self-image and artistic competence. A by-product of art therapy is the satisfaction that comes from discovering latent skills and sharpening them.

In addition to these concrete effects, the use of art in ongoing groups may have additional payoffs in exploring fantasy and imagination, working through conflicts among group members, and helping them establish rapport. Art seems to contribute to pleasure, whether it is pleasure derived from unconscious sources or simply the bubbly pleasure that comes from playing and being silly.

Spontaneous painting and modeling

Art in the context of therapy is a *spontaneous* activity in contrast to a planned, deliberate action, such as teaching arts and crafts to patient populations. Virtually all art therapists agree that a person's artistic talents or training are irrelevant to the use of art as a therapeutic device. What is important in art therapy is the act itself and what the end product reveals about the mental life of the artist. The art therapist encourages group members to depict their inner experiences as spontaneously as possible and not concern themselves with the artistic merits of their work.

Carl Jung believed imagination and creativity to be healing forces in human life. The role of fantasy in creative play has been described by Jung in the following way:

> It is not the artist alone, but every creative individual whatsoever who owes all that is greatest in his life to fantasy. The dynamic principle of fantasy is play, which belongs also to the child, and as such it appears to be inconsistent with the principle of serious work. But without this playing with fantasy, no creative work has ever come to birth [Jung, 1921/1970, p. 63].

Jung used the term "imaginative activity" to refer to a creative enterprise (Lyddiatt, 1971), in which the subject objectively observes a fragment of fantasy as it develops, without trying to affect it consciously. A good example of the spontaneous use of fantasy in art therapy is the scribble technique, in which a participant, without planning, draws a continuous flowing line without lifting the pen or brush from the paper. The purpose of the exercise is to liberate spontaneous expression. As group members scribble, unconscious material emerges from the psyche. They are then encouraged to look at the drawing to see if some design, person, or object that has been released from the unconscious through visual imagery can be identified. Art-therapy methods such as the scribble technique parallel Jung's use of "active imagination" exercises, in which patients are instructed to continue an interrupted dream sequence in fantasy.

Sublimation

Sublimation is described in psychoanalytic theory as a defense mechanism. It is a process whereby antisocial impulses are diverted to socially sanctioned behaviors that provide compromise gratification for the original impulse (Kramer, 1958). Although all defense mechanisms help the individual cope with anxiety, sublimation is especially adaptive in that it leads to the most socially esteemed results. According to psychoanalytic theory, artistic expression is one example of sublimation, in which artists sublimate their fantasies into creative visual images.

For art therapists with a psychoanalytic orientation, sublimation is a central concept since art can at the same time divert and help express feelings of anger, pain, anxiety, fear, and depression. Historically, the arts have helped us express and deal with the timeless conflict between our instinctive urges and the constraints and demands of socialized living. The spontaneous construction of a scene modeled in clay by a quiet, withdrawn man of 31 who had been training for the priesthood illustrates this conflict (Lyddiatt, 1971). The scene consisted of the figure of a man confessing to a priest, with the word "doubts" emblazoned over his head. Behind the priest was a fierce, devilish creature with sharp teeth, and a gentle mother embracing a child was positioned to the side. The figures appeared to signify the artist's dual and antagonistic perceptions of the church.

According to Edith Kramer (1958, p. 16), "Every work of art contains a core of conflicting drives which give it life and determine form and content to a large degree." Art, through its abstract and symbolic quality, allows us to express acceptable equivalents of our instinctive urges without being unduly offended or threatened by the thoughts and feelings underlying them. The artistic outlet provides the opportunity to give symbolic form to our fantasies and thus feel less overwhelmed by them.

Art therapists who are less loyal to traditional psychoanalytic theory claim that the Freudian concept of sublimation is too restrictive (Garai, 1978). They maintain that the creative, expressive drive should be seen as an autonomous, inherent quality of a person and not as a derivative of repressed sexual and aggressive energies.

BASIC PROCEDURES

The leader of an art-therapy group provides a maximum of materials and flexibility to stimulate artistic expression. The materials are generally as simple as possible in order to enhance fluid artistic expression. Plenty of paints of all colors, clay for modeling, and materials such as wood, stone, fabrics, and paper are available. Sometimes group members are encouraged to bring in other materials they find attractive, such as shells from the beach or bark from trees. The group setting should allow space for movement and noise. The therapist stays out of the way as much as possible to abet the creative process. Members are told to go with their feelings and not worry about the artistic quality of their work. When art therapy does enliven a dormant talent for painting, as sometimes happens, that is a bonus; it has nothing at all to do with art therapy, however. The art therapist does not even have to be an artist. An interest in the creative arts and knowledge of abnormal psychology and group dynamics are much more important.

The techniques chosen by art therapists depend on their own theoretical biases and the group's function. Initially, group art therapy stemmed from work with withdrawn, isolated individuals in medical settings (Garai, 1978). Patients became interested in one another's artwork and through this vehicle became increasingly verbal. Today, some patients seek art therapy because they are blocked in creative expression. Obsessive/compulsive individuals, for instance, are very controlled and intellectualized. Playing with clay or getting covered in finger paints can help them break through their rigid defenses. With schizophrenics and other severely disturbed patient groups, art therapists attempt to encourage a positive self-concept by being very supportive. The fragmented thinking of schizophrenics is revealed in pictures that are also fragmented. In many European hospitals, schizophrenic patients are discouraged from freely expressing their inner feelings in art (Plokker, 1964). They are directed to paint the external world of landscapes, portraits, and still life, and, in so doing, to minimize anxiety and concretize their diffuse thinking. A limitation with many such programs is that there is a preoccupation with evaluating the aesthetic quality of art productions and a relative neglect of the active psychotherapeutic treatment of schizophrenia.

Psychodynamic art therapy

Most art therapists practice psychodynamic art therapy, basing their procedures on the psychological contributions of Freud or Jung, who maintained that artistic creations symbolically represent the artist's unconscious processes. The work of Margaret Naumburg (1966) is representative of this approach, which assumes that group members' fantasies, daydreams, and fears can often be expressed more immediately in pictures than in words. In the process of depicting such inner experiences in an artistic mode, patients frequently become more verbally articulate. Most group leaders do not directly interpret artistic symbols, but help participants discover their meaning for themselves by establishing a nonjudgmental, accepting environment and encouraging them to free-associate to the artwork. It is considered crucial that group members themselves associate to their productions in order to achieve self-understanding. A few art therapists, however, prefer to decipher and interpret their patients' art for them. Bernard Levy (Ulman & Levy, 1980), for example, claims that art therapists' training in assessing the meaning and value of art gives them an edge over the patient's limited understanding.

As an example of learning about oneself through the visual images one creates, consider the case of a depressed 24-year-old woman who painted a black picture of herself in bed at the age of four clutching a pair of ballet shoes (Lyddiatt, 1971). As the woman was encouraged to associate freely to her painting, she eventually recalled that on that night her 2-year-old sister had disappeared and she had not learned until years later that her sister had died. Her grief about the episode had long been buried. By discussing these memories the woman was able to express her grief and minimize her depression. In other cases, spontaneous, rough sketches might be made in response to a disturbing dream or fantasy. Associating to the finished drawing can help clarify the experience. It is also possible for learning to occur on an unconscious level, so that the person feels emotionally relieved without ever consciously understanding the content of his or her work. Typically, however, the art therapist helps the group member move from the symbolic to the concrete and from the unconscious to the conscious, aiding the participant to reexperience past events that had been blocked and that interfere with development and growth.

One particularly popular technique is the use of group murals, in which participants either draw whatever they like on a common mural or contribute to a theme chosen by the group (Harris & Joseph, 1973). Group members are encouraged to comment on the drawings, while the therapist facilitates the group interaction. The following example illustrates how the interpretation of symbolic communications expressed in the group mural can yield insights into intrapsychic and interpersonal conflict areas (Garai, 1978):

> Harry, pointing to Susan's jail which has a slightly open window in the top area through which a little bird is trying to escape, says, "You seem to be stuck in your jail. You are desperately trying to get out, but your wings seem to be clipped." Susan answers, "That's my life story. I'm always trying to get out of my mother's grip, but her jail has too heavy bars. Nobody helps me to get out and I can't make it on my own." Then Susan begins to draw a green field with a wide open pasture where a huge butterfly with colorful wings buzzes over the grass and around Richard's horse, which has escaped from a ranch nearby. Richard then turns to Susan, saying, "You try to be like me . . . I have just gotten out of the confines of my stable . . . you would like to be free like a butterfly to join me." Josephine, who has added a snail which is sticking only its feelers out of its shell toward some large blades of grass on Richard's ranch, chimes in, "Yeah, you innocent little birdie or butterfly. . . . You always have an excuse that you are buzzing around all the men by sheer accident. You are a superma-nipulator!" [p. 103.][1]

One psychodynamically-oriented art-therapy approach has been created specifically for use with groups. This is the synallactic group image technique of G. Vassilious (1968). A primary advantage of this technique is that other group members share in the art work of a given individual. At the outset of each group session, the group votes on one member's painting to serve as the focus of that meeting. Paintings are generally done at home by each person and brought to the group. After the vote, the person who was selected expresses her feelings before, during and after she did the paint-ing. The person also says something about the meaning of the painting, perhaps giving the work a title or free-associating to it. Then the other group members add their reactions and associations to the painting. The group's reactions to and projections on the painting narrow to a theme, called the Collective Image, which will serve as the theme of the group session that day.

One such group cited by Kymissis (1976) consisted of patients, most of whom were mothers, who were in transition between living on a hospital ward and in the community. A group member painted a picture of a bear

---

[1]From "Art Therapy—Catalyst for Creative Expression and Personality Integration," by J. E. Garai. In H. H. Grayson and C. Loew (Eds.), *Changing Approaches to the Psychotherapies*. Copyright 1978 by Spectrum Publications, Inc. Reprinted by permission.

and her cub. The Collective Image that emerged was: "We are dependent on the therapist. We want him to feed us (with medications, instructions, etc.). But sometimes we have to play the role of mother and we can't accept it" (p. 24). These mothers were experiencing conflicts about raising their children. For example, one woman who had recently been divorced had given up a child she felt unable to care for. Like dreams from a Freudian perspective, the paintings are regarded as having a manifest content—the visual images themselves—and a latent content—the symbolic, often unconscious processes represented by the images. The synallactic group-image technique structures the group session, since the initial goal is to form a Collective Image in response to the selected artwork, which then represents the theme for the session. In addition, the method allows those who are easily threatened to communicate with each other through the go-between of the painting. People can talk about how a painting upsets them as a way of starting to deal with their own upset or anger.

Humanistic art therapy

Not all art therapists conduct their group work from a Freudian or Jungian perspective. Many are more humanistic and view art therapy as an opportunity to exercise the "creativity muscle." They stress the group member's active engagement with materials, the process of doing artwork, rather than the meaning of the finished product. Others have commented that art therapy trains the right hemisphere of the brain, that is, the intuitive, spatially-oriented functions (Virshop, 1978).

Janie Rhyne (1973) is a humanistic art therapist whose approach is loyal to Gestalt theory. From the Gestalt perspective, painting and sculpting are seen as experiential events that are a function of the ongoing, present-centered awareness of the participant. The concepts of figure and ground are directly applicable since the way we perceive visually is related to the way we think and feel. The art therapist helps participants to experience and disclose who they are and might become. In this endeavor, Rhyne offers group members a number of guidelines. Among them is the suggestion to trust their own perceptions of what is right; give themselves permission to play with the art materials and even to act foolish; do what is most pleasing without comparing their work with others; be aware that everyone is in a continual state of change and that artwork can express that excitement, experimentation, and growth.

Rhyne provides a large assortment of materials for members, including clay, paint, glue, and chalk. She suggests that members begin by consulting how they feel inside in the same way that a Gestalt therapist might focus on awareness of inner sensations. The idea is to trust this inner awareness to provide a direction to go in self-expression rather than actively to look for a problem to solve or an experience to recreate. Another Gestalt-oriented art therapist, Elaine Rapp (1980), notes that the anxiety of group members to participate in creating art can be further reduced by introducing each new experience as a "happening" rather than asking them to make something. For example, the leader might toss hundreds of sheets of tissue paper in the air accompanied by suitable music in the background. Group members will spontaneously float the tissues in the air, roll them, fling them at one another, and fashion them into articles of clothing. Eventually the leader places some white drawing paper in the middle of the room together with paint brushes and a diluted mixture of acrylic polymer gel. The leader then shows the group how to affix shaped pieces of tissue to the paper without ever actually telling the group to make a collage.

Leaders of Gestalt art groups are available as facilitators rather than directors. They encourage participants to live in the present and give total expression to what they feel. Therapists must be skilled at empathizing with clients' perceptions of their own artwork. Sometimes, of course, therapists may supplement the group member's perception with feedback of their own, but the artwork is never dissected in an analytical fashion to determine its "meaning." The introspective perceptions of the artist are always more informative than the outer reality of the finished product.

The Gestalt art-therapy group progresses in stages (Rhyne, 1973). Initially, the group stresses the encouragement of personal identity through drawing or modeling by oneself. Tasks are kept simple and non-threatening to allow the release of conscious controls and spontaneous expression. Participants move from exploring inner sensations and feelings to looking at themselves in space, time, and relationship to others. In the early stages, then, the work is highly personal and done alone. A direction might be suggested by the group leader, such as to model clay by first making a shape illustrating something you don't like about yourself and then making another shape to show something you do like about yourself. Alternatively, members might be asked to paint a feeling, mood, or fantasy, or to respond in art to a stimulus word such as *love, hate, beauty,* or *freedom* (Figure 8-1). Afterwards, group members may share their experiences about what they have made. There is always the possibility that repressed emotions will come to light when personal imagery is modeled. The group will deal with those feelings as they arise.

In a later phase, group members might be asked to choose a partner to get to know better. The pair might be given paper and crayons or chalk and use the art work as a bridge to nonverbally communicate their inner experiences to each other. Some couples cooperate, some compete, and some interfere with one another's productions. Participants are encouraged to share their reactions and observations afterwards, but are discouraged from analyzing, interpreting, or defending images that they have chosen. In one case a shy Japanese man was paired with an aggressive Caucasian woman (Denny, 1975). When the woman drew a bold red arrow straight at him, he responded with a weak, purple line that curled back on itself. As the woman became less direct in her overtures on paper, he became more approachable.

An alternative strategy is the use of clay sculpture to explore interper-

Figure 8–1. Feeling states: (a) sweaty hands; (b) soft insides; (c) headache; (d) wet throat; (e) tight mouth; and (f) heavy body. *(From The Gestalt Art Experience, by J. Rhyne. Copyright © 1973 by Wadsworth Publishing Company, Inc. Reprinted by permission of Brooks/Cole Publishing Company, Monterey, California.)*

sonal relationships. Group members are urged to close their eyes, imagine someone else with whom they have significant emotional ties, and to model in clay an image of the way they perceive that person. A clay effigy of an enemy could even be destroyed as an outlet for aggression. The leader can follow up artists' creations by asking how much energy they have invested in the other person and how to differentiate the identities of that person and themselves.

There are other exercises that are used at the group level. For instance, group members can use art media to visually represent their perceptions of group interactions and, in so doing, bring out submerged conflicts. Rhyne (1973) likes to ask participants to make a quick portrait of every other group member and exchange signed portraits. The exchange may be accompanied by a few statements between pairs, perhaps sharing the characteristics that led to a certain symbolic expression of the other person. Another option is to compare self-portraits with portraits of others to disclose disparities between how members see themselves and how others see them. A woman who perceives herself as lively and animated, for instance, might be viewed as big-mouthed and loud by other group members. This is exactly what happened in a group run by James Denny, another art therapist with an existential, humanistic focus. The woman drew herself in reds, oranges, and yellows, with humorous eyes and a flower in her mouth. Her male partner's drawing depicted her as wide-eyed, and smiling, too, but also as being quite overwhelming (Denny, 1975).

The humanistic approach to art therapy is used both in workshops for personal growth and creative development and in intensive individual or group therapy. The goal is to reach levels of psychological exploration agreed upon by both the therapist and client or leader and student (Rapp, 1980). On this self-discovery tour the art therapist must always remain flexible with the use of technique and never lose sight of the group member's ongoing needs. The group's supportive environment offers a nourishing community where participants can become creative in ways they never believed possible as they validate their subjective experiences in a visual mode.

APPRAISAL

Art therapy has historically been a method of choice with severely disturbed patients, children, and adolescents; in other words, groups that cannot easily verbally share their thoughts and feelings with a therapist. It is important to realize that other kinds of groups can also benefit from working therapeutically with art materials. For example, group leaders can facilitate their work with overly verbal members in this way. Art-therapy techniques have also been used to study families with problems by having family members collaborate on a project or produce individual perspectives of family transactions (Kwiatkowska, 1978). It has also been used with obese women, helping them reduce their isolation by interacting around their artwork.

The most frequent note of caution in regard to art therapy is its undisciplined use with fragile or disturbed individuals (Betensky, 1973). Creative self-expression in both art and dance therapy has the potential to release explosive emotional impulses. In the absence of firm and thoughtful guidance by a skilled group leader, some group members may feel overwhelmed by these feelings. Moreover, a psychotic individual, who may have ready access to traumatic early experiences that can yield much symbolically expressive art, may not be in a position to integrate and learn from unconscious expressions (Champernowne, 1970–71). In groups of college students this is not such a critical issue. But in order to make art expression therapeutic, it should ideally be part of a carefully thought-out program or group goal. At the very least, there must be an opportunity to verbally follow up nonverbal art activities.

A second limitation in the use of art for therapeutic purposes is that it is difficult to know what aspect of the method is responsible for any favorable changes that occur. This is one of the main disputes between psychodynamic schools, humanistic schools, and activity therapists. The process of painting, the finished product, and relationships with the therapist and other group members may all be responsible. Research is not available to provide a definitive answer.

A third drawback is that art therapy is sometimes contraindicated in that the highly personal nature of the task may encourage narcissism and self-absorption rather than sharing and relating. Moreover, some individuals are very resistant to expressing themselves through the vehicle of art, although to most people art is a particularly nonthreatening mode of expression.

During the last decade or so, art therapy has become increasingly professionalized in terms of establishing training programs and defining itself. Art therapists have also become venturesome in terms of emerging from the shadows of the psychiatric profession and expanding beyond the bounds of traditional psychoanalytic theory. The benefits of art therapy in the group context are likewise broader than helping resolve individual neuroses as part of a total treatment package. There is evidence that using artwork to express thoughts and feelings can enhance appropriate peer-relating behavior and self-esteem (Isaacs, 1977). There is also evidence that art has an educational value in developing cognitive and creative skills (Silver, 1978).

SUMMARY

Art therapy is a relatively new discipline. Margaret Naumburg has played an influential role in developing art therapy in the United States and promoting the idea that the inner self can be expressed in visual form through spontaneous painting, drawing, or sculpting. Freud's theory of the unconscious has been important in art therapy, as has Jung's emphasis on personal and universal symbols. Art therapy is practiced both as an adjunct to formal psychotherapy and as a method in and of itself.

Art therapy functions as an outlet for conflicts and strong feelings, facilitates therapeutic progress, aids in interpretative and diagnostic work, encourages discipline and control, develops sensory awareness, and improves self-image and artistic competence. In art therapy, spontaneous painting and modeling exist as a type of imaginative activity and not as a function of talent. Psychodynamically-oriented art therapists stress the concept of *sublimation*, the indirect gratification of antisocial impulses.

Leaders of art therapy groups typically encourage members to free associate and discover the meaning of their work for themselves. In some exercises, the whole group works together, such as in producing group murals and using the *synallactic group-image technique*. Humanistic group leaders stress the doing of the art and deemphasize the meaning of the work. They encourage members to trust their own perceptions and explore their creations by themselves and with other members.

Art therapy was initially practiced in hospitals and mental health clinics with very disturbed patients. Today art therapy reaches broader populations and has moved beyond its psychoanalytic roots.

REFERENCES

Betensky, M. *Self-discovery through self-expression*. Springfield, Ill.: Charles C Thomas, 1973.

Champernowne, H. I. Art and therapy: An uneasy partnership. *American Journal of Art Therapy*, 1970–71, *10*, 131–142.

Denny, J. M. Techniques for individual and group art therapy. In E. Ulman &. P. Dachinger (Eds.), *Art therapy*. New York: Schocken Books, 1975.

Freud, S. [*Introductory lectures on psychoanalysis Part II: Dreams*.] (J. Strachey, Ed. and trans.). London: Hogarth Press, 1963. (Originally published, 1922.)

Garai, J. E. Art therapy—catalyst for creative expression and personality integration. In H. H. Grayson &. C. Loew (Eds.), *Changing approaches to the new psychotherapies*. Jamaica, N.Y.: Spectrum, 1978.

Harris, J., & Joseph, C. *Murals of the mind: Image of a psychiatric community*. New York: International Universities Press, 1973.

Hodnett, M. L. Toward professionalization of art therapy: Defining the field. *American Journal of Art Therapy*, 1972–73, *12*, 107–118.

Isaacs, L. D. Art therapy group for latency age children. *Social Work*, 1977, *22*, 57–59.

Jacobi, J. *The inner kingdom of images*. Princeton, N.J.: Princeton University Press, in press.

Jung, C. *Collected Works* (Vol. 6). London: Routledge &. Kegan Paul, 1970. (Originally published, 1921.)

Kramer, E. *Art therapy in a children's community*. Springfield, Ill.: Charles C Thomas, 1958.

Kramer, E. *Art therapy in a children's community*. New York: Schocken Books, 1978.

Kwiatkowska, H. *Family therapy and evaluation through art*. Springfield, Ill.: Charles C Thomas, 1978.

Kymissis, P. Observations on the use of the synallactic group image technique in an aftercare group. *Art Psychotherapy*, 1976, *3*, 23–26.

Lyddiatt, E. M. *Spontaneous painting and modelling*. London: Constable, 1971.

McNiff, S. The effects of artistic development on personality. *Art Psychotherapy*, 1976, *3*, 69–75.

Naumburg, M. *Dynamically oriented art therapy: Its principles and practices*. New York: Grune &. Stratton, 1966.

Plokker, J. H. *Artistic self-expression in mental disease*. London: Mouton &. Co., 1964.

Prinzhorn, H. [*Artistry of the mentally ill*.] (E. Von Brockdorff, Ed. and trans.). New York: Springer, 1972. (Originally published, 1922.)

Rapp, E. Gestalt art therapy in groups. In B. Feder and R. Ronall (Eds.), *Beyond the hot seat: Gestalt approaches to group*. New York: Brunner/Mazel, 1980.

Rhyne, J. *The Gestalt art experience*. Monterey, Calif.: Brooks/Cole, 1973.

Silver, R. *Developing cognitive and creative skills through art*. Baltimore: University Park Press, 1978.

Ulman, E. Art therapy: Problems of definition. In E. Ulman & P. Dachinger (Eds.), *Art therapy.* New York: Schocken Books, 1975.

Ulman, E., & Levy, C. A. (Eds.), *Art therapy viewpoints.* New York: Schocken Books, 1980.

Vassilious, G. An introduction to transactional group image therapy. In B. Ries (Ed.), *New directions in mental health, Vol. 1.* New York: Grune & Stratton, 1968.

Virshop, E. *Right brain people in a left brain world.* Los Angeles: Guild of Tutors Press, 1978.

9

Theme-Centered Interaction

Theme-centered interaction (TCI) is a relatively new addition to the group movement and may not be as well known as some of the approaches so far discussed. The method is rapidly increasing in popularity, however, due in large part to the energy and influence of its creator, Ruth Cohn, a German-born experiential psychoanalyst and group psychotherapist. The theme-centered interactional group belongs within the humanistic tradition together with other process groups such as sensitivity groups and Rogerian encounter groups, yet has mainly been shaped by the philosophical background and psychodynamic training of its originator. The method's unique quality is its focus on a theme that structures the events of the group and around which interactional processes and its explicit philosophical basis can be explored. The approach has been referred to as "an experiential method (integrating educational, group-dynamic, and therapeutic features) which may be adapted to group needs, problem solving, and a variety of themes" (Gordon, 1972, p. 104).

HISTORY AND DEVELOPMENT

The history of the theme-centered interactional method reveals many of its distinguishing features. Ruth Cohn was a practicing psychoanalyst when she emigrated to the United States in 1941. She had been trained at the Zurich Psychoanalytic Institute and brought her practice in individual and group psychoanalysis to New York City. While supervising and training psychoanalysts in the 1950s she offered countertransference workshops to acquaint budding and experienced therapists with aspects of their own personality dynamics that might distort their perception of patients and interfere with their effectiveness in conducting therapy. In her typically self-disclosing way, Cohn asked her student group to remain silent while she free-associated to a case with which she was having difficulty. While listening, the group learned a great deal about their leader as well as her patient. They also related their own feelings, thoughts, and backgrounds to the case. With Cohn functioning as a participant/leader, a highly charged group atmosphere was created. As students began to present cases of their own and relate them to aspects of their own lives, the countertransference theme came alive. It became clear to the therapists that they were unconsciously repeating the same conflicts and interactional behaviors in the workshop that they experienced with their patients in therapy. Indeed, many times they "acted out" their patients in the group and the group became "the therapist." The group sessions were used to identify and dissolve this interference to effective therapy (called countertransference).[1] For example, one participant rationalized the rebelliousness of a patient who failed to pay his fees. He was shown that his own behavior in breaking a rule of silence during case presentations in the countertransference group was similar to the defiant behavior of his nonpaying patient and elicited a response from the group similar to the one his client elicited from him.

Although this supervision group was designed to be an educational workshop, its greater value was in the therapy it provided for its members. Rather than dismissing group incidents as interference with the workshop goal, Cohn's psychoanalytic training inspired her to "go with the resistance" and give precedence to events that appeared to be distracting the group from its purpose. She realized that these group interactions could be used profitably to elaborate the countertransference theme. In effect, students' therapy problems were related to developmental and personality issues within the students themselves. As group leader, Cohn tried to balance the group work between the theme itself and the ongoing interactions of the participants. She facilitated the group process by identifying points of contact between the countertransference issues of the individual and the events within the group that illustrated them.

Countertransference is a psychoanalytic concept particularly amenable to a theme-centered format. However, Cohn began to explore the viability of using other themes to bridge the distance between group process and group goals and concerns. By 1962, seven years after the first countertransference workshop, she was applying the technique for other purposes. In one case, employees in a large industrial organization met to discuss problems within the company's administration. As the group

---

[1]While "countertransference" is an accepted phenomenon today in all discussions of psychotherapy—it was at the time of the "countertransference" workshop labeled as a weakness of the therapist that needed to be "analyzed." It was in the open disclosure of countertransference as a fact of any therapist's life that this workshop became a guiding force in the experiential movement.

tackled conflicts and issues within the organization, problems in management relations came vividly to life within the group itself. In another instance, "Training in Emotional Skill" was used as a theme for a group of psychologists (Cohn, 1969). The power of a theme to act as a pivot around which important individual and group learning could turn became increasingly clear.

Although there has been a great deal of experimentation to broaden the applicability of a theme-centered approach to groups, TCI had its origin in education and retains a strong educational thrust. Ruth Cohn had long been intrigued by the contrast of the zestful, alive quality of many therapy groups with the languid, dull quality of so many classrooms. One function of the TCI movement has been to get teachers off the podium and into interaction with their students. As we shall see, TCI offers a more psychologically sophisticated approach to classroom learning than is usually the case, as well as a more structured approach to group psychotherapy and encounter. The main vehicle for teaching the theme-centered interactional method is the Workshop Institute for Living-Learning (WILL), an organization founded by Cohn in 1966. Today WILL trains teachers, therapists, business people and other group leaders in TCI and offers workshops for professionals and the public in major metropolitan areas in the United States, Canada, and Europe.

BASIC CONCEPTS

Living/learning

Ruth Cohn had to grow beyond her own psychoanalytic roots in order to fashion the theme-centered interactional approach and reveal so much of herself in the group. In truth, the method has borrowed more from the humanistic tradition and the existential principles of Western philosophy than from psychoanalytic theory (Rubin, 1978). The *living/learning* concept illustrates this philosophical heritage. The term was coined by Norman Lieberman at the time of the founding of WILL in 1966 (Cohn, 1971). It is meant to emphasize the fact that education, psychotherapy, and encounters can all provide people with a live learning experience. When lively people communicate with one another about issues, tasks, or themes, they are in a living/learning situation. This is in contrast to the "dead" learning that goes on in many classrooms, where a teacher spoonfeeds both facts and opinions to a passive, receptive student. The theme-centered interactional group aims to promote learning as a living experience, so that the therapeutic outcomes derive from an educational-growth model rather than a medical-cure model.

Buttressing the living/learning concept are three humanistic axioms accepted and upheld by theme-centered leaders (Ronall & Wilson, 1980):

- Human beings are discrete psychobiological units within a unified cosmos. In other words, all people are acknowledged to be simultaneously autonomous and interdependent. Group members are encouraged to value their differences from one another together with their needs for mutual feedback and nourishment.

- Life and growth, and decisions that encourage their unfolding deserve respect. Forces that promote this respect are seen as humane; forces that do not promote this respect are seen as inhumane. Within the group there is freedom for exploration, experimentation, interaction, acceptance of emotions, and open communication.
- Free decision-making is bounded by internal and external limits. At the same time, these boundaries are flexible and expandable. Group members are recognized to possess more behavioral freedom than they probably ever use and by the same token to be restricted in their behavior by virtue of reality constraints within the group and in the world at large.

Transference and countertransference

The psychoanalytic concepts of *transference* and *countertransference* are endemic to the TCI group. One definition of transference is "the process in which a person projects a pattern of adaptation which was learned, developed and adopted in a previous life situation to a current life situation; he then displaces the affect from that situation to the present situation" (Demarest & Teicher, 1978). Transference occurs in a group when members displace feelings that belong elsewhere onto another member or the leader. Typically, transference takes place when a participant behaves toward another member or the leader as if that person were someone else in the participant's life. The significant other might be a parent or spouse, a lover or a teacher—usually a figure from the distant past. The chosen group member might be someone whose physical characteristics or group behavior is unconsciously reminiscent of the significant other. Thus, members respond to one another on the basis of both here-and-now behaviors and unconscious needs. They may even distort each other's comments and attempt to push one another into specific roles for transferential reasons.

The interpretation of transference is a crucial aspect of psychoanalytically-oriented groups. At one extreme there are practitioners who merely do individual psychoanalytic therapy within the group setting, by attending to unconscious processes through exploring free associations, dreams, and resistances, focusing on intrapsychic processes, and analyzing transference phenomena. The virtue of the group setting for most psychoanalytically-oriented leaders, however, is that it allows for multiple interactions. We have already seen how the presence of other persons can provide a vehicle for encouragement and support. Likewise, transferences and reactions to them are multiplied in groups because of the potential for so many different kinds of relationships. In analytic group therapy, activating these transferences is critical to the regressive process, in which intense expressions of emotion and an exploration of childhood and the past are used to foster reconstructive personality change (Mullan & Rosenbaum, 1978).

At the other extreme are some psychoanalytically-oriented group therapists who combine group dynamics with group psychoanalysis. The Tavistock group, described in Chapter 2, illustrates this approach. Tavistock groups ignore individual transference that interferes with the development of group relationships and communication, but interpret group themes and the group structure that develops out of all members' interacting needs.

Theme-centered interactional group leaders recognize that participants' reactions to one another are based both on present behaviors and historical needs. As individual members try to impose their own influence on the group, certain tensions among them inevitably emerge. TCI leaders chart a course between two psychological realities. On the one hand, they recognize the way participants can distort group events and incorrectly attribute attitudes and motives to other members. On the other hand, they fall short of exploring the ultimate origins of any given behavior in a person's past history unless it relates directly to the chosen group theme.

In some TCI groups the issue of transference, or its parallel, countertransference, may serve as a theme. Countertransference is a leader's response to the unrealistic attitudes and expectations of group members. Clues to the presence of countertransference include: premature and unreasoning dislike for participants; an inability to empathize with them; an overemotional reaction to their troubles; an excessive liking for them; and defensive, argumentative, indifferent, inattentive, impatient, and angrily sympathetic feelings and behaviors in response to them (Cohen, 1952). These reactions apply to both group leaders (countertransference) and members (transference) and may indicate an opportunity for useful work on the theme of unrealistic attitudes and reactions.

The theme

The use of a *theme* is the primary distinguishing feature of the TCI group. It is the centerpiece around which the group performs. The theme provides a functional structure for the group without a preconceived agenda. The group leader, a delegated committee, or the group as a whole selects a theme as the focus for the group and as a way to encourage cohesiveness. Group members work on the theme or task while also becoming free with each other. Use of the word "theme" is certainly not limited to TCI groups, but the theme-centered interactional method has discovered a way of packaging a theme and resolving tasks while allowing individuals to become more aware and effectual in their thoughts, feelings, and actions.

The selection and wording of an appropriate theme is crucial. Therapy groups are said to have one (implicit) theme only: "I want to feel and function better" (Cohn, 1971). Working groups, on the other hand, might be concerned with many other themes. When a group leader initiates or is invited to a group or workshop without a clear understanding of the members' particular issues and concerns, the theme will reflect an assessment of their needs, such as "Sharing My Expectations With You" or "Finding My Wants and Sharing Them," or any formulation congenial to the group members' verbal styles.

Lieberman (Gordon, 1972) has divided themes into five groups:

- *Exploring* themes help participants develop interpersonal relationships and discover new interests. Participants relate to themes that are personally relevant. An example from a growth group might be "Getting to Know You, Letting You Know Me." A theme for a skills group would be "Discovering What I Do Best."
- *Expediting* themes aim to clarify dilemmas and impasses and provide a readiness for getting to work. An example is "Getting Things Done with You."
- *Experiencing* themes emphasize awareness in the here-and-now and are typically used with school, community, club, or family groups, which are already established. Representative themes include "Being Me and Relating to You" and "Finding Autonomy and Interdependence."
- *Experimenting* themes focus on increasing efficiency, playing with new and different ideas for overcoming persistent problems, and moving forward creatively. "Finding New Ways of Teaching Mathematics," "Finding New Ways of Contacting My Kids," and "Taking Risks with You Here-and-Now" are examples.
- *Evaluating* themes are used to help participants survey their lives and take stock of their accomplishments with an eye to future goals. Sample themes include "Experiencing Myself at Home (in My Community, at School, at Work)" and "Where I've Come From and Where I'm Going."

There is no limit to the number of conceivable themes for a group, but the wording is important. The statement of themes must be personal, positive, engaging, and open-ended. The use of gerunds in the theme reflects growth and movement. A theme is not a topic, such as "Juvenile Delinquency." Nor is it an agenda such as one might have in a business meeting. Positive wording, such as "Bridging My Loneliness," is more effective for therapeutic outcomes than negative wording, such as "Being Lonely." Themes awaken feelings and interests among the group members and help create a living/learning atmosphere by hooking into each participant's personal responses to an issue or task.

Dynamic balancing

Cohn (1970) offers the following description of the TCI group.

The Theme-Centered Interactional Workshop can be graphically seen as a triangle in a globe. The *triangle* presents the workshop setting, which is organized in awareness of dealing with the three basic factors of all interactional groups: 1) The individual: I, 2) the group: We, 3) the theme: It. The *globe* designates the environment in which the workshop takes place: time, location, make-up of the group and the auspices under which the workshop series takes place. The Theme-Centered Interactional Method gives equal importance to the three basic points of the triangle and their relationships, and keeps the "globe" in mind. The richness of this simple structure is evident if one visualizes the complicated structure of the "I" as a psychobiological unit, of the "We" as the interrelatedness of the group's members, and the theme as the infinite combination of concrete and abstract factors [Cohn, 1970, p. 24].

The important aspects of group functioning, described by the points of the triangle in Figure 9-1, are present in all groups. We have seen that groups in general can be distributed on a scale that reflects their relative emphasis on the "I," or individual member, versus the "We," or group dynamics. However, one of the unique qualities of TCI groups is the deliberate enunciation of these constructs and their interaction. It has been mentioned that one of the cardinal axioms or "givens" of TCI groups is the notion that human beings are both autonomous and interdependent. They are part of a larger universe as well as unique and responsible to themselves. The *I* point of the triangle reflects the autonomous dimension, the personal experience of each group member at any point in time. The *We* point refers to the interdependency of people and the observation that the group has a "we-ness" or life of its own.

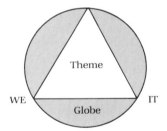

Figure 9-1. Triangle in the globe

Dynamic balancing is the process of trying to integrate the points of the I-We-It triangle within the group environment. It is a core concept in TCI. Groups that stress exclusively the I and We areas tend to be very emotional, affective experiences. Encounter groups are good examples of this emphasis. Concentration on the I and the We leads to concern about which participants feel scared or angry, and the sharing of such feelings is encouraged. In contrast to this "process" orientation, business and classroom groups or meetings with prepared agendas stress the It aspect by being mainly content-oriented. They stay with the It of working out production quotas, teaching curricula, ordering textbooks, or planning activities. Their effectiveness or lack of it is oftentimes dependent on their lack of attention to intrapsychic and interpersonal dynamics. A jealous member of an organization can hang up the group's process indefinitely; one angry teacher (or rebellious student) can thwart a carefully crafted program for an entire school.

According to TCI practitioners the I is most fruitfully explored and developed when group interactions take place around a theme since participants tend to pursue the theme in their own idiosyncratic ways. A TCI approach to teaching a college class on the topic of biological stress illustrates the living intersection of the points of the I-We-It triangle (Langler, 1973). In designing an approach to the subject the author spent some time considering the expectations for the course (It), his own expectations (I), and where the students might be (We). The theme "Experiencing and Understanding Biological Stress" was chosen as a way to integrate research findings on biological stress with students' personal experiences of the topic. The following introduction to the students provides them with an intellectual issue while requiring them to refer to their past experience and moving them to the here-and-now:

> Our topic today is "Experiencing and Understanding Biological Stress." As I think about biological stress, I recognize that when I feel I'm under stress various physical manifestations express themselves as tension, a headache, a general feeling of not well being. It also seems that I can correlate the colds I get with periods of stress. I also think that the death of people I've known in some instances could have been attributed in part to stress. What I would like you to do this morning is to think about what the words biological stress mean to you, moments in your own life when you felt you were under stress and what the physical manifestations might have been, or people you've known whose death you might in some part attribute to stress. It might also be interesting for you to share with the group whether you are feeling under any kind of stress now and what that feeling is. Finally I'd like all of us to ask what might account for these various things, particularly focusing on the nervous and endocrine systems [Langler, 1973, p. 2].[2]

The subsequent group discussion drew on the students' own impressions of biological stress and integrated their observations with the professor's contributions on the physiology of stress.

The group loses its balance and effectiveness when one point of the triangle predominates at the expense of the others. Take the example of a participant who goes into great detail in sharing her marital difficulties while exploring the theme "Handling My Anger Effectively." Other members might respond loudly to her and turn the group into a shouting match, providing a living example of the theme. Likewise, others might join with her and tie her experiences to their own thoughts and feelings. The group might also list viable options to handling anger inappropriately. In all of these cases, there is the possibility of positively converting whatever happens into further growth and learning. Members see how they handle anger elicited by one participant's domination of the group. The leader's

[2]From *Biology Unit on Biological Stress Taught Using the WILL Method,* by G. Langler. Unpublished manuscript, 1973, Oberlin College. Reprinted by the permission of the author.

role is to preserve the group's dynamic balance and illuminate the process for the members. The leader's ultimate goal is the gradual assumption of these functions by the group.

The globe in which the triangle is placed refers to the environment in which the group functions. This includes time, place, and avowed purpose of the group, and the factors that led to its inception. More subtly, the globe also includes the "values and influences" and "political/historical situations" of the environment (Ronall & Wilson, 1980). Thus, a group meeting the day after the assassination of a political leader would be influenced by that dramatic event. More commonly, the feeling that group members bring to the group—unacknowledged relief at getting out of work, curiosity about discovering the "truth" about Jack, anger at being coerced to attend, impatience to meet one's spouse's demand to be home early to babysit— are all part of the various "globes" of the group members. In theory, the globe concept is based on the action that the universe is indivisible and that all factors in the world are interdependent with all others.

Globe factors need to be referred to by the leader so that participants can be encouraged to share relevant resistances and clear the air emotionally to facilitate effective group functioning. When the leader is an outsider to an agency where the group members might be very familiar with one another, this is a globe factor apt to be especially significant (Shaffer & Galinsky, 1974). A sharp leader will research the situation and try to gain an understanding for the rationale of the group prior to entering. In one unfortunate case, Cohn offered a workshop on staff relations at a psychiatric clinic and found on her arrival that staff members who were in opposition to the medical director had not bothered to attend!

BASIC PROCEDURES

There is considerable variability in the techniques that TCI group leaders draw upon, based on life experience, training, and familiarity with the methods of encounter, Gestalt, psychodrama, and other therapies. In addition to employing techniques that overlap with other kinds of groups, there is a structured system of group-leading peculiar to TCI groups. It is sometimes difficult to differentiate between the methods and the guiding philosophy of TCI, since the guidelines of the process are seen as basic humanistic concerns and phenomena rather than as rules for conducting a group (Rubin, 1978).

Postulates

Two postulates flow directly from the underlying humanistic axioms stressing the twin needs for freedom and relationship. The first postulate is *you are your own chairperson*. This postulate stresses the fundamental, though always limited, autonomy of group members with the reminder that they are responsible for their own actions and decisions in the group. Chairpersons make themselves aware of their own needs and goals, as well as their perceptions of the realities of other people and circumstances—and act to satisfy and realize them while considering everyone involved. Leaders encourage participants to take responsibility for themselves in the group. They are urged to give and get what they want to give and get in the session and in their lives. If a participant wishes to remain silent, the leader merely attempts to help the member make that choice a conscious and enlightened one. Chairpersons may need the reminder that they are responsible for their actions and decisions, especially those that influence other people's lives. The postulate of being your own chairperson is not a rule that is arbitrarily forced on the group but an existential truth that is not within the power of any person to deny. Since people so often give up their power and wait for permission from others, this postulate helps encourage active awareness of each person's responsibility for giving and getting in the group.

The leader is governed by the same tenet. In fact, the postulate helps to remove the onus of authoritarianism from the leader and encourages members to expand their possibilities and choices themselves. "Being your own chairperson" is very different from "doing your own thing." Self-centered behavior has a detrimental impact on the other members and on the group process, whereas being one's own chairperson acknowledges an awareness of internal and external factors and of responsibility for actions and their consequences.

The second basic postulate of TCI groups is that *disturbances take precedence.* Within a group's life there are times that individuals may not be fully present and involved because of emotional interference. A disturbance is any thought or feeling that detracts from the individual's full presence in the group. It may be an external event, such as being demoted at work or having an argument with one's spouse, or it may be an interpersonal issue within the group, such as unfinished emotional business between two members. Disturbances may also be positive events, such as a promotion or a love affair. In any case, personal interference takes priority and is identified and handled by the involved individual. Disturbances of a group may sometimes have to take precedence over those of a person. In a task-oriented group, for example, the external situation may demand speedy action beyond an individual reaction. The discussion of personal issues might then have to be postponed.

The leader's role is to encourage group members to handle any disturbances so that they can be resolved sufficiently to allow the individual to attend to the present and the group to proceed. Because the postulate is often stated as a ground rule before the group begins, group members are expected and encouraged to disclose disturbances on their own. A sensitive leader, however, will be aware that a group member is upset or distracted and will assist that person in dealing with the disturbance.

Disturbances are particularly apparent when the group does not have a sensitivity or psychotherapy theme, such as a work group within an educational or organizational setting. For example, Ruth Cohn (1971) was asked to demonstrate TCI procedures in an academic seminar on economics entitled "Stock Market and Money Market." When she noticed that two women appeared to be daydreaming instead of listening to the lecture, she interrupted the seminar and asked the women to share their views about the lecture with each other within the group. The women admitted that they had little interest and no expertise in the subject. This admission stimulated a lively exchange that brought the women back into the flow of the group and the group back to the women.

The purpose of dealing with disturbances as they occur is simply to bring participants back to a point where they can once again involve themselves fully in the group. Often it is sufficient for members merely to share their concerns or upsets with the group. At other times, however, the member may be upset enough to warrant therapeutic work around the issue. Techniques borrowed from other perspectives, such as the Gestalt exercise of making the rounds, are useful tools to resolve disturbances (Shaffer &. Galinsky, 1974). The leader keeps in mind, however, that those with the disturbance will return to the theme as soon as they are able.

Disturbances usually relate to the theme. Imagine, for example, a parent group on the theme "Meeting the Challenge of Change." During one session the coleader is missing and one member is upset because of his absence. As the member talks about her feelings, the issue becomes a bridge to a discussion on meeting a new challenge created by an adolescent going away to school and stepping out of the group member's life. Such is the power of the theme.

Communication ground rules

A number of ground rules of communication have been suggested to aid in the implementation of the two basic postulates in TCI groups (Rubin, 1978). These auxiliary rules are not necessarily presented to the participants at the outset of the group, but are frequently used as reminders or guidelines by the leader to enhance group functioning.

1. *Speak for I.* Participants are encouraged to speak in the first person singular to emphasize that individuals are personally responsible for their opinions or feelings. "We," "everybody," and the indefinite plural "you" tend to be used to avoid potential disagreement or to suggest agreement without verification. By staying with the first person singular, members are urged to check out the views of others and to avoid projecting their own attitudes and feelings onto them.

2. *Make the statement behind the question.* Questions are reserved for information-seeking. Gestalt therapists have pointed out that questions often disguise hidden statements (for example, "Do you really think this program will work?" might disguise the opinion that the program won't work). Asking a question often involves very little disclosure and risk, whereas making a personal statement suggests authentic communication

and helps develop self-awareness. TCI participants are encouraged to at least state their own views prior to asking questions.

3. *Hold off making personal interpretations of others as long as possible.* At their best, interpretations of others' behaviors are a gift of insight. More often they put people on the defensive.

4. *Avoid generalizations.* Generalizations change the direction of the group process. This may or may not be desirable. Group members are urged to stay concrete and specific. Judicious use of generalizations can be helpful in bridging the way from topic to topic.

5. *Acknowledge the subjectivity of your perceptions of others.* Group members are reminded that their opinions of others are only that, opinions, and that no one has a monopoly on the truth. Group members are encouraged to admit that their perceptions are biased and to share what they mean with one another. In this way, scapegoating is avoided and personal attacks are discouraged.

6. *Side conversations are important.* In the same way that disturbances take precedence, so may side conversations between two or more group members. Side conversations are often rich in relevant group material, and they may reflect the inhibitions or hostilities of members. The leader will gently invite members to share side conversations with the group, and the participants then decide whether they wish to do so.

7. *Speak one at a time.* Obviously, when two or more members speak at the same time, the group loses cohesion and gains confusion. Members are encouraged to speak in turn.

8. *When two or more people want to speak at the same time, let them resolve the issue.* The persons wishing to speak are each encouraged to briefly share with one another their concern for instant relief. A decision on the order of speaking is then resolved on the basis of the ensuing discussion. The involved members, not the leader, make this decision.

9. *Be selectively authentic in communicating.* Communications are to be both authentic and selective: authentic in the sense of being genuine and sincere; selective in the sense that not everything on a group member's mind can be nor should be shared. Members are encouraged to be aware of their thoughts and feelings and attentively choose what they say and do. As their own chairpersons, they determine what to share with the group with the assurance of still being authentic without bowing to group pressure.

Selective authenticity is also a value for group leaders. They, perhaps more than anyone, must integrate their own needs for giving and receiving with their leadership function. The leader often has to stay with comments that will enhance the group's interaction. A leader's disclosure of anger toward a group member might or might not be appropriate. With regard to leader authenticity, "To give less than needed is theft; to give more is murder" (Cohn, 1971, p. 270). If the participant could actually benefit in self-understanding beyond feeling deprecation, such sharing might be useful. This might especially be the case when feelings of anger are shared by many other members. In any case, timing and sensitivity predominate. Since disturbances take precedence there might be times when leaders become distracted and need to share that material to preserve their participant-presence in the group. Authenticity around the group theme is necessary; a leader's selectivity may decrease during the course of a group as relationships become stronger. An example would be the leader who shares her own teaching experiences in a group on "Improving My Teaching Skills" or her work with a particular patient in a countertransference group.

Beginning the group

The leader's function at the beginning of the TCI group is more structured than in many other groups, and nowhere is this structure more apparent than in the opening session. In the same way that William Schutz might begin an encounter group with a nonverbal, energizing exercise, Ruth Cohn makes an effort to establish an involved, but nonthreatening mood. She attempts to reduce anxiety, create a constructive group climate, and concurrently orient the participants toward thinking about the theme. Her favorite opening in early days was known as the "triple-silence technique" (Cohn, 1969). There are usually three periods of silence. During the first, group members are invited to sit quietly, with eyes closed. They are instructed to tune into themselves, focus on the "I" of the triangle, and collect any thoughts or feelings about the theme's relevance for them when they first decided to attend the group. After a few minutes of silent reflection, the leader offers a second suggestion, namely to return to the group with open eyes and experience what it is like to be in the group at that moment. This is a here-and-now step, focusing on personal feelings and sensations related to other group participants, the We part of the triangle and the globe. The third silence involves a task, prepared in advance by the leader, that attempts to pull together the I, We, and It dimensions, so that each participant has a mental TCI experience. Participants might be asked to look at the group and select one group member they believe might enhance their work in a workshop with the theme "Learning to Give and Take."

At the end of the triple-silence period, group interaction begins. The leader gently invites the participants to share as many thoughts and feelings generated by the techniques as they wish. The ground rules for the group are informally related at this time. Members are reminded, for instance, that they are their own chairpersons and must take responsibility for getting from and giving to the group what they wish; and that disturbances to the theme take precedence, so that feelings of boredom, anger, and other distractions from complete participation can emerge and be dealt with.

Cohn likes the use of meditative silence in groups to encourage members to concentrate on thoughts about the theme, being in the group, or task instructions. She cautions, however, that the triple-silence technique may be too threatening as an opener with a group in which an inordinate amount of anxiety or defensiveness can be anticipated. In such cases, silence may actually increase the anxiety level. Consequently, groups that have been coerced into attending a workshop, for instance, may benefit from a different kind of opening to reduce members' apprehensiveness. For instance, group leaders might share personal aspects of their background and their rationale for being at a workshop before inviting the group to begin.

Other openings can be specifically tailored to the group's theme. In a weekend workshop on the second-chance family, participants were initially asked to do three things on the theme "Reliving My Early Family Memories" (Challis, 1979):

- Picture a scene that you remember from your childhood while you were sitting at the family table.
- Imagine you are taking a snapshot of that family scene.
- Now, if you want, change the scene in any way you wish.

Participants were given the opportunity to share their scenes and memories in pairs and to form simulated families and work through some unfulfilled childhood needs.

Any opening that stimulates group members to find their own entry into the theme can be employed. Appropriate openings lead to productive group interaction related to the theme. The leader acts to maintain the group's dynamic balance and further the intensity and meaningfulness of the group process. As well as balancing the I-We-It triangle, the leader also models characteristics of self-actualization for participants by responding authentically, taking responsibility for thoughts and feelings, and listening actively to and sometimes reflecting the comments of others. In other words, leaders are really participant/leaders. Cohn notes that there is a tendency in new groups for members to direct most of their initial comments to the leader rather than to one another. She maintains that the TCI leader can respond directly and openly to promote a constructive group atmosphere. Unlike analytic group therapy, in which the leader can choose to ignore participants' comments or questions or deflect them by use of interpretations or indirect responses, the TCI leader typically responds directly and authentically. Thus, Ruth Cohn might answer the person who discloses feelings of anxiety by sharing some feelings of her own. To a person asking for suggestions on how to solve a particular problem, she might ask for more detail about the problem, or she might reveal examples of problem solving from her own life or practice. Members would thus be guided to find their own solutions. In any case, Cohn would emphasize the positive aspects of the member's comments. Negative feelings, she believes, can be integrated better when group members have achieved a sense of trust and caring for each other.

Perhaps the single most important aspect of leadership, particularly during the opening segments of the group, is clearly conceptualizing the time/space human-situation environment that constitutes the globe. Cohn (1971) stresses the importance of pregroup work to get information on who is seeking the workshop, who is resistant, who is paying, and what the room conditions and time constraints are. Once she has as much information as possible, she uses her own fantasy to experiment with themes, imagine the responses of the participants, and think of introductory procedures and their impact on the anxiety, experience, need, and excitement levels of the group. In other words, group leaders think through their own I needs, the hypothetical needs of the group, and what the task of the first session needs to be.

The leader as guardian of the method

Throughout the group's life, the leader acts as the *guardian of the method* and performs a number of balancing acts. One tightrope is between the I-We-It points of the triangle. Encouraging group members to move beyond their personal feelings and attend more closely to the theme can be tricky. People are generally more invested in themselves and their own dynamics than in a work theme.

Challis (1972), for example, notes that all members of new groups are concerned to greater or lesser degrees with four self-oriented issues:

- identity—who am I and what am I to be in this group?
- control/power—fencing with one another for control and influence;
- individual needs/group needs—hoping and waiting for the group to meet my individual needs;
- acceptance/intimacy—will I be liked and how close to others do I have to get?

These emotional issues are legitimate concerns of group members in the group's early stages. The leader's ability to redirect these concerns without sacrificing valuable member input and cutting off the flow of the group is crucial.

The "snapshot technique" is used in the TCI method to help the group make transitions (Shaffer & Galinsky, 1974). At a given moment the leader interrupts the group process and asks members to pinpoint their inner thoughts or feelings. Then the leader asks each member in turn to describe very briefly his or her experience at that moment. Members are asked not to interrupt each other and to proceed swiftly around the circle. In this way, the group conducts a brief illumination of itself to find out where the We is. Participants are encouraged to offer impressions as terse as "I'm scared" or "very peaceful."

The leader acts as guardian of the method and directly encourages living/learning primarily by trying to maintain a dynamic balance between the I-We-It factors. In flowing TCI groups the leader intervenes less and less. However, leaders remain essential for theme-centered interactional groups, even though members may be experienced leaders themselves. If members have to divide their attention and take over the balancing task, the effectiveness of their work may suffer. Sometimes individuals monopolize the group or suffer quietly. Other group members might allow this to happen without comment. At such times, leaders use their judgment to remedy the situation. They might make use of encounter methods, psychodrama, Gestalt techniques, or any other aspects of their training that might help to promote the group experience. A psychoanalytically trained TCI leader, for example, might interpret some group behavior in the light of transference phenomena. However, participants are always their own chairpersons, and remain responsible for their own growth and for solutions to their own disturbances. Members, however, are not asked to be aware of the group process at all times, as leaders are.

In groups that have themes that are strongly interpersonal, such as "Being in This Group My Way" or "Discovering My Relatedness to You," the theme itself merges easily with the We and I dimensions. In groups that have more academic themes, dynamic balancing insures a personalization of the subject to stimulate the group. When the group's theme is not a therapeutic one, the leader needs to exercise authority to guard the theme. The leader of nontherapy groups must perform a balancing act—encouraging a sufficiently personal level of group interaction while avoiding dealing with serious pathology. The leader will choose not to explore the intense personal experiences of disturbed members but will stress facts that support self-esteem and that relate to other group members and the theme. A man's severe communication problems, for example, may be identified as a symptom of his need for recognition and used as a stimulus for exploring his interactional style in the group.

Just as in therapy groups, where the implicit theme is "Getting Well," awareness of self and others in TCI groups is relevant to the theme. In some groups (for example, Tavistock groups), the leader deliberately comes on like a parental authority figure with whom the members struggle. In the TCI group, leaders stay with their own here-and-now experiences in an open, courageous way. While leading a group with the theme of "Growing in Relation to My Authority Figures," Ruth Cohn responded in the following way to one of the group members (Cohn, 1972, p. 871):

Group leader:	Elaine, you look at me as if I had all the answers to your questions. I feel uncomfortable when you look at me this way.
Elaine:	But you are the expert here. You must know how to handle these girls.
Group leader:	I am really less of an expert with high school girls than you. But I wonder whether words like "expert" and "handle" get in your way of being alert to your own convictions and feelings—and maybe the girls?

For Elaine, the leader is the authority; for other group members other authorities—the government, the school system, and parents—have been mentioned earlier in the group. In this excerpt, the leader deals with Elaine's indirect request for personal help and attention with an elaboration of the group theme and with the intent of returning the power back to Elaine. She says "I would like you to remember how it was to be 15 years old. Take your time to remember and now pretend you are 15 years old. Remember a situation where your father, mother, or a teacher told you what you ought to do." Gradually, members pick up on Elaine's memories and share their own accounts of feeling insecure, rejected, exasperated, or dependent in dealing with parental authority. This stimulates a sense of kinship within the group and helps members explore their own personal issues of authority.

APPRAISAL

The theme-centered interactional method has not generated the same amount of attention or sensationalism in North America as other contemporary groups have. One reason for this relative lack of press is that TCI does not actively reject many of the tenets of traditional group therapy. Because of its relative loyalty to traditional psychoanalytic concepts, many traditional group leaders have little trouble accepting TCI, learning about it, and actually incorporating it into their practice. One therapist, for example, amended her more traditional approach with seven uninvolved group members by giving the group a theme on the topic of isolation and setting a ten-session limit (Buchanan, 1969).

As with so many other experiential group approaches, there is a dearth of empirical research evaluating the effectiveness of TCI and the contributions of its respective components. There are no good data, for instance, showing to what extent organizational groups that use the TCI format meet their immediate and long-range objectives. The few studies that do demonstrate an increase in self-esteem or positive behavorial changes as a result of participating in a TCI growth group remain unpublished (see Challis, 1974; Sheehan, 1977).

I have tried to indicate that TCI occupies a comfortable seat within the domain of legitimate group therapy and education. TCI falls solidly within humanistic pioneering. TCI leaders are truly participant/leaders: they try to give to and get from the group and deal with and share their own disturbances while encouraging others to do likewise. The focus is on modeling an authentic and personal experience for the participants rather than on curing pathology. Consequently, the method requires the presence of leaders who do not put their own needs before the needs of the group members. However, leaders must be comfortable drawing upon experiential techniques from other sources, such as Gestalt and encounter. This is because TCI is more a conceptual framework for structuring and viewing a group than an arsenal of techniques.

A central virtue of the TCI approach is its potentially broad range of application. It is one of the relatively few group methods that is equally at home in therapeutic, educational, and organizational contexts. The method can be easily adapted to suit virtually all populations and types of group work. The idea of fitting complex problems and needs into workable themes has a logical appeal. Moreover, there is no limit to the kinds of themes that may be fruitfully explored in a group setting. These include personal themes that reflect concerns about loneliness, alienation, life goals, and sexuality, and themes that emerge naturally within given groups, such as delegating work, clearing communication channels, and teaching subject matter. A skilled TCI group leader has a powerful conceptual tool in hand with which to further personal development as well as professional skills and societal awareness.

SUMMARY

The theme-centered interactional approach to groups was developed by Ruth Cohn, based on her psychoanalytic training and her commitment to humanistic ideals. The Workshop Institute for Living-Learning, operating in both Europe and North America, is the main vehicle for TCI training.

The basic concepts underlying the theme-centered interactional approach include *living/learning transference and countertransference,* the *theme,* and *dynamic balancing.* Living/learning implies that education, psychotherapy, and encounter can share a commitment to a live learning experience. Transference and countertransference are psychoanalytic concepts. TCI groups stress that members' reactions are based on both present behaviors and historical needs. The theme is the most distinguishable feature of the TCI group. A group theme should be personally engaging and live, offering a structure but not an agenda for the group. Dynamic balancing suggests the need to integrate the individual, the group, and the theme on a continuing basis and to do so within the reality of the globe, or outside environment.

The TCI group emphasizes the postulates that *each member is his or her own chairperson* and that *disturbances take precedence.* Several communication ground rules, such as the need for members to speak for themselves, exist as reminders to enhance group functioning. The group leader uses opening techniques to involve members, reduce their feelings of being threatened, and orient them to the theme. The leader does considerable preparation to select an appropriate theme and subsequently acts as *guardian of the method,* intervening when necessary to insure that the triangle in the globe remains in dynamic balance.

The theme-centered interactional group exists somewhere between education and therapy and has a very broad range of application. It is easily adapted to serve educational, therapeutic and organizational populations with diverse needs.

REFERENCES

Buchanan, F. S. Notes on theme-centered time-limited group therapy. In H. M. Ruitenbeek (Ed.), *Group therapy today.* New York: Atherton Press, 1969.

Challis, E. *The dynamics of groups.* Unpublished manuscript. York University, 1972.

Challis, E. *Freedom is a constant struggle: Moving from stereotype to personhood in a male-female consciousness-raising workshop.* Unpublished doctoral dissertation, Union Graduate School, 1974.

Challis, E. Personal communication, Sept. 13, 1979.

Cohen, M. B. Countertransference and anxiety. *Psychiatry,* 1952, *15,* 231–243.

Cohn, R. C. From couch to circle to community: Beginnings of the theme-centered interactional method. In H. M. Ruitenbeek (Ed.), *Group therapy today.* New York: Atherton Press, 1969.

Cohn, R. C. The theme-centered interactional method: Group therapists as educators. *Journal of Group Psychotherapy and Process,* 1970, *2*(2), 19–36.

Cohn, R. C. Living-learning encounters. In G. Gottsegen, M. Gottsegen, & L. Blank (Eds.), *Confrontation: Encounters in self and interpersonal awareness.* New York: Macmillan, 1971.

Cohn, R. C. Style and spirit of the theme-centered interactional method. In C. J. Sager & H. S. Kaplan (Eds.), *Progress in group and family therapy.* New York: Brunner/Mazel, 1972.

Demarest, E. W., & Teicher, A. Transference in group psychotherapy. In H. Mullan & M. Rosenbaum (Eds.), *Group psychotherapy: Theory and practice* (2nd ed.). New York: Free Press, 1978.

Durkin, H. E., & Glatzer, H. T. Transference neurosis in group psychotherapy: The concept and the reality. In L. R. Wolberg & E. K. Schwartz (Eds.), *Group therapy: 1973. An overview.* New York: Intercontinental Medical Book Corp., 1973.

Gordon, M. *Theme-centered interaction.* Baltimore: National Educational Press, 1972.

Langler, G. *Biology unit on biological stress taught using the WILL method.* Unpublished manuscript, Oberlin College, 1973.

Mullan, H., & Rosenbaum, M. Transference and countertransference. In H. Mullan & M. Rosenbaum (Eds.), *Group psychotherapy: Theory and practice* (2nd ed.) New York: Free Press, 1978.

Ronall, R., & Wilson, B. J. Theme-centered interactional groups. In R. Herink (Ed.), *Psychotherapy handbook.* New York: New American Library, 1980.

Rubin, S. S. *An introduction to the theme-centered interactional approach.* Unpublished manuscript, 1978. (Available from WILL, 126 W. 11th St., New York, N.Y. 10011.)

Shaffer, J. B. P., & Galinsky, M. D. *Models of group therapy and sensitivity training.* Englewood Cliffs, N.J.: Prentice-Hall, 1974.

Sheehan, M. A. C. *The effects of theme-centered growth groups on the self-concept, self-esteem and interpersonal openness of adults.* Unpublished doctoral dissertation, Columbia University Teacher's College, 1977.

10

Transactional Analysis

Eric Berne, a San Francisco-based psychiatrist who founded transactional analysis (TA), once had as a patient a successful lawyer. The lawyer related a story about a hired hand at a ranch who received help in unsaddling his horse from a vacationing 8-year-old boy in a cowboy suit. "Thanks, cowpoke," said the hired hand.

"I'm not really a cowpoke, I'm just a little boy," replied the youngster.

Then the patient confessed to Berne "That's just the way I feel. I'm not really a lawyer. I'm just a little boy" (Dusay & Steiner, 1972, p. 77).

Stimulated by this dynamic man's perception of himself as a little boy, Berne began to view the behavior and feelings of people as being somehow derived from three distinct intrapsychic processes that he called ego states and labeled Child, Adult, and Parent. These ego states are the basic concepts behind a structural analysis of personality and are the building blocks of transactional analysis. TA has been popularized by books such as *Games People Play* (Berne, 1964), *I'm OK, You're OK* (Harris, 1969), and *Born to Win* (James & Jongeward, 1971). However, Berne's basic theories of personality and psychotherapy had actually been developed in publications during the 1950s. He was apparently embarrassed by the unexpected commercial success of *Games People Play*, a book intended for use by professionals already interested in TA, fearing that his professional credibility might be compromised by its best-seller status (Holland, 1973).

HISTORY AND DEVELOPMENT

Trained as a Freudian psychiatrist, Berne broke with the psychoanalytic movement in 1956, though he remained cordial to it throughout his career. At one point he suggested that if TA were an apple, then psychoanalysis might well be the core (Holland, 1973). He was particularly indebted to his own analyst, Paul Federn. Berne was also influenced by less orthodox psychoanalysis. There are theoretical links between transactional analysis and W. R. D. Fairbairn's object-relations theory, and between Berne's concept of life scripts and Alfred Adler's notion of the "style of life."

One of Berne's first professional experiences was in an army hospital during World War II. He became interested in group therapy after the following incident took place in the hospital. The soldiers, forbidden from keeping liquor on the premises, were in the habit of secreting alternative toxic substances, such as shaving lotion, around their barracks. Frustrated with the ineffectiveness of periodic room searches, Berne called a ward meeting of patients to discuss the medical disadvantages of drinking shaving lotion. Surprisingly, the patients' response to the meeting was very enthusiastic, and he scheduled daily group discussions with them thereafter (Berne, 1966). Today TA is generally practiced in a group format, where its advantages are most apparent.

During the 1950s Berne developed the concepts that form the basis for current TA groups. The identification of Parent, Child, and Adult ego states appeared in a 1957 *American Journal of Psychotherapy* article. His first book on TA appeared in 1961. He wrote a total of eight books and many articles before his death from a heart attack in 1970. In addition to being an original thinker, prolific writer, and revered therapist, he trained and inspired a host of other therapists. His ideas were distilled and rehashed in group "seminars" regularly scheduled in the San Francisco area that included a growing body of professional disciples. The original seminars consisted of seven people who met to discuss and supervise cases and talk about TA theory and method. From this nucleus arose the International Transactional Analysis Association in 1964. Today this professional organization offers elaborate training, supervision, and certification in TA practice, and publishes the *Transactional Analysis Journal*.

Transactional analysis developed partly in response to Berne's exasperation with orthodox psychoanalysis, which he criticized for its slow pace and complexity. The language of TA, on the other hand, is down to earth, even earthy. Berne loved to invent words and phrases, and some of his favorite terms, like "racket" and "game," have become part of the universal psychotherapy lexicon. Within his active, streamlined approach to working with groups, however, lies a fairly sophisticated theory. Although the basic work was complete several years prior to Berne's death, others have subsequently worked to embellish the original theories and to expand the application of TA to schools, organizations, and mental-health systems.

BASIC CONCEPTS

There is a historical progression of concepts in transactional analysis that provides a systematic way to learn about and understand Berne's theories. The basic framework is known as *structural analysis*. Structural analysis focuses on the intrapsychic processes or the make-up of the individual personality. Once this aspect was formally concretized, Berne began to look at interactions among people, particularly among clients in therapy groups. His description of the ways people relate to each other became known as *transactional analysis*. After examining transactions for some time, Berne became aware of certain repetitive features to particular transactions that were designed to make participants feel sad, guilty, angry, or victorious. He called these features "games" and developed *game analysis*. Finally, Berne found that it was often difficult for people to give up destructive games because of an apparent investment in a particular life goal. In other words, group members often seemed to repeat games as if compulsively acting out parts of an ongoing drama. Berne's work in this area culminated in *script analysis*.

Ego states (structural analysis)

Structural analysis is the foundation for transactional, game, and script analysis, not only historically, but also theoretically and conceptually. With his roots in classical psychoanalysis, Berne quite naturally focused on intrapsychic processes before exploring relationships between people, and though he dispensed with some of the more awesome-sounding Freudian labels, his way of conceptualizing personality retains a strong psychoanalytic flavor. Personality consists of three discrete, functional structures known as *ego states*. Each ego state represents a particular pattern of thinking, feeling, and behaving and is based on one of Berne's three pragmatic absolutes, illustrated in Figure 10-1 (Berne, 1961):

- Every grown-up individual was once a child. To represent this child in each of us, there is a Child[1] ego state.
- Every human being with sufficient brain-functioning tissue is potentially capable of adequately testing reality. This ability to organize data and reach rational decisions is within the domain of the Adult ego state.
- Every individual who survives into adult life has had either functioning parents or someone *in loco parentis*. The parenting agent lives on within each personality as the Parent ego state.

In TA theory, the personality naturally differentiates these three ego states, which are capable of functioning harmoniously together. This is in contradiction to psychoanalytic theories, which maintain that the frag-

---

[1]Capitalizing Child, Adult, or Parent indicates an ego state in TA terminology, not a real child, adult, or parent.

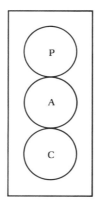

Figure 10-1. Parent, Adult, and Child ego states

mentation of the personality into components is the result of trauma and indicates pathology. There is certainly a superficial similarity between the Parent, Adult, and Child ego states and the Freudian constructs of super-ego, ego, and id. However, Berne noted significant differences between them as well and viewed the ego states as psychological, historical, and behavioral realities (Berne, 1966).

The ego states are somewhat more complex than the pragmatic absolutes might suggest. The Parent reflects the individual's real parents or parenting agents. It is a historical record of the important things that parent figures did to or around a person. Many of the beliefs, prejudices, values, and attitudes that we represent as our own were actually taken in long ago from external sources. Berne insisted this process was automatic, whereas others claim children play an active role in screening and processing what they perceive in the world. The Adult represents objectivity, reason, organization, reliability, and intelligence. It functions in somewhat the same manner as a computer, assessing reality, testing probabilities, and making rational decisions. The Adult deals with the facts. The most primitive ego state, the Child, exists as a relic of the person's childhood, consisting of the feelings, behaviors, and thoughts the person had as a child.

The ego states can be further broken down both structurally and functionally in second-order analyses. A structural analysis refers to the content of an ego state, whereas a functional analysis refers to the process of an ego state, that is, how an ego state is used. Structural and functional divisions of the three ego states are illustrated in Figure 10-2. Structurally, the Child ego state consists of a C_1 (Child in the Child), the uncensored feeling state of the young infant; A_1 (Adult in the Child), the intuitive, creative, curious infant that Berne called the "Little Professor," who signals the beginnings of primitive thinking; and P_1 (Parent in the Child), comprising the infant's early nonverbal perception and incorporation of the parents' behaviors and feelings.

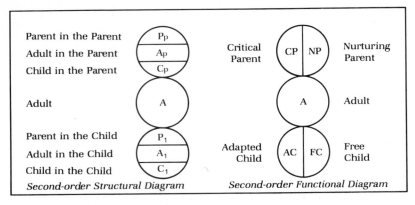

Figure 10–2. Structural and functional divisions of the three ego
states

Functionally, the Child operates as a Free or Natural Child and as an
Adapted Child. The Free Child is spontaneous, creative, playful, autonomous, and self-indulgent. As long as its natural impulses are processed
through the Adult, the Free Child behaves within realistic limits. The
Adapted Child is restrained, not by Adult processes, but by the influence of
parental rules and prohibitions. The Compliant aspect of the Adapted
Child tries to placate and please others. The feelings associated with it are
fear, guilt and shame. The Compliant Child's balancing aspect, the Rebellious Child, feels anger and resentment and acts to contradict the Parent.
In both aspects, the Adapted Child bases all actions and feelings in
response to the Parent.

The Parent can likewise be dissected structurally and functionally.
Structurally, the Parent is divided into the Parent, Adult, and Child of the
real parents. Functionally, the Parent is divided into a Nurturing Parent,
which is protective, caring, supportive, worried, and reassuring, and a
Critical or Controlling Parent. The Critical Parent provides both constructive and destructive criticism, though this part of the Parent ego state is
typically considered to be the bad parent, who is punitive, demanding, and
opinionated. The Critical Parent is reflected in a person's arbitrary and
nonrational attitudes and prohibitions.

One of the goals of the TA group is to enable people to develop ready
access to all ego states and be able to make choices that are consistent with
what people need and want based on a perception of what is available and
safe. Each ego state has inherent advantages and disadvantages. The Child
can be joyful and energetic, but also experience sadness and fear; the Adult
can think through complex ideas, but also make poor use of information;
the Parent stores a wealth of knowledge and experience with which to
nurture and support, but can also misguide and send harmful messages to
the Child.

One ego state is usually dominant in a person's behavior, and the diagnosis of ego states is often a prominent activity in TA groups. It is possible for a person to operate in more than one ego state at a time, such as the inhibited man who ventures to have fun at a party with his enthusiastic Child while his Parent reminds him how he is embarrassing himself. The following self-statement incorporates all of one person's ego states (Woollams & Brown, 1979):

> A college student discussing her roommate says: "She's a foolish, irresponsible, silly girl (Critical Parent), who needs me to smooth the way for her, so I go out of my way to help her (Nurturant Parent). Sometimes I wonder if that's a good idea (Adult), but I want to be a helpful person like mother taught me to be (Adapted Child) even though I feel like telling her to leave me alone (Free Child)" [p. 23].

Transactions

A *transaction* is an exchange of strokes between two people, made up of a stimulus and a response between two ego states. *Strokes* are units of recognition, somewhat akin to social reinforcers. They are the most basic units in transactional theory and, according to Berne, have a definite survival value. They are manifested by physical stroking or touching, or by verbal or nonverbal signs of recognition. The infant receives both nonverbal strokes, such as cuddling, rocking, nursing, and holding, and verbal strokes such as singing, cooing, and speaking. In time, strokes become less physical and more verbal and psychological and can be communicated by facial expression, gesture, and body language alone. They can be unconditional or conditional, positive or negative. Positive strokes, sometimes referred to as Warm Fuzzies, make the recipient feel warm, important, and worthy. Negative strokes, or Cold Pricklies, though creating feelings of worthlessness and discomfort, are, according to Berne (1977), still better than no strokes at all.

Most of us would like to receive positive, unconditional strokes for just being. "I love you just as you are" is the epitome of this kind of stroke. More common are conditional strokes, which imply that people are desirable or to be loved as long as they are cute or smart or hang around with the right kind of people. The Adapted Child eventually works to enhance attributes that are being stroked by important parenting figures. Many group participants are their own worst enemies in the sense that they give themselves negative self-strokes. The Critical Parent demands perfection and they repeatedly tell themselves "You sure are stupid" or "You should have done better!" Most of us live in a chronic state of stroke deficit and are uncomfortable with giving and receiving positive strokes (Steiner, 1971a). When someone offers a compliment such as "You're very smart," the Critical Parent silently replies "Yes, but I'm not very attractive." TA offers techniques to discourage such self-persecution and release the Free Child from the clutches of the Critical Parent. TA groups also encourage participants to develop and change their stroking patterns.

In TA groups, behavior is best understood by looking at transactions between the participants. Berne considered group dynamics important considerations in treatment. He did not endorse the Freudian concept that the group member psychologically identifies with the leader, nor the notion that the group recreates a family constellation for each participant, since the group process appeared more complex than either theory would permit (Dusay & Steiner, 1972). He viewed group process as the transactions that occur across any boundary of the group structure. For Berne, the transactions that take place between the leader and the group members and, less significantly, among the members themselves, determine the cohesion of the group. A rough index of group cohesion is the attendance rate (Berne, 1955).

There are three kinds of transactions: complementary, crossed, and ulterior. In a complementary transaction, the response comes from the ego state of the person at whom the stimulus was directed and is returned to the same ego state of the person who initiated the transaction. For example, Agnes asks Bernie "What time is it?" (Adult to Adult), and Bernie replies "It's noon" (Adult to Adult). Complementary transactions are clear and understandable even when the transaction is Parent to Child and Child to Parent. Each person feels understood and connected to the other.

In a crossed transaction (Figure 10-3), the response comes from a different ego state than the one to which the stimulus was directed. Agnes asks Bernie "What time is it?" (Adult to Adult) and Bernie says "Why don't you get your own watch?!" (Parent to Child). In the crossed transaction, there are misunderstandings and a tendency for arguments, hurt, and anger. However, this type of transaction is still clear and there are no doubts about the level of misunderstanding.

The ulterior transaction is not crossed, but it contains a hidden message intended to influence other people without their awareness. The transaction occurs at two levels simultaneously, the social level and the psychological level. On the social level the transaction is superficially

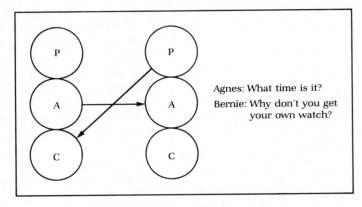

Figure 10–3. Crossed transaction

plausible; on the psychological level there is a concealed motive. The man who uses his Adult to invite a woman to "come over for a drink" may be sending a different message from his Child to her Child. A student who habitually turns in sloppy assignments may be inviting a Parent criticism to his Child.

Transactions are used to structure time and to receive strokes. Group members are always free to respond from any ego state depending upon the kind of stroke they wish to give or receive. People who feel relatively good about themselves are freer in their options and not as likely to be hooked by a particular state of another person. This is sometimes difficult. For example, a Critical Parent statement such as "Stop what you're doing, you're doing it all wrong!" or "You never do anything right!" can easily hook Adapted Child feelings. The following replies to that statement have been described by Woollams and Brown (1979, p. 74) as "Parent shrinkers" in that they avoid an Adapted Child response and invite initiators out of their Critical Parent:

- *Adult with Little Professor:* I acknowledge your intention to invite me into some ill-chosen response, but considering the relative lack of merit in your rather vociferous remark, I respectfully decline.
- *Adult:* Yes, you may be right about that. What do you suggest that I do?
- *Free Child:* Have you heard the one about . . .
- *Nurturing Parent:* Oh, dear, are you feeling well? You look *so* tired.

Past transactions are critical in accounting for present ego-state development. *Injunctions* are messages from the Child ego state of the parents, usually made without the awareness of the Adult, based on the parents' own circumstances in life. Injunctions generally begin with the word "Don't," such as "Don't be close" or "Don't be a child." The most devastating injunction is "Don't be," which is an invitation to suicide (Goulding, 1972). If the child obeys the injunction, at some point he makes the decision "If things get too bad, I'll kill myself" or "I'll get you even if it kills me" or something equally destructive. Although Berne believed that an injunction is "inserted in the child like an electrode" (Berne, 1972, p. 116), other TA practitioners maintain that the child has some power to accept or reject messages and may actually misinterpret or invent some parental messages (Goulding & Goulding, 1979).

According to TA theory, emotional problems are learned behaviors based on childhood decisions and represent compromises between satisfying the child's own needs and getting along with (getting strokes from) parent figures (Woollams & Brown, 1979). By the age of 4 or 5, children have learned how best to manipulate the environment and control their own behavior in order to receive the maximum number of strokes. At this point, children make their principal decision, based on their experience of the world, of what they can expect from life and how they had best relate to the world. The kind of decision the child makes depends on the combination of positive and negative strokes received and on the consistency of parental messages. By the time children reach school age, they have been exposed to almost every kind of parental attitude and further messages merely reinforce what has previously been inscribed. Most important, this decision, made by the child at a very early age, becomes fixed as a style of relating to others through adulthood.

Berne (1966) described four basic existential positions that individuals may adopt and defend throughout their lives as a result of the early decision: I'm OK, You're OK; I'm OK, You're not OK; I'm not OK, You're OK; and I'm not OK, You're not OK. Those who select the I'm OK, You're OK position have decided they are worthwhile and important, that others are basically good, and that all of life's opportunities are available to them. Those who select the I'm OK, You're not OK position are likely to experience others as dangerous or untrustworthy and life as a "survival of the fittest." In its extreme form, this position represents the paranoid personality. The I'm not OK, You're OK position represents the world view of the depressive, and the I'm not OK, You're not OK decision, at its extreme, reflects the schizophrenic's existential position.

When children adopt a position, they also adopt a series of defenses for their world view. Influences that appear to threaten the world view are avoided. Berne (1966) cites the following as an example of pathological development. Rita used to run to greet her father every night when he came home from work. However, she became bewildered as Father would at times be warm and nurturing, whereas at other times he would talk roughly to her and push her away. As the unpleasant occasions became more frequent, she refrained from greeting him at all. Consequently, when he arrived in a good humor, he would reprove her for neglecting him, but if she approached him when he was in a bad mood, he would reject her. When Rita was about 4, Father and Mother had a particularly terrible argument. Rita burst into tears, fearful and bewildered. At that moment, she decided that "Men are beasts." The position taken was one of I'm OK, You (men) are not OK. As an adult, Rita found herself involved with a series of abusive men. Nonabusive men bored her because they threatened her existential position and her decision about men. It had become necessary, in order to protect the psychological investment she had in her decision, to prove that even benevolent-looking men were, underneath the superficial pleasantries, beastly.

The social interactions of the adult are related to the original decision and existential position adopted as a child. The decision will continue to influence how the person thinks, feels, and behaves throughout life. A primary goal of TA is to move group members toward an I'm OK, You're OK life position. People who view themselves and others as OK are also referred to as Winners (James & Jongeward, 1971). Winners seek authenticity in themselves and in relationships, whereas losers feel okay only if something is changed in their lives. They spend their energy lamenting the past and pinning their hopes on the future.

Games

Sets of transactions such as rituals, activities, and pastimes are task-oriented or stylized interactions that are used to structure time and receive strokes. They consist of honest, nonmanipulative transactions. *Games*, however, are fundamentally dishonest. The game is a series of ulterior transactions leading to a particular, usually unpleasant, outcome known as the payoff, which provides both primary and secondary gains for each player. Berne used his Little Professor to come up with many colorful names for psychological games, including Alcoholic, Cops and Robbers, Uproar, Rapo, Wooden Leg, and Now I've Got You, You Son of a Bitch.

In the game "Why Don't You? Yes, But . . .," often played in groups, the principal player consistently asks for suggestions or advice and just as consistently rejects any that are offered. The other group members assume that the initiator of this game is relating from the Adult ego state—that he or she is attempting to solve a real problem in a concrete manner—so they offer suggestions from their Adults. However, the initiator is actually in the Child and believes that the suggestions are from the respondents' Parents. The payoff is the good feeling the initiator gets for rejecting the group's suggestions, proving that Father doesn't know best. There is a payoff for the group as well, since the initiator's con only works when the members are receptive or easily hooked. This payoff may be a feeling of frustration and irritation that can lead to a justified venting of anger, despair, or guilt at a later time. The primary gain of any game is to receive strokes and to maintain and defend an original decision about the world and the people in it. The game is a rich source of strokes and reinforces life positions—that children are no good or are ungrateful and that parents are no good or are bullying.

People are usually playing a game when they engage in a series of transactions and at least one player feels badly or is injured in some way. The bad feelings after a game are called *racket* feelings. They generally involve the repetition of some unfinished psychological business. The racket feelings that group participants smugly walk away with are anger or depression. These feelings were probably ways of getting strokes from family members and helped avoid genuine feelings that were discounted[2] or not stroked. Racket feelings are adaptive substitutes for Free-Child feelings or those the Parent deems not OK. Consider a group session in which one member fails to complete a task he agreed to do. Different participants may react with unique, predictable racket feelings: one is furious at the neglectful member; one is confused about what happens next; one feels very let down; one feels protective of the offender; one feels

---

[2]A discount refers to a lack of attention or negative attention that carries a not-OK message.

smugly superior; and one passively defers to the others. A Free-Child response would allow a better resolution of the problem: the expression of annoyance together with adult, mutual problem-solving behavior.

Scripts

Beyond transactions lies the master plan organizing the individual's life, known as the script. The study of scripts was the final step in Berne's development of TA theory (Berne, 1972), and has been elaborated on by Steiner (1974) and Crossman (1966). A script is a personal life plan shaped by a series of decisions made early in life as a strategy for survival. When parents communicate a sense of worth to a child, he or she adopts a constructive life script, invested with feelings of OK-ness and trust in oneself and the future. More destructive life scripts derive from decisions made to deal with negative and conditional messages. The child's existential position thus carries with it its own particular script-ending.

According to Berne, important life decisions are made in the first two or three years of life and most of the remaining scripts are acquired before the age of 6. The main determinants of individuals' scripts are the Child ego states of their parents as communicated through injunctions (Steiner, 1974). Although many injunctions are overtly specified, such as "Don't cry in public" or "Don't hit smaller children," others are inferred, so that a child who is scolded for displaying emotions may receive the message "Don't feel." Commonly communicated themes such as "You'll never amount to anything," "Don't ever trust anyone," or "You're a nuisance!" are translated into decisions and lifelong scripts such as "I'll never trust anyone," "I've got to be strong," and so on. The total process, in other words, begins with injunctions implanted by strokes, and leads to decisions and scripts that support the injunctions. The chosen life script, of course, has to be consistent with one's existential life position.

A secondary source of scripts are messages from the Parent ego states of parent figures. These messages, called "counterinjunctions" or "drivers," also restrict the child's personal growth and development. Kahler (1975) has identified the most common drivers as: Be Perfect, Be Strong, Hurry Up, Try Hard, and Please Me. They are socially acceptable statements but ultimately destructive because they imply that children are OK only if they follow the directive. Since no one can be perfect or totally strong, fast, successful, or pleasing, drivers are fuel for fleshing out the details of losing life scripts.

According to Berne, a person's script is clearly advertised in body movements, gestures, postures, mannerisms, and symptoms. He believed that fantasies and fairy tales, remembered from childhood, are instrumental in script development. Little Red Riding Hood, for instance, reflects the message "Be a good, helpful girl," with the implication that she will eventually be rewarded for her effort. Women who live this fairy tale tend to gradually wither away while being cute and indulged, and victimized by others. Other scripts are predictable from a person's culture of origin.

Women have been scripted as inferior, supportive characters to the accomplishments of men in our culture for many generations (James, 1973). The following script matrix shows how Miss America can be scripted, with father supplying the Child script message and mother providing the Adult information (Steiner, 1974):

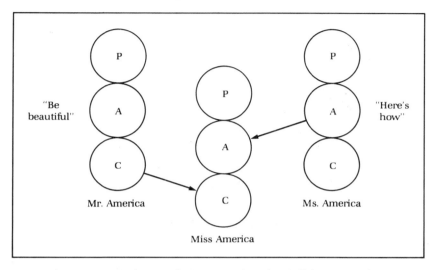

Figure 10–4. Script matrix: How to raise a beautiful woman. *(From Scripts People Live: Transactional Analysis of Life Scripts, by C. Steiner. Copyright 1974 by Grove Press. Reprinted by permission.)*

Of course, not all parental influences on children are negative. "Permissions" and "allowers" are positive, growth-enhancing messages that encourage self-esteem and freedom of choice. There is some disagreement among practitioners whether the long-range goal of TA is to produce a script-free individual or eliminate counterproductive scripts and replace them with scripts that reflect I'm-OK feelings. In any case, the TA group is a place where scripts are regularly confronted and not allowed to proceed unchallenged.

BASIC PROCEDURES

Practitioners of transactional analysis use specific procedures to help participants deal with ego states, transactions, games, and life scripts. Structural analysis is used to help group members conceptualize and segregate ego states and establish the predominance of Adult reality-testing functions free of the contaminations of Child and Parent influences (Berne, 1961). Transactions between group members are examined to help individuals eliminate their tendencies to manipulate others and respond insightfully to the manipulations of others. When games become apparent, they are commented upon and analyzed to help group members experience a broader range of choices and attain game-free relationships. Finally, group members are encouraged to examine their scripts and redecide their original existential positions in order to free themselves from the compulsions of actualizing pathological life plans.

Contracts

Eric Berne believed in a straightforward, economical form of therapy. Statements that might be appropriate in other experiential groups, such as "What does the group think or feel about that?" are not considered fruitful in transactional analysis (Dusay & Steiner, 1972). Rather, the group sessions revolve around a series of individualized contracts. TA contracts outline the goals and conditions of treatment and are used as an index of individual progress or improvement. The goals are, of course, chosen by the participant and not by the group leader. The contract is a description of behavior as opposed to vague feeling states. In other words, a group member would not contract to be happier and more satisfied with life, but might contract to have fewer arguments with family members or to work more responsible hours at a job. Contracts are sufficiently concrete to answer the question "How will *you* know and how will *we* know when you get what you are coming to the group for?" (Dusay & Steiner, 1972, p. 94). Thus, it is often helpful to elicit behavioral examples to arrive at a good contract. The member might be asked to bring a problem into the here-and-now and play the roles of each person in the scene to illustrate the problem.

The contract is an opportunity for the Adult and the Child ego states to reveal what they want or need. It is generally assumed that the Parent is regularly expressing its demands. Most important, the contract engages the Adults of the participants in a collaborative, cognitive procedure. The use of contracts between the group leader and the participants assumes mutual consent and the democratic flavor of two equals negotiating with each other. This is quite different from the psychoanalytic point of view and, in some ways, Berne's decision to call group leaders "therapists" and group members "patients" is a misleading legacy from the medical model under which he was trained.

Group leaders do not accept contracts they are not comfortable with or do not think are realistic. To become a millionaire is probably an unrealistic therapy goal; to have a steady job or graduate from a university is reasonable. To become Don Juan is grandiose; to get and maintain an erection at least once a week is workable. The nature of the contract will influence the direction of the therapy. Many college students come to groups with nonspecific complaints regarding feelings of alienation, lack of meaning, or boredom. For them, a TA group leader might work on time structuring, helping the person give up rituals, pastimes, and games that have little stroke value, and substitute more meaningful endeavors.

Contracts can change and be added as the group progresses. Although some contracts reach far into the future, others represent short-term goals, including changes to be fulfilled in a single session. A Hurry-Up person, for example, might initiate the process of slowing down by agreeing to take a 15-minute break each day. Some contracts take precedence because of their seriousness. The Gouldings (Goulding & Goulding, 1979) believe that potentially suicidal or homicidal people need to make no-suicide and no-homicide contracts before any other therapeutic business takes place and suggest several guidelines for instituting them successfully.

Personal work in TA groups does not typically begin until a member has contracted to work. TA group leaders are not particularly invested in the group process. On the other hand, the content of a contract must never be allowed to take precedence over relationship issues between the leader and a member or among members. Here-and-now issues in the life of the group come first, whether they be major life events such as divorces and job changes, or friction between members.

Protection, permission, and potency

The first rule of TA therapy has been described as "The therapist should remain in an OK position both during and after therapy" (Woollams & Brown, 1979, p. 234). This means that group leaders take care of their own psychological needs and do not discount any of their own ego states even if the group is not going well. By feeling OK about themselves, they model OK feelings in the group. Skilled group leaders use all their own ego states when conducting the group. The Parent protects and supports; the Adult analyzes and gives information; the Child offers creativity and enthusiasm, and models how to feel and have fun. Perhaps really effective therapists can be distinguished from mediocre ones by the intuitive power of their Little Professors to jump at quick and accurate insights. While maintaining access to all ego states, group leaders use their Adult to continually process what is occurring in the group. Skillful leaders do not become rescuers. A Rescuer is someone who does more than 50% of the other person's work in therapy (Steiner, 1974). By supporting equality and believing that people are not helpless, one can find ways for group members to use their own power rather than having them remain Victims dependent upon the leader's power. As a general rule, it is easier to hook someone else's Adult by being in one's own Adult.

Protection, permission, and potency are three elements that a group leader provides in a TA group. Protection implies that the leader is professionally qualified to lead the group and agree to goals stipulated by members' contracts. Protection also involves insulating the group members from physical harm and being reasonably available to them. When members are particularly upset or distraught, leaders may temporarily use their Parent to nurture and protect the client's scared or confused Child. This support is temporarily offered to bring a member through a crisis or permit experimentation with difficult new behaviors and experiences. Stroking a member, physically or verbally, may be helpful as long as it facilitates meeting a contract or does not play into a negative script.

Excessive use of a leader's Parent invites an Adapted Child response from the group and no real growth in Adult functioning.

Permissions are part of any group leader's behavior repertoire and involve granting members positive allowance to change and grow to counteract the negative injunctions learned in childhood. By structuring the group, giving didactic explanations, and suggesting experiments, the leader is implicitly permitting change. The TA therapist gives clients permission to use their ego states—to think straight as an Adult, to experience the freedom of the Natural Child and, less frequently, to draw on the resources of the Critical and Nurturant Parents. The leader's comments and interventions are designed to use the group constructively, and to have clients experience their ego states, stop playing games, and overcome script injunctions.

Potency refers to the leader's ability to use timely, curative interventions. According to Dusay and Steiner (1972), there are four curative factors in any group: the natural drive that humans have toward health and growth; the recognition of group members as human beings and the attainment of strokes; the corrective emotional experiences that come from confrontations and encounters with other group members; and the specific behavior of the leader. The leader's interventions vary from group to group. Berne (1966) described four types of operations appropriate to TA groups: decontamination, recathexis, clarification, and reorientation. Decontamination refers to clarifying ego states and the structure of the individual personality. Recathexis has to do with encouraging the experience of different ego states. Clarification refers to the members' attainment of Adult control to prevent them from inadvertently sliding into Parent or Child. Reorientation, the last step, consists of changing the life script and experiencing life differently, viewing oneself and others as basically OK.

Analysis of ego states, transactions, and games

To effect the processes of decontamination and recathexis, the group leader and the members become skilled at diagnosing ego states. The identification of ego states is accomplished in at least four ways: (1) members' behavior and their use of words, voice quality, gestures, facial expressions, and attitudes reveal the ego state predominating at any time; (2) ego states are also evident by observing transactions between people; (3) a person's past history and family relationships reveal a great deal about ego-state functioning; and (4) group members can learn to identify their own ego states, particularly after a significant experience such as a group encounter.

Intuitive therapists are very adept at spotting hidden Child, Adult, or Parent messages. Some group leaders use structured techniques to diagnose ego states. Empty-chair techniques, borrowed from Gestalt therapy, are employed by having the person "place" each ego state in a different chair and encouraging an interaction among them. In another technique, known as "script rehearsal" (Dusay, 1970), two or more group members enact a scene that represents a problem for at least one of them. Meanwhile, other group members stand behind the main participants and act as Parent ego states, others sit on the floor and respond as Child ego states, while someone else observes and takes notes from the Adult state.

The first step for the group leader is to help participants distinguish between Child and Adult mode behavior. Adult boundaries are first strengthened by "decontaminating" the Adult from the Child and the Parent. The person needs to think clearly, and the wishes and fantasies of the Child or the intrusiveness of the Parent can contaminate straight thinking, as in the hallucinations of the severely disturbed schizophrenic. The goal of understanding and strengthening Adult functioning is not to be confused with gaining insight into intrapsychic and group dynamics. Structural analysis is used to help group members maintain control of intrapsychic processes in stressful situations. Berne strongly believed that people have to live successfully in the world first and concern themselves with insight later on.

Second, the Natural Child and the Little Professor are freed from the overbearing influence of the Adapted Child (James, 1977). Only then are members introduced to their Parent ego states. According to Berne, differentiation between Child and Adult is less threatening for people than dealing with the Parent. In the first place, the Child is most vulnerable to the Parent, so that by introducing the Parent last, the Child is able to express itself with fewer Parental restrictions. Second, it is important to wait until the Child is differentiated before focusing on the Parent because the Child can learn from experience. Theoretically, the Adult is strengthened as the Child grows. Once both Child and Parent are differentiated, the Adult can observe the conflict between them and can ensure that the expression of each is relegated to appropriate times and places.

One of the benefits of structural analysis is that group members learn about the relative strength of their ego states and may then wish to assume a contract to balance them. For example, a grim, self-critical man may want to expand the functioning of his Natural Child and start having some fun. This situation is common among men in our society, since they tend to have strong Adults and need to develop their Nurturant Parent and accept the feelings of their Natural Child. Women, on the other hand, have tended to overdevelop their Nurturant Parent while discounting their Adult power and rationality. People who have been severely discounted in one or more of their ego states, such as the schizophrenic patient, may benefit from "reparenting," a TA-oriented treatment originated by Jacqui Schiff (1975).

Diagramming ego states is a useful conceptual device. Many group leaders make use of a blackboard and chalk to draw ego states and transactions to crystallize learnings. Berne believed that structural analysis had to take place prior to instituting work on a transactional level or dealing with games or scripts. Current thinking is not consistent with this position. Some TA therapists use ego-state analyses to add conceptual understanding to therapy work that has already taken place but rarely ask the standard TA question "What ego state are you in?" Others pay minimal attention to ego-state diagnosis and go directly to redecision work (Goulding & Goulding, 1979).

The group provides an ideal environment for analyzing transactions and games since interactions between participants provide a wealth of clinical material. The group operates in the here-and-now, whereas transactions between group members provide abundant evidence of the past manifesting itself in the present. Any statement is grist for the group leader's mill, since it is a sample of the member's transactional behavior. For example, group members may apologize for being late for their first group meeting (Berne, 1966). The leader may interpret this as the beginning of the "Schlemiel" game, in which the player seeks to gain absolution for being destructive. Instead of responding to a member's Child, the leader tries to intervene with the Adult: "What response do you expect when you say that?" If the participant feels threatened or humiliated by the group leader the leader pursues that response, which originates in the Child, using the transaction as a vehicle to reach important clinical material.

As the group progresses, the leader analyzes the ulterior transactions among group members, indicating when they have manipulated others or have been hooked by the manipulations of others. As Holloway (1977, p. 218) puts it, the leader acts as a "friendly detective who will present evidence of incongruities." Some participants may be easily hooked into providing Parental nurturance by a client who weeps or complains from the Child. In the group, the apparently successful manipulations of, for example, the complaining Child, receive less and less reinforcement as group members learn to understand and control their own behavior. Consequently, the group provides an environment for strengthening Adult behavior and control by differentially reinforcing one another's behavior.

Game analysis involves a similar approach. The leader describes the subversive elements of the participants' functioning, indicating both the psychological and social advantages of the game for all players. Basically, leaders have the option to expose, play, ignore, or offer an alternative to games they see being played. If group members ask "What are we doing here?" they are apt to be confronted and asked to explain their question. More supportive therapy groups would answer the question directly. Psychoanalytic groups or Tavistock groups might view the question as reflecting group issues of authority and rebellion. A TA leader would probably see the question as an instance of the "Psychiatry" game, in which the member overtly complies and covertly rebels (Berne, 1966).

In one instance, a woman in a group played a heavy game of "Kick Me" in her life and in the group. Outside the group she had been fired from 30 jobs, and she was only 32 years old! Inside the group she would tell a story about her life during each group session and change the facts every time. The group members became predictably irritated with her and their Parent ego states were hooked by her Child and kicked her accordingly. The leader successfully interrupted the game by giving the group members permission not to kick her after explaining the game's dynamics. No matter how hard she played, the group members refused to jump on her and, in fact, stroked her for other behaviors. This intervention succeeded in interrupting her game both inside and outside the group.

Script analysis and redecision work

If the short-term goal of TA groups is to fulfill contracts, then the long-term goal is to rewrite life scripts. Group leaders should be aware of the psychological impact of their messages to be sure that they do not reinforce the clients' scripts. According to Berne, most people come to therapy to learn how to play their games better, that is, without the inevitable pain and disappointment but also without giving up sources of strokes. He believed that the therapist has a special responsibility and a special power to tackle and subdue outdated scripts. TA therapists aim to place more power in the hands of group members and less in the hands of the therapist.

Script analysis requires a comprehensive assessment of ego states, simple and stereotyped transactions, and complex transactions involving several people in a long-range life plan. The script is a transference phenomenon, derived from the drama of the original family. By living out their scripts, clients try to recapture or augment the gains of the original family experience. The leader may elicit information about the family drama by taking a history of participants' childhood experiences and their descriptions of family members. Another technique is to ask clients to represent the family theatrically. They are asked "If your family were put on the stage, what kind of play would it be?" (Berne, 1977). Participants are also asked to outline the plot and to give each character their lines. These techniques help retrieve early experiences from memory and provide a nonthreatening framework for discussing parental influences, conflicts, fears, and disappointments.

Information about scripts can also be obtained using a long list of questions conceived by Berne and his followers (James, 1977). Examples include "What was your parents' favorite slogan or precept?" "What kind of life did your parents lead?" and "What did you have to do to make your parents smile or chuckle?" The rationale for this type of inquiry is that the parental influence remains alive in clients' daily transactions and long-term plans and goals (James, 1977). Aspects of members' scripts are also manifested in their transactions with other group members. They are more likely, for instance, to relate comfortably with individuals whose scripts are either similar to or dovetail with their own (Steiner, 1974).

Finally, didactic devices such as Karpman's (1968) drama triangle can be used to identify scripts and games. The three points of the triangle refer to the positions of Victim, Rescuer, and Persecutor (see Figure 10-5). Victims suffer, act helpless, and experience themselves as not OK. Rescuers feel OK only as long as they are helping someone else. In reality they need others to

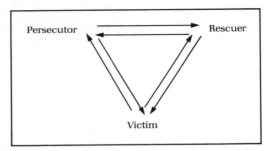

Figure 10–5. Karpman's Drama Triangle

remain Victims to play their game. Persecutors criticize and abuse others and invite them into the Victim position. Most group members have a favorite position where they spend most of their time, but a well-played game allows for movement around the triangle. For instance, a man may act like a Victim—pleads that he can't possibly participate in a group activity and acts helpless. A woman in the group, a friendly Rescuer, steps in, lending good cheer and a helping hand. The Victim, however, becomes increasingly dependent and ineffectual, so that the Rescuer becomes frustrated and angry, actually shifting to the Persecutor role. Or, if the Victim fails at a task, he may turn on the Rescuer, blaming her for causing the problem. In this case, the original Victim becomes the Persecutor and the original Rescuer feels like a Victim. The net result is a payoff of racket feelings and a perpetuation of self-defeating roles. The antidote is awareness and conscious efforts to step out of an escalating cycle.

TA operates within a decisional model. It assumes that early life decisions get people into trouble and that these decisions can be changed in the present. Berne (1966) cites one case in which a resistant woman answered the leader's question of "Why don't you want to get better?" with the answer "Because getting better would mean doing the things my parents always wanted me to do, and I have to spite them." The group leader replied with the following anecdote: "One night in the middle of winter a policeman found a drunk sitting on a doorstep, shivering and shaking and freezing, and he asked him what he was doing there. The drunk said, 'I live here,' so the policeman said, 'Then why don't you go in?' The drunk said, 'Because the door's locked,' so the policeman said, 'Why don't you ring the bell?' The drunk said, 'I did, but they didn't answer,' so the policeman said, 'Then why don't you ring again? You'll freeze to death out here.' And the drunk said, 'Oh, let them wait' " (Berne, 1966, p. 255). In other words, the leader was trying to cure the member of the game "Ain't it Awful" and hook her Child into allowing her Adult to give up getting back at her parents and make a decision to move ahead with her own life. One of life's most difficult lessons seems to be for people to do what they want to do in spite of the fact that someone else also wants them to do it!

The group must provide an atmosphere that suggests a new experience for the participant rather than a place to live out an old script. Script processes can be taught didactically to group members, and with mild scripts, cognitive understanding may be sufficient to carry out decisions that counter the script. With more serious scripts, however, the redecision process must occur with Child ego states not as accessible to Adult reasoning. To reach the Child, TA groups rely on methods adapted from other therapy approaches, including encounter techniques, Gestalt empty-chair work, psychodrama scenes, and bioenergetic rage release. In redecision therapy (Goulding & Goulding, 1979), which integrates TA with Gestalt therapy, group members work to break out of impasses, points at which a person is stuck between two positions. Impasses, like scripts, often have their origin in messages received in childhood and decisions made about them. Unlike the pure experiential focus of Gestalt groups, redecision-therapy groups also stress cognitive understanding. Participants are frequently invited to experience and enjoy their Child and create fantasy scenes in which they can give up unwise decisions made in childhood and improve upon the original scene in the present. In the following excerpt, a woman separated from her husband is having difficulty relinquishing the ex-spouse from her life and allowing herself to grow without him (Goulding & Goulding, 1979). Bob is the group leader:

> *Sue:* There's nothing I can do. He keeps phoning me, and . . .
>
> *Bob:* You must have a very strange telephone. One that sticks to your hand so you can't hang up (group members laugh).
>
> *Sue:* I see the point, but . . .
>
> *Bob:* *But.* But you are going to keep talking to him and being angry just as long as he dials your number.
>
> *Sue:* Well, you shouldn't just . . . give up on somebody.
>
> *Bob:* Shut your eyes and repeat that statement. "You shouldn't just give up on somebody." See how that fits your past [p. 181].

Sue saw that she was unsuccessfully working to make her ex-husband happy in the same way that she had struggled with her father. Her redecision in the fantasy scene to go outside and play and leave her father to drink if he chose to led to a real-world decision not to take charge of her ex-husband's depression and stay angry at her failure to help him.

Much of the thrust of the TA method is cognitive and educational. At one time it was thought that redecisions could be made directly by the Adult based on the rational processing of new information offered by the group leader and fellow participants. It has recently become clear, however, that the source and quality of the original decision will influence the direction of the prescription. According to Robert Goulding (1974) there are three kinds of childhood injunctions. A first-degree injunction, from the parent's Parent, is the most simple. An example is a Parental message to work hard and not have any fun. A second-degree impasse is between the parent's Child and the child's Child and is more destructive (for example, "Everything is your fault, so go away."). Finally, a third-degree impasse is between the Adapted Child and the Free Child, such as in severe depression, when the Free Child is totally squashed. The latter two impasses require more regressive work than the first and the involvement of the group member's Child.

The importance of identifying injunctions, rackets, and decisions and making redecisions is apparent in the TA treatment of phobias. In the following example, several group members have admitted to an irrational fear of heights. In fantasy, the group has been encouraged to slowly climb a ladder and visualize their parents' responses to a declaration that they will not fall off or jump off the ladder:

Bob:	Do any of you have any response from your mothers?
Beth:	*(As her mother)* Get off that ladder, I told you.
Bob:	Answer her back.
Beth:	No way. (laughter)
Bob:	Any other responses?
Al:	Mine doesn't mind my climbing but is having such a fit that I said, "Fuck."
Cindy:	Mine says, "You are making me nervous."
Bob:	Answer.
Cindy:	(not audible)
Bob:	Yell so she can hear!
Cindy:	*I* am not nervous!
Brad:	Mine says, "Be careful!"
Mary:	What does that mean? Answer her.
Brad:	It just means. . .you know. . .take good care of yourself and hang on tight or you'll fall.
Mary:	Respond.
Brad:	Don't worry, I'll hang on tight.
Mary:	Find a way to respond that is safe and not compliant.
Brad:	I will take care of myself.
Bob:	Any other mothers have anything to say?
Dee:	Mine sits and smiles and says, "You think you are brave. Wait until you get higher. The ladder will slip."
Bob:	Answer that. First, ask your friends if they are holding the ladder tightly or will they push it over when you get higher?
Dee:	Will you push it over?
Group:	NO.
Bob:	Believe them?
Dee:	Absolutely.
Beth:	I am climbing fine. My mother is warning me about dizzy spells.
Bob:	Answer.

Beth: I am strong, and I am not sick, and I never had a dizzy spell in my entire life in spite of all your talk about dizzy spells. I am perfectly safe. Hey, that's true. All my life I have been phobic because of your damn fake dizzy spells. And you...you, mother, never had dizzy spells either. You faked your dizzy spells to get your way. Hey, I am not scared anymore. I am very happy about that.

Bob: Any fathers have anything else to say?

Al: My father wants me to go faster.

Bob: Answer.

Al: I am enjoying myself, and I don't have to go faster. I'll take my time.

Bob: Ready for the third rung? OK. The hand moves higher on the ladder. (realizing his switch from the imperative) Move up the second hand, get a firm grip, move up one foot to the next rung, get well balanced, now move up your second foot. Is anybody scared?

Cindy: I am.

Bob: Go back to the second rung. What do you experience?

Cindy: My stomach gets fluttery and I feel breathless.

Bob: You flutter your stomach and hold your breath. Tell your mother that. "When I get this high I flutter my stomach and hold my breath."

Cindy tells mother that.

Bob: What does she say?

Cindy: Of course, because you are scared!

Bob: Answer.

Cindy: I don't want to do that. I want to get to the top.

Bob: Don't want to. (Bob is reminding her of the difference between want and autonomy; people can "want" forever, and not "do" anything.)

Cindy: I am breathing easier now, and I am not fluttering my stomach. I am not scaring myself.

Bob: Tell your mother: I'm not going to fall or jump off.

Cindy: I'm not going to fall or jump off, and that ladder is not going to break down under me.

Bob: Has she any response?

Cindy: No, but she doesn't believe I'm safe.

Bob: Will you tell her, I don't give a fuck whether you believe me or not?

Cindy: I don't. I don't give a fuck whether you believe me or not. That's your problem.

Bob: Want to go to the third step now?

Cindy: Yeah.

Bob: What do you experience?

Cindy: This time I'm fine.

Bob: *(to group)* Any other trouble on the third rung?

Ann: I feel proud of myself, and I am pounding my heart...

Bob: What are you saying inside your head? To get you to beat your heart faster.

Ann: I might fall off and kill myself.

Bob: Will you take the other side: I WON'T fall off...

Ann: I don't know.

Bob: Who is in charge of your falling?

Ann: I am. I WON'T fall. I won't kill myself.

Bob: Say it again.

Ann: I won't fall. I won't kill myself. I see mother running out of the room, and hiding her face in a pillow, while my father is cheering.

Bob: What does he say?

Ann: He says you are a really good girl to climb when you are scared.

Bob: Tell him you are a woman, not a girl, and whether or not you are scaring yourself *now.*

Ann: I'm great now. I am a woman, and I am not scaring myself.

Bob: True? (not sure about her) (She nods.) Great. Everybody OK? Anybody not feeling good? (looks around) OK, will you look down on this gang helping you by holding the ladder and tell them, "I can see further than you can, down there on the ground." [Goulding & Goulding, 1979, pp. 266–269].[3]

At the conclusion of the fantasy experience, the group is encouraged to climb an actual ladder and reinforce their newly discovered fearlessness. The therapists claim that the direct confrontation of Parent injunctions through fantasy and role-playing leads to quick, effective cures for acute and long-standing fears.

APPRAISAL

One of the virtues of transactional analysis is the ease in understanding its concepts and methods. The division of a person's functioning into distinct ego states has a common sense reasonableness to it, reflecting the way we have historically thought of people as having a multiple nature. To some, TA offers the profundity of psychoanalysis without having to come to terms with its elaborate and sometimes mystical superstructure. TA practitioners, however, point out that though an appreciation for historical antecedents of current behavior may be important, there are fundamental differences in value and approach between TA and psychoanalysis. TA is

---

[3]From *Changing Lives through Redecision Therapy,* by M. M. Goulding and R. L. Goulding. Copyright 1979 by Brunner/Mazel. Reprinted by permission.

positive and optimistic. It joins the experiential groups that have previously been discussed in their commitment to give group members the opportunity to make their own autonomous decisions. Anyone can use TA, evidenced by its application to healthy individuals as well as emotionally disturbed populations. TA is pragmatic. Eric Berne continually asked for evidence of "cures" and grew impatient with methods that always seemed to be moving toward a goal but rarely got there.

One of the shortcomings of TA may be that people are not quite as reasonable as the theory would suggest. In the early days of TA, and to a lesser extent today, the assumption is that with enough information and reason, people are capable of change. They simply receive new information, process it, make a decision, and alter their behavior. Theoretically, change occurs when information embedded in the Child ego state is made conscious and available to the Adult (Berne, 1961). In practice, change is not always so direct. Consequently, proponents of TA have been forced to draw upon the methodologies of other group approaches that drive the information home on an experiential level. To this end, encounter, Gestalt, psychodrama, body therapies, and other techniques previously discussed are adopted. Leaders of TA groups are generally comfortable introducing whatever method works to fulfill stated goals.

Any group of adherents of a psychological method who devise their own vocabulary and establish their own accrediting body and professional journal run the risk of becoming a cult. It is true that members of TA groups usually have to become acquainted with a basic vocabulary including terms such as Parent, Adult, Child, game, racket, decision, script, stroke, discount, and contract. Some TA leaders get very wrapped up in disseminating a huge vocabulary of cute catch phrases, and the primary activity of a group session seems to be an intellectual contest to accurately label a particular behavior or transaction. This kind of endeavor is not only unnecessary, but probably injurious, in that group members may begin to experience themselves as mechanical dolls playing disconnected roles. The most progressive TA group leaders virtually ignore jargon and get on with the work.

TA groups, as I have mentioned, do not pay much attention to group process and development of group norms. Like Gestalt and body-therapy groups, the work is generally done with one person interacting with the leader. Nonetheless, there is reason to believe that TA groups go through stages similar to those traversed by other experiential groups, so that interactions among members increase and interactions between the leader and a given member decrease as the group progresses (Misel, 1975). There are also group leaders who seek to integrate TA with process models of group functioning (Peck, 1978).

TA proponents clearly advocate the group format as the very best possible arena for change. Problems are viewed as existing between people rather than within isolated individuals, and TA has developed the study of interpersonal communication into an art form. A tremendous amount of

Adult information is available in the combined resources of the many personalities present in the group. Support and encouragement is always at hand to give reassurance that change is possible. And the group is used to reinforce new decisions made by individual participants. Group members freely intervene during the course of the session and random remarks are looked at for the ways in which they reflect games or constitute ulterior or crossed transactions. Moreover, participants are stimulated by the work of others and learn to use it for themselves.

Today, transactional analysis is a fairly complete conceptual system. Contemporary practitioners have struck out in many different directions from the position advocated by Berne. One account (Goulding, 1976) indicates that there are at least four different TA models operating today: the Bernian model; the Schiff-reparenting model (Schiff, 1975); the Asklepieion model (Groder, 1976); and the redecision model (Goulding & Goulding, 1979). The scope of the applicability of TA is impressive, spanning the gap between kindergarten children (Grieve, 1978) and bureaucratic organizations (Frank, 1975), and including alcoholics (Steiner, 1971a) and the mentally retarded (Cheney, 1970).

There are a large number of position papers, case studies, and research reports on TA available in the literature. However, there are not many empirical studies substantiating the effectiveness of TA with various populations that also honor the tenets of rigorous research, such as the use of adequate control groups, sound and unbiased measures, and sufficient follow-up. Berne initially noted that the structural analysis of ego states had experimental support in the laboratory work of Wilbert Penfield (1958). Penfield stimulated the temporal cortex of the brain with weak electric currents and found that past events appeared to be recorded in detail together with feeling states associated with the events. This finding encouraged the investigation of a person's ego states in search of evidence of early parental messages and injunctions. More recent work has shown that Parent, Adult, and Child communications can be reliably observed and recorded (Baker & Holden, 1976). Among the very few studies that have incorporated control groups and statistical measures are Groder's (1976) use of TA to treat hardened criminals in a maximum-security facility and Amundson and Sawatzky's (1976) use of TA as part of an educational program for children. In Groder's program, group sessions resulted in significant changes on personality instruments such as the MMPI and CPI and behavioral changes, including the disappearance of infractional behavior. In Amundson and Sawatzky's study, the treated children increased on measures of self-esteem and peer acceptance.

SUMMARY

Transactional analysis (TA) was developed by psychiatrist Eric Berne, who viewed psychoanalysis as overly slow and unnecessarily complex. The basic concepts underlying TA include *ego states, transactions, games,* and *scripts. Structural analysis* is the exploration of ego states, the distinct patterns of thinking, feeling, and behaving found within an individual and labeled the *Parent, Adult,* and *Child.* Functionally, the Parent can be broken down into the Critical Parent and the Nurturant Parent, and the Child includes the Free Child and the Adapted Child.

Transactions are stimuli and responses between ego states. Transactions between individuals are typically *complementary, crossed,* or *ulterior. Injunctions* are messages from the Child of a person's parent that later inhibit the free functioning of that person as an adult. TA theory outlines four basic existential positions, including the ideal I'm OK—You're OK position.

Games are ulterior transactions leading to outcomes that have primary and secondary gains for each player. Examples of games are Rapo and Now I've Got You, You Son of a Bitch. Scripts are master plans for organizing one's life and originate in childhood. They may be diagnosed from group behavior as well as from favorite slogans and fairy tales.

TA groups revolve around *contracts* with individual participants specifying the goals and conditions of treatment. The group leader provides *protection* for the group members, *permission* to experiment with change, and *potency* in the form of timely interventions. The leader helps to analyze ego states, transactions, games, and scripts. The short-term goal of TA is to fulfill contracts; the long-term goal is to rewrite life scripts. Changing scripts involves *redecision* work and specific learning devices such as the *drama triangle.*

TA groups have an educational and cognitive thrust and use the group to provide support for working on contracts and to solicit Adult information from participants. Transactional analysis is relatively easy to understand, to the extent that some people criticize it for being overly reasonable. Although the group process is not emphasized by TA practitioners, the group setting is ideal since the approach insists that problems exist largely between people.

REFERENCES

Amundson, N. E., & Sawatzky, D. D. A summative evaluation of the "Transactional Analysis with Children" educational program. *Transactional Analysis Journal,* 1976, *6,* 326–328.

Baker, E. E., & Holden, J. D. An investigation of transactional analysis postulates involving the Parent, Adult, and Child ego state model. In G. M. Goldhaber & M. B. Goldhaber (Eds.), *Transactional analysis: Principles and applications,* Boston: Allyn & Bacon, 1976.

Berne, E. Group attendance: Clinical and theoretical considerations. *International Journal of Group Psychotherapy,* 1955, *5,* 392–403.

Berne, E. *Transactional analysis in psychotherapy.* New York: Grove Press, 1961.

Berne, E. *Games people play.* New York: Grove Press, 1964.

Berne, E. *Principles of group treatment.* New York: Oxford University Press, 1966.

Berne, E. *What do you say after you say hello?* New York: Grove Press, 1972.

Berne, E. *Beyond games and scripts.* New York: Grove Press, 1977.

Cheney, W. D. T.A.'s widening use with the mentally retarded. *Transactional Analysis Bulletin*, 1970, *9*, 104–105.

Crossman, P. Permission and protection. *Transactional Analysis Bulletin*, 1966, *5*, 152–154.

Dusay, J. M. Script rehearsal. *Transactional Analysis Bulletin*, 1970, *9*, 117–121.

Dusay, J. M., & Steiner, C. M. Transactional analysis in groups. In H. I. Kaplan & B. Sadock (Eds.), *New models for group therapy*. New York: Jason Aronson, 1972.

Frank, J. S. How to cure organizations. *Transactional Analysis Journal*, 1975, *5*, 354–358.

Goulding, M. M., & Goulding, R. L. *Changing lives through redecision therapy*. New York: Brunner/Mazel, 1979.

Goulding, R. L. New directions in transactional analysis: Creating an environment for redecision and change. In C. J. Sager & H. S. Kaplan (Eds.), *Progress in group and family therapy*. New York: Brunner/Mazel, 1972.

Goulding, R. L. Thinking and feeling in transactional analysis: Three impasses. *Voices: The Art and Science of Psychotherapy*, 1974, *10*, 11–13.

Goulding, R. L. Four models of transactional analysis. *International Journal of Group Psychotherapy*, 1976, *26*, 385–392.

Grieve, J. H. *Effects of teacher methods using transactional analysis strategies on achievement and emotional adjustment of kindergarten children*. Unpublished doctoral dissertation, University of Michigan, 1978.

Groder, M. G. Asklepieion: Effective treatment for felons. In G. M. Goldhaber & M. B. Goldhaber, *Transactional analysis: Principles and applications*. Boston: Allyn & Bacon, 1976.

Harris, T. *I'm OK, You're OK*. New York: Harper & Row, 1969.

Holland, G. A. Transactional analysis. In R. Corsini (Ed.), *Current psychotherapies*. Itasca, Ill.: F. E. Peacock, 1973.

Holloway, W. H. Transactional analysis: An integrative view. In G. Barnes (Ed.), *Transactional analysis after Eric Berne*. New York: Harper's College Press, 1977.

James, M. The downscripting of women for 115 generations: A historical kaleidoscope. *Transactional Analysis Journal*, 1973, *3*, 15–22.

James, M. *Techniques in transactional analysis*. Reading, Mass.: Addison-Wesley, 1977.

James, M., & Jongeward, D. *Born to win*. Reading, Mass.: Addison-Wesley, 1971.

Kahler, T. Drivers: The key to the process of scripts. *Transactional Analysis Journal*, 1975, *5*, 280–284.

Karpman, S. B. Fairy tales and script drama analysis. *Transactional Analysis Bulletin*, 1968, *7*, 39–43.

Misel, L. T. Stages of group treatment. *Transactional Analysis Journal*, 1975, *5*, 385–391.

Peck, H. B. Integrating transactional analysis and group process approach in treatment. *Transactional Analysis Journal*, 1978, *8*, 328–331.

Penfield, W. *The excitable cortex in conscious man*. Springfield, Ill.: Charles C Thomas, 1958.

Schiff, J. L. *The cathexis reader: The transactional analysis treatment of psychosis*. New York: Harper & Row, 1975.

Steiner, C. M. *Games alcoholics play*. New York: Grove Press, 1971. (a)

Steiner, C. M. The stroke economy. *Transactional Analysis Journal*, 1971, *1*, 9–15. (b)

Steiner, C. M. *Scripts people live: Transactional analysis of life scripts*. New York: Grove Press, 1974.

Woollams, S., & Brown, M. *The total handbook of transactional analysis*. New York: Prentice-Hall, 1979.

11

Skill-Training Groups

The group approaches presented and discussed in the preceding chapters are part of the human-potential movement. In contrast, skill-training groups draw more from behaviorism and behavior therapy than any other single source. Skill-training groups, alternately called life-skills groups, attempt to teach adaptive skills instrumental in meeting important life demands. These skill groups are much more structured than any approach discussed so far. Both their structured, systematic quality and the concepts they have adopted ally them with the behavioral perspective.

HISTORY AND DEVELOPMENT

The behavioral learning model is very different from both Freud's psychodynamic model, which has been the dominant force in psychotherapy during this century, and from the humanistic model championed by Carl Rogers and like-minded practitioners. The behavioral model was developed in the laboratory, and continues to be dedicated to scientific precision, careful measurement, and the controlled manipulation of observable events (Kanfer & Phillips, 1970). Many of the fundamental laws of learning formulated by behaviorists were derived from experiments with small animals in controlled laboratory settings. Most introductory psychology students are familiar with Russian physiologist Ivan Pavlov's discovery of conditioned reflexes. From his original interest in the way organisms adapt and learn to respond to changes in their environment, Pavlov attempted to condition dogs to salivate at the sound of a bell that had previously been paired with the presentation of meat powder. From these early experiments, the study of the laws of behavior has flourished and now includes the treatment of human problems. The original use of the term behavior therapy is independently attributed to Arnold Lazarus in 1958 and to Hans Eysenck in 1959 to describe the application of experimental psychology to problems of human behavior. Today the role of behavior therapy is extremely powerful in devising pragmatic treatment strategies for a large number of psychological problems and in documenting treatment effectiveness through carefully controlled research.

Behavior therapists are just beginning to develop methods for working with groups. Initially, the clinical application of behavioral principles to groups was stimulated by laboratory experiments showing that learning-theory variables such as reinforcement contingencies could influence the verbal output and leadership status of group members (Liberman & Teigen, 1979). From that point, behavioral clinicians infused conventional group-therapy formats with behavioral techniques. Moreover, behavior therapists were the most active in translating the procedures of other group approaches into the language of social-learning theory (see Liberman, 1970). That is, they were interested in demystifying the interventions used by group leaders or members by reducing interactions to explicit stimuli and responses. For example, the caring presence of other clients with similar problems may aid the anxious participant through what the learning theorist calls "desensitization," while their supportive reactions may "reinforce" some behaviors.

More recently, the behavioral group leader has become more directive in structuring the group format to take advantage of specific behavioral techniques and in discouraging spontaneous group processes. By and large, the behaviorally-oriented group has simply extended individual therapy procedures. Most behavior therapists who run groups do so to conserve time and money and tend to ignore the influence of group dynamics. For instance, several clients suffering from irrational fears might be brought together and treated with a conditioning procedure such as systematic desensitization. This approach is ostensibly conducting individual therapy in a group context, in the same way, incidentally, that many Gestalt or transactional-analysis therapists do one-to-one work in a group.

A number of behavior therapists do see the possibility of combining behavioral techniques with more traditional group therapy, capitalizing on the diverse experiences of group members and a wider support system for learning life skills (Lazarus, 1968). Behavioral problems almost inevitably involve interactions with other people. This is clear when a person suffers deficits in conversational skills, dating, or intimate relationships. However, even in the case of anxiety symptoms or problem behaviors such as smoking or overeating, there is usually an interactional component. The presence or absence of other people may encourage the behavior. The group becomes a microcosm representing the real world. It is a social network in which social skills can be realistically assessed and practiced. Groups, moreover, act as balancing agents that help appraise therapists and prevent them from imposing their own values on clients. Whether the group is called a therapy group, a training group, or a skill-training group, the same laws of learning apply. What varies is the composition of the group and its behavioral targets.

BASIC CONCEPTS

Central to a behavioral approach is a focus on observable behaviors. Freudian concepts such as repression, the unconscious, and transference are forthrightly rejected or at least translated into less mystical language. Behavior therapists deal with problem behaviors directly and do not generally concern themselves with the historical roots or underlying causes of current difficulties. Behaviorists recognize that past events may be instrumental in forging current problems, but choose to attack the behaviors themselves and the environmental factors that maintain them. Looking at behavior in its environmental context is crucial. Sometimes the recommended intervention consists of changing the context or the responses that maintain a behavior rather than altering the behavior itself. It is not relevant here to evaluate the relative merits of behavior therapy. It is important, however, to keep the foregoing principles in mind, since skill-training groups rely on behaviorism for much of their conceptual grounding.

Educational model

Skill-training groups attempt to merge didactic and experiential learning. Many of the exercises are experiential, but the group format is clearly *educational*. This is consistent with behavior therapy's departure from a medical-treatment model and its adherence to a problem-solving, skill-oriented approach. A skill-training group resembles a programmed course of instruction more than a set of psychotherapy sessions. Group members are not viewed as patients with diagnoses but as students who wish to enhance their lives and correct deficits they assess in themselves (Factor & Daubenspeck, 1979). Rather than offering treatment, group leaders provide systematic instruction to change attitudes and behaviors and fulfill member goals.

Skill-training group leaders are more interested in research on developmental tasks than in abnormal psychology. Best-sellers such as Gail Sheehy's *Passages* (1976) and Daniel Levinson's *The Seasons of a Man's Life* (1978) have noted that we move through predictable life stages, and that each stage includes certain challenges and a set of skills necessary to meet those challenges and to continue to mature. For instance, the person contemplating marriage will need an expanded repertoire of skills to cope with meshing two unique personalities and life styles into a single, intimate living unit. If the necessary skills are not obtained during a developmental stage, the person is at a disadvantage in meeting future needs and responding appropriately to life stresses.

One critical period is the stage of late adolescence and early adulthood, when a number of important life choices are being confronted for the first time. The acquisition of skills in the areas of interpersonal relationships, the negotiation of needs, and the management of anxiety predict future success or failure in developing intimacy, becoming independent, and developing competence in life and work. There are innumerable reasons why someone develops deficits in these developmental areas, including the absence of an appropriate parental role model, an unsupportive or impoverished environment, lags in physical development, lack of opportunity to practice a skill, traumatic experiences, and emotional blocks. In skill-training groups, deficits in psychosocial skills are defined and assessed as concretely as possible.

The group experience can either facilitate or interfere with the learning process. Experimental research with small groups suggests that the group has advantages over the individual in problem solving (Cartwright & Zander, 1968). A group can, under facilitative conditions, divide the labor, save time, and generate higher quality solutions than an individual. However, members' personal defensiveness, needs to conform, and needs for power can interfere with the learning process. Some behaviorists design groups to deliberately create an optimal learning climate by building cohesiveness, altering the group's communication structure, equalizing power, and establishing group as opposed to individual goals.

Goal setting

Skill-training groups aim to cultivate behaviors that are viewed as desirable by either the group member or society. Any other effects of the group, such as enjoying the experience, learning about other participants, and general personality change and growth are viewed as by-products to the *specific goal* of the group. The groups try to help participants develop critical emotional and interpersonal skills that are clearly specified in a contract between the group leader and the individual. Unlike the group leader in sensitivity or encounter groups, the leader of a skill-training group is obliged to keep the group from wandering from its stated purpose and into areas of general personality reorganization.

The kinds of life skills taught in groups include such basic behaviors as anxiety management, career planning, decision making, parenting, communication skills, and assertiveness training (Drum & Knott, 1977).[1] The goal may be broad or narrow, so that some skill-training groups attack

[1]Drum and Knott (1977) have described two other kinds of structured groups in addition to life-skills groups. These are life-theme groups and life-transition groups. Both approaches share a conceptual base with life-skills groups but are less clearly behavioral in focus. Life-theme groups help people examine basic values and beliefs rather than develop interpersonal skills. Examples include consciousness-raising groups for men or women, values-clarification groups, and groups on loneliness and human sexuality. Life-transition groups are responses to major life changes or are used to help pave the way to new stages in living. Examples include groups to deal with the death of a family member, divorce, career changes, or physical disability.

anxiety or lack of assertiveness in general, whereas others focus on a particular kind of anxiety, such as a fear of flying, or another specific target, such as weight loss or smoking. For groups of severely disturbed patients, the skill training may be rather rudimentary, such as learning how to eat without spilling. With healthier groups the goals become increasingly sophisticated.

Regardless of the group's theme, the intention is to establish problem-solving skills for the future and to combat the specific problem that brought the member to the group. A skill-training program that grew out of such an emphasis is relationship-enhancement therapy (Guerney, 1977). In this approach, members of a social unit learn specific interpersonal skills for expressing themselves without arousing defensiveness and hostility in others. Four sets of behavioral skills are demonstrated and practiced: expressing—becoming aware of and communicating feelings, perceptions, and desires pertaining to the relationship; empathic responding—fully understanding and communicating this understanding to the expresser; mode switching—moving appropriately between expressing and empathic responding; and facilitating—learning to effectively teach the aforementioned skills to others. The relationship-enhancement method has been used successfully in filial groups to teach parents to conduct therapeutic play sessions with their children (Guerney, 1977) and to teach troubled husbands and wives to use therapeutic skills with one another (Collins, 1977). It can also be effective in enriching relationships that are already satisfactory.

A second skill-training approach, focusing on very practical, adaptive behaviors, is called structured-learning therapy (Goldstein, 1973; Goldstein, Sprafkin, Gershaw, & Klein, 1980). This approach is tailored to people who lack developmentally appropriate behavior skills, such as social skills, planning skills, and skills for dealing with stress. The structured-learning therapy group has been directed at teaching prosocial skills to unsophisticated working-class clients, ex-hospital patients, and behaviorally disordered adolescents, for example, using modeling, role-playing, performance feedback, and transfer-of-training techniques.

Goals in skill-training groups are generally individualized. Some therapists also include group goals intended to facilitate individual goals (Rose, 1977). To encourage more or less equal participation by the members, for example, one group goal might be to insure that no one talks more than 25% of the time. Similar group goals might revolve around the expression of affection between group members, distribution of work, leadership and governance, and an increase or decrease of specific activities. Group goals are introduced to increase the motivation of the group or to modify the group interaction pattern in a positive direction. In general, these group goals are secondary to individual goals.

Because skill-training groups are highly structured and attainment of goals is most prominent in the participant's mind, there is usually a time limit for accomplishing goals and an incremental building of skills from session to session. Leaders structure the content of each session, and they actively lead the group to facilitate meeting goals. In part, this no-nonsense approach to group therapy is a rejoinder to those who believe that some groups operate only to train people to become good group members, but leave them without visible behavioral changes to use in their home environments.

Measurement and evaluation

A third concept relevant to skill-training groups, as well as all behaviorally-oriented groups, is *measurement and evaluation*. Since the time when experimental psychologists began measuring simple stimulus/ response relationships in controlled laboratory settings, the behavioral model has been committed to a research orientation. It is important to know not only that something has changed but to demonstrate that change and attribute it to the correct antecedent variables. In behavioral groups it is not unusual to use a host of paper-and-pencil tests, measuring devices, and behavioral observations to monitor progress throughout the course of the group.

Problems are carefully defined according to their rate and intensity of occurrence. Most problems are either *excesses* (too much smoking, too many arguments, too much fear) or *deficits* (too little sleep or exercise, too few sexual relationships). Members are encouraged to learn the skills of self-observation and to record data on themselves. Responses can be counted, timed, or rated, and there are scales and checklists to do so objectively. It is also important for group members to recognize that problems occur in the context of the environment. An anxious person is probably not always anxious, but more or less so depending upon moment-to-moment environmental contingencies (Mischel, 1973). Or as one pundit put it, "When I'm out among friends, I'm the life of the party, but when I'm home by myself, I seem to clam up!"

Measuring a response includes noting the circumstances under which it occurred. If someone admits to a fear of public speaking, for instance, it might be important to assess how extreme the fear is, how it manifests itself, and under what circumstances the person is afraid. To measure these variables, there are fear inventories that rate feelings of anxiety in relevant situations; there is physiological recording equipment to monitor physiological indices of fear and anxiety, such as heart rate, pulse, and sweating; and there are behavioral exercises, such as giving a trial speech in front of an audience and being evaluated on the performance.

One of the reasons for focusing on overt behaviors is that they can be more readily measured. It is very difficult to know if someone's "personality" or "self-concept" has changed after a group experience. It is much easier to see that a person can give a five-minute speech in front of an audience of 20 peers without stuttering. Behaviorists know that the hidden expectations and pressures for a group member to behave in a certain, pleasing way, called the "demand characteristics" of the situation, as well as the wish on the part of the group leader to forge a successful group experience, can color the leader's perception of the group's success or failure. Scientific measurement procedures act to overcome this bias. In skill-training groups the leader will spend as much time and effort structuring the group and evaluating its outcome as in actually conducting sessions.

In a carefully crafted group experience the problem behavior is measured periodically from the beginning to the end of the group program. Initial measurements are used to provide a baseline of a problem's frequency, duration, and intensity prior to treatment. This information helps to fashion a reasonable goal. The group's success can be evaluated by the extent to which the relevant behaviors deviate from the baseline at the end of treatment. To ascertain that the group experience itself was responsible for changes, as opposed to statistical regression or extratherapeutic factors such as maturation or the influence of other life experiences, various experimental designs can be used. Most of these employ a control group of clients who do not receive treatment or receive a different kind of group experience. Time-series designs are used for the same purpose (Hersen & Barlow, 1976). These are statistical instruments for measuring change among small numbers of subjects over time when control groups are not available.

BASIC PROCEDURES

Of the various skill-training groups, the type that best illustrates the teaching of an important life skill with the use of behavior-therapy methods is assertiveness training. Moreover, the methods that comprise assertiveness-training groups are representative of behavioral methods in general. Consequently, the remainder of the chapter focuses on assertiveness training as a model of skill training.

Assertiveness training was originally popularized by the publication of Alberti and Emmons' *Your Perfect Right* in 1970. The authors were influenced by the human-potential movement and the humanistic value system that permeates most group approaches discussed in this book. As such, Alberti and Emmons took a behavior-therapy technique for treating neurotic anxiety conditions and translated it into a behavioral/humanistic approach for enhancing self-esteem (Alberti, 1977). The roots of assertiveness training go back at least as far as Andrew Salter's (1949) conditioned-reflex therapy. Salter, a laboratory behaviorist, based his work on Pavlov's categorization of excitatory and inhibitory brain processes. Salter proposed that nonassertive individuals develop inhibitory personalities through a learning history in which they are punished for excitatory social behaviors. He designed procedures to activate the excitatory processes in the brain and reduce (decondition) inhibiting anxiety. Salter's techniques to build excitatory feelings and increase behavioral freedom antedate many of the methods of current assertiveness training. An example is his emphasis on expressing feelings directly, which he called "feeling talk." A few years later Joseph Wolpe (1958) applied the term assertiveness to openness in interpersonal behavior. He noted that many individuals are unable to express appropriate feelings or actions in interpersonal relationships because of the crippling presence of anxiety. Wolpe found that individuals' assertive expression of their thoughts and feelings in social situations can overcome the interfering anxiety response. The rationale behind the method is Wolpe's reciprocal-inhibition principle, which states "If a response inhibitory of anxiety can be made to occur in the presence of anxiety-evoking stimuli it will weaken the bond between those stimuli and the anxiety" (Wolpe & Lazarus, 1966, p. 12).

Groups for reducing fear and avoidance patterns and assertiveness training have moved far beyond Salter's and Wolpe's seminal concepts. Lange and Jakubowski (1976) divide current assertiveness-training groups into four types depending upon the structure of the group sessions: (1) groups organized around a set of specific role-playing exercises; (2) groups in which each session revolves around a particular theme, such as learning to give constructive criticism; (3) groups that combine role-playing with a variety of other procedures such as consciousness raising, parent-effectiveness training, fair-fight training, conflict-resolution training, or transactional-analysis script analysis; (4) groups that are relatively unstructured and flow with the ongoing needs of the individual members.

Assessment

An assessment of assertiveness-skill strengths and deficits is generally performed in the group's early stages. There are at least 17 assessment inventories available to gauge the kinds of assertiveness problems group members may have (Kelley, 1979). One example is the Rathus Assertiveness Schedule (Table 11-1). Essentially, being assertive means that you can recognize and express your wants, needs, likes, dislikes, and expectations. Most assertive behaviors can be divided into request or refusal responses with significant others or with strangers (Cottler & Guerra, 1976). A social-request response would be asking someone for a date or asking a stranger for the time. A protective or refusal response would be rejecting the offer of a relative to spend the weekend or saying no to a salesman. The components of an assertive response could include eye contact, body posture, gestures, facial expression, and nonverbal speech characteristics, as well as the verbal content of the response.

Whether or not a formal assertiveness inventory is employed, a group leader will encourage a dialogue with participants to help identify and specify the difficulties each has in acting assertively. Members are encouraged to evaluate their own behavior and present examples of assertive and nonassertive actions from their lives. Leaders patiently communicate the nature of assertive behavior and how it can be distinguished from nonassertive and aggressive behavior. They emphasize the disadvantages of

TABLE 11-1.   Rathus Assertiveness Schedule

Directions: Indicate how characteristic or descriptive each of the following statements is of you by using the code given below.

+3 very characteristic of me, extremely descriptive[1]
+2 rather characteristic of me, quite descriptive
+1 somewhat characteristic of me, slightly descriptive
−1 somewhat uncharacteristic of me, slightly nondescriptive
−2 rather uncharacteristic of me, quite nondescriptive
−3 very uncharacteristic of me, extremely nondescriptive

_____ 1. Most people seem to be more aggressive and assertive than I am.*
_____ 2. I have hesitated to make or accept dates because of "shyness."*
_____ 3. When the food served at a restaurant is not done to my satisfaction, I complain about it to the waiter or waitress.
_____ 4. I am careful to avoid hurting other people's feelings, even when I feel that I have been injured.*
_____ 5. If a salesman has gone to considerable trouble to show me merchandise which is not quite suitable, I have a difficult time in saying "No."*
_____ 6. When I am asked to do something, I insist upon knowing why.
_____ 7. There are times when I look for a good, vigorous argument.
_____ 8. I strive to get ahead as well as most people in my position.
_____ 9. To be honest, people often take advantage of me.*
_____ 10. I enjoy starting conversations with new acquaintances and strangers.
_____ 11. I often don't know what to say to attractive persons of the opposite sex.*
_____ 12. I will hesitate to make phone calls to business establishments and institutions.*
_____ 13. I would rather apply for a job or for admission to a college by writing letters than by going through with personal interviews.*
_____ 14. I find it embarrassing to return merchandise.*
_____ 15. If a close and respected relative were annoying me, I would smother my feelings rather than express my annoyance.*
_____ 16. I have avoided asking questions for fear of sounding stupid.*
_____ 17. During an argument I am sometimes afraid that I will get so upset that I will shake all over.*
_____ 18. If a famed and respected lecturer makes a statement which I think is incorrect, I will have the audience hear my point of view as well.
_____ 19. I avoid arguing over prices with clerks and salesmen.*
_____ 20. When I have done something important or worthwhile, I manage to let others know about it.
_____ 21. I am open and frank about my feelings.
_____ 22. If someone has been spreading false and bad stories about me, I see him (her) as soon as possible to "have a talk" about it.
_____ 23. I often have a hard time saying "No."*
_____ 24. I tend to bottle up my emotions rather than make a scene.*
_____ 25. I complain about poor service in a restaurant and elsewhere.
_____ 26. When I am given a compliment, I sometimes just don't know what to say.*
_____ 27. If a couple near me in a theatre or at a lecture were conversing rather loudly, I would ask them to be quiet or to take their conversation elsewhere.
_____ 28. Anyone attempting to push ahead of me in a line is in for a good battle.
_____ 29. I am quick to express an opinion.
_____ 30. There are times when I just can't say anything.*

[1]Total score obtained by adding numerical responses to each item, after changing the signs of reversed items.
*Reversed item.
From "A 30-item schedule for assessing assertive behavior," by S. A. Rathus, *Behavior Therapy*, Vol. 4, 1973. Reprinted by permission.

being nonassertive and stress that assertiveness increases viable options and control over one's life. With this change comes increased self-respect.

The nonassertive person holds back feelings because of anxiety, guilt, or lack of social skills. The aggressive person violates the rights of others through domination, humiliation, or degradation. Aggressiveness is not based on mutual respect but consists of trying to meet your needs at the expense of someone else's self-respect. The distinction between a nonassertive response, an assertive response, and an aggressive response is clarified by discussing specific situations and exchanging opinions in the group.

To overcome anxiety, make up for deficiencies, and learn assertive skills, group members must believe it is all right to act assertively. The group leader plays a central role in making a positive case for assertive behavior. Kelley (1979, pp. 58–59) has assembled a list of basic human rights that support assertiveness:

- the right to be left alone
- the right to be independent
- the right to be successful
- the right to be listened to and taken seriously
- the right to get what one pays for
- the right to have rights; that is, to act in an assertive manner
- the right to refuse requests without feeling guilty or selfish
- the right to ask for what you want
- the right to make mistakes and be responsible for them
- the right to choose not to assert oneself

Group members are shown that assertiveness should not be confused with interpersonal insensitivity or restricted to the expression of negative feelings. An equally valid component of assertiveness training is learning to express positive, caring responses to others. Participants are also told that having the right and the ability to act assertively does not imply necessarily having to do so in any and every situation.

Another approach to describing assertive behaviors is Lange and Jakubowski's (1976) categorization of six types of assertiveness. Basic assertion is a simple statement of personal feelings, thoughts, opinions, or rights. Examples include saying "I'd like to leave now" or "I like you a lot." Empathic assertion indicates a recognition of the other person's feelings or position followed by an assertive statement. The statement "I know that you want to come along, but this time I want to go by myself" communicates empathic understanding plus an assertive position. Escalating assertion is a gradual build-up from a minimally assertive, relatively effortless statement to a stronger statement when the minimal response is ineffective. Requesting that someone quiet down in a movie theater might take this form. Confrontive assertion is used when words don't match actions. The process involves stating what people had indicated they would do, what they actually did, and what the speaker wants. "My understanding was that you would have the money today. Now you say you did not bring the money. I would like to know why you don't have the money with you, and when you will have it" is an example of confrontive assertion. In an I-language assertion, speakers must objectively describe another's behavior, indicating its effect, describe one's own feelings, and state what they want. This type of assertion response is particularly helpful in sharing negative feelings. An example would be: "You didn't wash the dishes again last night. When I brought my date home the kitchen was a mess and I felt embarrassed and upset. I would like you to do your share of the housework on time." Finally, assertion and persuasion involve using timing and tact to be influential in groups without being aggressive.

Behavior rehearsal

Behavior rehearsal is the primary vehicle for skill training in the assertiveness group. The technique consists of role-playing a situation that has created or can be anticipated to create some difficulties for the group member. Other group members and the leader participate by coaching and playing the roles of significant others in the interaction. In a structured group the leader might begin by introducing situations that are commonplace and likely to be troublesome for most nonassertive participants. Typical exercises draw upon both request and refusal responses. Examples include dealing assertively with salespersons, waiters, and garage mechanics, handling criticism and anger, and various conversational skills, such as being attentive to information offered by others, giving and receiving compliments, self-disclosure, changing topics, breaking into or terminating conversations, and dealing with silences.

In the early stages of the group, situations are presented that constitute only low-level threats for the participants. One way to begin a large group, for example, is to have members make eye contact with one another, introduce themselves, and then state what they liked about the other person's introduction (Lange & Jakubowski, 1976). As the group progresses, more challenging behavior rehearsals are introduced. Over time, most assertiveness-training groups become less structured, so that participants supply their own unique difficulties from the real world to role-play within the group. The role-playing, of course, somewhat resembles the content of a psychodrama session and, as such, bears the mark of Moreno's work. The idea is not, however, to relive an emotionally charged experience for catharsis or emotional discharge. The scenes deal exclusively with assertiveness issues and building an adaptive behavioral repertoire.

Behavioral principles are employed in the behavior-rehearsal procedure. First, the group leader or another group member might *model* a better way of handling the situation. Modeling is a behavioral technique that has been shown to be effective in developing new responses or strengthening weak ones (Bandura, 1971). By observing the model's assertive responses and their impact, group members vicariously learn the skill. In some groups, audio or video tapes of models engaged in assertive behavior are used. Modeling is especially useful when a group member has a very limited idea of what a good assertive behavior would be in a given situation. Less naive groups can jump directly into the rehearsal phase. The group members who play the various roles in a scene become more involved in the group process and also learn behavioral responses for their own use. A typical behavior-rehearsal sequence might go like this:

(In this situation Marge is trying to build up the courage to face her parents and inform them of her decision to move away from home and live with two girlfriends. Two group members have been chosen to play her parents.)

Marge: Mom, dad, I have something to tell you. I...uh...am thinking of...um...maybe moving into an apartment.

Dad: An apartment? What for? Don't you like living here anymore?

Marge: Yes, of course I do. It's just that I'm 19 now and Joyce and Sue really want me to move in with them.

Mom: Well, dear, we don't know anything about these friends of yours.

Marge: They're really nice and, uh, besides, I've made up my mind. I'm going to do it and that's that.

Leader: Okay, let's stop for a minute. Group, what was assertive about Marge's behavior?

Group member 1: Well, Marge, I liked the way you made eye contact and spoke in a loud, firm voice.

Group member 2: I think you started out well by telling your parents that you wanted to talk with them.

Leader: That's great. Marge, what did you think was assertive about your approach?

Marge: I was pretty calm at the beginning and I spoke up, which I tend not to do.

Leader: Yes, that's excellent. How might you improve?

Marge: I got defensive when my father tried a guilt message and at the end I lost my temper when my mother started interrogating me.

Leader: Okay, good insight. Anyone else? Any suggestions?

Group member 3: At the beginning you sounded tentative, Marge. Instead of informing them of a decision you had made, you sounded as if you were seeking their approval. Maybe you could tell them right off that you hope they will approve but you intend to move in any case.

Group member 4: I noticed a sheepish grin right before you made a strong statement.

Leader: That's very helpful feedback. Marge, would you like to try again and use what you have learned?

(After perfecting the interaction with relatively benign parents, the leader might ask Marge if she would like to

try again with somewhat more negative parents so that she is prepared to meet any contingency.)

Usually, only small chunks of a complex behavior are attempted at one time. After a couple of transactions the rehearsal is interrupted by the leader to solicit feedback from the group members. The defined client and the group are asked for their impressions of what was assertive and what was not and for their suggestions for experimentation or improvement. The leader may assist by coaching the group member in the role-playing situation. Coaching is an intervention in which the leader prompts and aids members when they encounter difficulties, giving hints, feedback, and support along the way.

Another component of the behavior-rehearsal procedure is *reinforcement*. Reinforcement is a fundamental behavioral concept and is the cornerstone for most behavior-change methods. Technically, there are several ways of defining reinforcement. According to the operant psychology of B. F. Skinner (1953), reinforcement involves the occurrence of an environmental event or stimulus that increases the likelihood of a response that precedes it. For our purposes, reinforcers are rewards or, more specifically, the positive reactions and encouragement offered by the leader and group members. Most important, a member is reinforced for any sort of improvement rather than only for the completion of a complex assertive sequence. The process of offering reinforcement in small steps as the response gradually approximates a complete and proficient set of behaviors is called "shaping." In behavioral groups, reinforcement generally applies to shaping the behavior of individual participants toward their goals. In some instances the interactions or task performances of the group as a whole may be modified by using group contingencies to reinforce all the members following accomplishment of their objectives (Feldman & Wodarski, 1975). In other situations, students in a classroom, convicts in a prison, and patients on a hospital ward might participate in a behavioral program in which they are rewarded with tokens or privileges for meeting stated goals.

Modeling, coaching, and reinforcement are key components of the behavior-rehearsal technique, though there is disagreement about what combination of components is optimal (McFall & Twentyman, 1973). The group leader's use of behavior rehearsal may be summarized in the following seven steps (Fensterheim & Baer, 1975):

- defining the behaviors that need training
- coaching and instructing the client's performance of a scene
- repeating the scene, hopefully with some improvement
- modeling the desired behavior
- using a graduated, hierarchical approach in cases where the problem is too difficult or anxiety arousing
- practicing the behavior over and over during the group session

- receiving feedback about the client's behavior in the home environment

Relaxation training

Very nonassertive people often experience considerable anxiety in interpersonal situations. Prior to introducing behavioral skill training in assertiveness groups, the leader often teaches relaxation techniques for inhibiting the anxiety response. Many behavioral groups rely almost exclusively on relaxation training to overcome general anxiety or specific fears.

There are a number of different approaches to relaxation training. Most are based on Jacobson's (1938) progressive-relaxation procedure in which muscle groupings are alternately tensed and relaxed. By clenching a fist, for example, and then unclenching it, thus releasing tension, the client learns to differentiate between states of tension and relaxation and ultimately to relax the muscle at will.

Relaxation training is sometimes combined with an imagery procedure, as in systematic desensitization. In this technique, relaxation training is coupled with two additional steps. First, a fear or anxiety problem is divided into a hierarchical sequence beginning with situations that cause little anxiety and progressing to situations that create a great deal of anxiety. A would-be public speaker, for example, might not find speaking to one friend alone in a room overly threatening, but cringe at the thought of addressing a classroom full of colleagues. A person with a fear of spiders might regard looking at a small spider in an illustrated book as mildly anxiety arousing, but would find touching a harmless spider as extremely intimidating.

The second step in the desensitization procedure is to combine the relaxation response with the image of a feared object. Clients are asked to close their eyes, relax, and visualize an item low on the anxiety hierarchy. The moment clients report feeling anxious, the therapist asks them to terminate the image immediately and relax. The sequence is repeated and refined until the person is able to visualize the entire hierarchy of scenes without becoming anxious. It is very important that anxiety be kept to a minimum, since the anxiety response itself may otherwise be reinforced. The idea is to replace the anxiety response with relaxation in the threatening situation.

The systematic-desensitization technique was introduced by Joseph Wolpe (1958) and explained by the reciprocal-inhibition principle discussed earlier. In recent years the technique has become a basic part of the arsenal of behavior therapists operating individually or in groups. Systematic desensitization has been used effectively with a number of problems, including fear of public speaking (Paul, 1966), test anxiety (McManus, 1971), social anxiety (Paul & Shannon, 1966), and sexual dysfunctions (Lazarus, 1968). When desensitization is accomplished in real life, rather than in imagery, that is, by asking clients to gradually confront a live audience or spider while in a relaxed state, the technique is called *in vivo* desensitization.

The actual desensitization procedure is usually not part of an ongoing assertiveness-training group. However, the hierarchy concept is retained by having members tackle progressively more challenging and formidable assertive encounters. Moreover, participants are urged to try a "minimal effective response" to accomplish a goal before escalating to heavier artillery. In other words, one might say "I wonder if you could be more quiet. I'm having a hard time hearing" in a noisy movie theater before resorting to more forceful measures.

One impromptu indication of the anxiety level a participant experiences in a situation demanding an assertive response is obtained by use of the Subjective Units of Discomfort (SUD) scale (Cottler & Guerra, 1976). Zero on the scale denotes a very relaxed and comfortable state while 100 denotes the worst possible state of panic. Group members are taught to rate their anxiety or discomfort numerically, using tension cues such as shortness of breath, sweating, pounding pulse, muscular tightness, and feelings of panic. The SUD scale has a wide range of application. It can be used within the group session to reflect the anxiety a participant experiences while imagining an assertive situation or rehearsing a confrontation. It can be used at home to gauge the threat of a situation and to measure progress. Assertive action is one indicator of success; assertive action while feeling relatively relaxed is even better.

Cognitive restructuring

Attacking the belief system of nonassertive group members can also be accomplished by using cognitive-restructuring techniques. Such techniques fall within a cognitive/behavioral extension of orthodox behavior therapy.

I have already discussed the development of a belief system that places a high premium on personal rights. However, people also operate with irrational assumptions of which they are hardly aware. Albert Ellis (1962) has enumerated 11 irrational beliefs that he maintains lead to emotional problems. Prominent among these are the ideas that you must have approval and love from the significant people in your life, and that you must be thoroughly competent, adequate, and achieving in all possible respects in order to be worthwhile. Ellis insists that these ideas are patently illogical and personally destructive because they lead to emotional disturbance when we do not receive approval or love or when we fail in some enterprise. These eventualities are absolutely unavoidable and commonplace, of course, so that maintaining this irrational belief system insures a life of frustration and disappointment. There is a tendency among many people to experience a small failure, magnify the impact of the experience by contaminating it with their irrational beliefs, and then feel awful.

Ellis' rational-emotive therapy (RET) is a way of diagnosing irrational beliefs and systematically substituting rational ideas in their place. His RET groups spend considerable time attacking and breaking down the irrational components of a person's thinking and encouraging the substitution of more reasonable ideas and conclusions (Ellis, 1974). A person who feels devastated and unworthy as a result of a rejection, for example, learns to apply standards of reasonable evaluation and perceive the event as unfortunate and perhaps even informative because, though it's nice to be loved by a particular person, it is not critical to one's well-being and survival.

Lange and Jakubowski (1976) have made cognitive restructuring methods an integral part of their assertiveness training groups. Group members are taught to recognize irrational assumptions and replace them with rational alternatives. Often the resistance to acting assertively is a fear of a catastrophic outcome. The reason that a woman might not approach a man and ask him out, may be a fear that something awful will happen. The something awful is usually a rejection, which implies she may feel totally humiliated and worthless. The rational alternative is to say "Well, he turned me down and though I hurt a little I'm still a worthwhile person. Besides, why do I want a man who can't tolerate an assertive woman?" In other cases the resistance to acting assertively is a fear of hurting others, looking foolish, or expressing anger. In all likelihood, the more group participants think rationally, the more likely they will act assertively.

Homework

Behavior therapists are very concerned about the gap that often exists between the group experience and the retention of new skills and their application in the home environment. One way to encourage generalization of changes in assertiveness to the outside world is to assign homework. At the very least, members are asked to bring in recent incidents in which they incurred difficulty being assertive and to present the incidents for sharing and rehearsal in the group. Members can also describe assertive responses they have avoided but will now attempt. Cottler and Guerra (1976) ask participants to use a "homework diary" to record between-session assignments, including what was done, SUD ratings, how successful the experience was, and suggestions for improvement.

Homework assignments begin at low levels of stress in order to maximize the probability of a successful outcome. Success encourages further experimentation and more success. The assignments can be individualized according to the particular sphere of problems encountered by each group member. Asking a telephone operator for a number and address or borrowing a cup of sugar from a neighbor might be low-level assignments; approaching a professor about a low grade or starting a conversation with a stranger while waiting in line might be more advanced skills. Some assertiveness group leaders encourage rather forced and pushy interactions, such as going to a gas station, asking for fifty-cents worth of gasoline and requesting that the oil be checked and the windows cleaned. It may be better to stick with behaviors that do demand assertiveness, are realistic, and retain sensitivity to others. The idea is to overcome inhibition and to develop and polish a useful set of skills, not to screw up one's courage to undergo a *rite de passage* to impress the group and the leader.

Additional techniques

Up to this point I have discussed the active role the assertiveness-group leader plays in orienting members to the topic, assessing problems, implementing specific change procedures, and evaluating effectiveness. The leader relies on modeling, desensitization, cognitive restructuring, and behavior rehearsal, as well as on facilitative group behaviors such as providing open and honest feedback and reinforcing progress toward a goal. Skillful leaders also try to alter group norms, communication styles, and patterns to give all participants a more or less equal opportunity to work and to encourage members to help one another. Gradually the therapist may become less of a leader and more of a consultant, as individuals take an increasing amount of responsibility for their own progress and for applying their skills outside the group.

There are a number of specific techniques favored by group leaders that are unique to assertiveness training. For instance, the "broken record" is a repetition of the assertor's position in spite of pressure and criticism from others to yield or compromise. Without resorting to defensiveness or explanation, individuals may repeat their demands or point of view like a broken record:

Salesman:	Here's a handy-dandy tool kit I'd like to show you.
Client:	No, thank you, I'm not interested in buying a tool kit today.
Salesman:	Well, this kit is the most versatile on the market and can save you lots of money.
Client:	I believe you, but I'm not interested in buying one.
Salesman:	Aren't you interested in saving money?
Client:	I'm still not interested in buying a tool kit.
Salesman:	This is your last chance to get one and you're the only person on the block without one.
Client:	I'm not interested.

Refusing someone's requests or making one of your own may require repetition of the essential point several times.

A more controversial technique is "fogging," suggested by Manuel Smith (1975). Fogging is recommended as a passive, noncombative response to persistent critics or naggers. The fogger acknowledges that what the critic says may have some merit without directly taking issue or totally acquiescing. For example, when mother says "You never did know how to dress with any taste," the fogger might respond "You may be right, mother, I don't know much about dressing stylishly." When mother continues "When you dress that way, I bet the boys get the idea that you're a tramp," the fogger comes back "You may be right." The problem with the technique is that though it may prevent the escalation of a potentially fiery conflict, it is basically a manipulative and dishonest communication that does nothing to enhance the long-term relationship between two people.

These are only two samples of specific interventions that might be used in an assertiveness-training group as skill-building exercises or recommended solutions for particular problems. Creative group leaders have concocted many other techniques to supplement standard procedures.

APPRAISAL

The systematic, structured, skill-training approach to groups seems to be on the upswing. In one sense it is surprising that behaviorists have not made more use of the group format, given the advantages of a group for learning new behaviors and attitudes. This school has consistently stressed the need to obtain representative samples of a client's behavior before, and while, proceeding with treatment. The group setting, of course, affords a much broader, more thorough sampling of interpersonal behaviors than an individual meeting between a therapist and a client. In individual sessions, clients can plead that others complain about their tendency to be critical, while remaining helplessly blind to their own behavior. A firsthand view of the critical behavior within the group helps the therapist assess the difficulty and provide feedback to the client.

Behavioral techniques are the favorite tools of group leaders teaching a number of critical life skills, including parenting (Patterson, 1976), weight control (Wollersheim, 1977), anger control (Novaco, 1975), and communication within couples (Birchler, 1979). Most of these group programs deal with individuals who already claim to have problems in an identified area. There is currently a need for more life-skills intervention efforts at a prevention level, to teach problem-solving methods so that problems are nipped in the bud or avoided altogether. A popular example of a preventive skill-training approach is parent-effectiveness training (Gordon, 1970).

It has been noted that structured groups, through their goal-directedness and concrete focus, help to demystify the process of self-discovery (Drum & Knott, 1977). The issue of how much or how little structure is optimal in a group is a controversial one. Most experiential groups, as we have seen, emphasize self-exploration and growth within a safe, relatively unstructured environment. The counterargument states that when goals are made clear, desired behaviors are identified, and group process is explained, the therapeutic work takes place more quickly. Proponents of skill-training groups point to small-group research suggesting that a lack of structure early in the group's life adversely feeds on the participants' confusion, distress, and tendency to drop out (Bednar, Melnick, & Kaul, 1974). Structure in the early stages, in the form of didactic explanations, norm setting, and interpersonal exercises, can promote desirable group development. In the ambiguity of a new group situation, evolution seems to proceed from structure to increased risk taking to increased cohesion to increased personal responsibility and growth (Bednar, et al., 1974).

When group process is viewed as educational and problem solving, therapeutic risk taking and change become relatively nonthreatening. At the same time the learning process is not as dry as teaching parched students in the arid atmosphere of the classroom. The topic is learning about self, the most exciting quest of all, and the vehicle of the group implies the enthusiasm of a here-and-now, sharing experience. One needs to remember, however, that the purpose of a skill-training group is skill acquisition. Consequently, the potential for self-discovery may be somewhat muted or restricted in comparison to other group approaches that offer a more open format. Moreover, though group members may more easily meet their practical goals, the very directive role of the leader carries the danger of breeding dependence and discouraging self-reliance. Perhaps the strongest limitation of behaviorally-oriented, structured groups at this time is that their leaders are often naive regarding factors of individual resistance and group dynamics that affect the participant's willingness to open up, experiment, and grow.

The important life skill of being comfortably assertive seems to be most advantageously learned in groups. The diverse life experiences of the group members provide a fertile field for generating, practicing, and feeding back assertive, nonassertive, and aggressive responses. The opportunities to develop and rehearse realistic and generalizable behaviors and strategies are improved when other participants can play other roles, contribute ideas, offer support, and reinforce progress. One of the reasons for choosing assertiveness training as a model skill-training group is the relatively large amount of documented evidence attesting to its effectiveness. Since the first experimental study on assertiveness training conducted by McFall and Marston (1970), the literature has grown quickly. Studies have demonstrated the positive use of the approach with groups as general as women (Wolfe & Fodor, 1975) to those as narrow as sexual offenders (Laws & Serber, 1975) and psychiatric inpatients (Hersen & Bellack, 1976). At least two review articles (Rich & Schroeder, 1976; Galassi & Galassi, 1978) have tackled the methodological issues in assertion-theory research. In comparison to most other experiential groups, a commitment to ongoing research evaluation has been maintained in this area.

Finally, there is an important interface between assertiveness training and other experiential groups discussed earlier. It is becoming increasingly clear that the ability to act assertively carries with it an increase in personal self-esteem. Those who cannot or do not behave assertively to defend their own rights and satisfy their own needs and wants while remaining sensitive to the needs of others are apt to feel helpless, even worthless. A common thread present in all experiential groups is that participants strive to nurture the ability to freely choose their actions and to increase their behavior potential. Assertive responses are but one type of action that goes into becoming a mature and fulfilled person.

SUMMARY

Behavioral approaches to psychotherapy have their origins in the psychology laboratory, including the early contributions of Pavlov on conditioned reflexes and Skinner in operant conditioning. In the past, behavioral groups have relied on transferring individual methods to the group context. More recently, behavioral practitioners have developed techniques that capitalize on the potential of the group for eliciting change.

Skill-training groups are rooted in behavioristic concepts, including a focus on observable behaviors and an educational, problem-solving model based on the learning of developmentally important life skills. Specific goals, such as the skills worked on in *relationship-enhancement therapy* and *structured-learning therapy* groups, are encouraged. Finally, all behavioral groups are concerned with measurement and evaluation of effects.

Procedures typically found in skill-training groups are exemplified by *assertiveness-training groups*. Assertiveness training developed out of Salter's *conditioned-reflex therapy*. Assessment of the problem includes the use of inventories such as the Rathus scale, the presentation of basic human rights, and differentiation among various types of assertiveness. *Behavioral rehearsal,* in which challenging situations are role-played, is the key technique used in skill-training groups. The procedure consists of modeling, coaching, and reinforcement. *Relaxation training* and *desensitization* are often used to reduce undue anxiety. *Cognitive restructuring* involves exploring the irrational assumptions behind one's beliefs and behaviors. *Homework* in the form of diaries or behavioral assignments is also typical of skill-training groups. Finally, interventions specific to assertiveness training include the *broken record* and *fogging*.

Skill-training groups are on the upswing and have been used to develop critical life skills such as parenting, weight control, anger control, and sexual responses. One of the advantages of all behaviorally-oriented groups is a strong commitment to empirical research. There is good evidence indicating that assertiveness-training groups, for example, lead to greater freedom and enhanced self-esteem. As with all experiential groups, an increase in self-esteem goes hand in hand with an increase in behavior potential among group members.

REFERENCES

Alberti, R. E. Issues in assertive behavior training. In R. E. Alberti (Ed.), *Assertiveness: Innovations, applications, issues.* San Luis Obispo, Calif.: Impact, 1977.

Alberti, R. E., & Emmons, M. L. *Your perfect right: A guide to assertive behavior.* (2nd ed.) San Luis Obispo, Calif.: Impact, 1974.

Bandura, A. Psychotherapy based on modeling principles. In A. E. Bergin & S. L. Garfield (Eds.), *Handbook of psychotherapy and behavior change.* New York: John Wiley & Sons, 1971.

Bednar, R. L., Melnick, J., & Kaul, T. J. Risk, responsibility, and structure: A conceptual framework for initiating group counseling and psychotherapy. *Journal of Counseling Psychology,* 1974, *21,* 31–37.

Birchler, G. R. Communication skills in married couples. In A. S. Bellack & M. Hersen (Eds.), *Research and practice in social skill training.* New York: Plenum Press, 1979.

Cartwright, D., & Zander, A. (Eds.), *Group dynamics: Research and theory.* Evanston, Ill.: Row, Peterson, 1968.

Collins, J. D. Experimental evaluation of a six-month conjugal therapy relationship enhancement program. In B. G. Guerney, Jr. (Ed.), *Relationship enhancement: Skill-training program for therapy, problem prevention, and enrichment.* San Francisco: Jossey-Bass, 1977.

Cottler, S. B., & Guerra, J. J. *Assertion training.* Champaign, Ill.: Research Press, 1976.

Drum, D. J., & Knott, J. E. *Structured groups for facilitating development.* New York: Human Sciences Press, 1977.

Ellis, A. *Reason and emotion in psychotherapy.* New York: Lyle Stuart, 1962.

Ellis, A. The group as agent in facilitating change toward rational thinking and appropriate emoting. In A. Jacobs & W. W. Spradlin, *The group as agent of change.* New York: Behavioral Publications, 1974.

Factor, D. C., & Daubenspeck, P. A. *Introduction to the skills approach in mental health services: An educational model of therapy.* Paper presented at the annual meeting of the Ontario Psychological Association, Toronto, February, 1979.

Feldman, R. A., & Wodarski, J. S. *Contemporary approaches to group treatment.* San Francisco: Jossey-Bass, 1975.

Fensterheim, H., & Baer, J. *Don't say yes when you want to say no.* New York: David McKay, 1975.

Galassi, M. D., & Galassi, J. P. Assertion: A critical review. *Psychotherapy: Therapy, Research, and Practice,* 1978, *15,* 16–29.

Goldstein, A. P. *Structured learning therapy: Toward a psychotherapy for the poor.* New York: Academic Press, 1973.

Goldstein, A. P., Sprafkin, R. P., Gershaw, N. J., & Klein, P. *Skill-streaming the adolescent.* Champaign, Ill.: Research Press, 1980.

Gordon, T. *P.E.T.: Parent effectiveness training.* New York: Peter H. Wyden, 1970.

Guerney, B., Jr. *Relationship enhancement: Skill training programs for therapy, problem prevention, and enrichment.* San Francisco: Jossey-Bass, 1977.

Hersen, M., & Barlow, D. H. *Single case experimental designs.* New York: Pergamon Press, 1976.

Hersen, M., & Bellack, A. S. Social skills training for chronic psychiatric patients: Rationale, research findings, and future directions. *Comprehensive Psychiatry,* 1976, *17,* 559–580.

Jacobson, E. *Progressive relaxation.* Chicago: University of Chicago Press, 1938.

Kanfer, F. H., & Phillips, J. S. *Learning foundations of behavior therapy.* New York: John Wiley & Sons, 1970.

Kelley, C. *Assertion training: A facilitator's guide.* La Jolla, Calif.: University Associates, 1979.

Lange, A. J., & Jakubowski, P. *Responsible assertive behavior.* Champaign, Ill.: Research Press, 1976.

Laws, D. R., & Serber, M. Measurement and evaluation of assertive training with sexual offenders. In R. E. Hosford, & C. S. Moss (Eds.), *The crumbling walls: Treatment and counselling of prisoners.* Champaign, Ill.: University of Illinois Press, 1975.

Lazarus, A. A. Group therapy of phobic disorders by systematic desensitization. *Journal of Abnormal and Social Psychology,* 1961, *63,* 504–510.

Lazarus, A. A. Behavior therapy in groups. In G. M. Gazda (Ed.), *Basic approaches to group psychotherapy and group counseling.* Springfield, Ill.: Charles C Thomas, 1968.

Levinson, D. J. *The seasons of a man's life.* New York: Knopf, 1978.

Liberman, R. P. A behavioral approach to group dynamics: I. Reinforcement and prompting of cohesiveness in group therapy. *Behavior Therapy,* 1970, *1,* 141–175.

Liberman, R. P., & Teigen, J. Behavioral group therapy. In P. Sjöden, S. Bates, & W. S. Dockens III (Eds.), *Trends in behavior therapy.* New York: Academic Press, 1979.

McFall, R. M., & Marston, A. R. Behavior rehearsal with modeling and coaching in assertive training. *Journal of Abnormal Psychology,* 1970, 76, 295–303.

McFall, R. M., & Twentyman, C. T. Four experiments on the relative contributions of rehearsal, modeling, and coaching to assertion training. *Journal of Abnormal Psychology,* 1973, *81,* 199–218.

McManus, M. Group desensitization of test anxiety. *Behavior Research and Therapy,* 1971, *9,* 55–56.

Meichenbaum, D. *Cognitive-behavior modification.* New York: Plenum Press, 1977.

Mischel, W. Toward a cognitive social learning reconceptualization of personality. *Psychological Review,* 1973, *80,* 252–283.

Novaco, R. W. *Anger control: The development and evaluation of an experimental treatment.* Lexington, Md.: D. C. Heath & Co., Lexington Books, 1975.

Patterson, G. R. *Living with children.* Champaign, Ill.: Research Press, 1976.

Paul, G. L. *Insight versus desensitization in psychotherapy: An experiment in anxiety reduction.* Stanford: Stanford University Press, 1966.

Paul, G. L., & Shannon, D. T. Treatment of anxiety through systematic desensitization in therapy groups. *Journal of Abnormal Psychology,* 1966, *71,* 124–135.

Rathus, S. A. A 30-item schedule for assessing assertive behavior. *Behavior Therapy,* 1973, *4,* 398–406.

Rich, A. R., & Schroeder, H. E. Research issues in assertiveness training. *Psychological Bulletin,* 1976, *83,* 1081–1096.

Rose, S. D. *Group therapy: A behavioral approach.* New York: Prentice-Hall, 1977.

Salter, A. *Conditioned reflex therapy.* New York: Farrar, Straus & Giroux, 1949.

Sheehy, G. *Passages.* New York: E. P. Dutton & Co., 1976.

Skinner, B. F. *Science and human behavior.* New York: Macmillan, 1953.

Smith, M. J. *When I say no I feel guilty.* New York: Dial Press, 1975.

Wolfe, J., & Fodor, I. G. A cognitive/behavioral approach to modifying assertive behavior in women. *The Counseling Psychologist,* 1975, *5,* 45–52.

Wollersheim, J. P. Obesity and behavior therapy groups. *Behavior Therapy,* 1977, *8,* 996–998.

Wolpe, J. *Psychotherapy by reciprocal inhibition.* Stanford: Stanford University Press, 1958.

Wolpe, J., & Lazarus, A. A. *Behavior therapy techniques.* New York: Pergamon Press, 1966.

12

Experiential Exercises

In this chapter, a variety of experiential exercises are offered to supplement the conceptual material presented in preceding chapters. Structured exercises are important in two ways: first, they aid group process and help achieve focused learning; second, by means of such exercises, group members actively facilitate group or individual goals. The learning stimulated by the exercise depends upon which exercise is used and when and how it is employed. For group members, new issues emerge as a result of participation in the exercise. New feelings are often generated and explored. And sometimes new behaviors are practiced or modeled. In addition, good experiential exercises can pull a group together by reducing barriers to openness, and they can push members further along the road to self-discovery.

The use of structured exercises within the experiential-group field ranges from the traditional T-group, in which the group leader (trainer) provides no structure at all, to the skill-training group, which may consist entirely of a series of uniform exercises. Group leaders who shy away from exercises generally believe that their use deprives members of the responsibility for structuring their own experience and that they are an artifice that deadens a potentially enlivening, spontaneous happening. Those who advocate the frequent use of exercises believe that they help to assess and highlight group concerns and resolve individual and group issues more expediently than the natural flow of events can.

Opinion also differs regarding when in the group's life exercises are most appropriate. Many therapists claim that the group needs to struggle on its own at first, and that introducing exercises prematurely discourages the expression of important individual feelings. Later, group members may benefit from exercises that deal with predictable group issues, such as power struggles, lack of intimacy or cohesiveness, or dissatisfaction with the leader. Other group leaders argue that a structured approach is particularly important in the early stages of an ongoing group in order to motivate participants and point them in a fruitful direction (Bednar & Melnick, 1974).

Despite so much apparent disagreement, there is a relative consensus that experiential exercises should not be used arbitrarily or indifferently. Group leaders who rely predominantly on the use of exercises risk turning their groups into an endless series of parlor games and making themselves little more than carnival barkers. Too often, unskilled or untrained leaders use structured exercises to camouflage their ignorance of leadership skills. This is an especially precarious strategy when the leader does not understand the rationale for or the potency of an exercise.

The use of exercises is largely a matter of personal preference. As group leaders acquire more experience, they are less apt to follow a formal agenda of structured exercises and instead tend to intuitively draw upon a large reserve of techniques to illustrate or deal with group issues. The experienced group leader will make a well-timed intervention and choose a specific technique or activity for a specific purpose. Leaders who contemplate the use of an exercise must ask themselves how it fits into their theory of group behavior, what the exercise will mean to the members, and if the issue involved warrants the time the exercise requires.

In short-term groups, such as workshops, marathons, or classes surveying various group approaches, the use of exercises may be very appropriate. Exercises have the power to demonstrate concepts much more quickly and vividly than words. Elizabeth Mintz (Morris & Cinnamon, 1976) gives a compelling example of this phenomenon. The game of "open the fist" invites participants to try to open a partner's clenched fist without being told how to proceed. Those who use gentle persuasion invariably do better than those who employ force, which immediately brings home the lesson that tact is more effective than violence.

The following exercises illustrate the kinds of activities that occur in each type of group previously discussed. Since the groups themselves overlap along certain dimensions, it is important to realize that a given exercise is not necessarily exclusive to a single group approach. However, an effort has been made to select exercises that accurately exemplify the concepts and practices of that approach. Some are original and some are adapted from other sources. They are broad in scope but they are certainly not comprehensive, and the chapter is not intended as a handbook for the potential group leader.

The exercises can be used to develop a session or sessions to demonstrate a given group approach.[1] The exercises associated with each type of group cover a range of activities and are generally organized from introductory to advanced levels. Each exercise includes guidelines for the time and expertise required for its use. Some leaders prefer to jump into an experience first and then conceptualize it. Others prefer to explain the rationale for the exercise prior to experiencing it. In either case it is very important to allow participants the opportunity to debrief after each experience and share their reactions and feelings. Those leaders who favor emotional expressiveness at the expense of cognitive integration may fear "talking away" the experience. In most groups, however, there is a concern for understanding the implications of an experience for one's life and development.

Another recommendation is that participation be voluntary so that members have the opportunity to withdraw from an exercise without losing face. It is also a good idea to ask the group at the outset if some issue of greater priority needs attention. Finally, it is critical for leaders and members alike to keep in mind that it is far more important to deal with the feelings and behaviors generated by the exercise than to finish it. The exercise is a means to exploring individual and group issues, not an end in itself.

My final suggestion is that readers engage in the exercises in the spirit of experimentation and innocent pleasure. Have fun!

T-GROUPS

Traditional T-groups are unstructured and rely on group members' initiative to provide an agenda. The following exercises are representative of those used in structured T-groups.

Who am I?

Purpose: This exercise is a potential T-group opener particularly appropriate for a group of strangers meeting for the first time. It is a good way of breaking the ice and getting to know one another quickly.

Time required: 30 minutes.

Materials: paper, pencils, pens.

Preparation: No special training is required.

Procedure: Give each group member a pencil and paper. The group members are given the following instructions:

---

[1] In addition to exercises that illustrate a particular group method, there are other strategies useful in designing a classroom survey of experiential groups. One is to ask group members to keep, as a learning tool, a diary of feelings, impressions, and insights that reflect the ongoing group experience. A second strategy, useful when the class is large, is to take a few minutes of each session for participants to meet in established three-person minigroups. The minigroup is a place where members, who may not be sharing all the same experiences in the large group, can gather to bring one another up to date on progress toward personal goals for the group experience and to offer and receive suggestions and encouragement.

Make a list from 1 to 10, and answer the question "Who am I?" ten times. Use whatever characteristics, traits, interests, or feelings you would like to use to describe yourself, beginning each sentence with the words "I am...."

When you have finished your list, pin it to your lapel or to the front of your shirt or blouse. Now move around the room, approaching other group members by reading their lists and sharing your own. Feel free to comment on other people's lists. (As an alternative, group members may read their lists aloud to the rest of the group.)

Lost at sea

Purpose: This exercise explores the group decision-making process. It teaches the effectiveness of consensus-seeking behavior in task groups. It also provides information concerning communication, leadership, and dominance patterns within the group and can help contribute to cohesiveness among group members (Jones & Pfeiffer, 1975, pp. 31–32).

Time required: 1½ hours.

Materials: Copies of the instructions and worksheets and pencils.

Preparation: The leader should be skilled in examining group process.

Procedure: Each individual in the group is given the following instructions and asked to complete the task in 15 minutes:

You are adrift on a private yacht in the South Pacific. As a consequence of a fire of unknown origin, much of the yacht and its contents have been destroyed. The yacht is now slowly sinking. Your location is unclear because of the destruction of critical navigational equipment and because you and the crew were distracted trying to bring the fire under control. Your best estimate is that you are approximately one thousand miles south-southwest of the nearest land.

Below is a list of fifteen items that are intact and undamaged after the fire. In addition to these articles, you have a serviceable, rubber life raft with oars large enough to carry yourself, the crew, and all the items listed below. The total contents of all survivors' pockets are a package of cigarettes, several books of matches, and five one-dollar bills.

Your task is to rank the 15 items below in terms of their importance to your survival. Place the number 1 by the most important item, the number 2 by the second most important, and so on through number 15, the least important.

_____ Sextant

_____ Shaving mirror

_____ Five-gallon can of water

_____ Mosquito netting

_____ One case of U.S. Army C rations

_____ Maps of the Pacific Ocean

_____Seat cushion (flotation device approved by the Coast Guard)

_____Two-gallon can of oil-gas mixture

_____Small transistor radio

_____Shark repellent

_____Twenty square feet of opaque plastic

_____One quart of 160-proof Puerto Rican rum

_____Fifteen feet of nylon rope

_____Two boxes of chocolate bars

_____Fishing kit

After the individual rankings have been completed the group has 45 minutes to complete the following task:

This is an exercise in group decision making. Your group is to employ the group consensus method in reaching its decision. This means that the prediction for each of the fifteen survival items must be agreed upon by each group member before it becomes a part of the group decision. Consensus is difficult to reach. Therefore, not every ranking will meet with everyone's complete approval. As a group, try to make each ranking one with which all group members can at least partially agree. Here are some guides to use in reaching consensus:

1. Avoid arguing for your own individual judgments. Approach the task on the basis of logic.
2. Avoid changing your mind if it is only to reach agreement and avoid conflict. Support only solutions with which you are able to agree at least somewhat.
3. Avoid "conflict-reducing" techniques such as majority votes, averaging, or trading in reaching your decision.
4. View differences of opinion as a help rather than a hindrance in decision making.[2]

After the group ranking is completed, look up the correct order in the Appendix. At this point you can compare the accuracy of individual rankings with the group consensus data. Spend some additional time discussing the decision-making processes that were involved in reaching the group's ranking. What behaviors helped or hindered the process of reaching consensus? What patterns of leadership emerged? Who participated and who did not? Who was influential? Why? What was the atmosphere of the group during the discussion? Were the major resources of the group used optimally? What covert pressures were used by group members to lobby for their views? How could group decision making have been improved?

[2]This exercise is reprinted from: J. E. Jones and J. W. Pfeiffer (Eds.), *The 1975 Annual Handbook for Group Facilitators.* San Diego, CA: University Associates, 1975. Used with permission.

An alternative to these instructions is to have one or more nonparticipating process observers who can provide feedback about group or individual behavior at the conclusion of the task.

Simulation skits

Purpose: This set of exercises can be used to practice communication skills within the group. The format allows for rehearsal of a range of useful skills as well as the opportunity to give and receive feedback.

Time required: 1 hour.

Materials: None.

Preparation: No special training is required.

Procedure: Three group members volunteer to begin. Each volunteer chooses one of the styles of communicating described by family therapist Virginia Satir (1972). These four styles describe communication stances that people may adopt when they experience conflict or stress.

1. The *placater* is a pleaser, a yes-person, continually apologizing and attempting at all costs not to make waves. Placators look helpless, feel worthless and usually express themselves by whining.

2. The *blamer* is the opposite of the placater, a perennial fault-finder and provoker. Blamers act superior and externalize their own shortcomings. They may point a finger accusingly, speak in a loud, tyrannical voice, and have tight muscles throughout the face and body.

3. The *computer* is the ultrareasonable, calm, cool, and collected individual who avoids feelings and emotionality like the plague. The computer talks in a monotone, stays abstract, and looks stiff and constricted.

4. The *distracter* makes comments that are unfocused, irrelevant, and perplexing. Distracters' body stances look disjointed and lopsided, and their voices may be out of tune with their words.

The volunteers are asked to choose styles that are new to them, styles that may be a little uncomfortable and that may broaden the volunteers' behavioral repertoires. Then they choose any topic and get involved in a discussion with one another, staying in their chosen roles. The remaining group members observe the interaction. After five minutes, the observers are invited to comment on their perceptions of the discussion. Then the volunteers share with the group how they felt in their roles. By experimenting with alternative ways of communicating, the participants can learn to approach one another in more congruent and less defensive ways.

Now repeat the procedure with three new group members. Try to give everyone a chance to participate at least once.

Other communication skills can be explored in the same "fishbowl" format, in which a few participants simulate various behaviors and the rest of the group looks on. Practice behavior description by choosing four or five members to adopt particular roles in a simulated interaction on a given topic. In arguing the merits of abortion, for example, a man might be coached by the leader to argue for the exact opposite of his own position;

another could be asked to support the dominant member of the discussion; a third person might be asked to try to steer the others from the topic; a fourth could be asked to tear apart the dominant individual's ideas. The number of possible roles to adopt are limited only by your own or the leader's imagination.

The discussion between the four or five members provides data for the observers to practice their skills in behavior description, that is, they avoid labeling and ascribing motivation to the featured participants. Again, keep going until everyone has had the opportunity to be part of a skit.

Task and maintenance roles

Purpose: In this exercise group members are provided with feedback about their typical interactional behavior. Task and maintenance roles are assessed to enable participants to evaluate their contributions to the group. Members learn which behaviors are overrepresented and which are underrepresented in the group.

Time required: 1 hour.

Materials: Description of task and maintenance behaviors.

Preparation: No special training is required.

Procedure: Half of the group sits in the center of the room; the remaining half forms a circle around them. Each person in the outer circle is asked to observe the behavior of someone in the center. The participants are instructed as follows:

If you are in the inner circle, you will be engaging in a discussion for 15–20 minutes. Any topic will do, although open-ended ones are best. During this discussion you will be observed by a person in the outer circle.

If you are in the outer circle, note how frequently your partner engages in various task and maintenance behaviors. Task behaviors include initiating, elaborating, clarifying, testing, and summarizing. Maintenance behaviors include relieving tension, compromising, harmonizing, encouraging, and gate keeping. (A description of each behavior can be found in Chapter 1.) Note if these behaviors are productive or counterproductive to the group goal. Record specific counterproductive behaviors: withdrawing, shifting topics, seeking recognition, dominating, aggressing, and being disruptive or irrelevant. After 15–20 minutes, share your observations with your partner about his or her group behavior.

Partners then switch roles, and the process is repeated. Conclude the exercise by discussing the frequency and distribution of various task and maintenance and behaviors in the group.

ENCOUNTER GROUPS

Microlab

Purpose: The microlab approach (Schutz, 1971) is a way of becoming acquainted with a wide variety of encounter concepts and techniques on an experiential level. The exercises are quite comprehensive and can serve as an adequate introduction to encounter groups.

Time required: 2–2½ hours.

Materials: None.

Preparation: The leader should be experienced, since some of the exercises may generate strong feelings among the participants.

Procedure: The group should be seated comfortably in a circle on the floor while the rules of open encounter are briefly reviewed, including the importance of communicating openly and honestly, concentrating on feelings, being attentive to the body, remaining in the here-and-now, and taking personal responsibility for behavior. In addition, members should refrain from drinking coffee, eating food, smoking cigarettes, and consulting wrist watches during the microlab.

The warm-up exercise in a microlab should be energizing, provide relief from nervousness or tension, and divert attention from external concerns to the present and the group experience. The group should allot 5–10 minutes for the warm-up exercise:

Close your eyes and breathe deeply for one or two minutes. Concentrate on your breathing and feel the energy flow through your body. Now, open your throat and let a sound come out of your mouth. At the same time, slowly rise to your feet. Let the sound get louder and louder and louder. At the same time, pound your arms up and down as if you were pounding on a table. Hold the sound at its loudest level for a while, and then gradually let it become softer and softer until you are quiet. Continue to breathe in complete silence. Slowly let your body sink to the floor until you are lying on your back concentrating on your breathing. Softly form the syllable OM and hum it each time you exhale. Feel the electricity in the room and in your body as you breathe deeply. Finally, return to a restful silence.

At this point, if your group is large, divide into smaller groups. A group of five or six people encourages more intense encounter for each participant then a larger group. The members try to link up with people they do not know well and sit on the floor in a circle. The following activities are a selection from many imaginative possibilities (Schutz, 1971). It is usually a good idea to balance verbal exercises with nonverbal exercises and individual experiences with interpersonal experiences. Follow each exercise with a short encounter session in which the participants share feelings and perceptions.

Encounter.   Have an encounter for about five minutes. Remember the ground rules: be open and honest, talk about your feelings, and stay in the present.

After five minutes the leader should interrupt and find out how it went. Some groups may wander off into telling anecdotes rather than engaging in valid encounter. The leader will remind the groups of the ground rules and ask them to have another five-minute encounter, trying harder to observe the rules.

Breaking in.   Decide which member of your group feels most left out of the group. Everyone else stands up and makes a circle by interlocking arms. The left-out individual stands on the outside of the circle and tries to physically break into the group while the group tries its best to keep him or her out. This activity will help you contact feelings of exclusion/inclusion and will help to build group cohesiveness.

Loneliness.   Think of the time you were most lonely in your life. As you sit quietly in your subgroup, try to recapture those feelings for a couple of minutes. Now share these experiences with each other. (This exercise will help to deepen the interpersonal relationships among group members.)

Trust fall.   For this exercise, you will need a partner. One person will fall and the partner will catch. If you are the catcher, stand about three feet behind your partner so that you can break her fall. If you are the faller, relax and fall backward into the arms of your partner. Try to fall without moving your feet or catching yourself. Notice your feelings as you prepare to fall or catch. Switch around so that everyone has an opportunity to both fall and catch. (This exercise is excellent for exploring the issue of trust.)

Impressions.   In this exercise, members share their main impressions of one another.
Sit in front of each member in turn and look the person in the eye. You can touch him or her if you wish. Briefly share how you feel about the person, stating both positive and negative feelings. Speak loudly enough for the group to hear. Be brief. When you finish, it's the next person's turn to go around the circle, facing one person at a time. Whenever it is your turn to listen, do not question or respond but try to learn something from the feedback you receive.

Arm wrestling.   Lie on the floor facing a partner. You are going to have an arm-wrestling contest with every person in your group. Put your right elbow on the floor, clasp hands, and use your left hand to support your opponent's elbow. (If you feel that certain group members are at a physical disadvantage, you may wish to allow them to use two arms in their contests.) Make lots of noise and ham it up.

Wise man.   Close your eyes and imagine a green meadow. Look for an old oak tree at the end of the meadow. Under the tree is a wise old man who will answer any question you ask him. Go up to him, ask him any question you wish, and listen to his answer. Behind him, a calendar is nailed to the oak tree. Read the date on the calendar. Then open your eyes and share your fantasy with your group.

Body lift.   Use this exercise if there is a person who still feels uncomfortable or ill at ease in the group, or who wants some nurturance from group members. Have the person lie on the floor with eyes closed. The members form a circle and gently pick the person up. Very slowly they raise the person over their heads, gently rocking his or her body back and forth. Then they slowly lower the person back to the ground.

Last meeting.   Close your eyes and imagine that the group is over. You are on your way home. Think of the things you did not say to the group but wish that you had said. After a few minutes, open your eyes and say those things. Then, without making a sound, continue to say goodbye to the group. (This exercise is a good way to conclude the microlab.)

Trust walk

Purpose: The trust walk is a well-known encounter activity that is used to expand sensory awareness and promote interpersonal trust.

Time required: 1 hour.

Materials: Blindfolds and sufficient space to explore, preferably outdoors.

Preparation: No special training is required.

Procedure: The group is instructed as follows:

Divide into pairs, choosing a partner unfamiliar to you. One person in each pair begins as leader, while the other is the blindfolded follower. After half an hour, reverse roles. The exercise is carried out *nonverbally*.

When you are in the leader's role, hold your partner by the hand, arm, or waist and take him or her on a sensory exploration. Do not talk, but guide your partner physically to avoid hazards such as steps, trees, or walls. Bring your partner into contact with interesting textures, such as leaves and bark, curtains and rugs, and other blindfolded group members. Try to get your partner to smell flowers, to feel the sun's heat or the chill of an air conditioner, to listen to birds or distant conversations and to walk and run over diverse terrain. Stop after 20–30 minutes and remove your partner's blindfold. Then share your feelings about leading and being responsible for the welfare of another.

As follower, pay attention to how you feel about putting complete trust in another person to take responsibility for your experiences and your welfare. Allow yourself to yield and to experience each new sensation. After your experience as follower, share your feelings with your partner.

Couple communication

Purpose: The following exercises can provide an opportunity to meet a number of unfamiliar group members and to experiment with verbal and nonverbal communication. These exercises are generally used early in the group's life.

Time required: 30 minutes.

Materials: None.

Preparation: No special training is required, but the leader should be prepared to deal with any strong reactions generated by the touching segments of the exercises.

Procedure: Mill around in a group until you find a partner. Together, do the first communication exercise below. After about five minutes move on to a new partner and do the second exercise. (Repeat for the last two exercises.)

Back to back.   Sit on the floor back to back. Try to carry on a conversation. After a few minutes turn around and share your feelings about the experience.

Sitting and standing.   One partner sits while the other stands. Try to carry on a conversation from these positions. After a few minutes reverse positions so that each of you experiences both the "up" and "down" perspectives. After a few more minutes, share your feelings about the experience.

Eyes only.   Make eye contact with your partner and communicate with your eyes only. After a few minutes, verbally share your feelings about the experience.

Face exploration.   When you find your next partner, do not speak. Instead, sit facing each other and explore your partner's face with your hands. Then let your partner explore your face. Finish by sharing your experiences. (This exercise may be quite threatening for many individuals. Be sure to allow the participants sufficient time to share their feelings about touching and being touched by people of both the opposite sex and the same sex.)

Living hands

Purpose: This nonverbal encounter exercise is very powerful for generating both feelings of competition and feelings of intimacy. It is excellent for exploring the issues of touch, intimacy, and competition with members of both the same sex and the opposite sex.

Time required: 1–1½ hours.

Materials: Blindfolds and chairs.

Preparation: The leader should be experienced, as the exercise can generate strong feelings.

Procedure: Arrange the chairs in the room so that they are facing each other about two feet apart. Remove rings and watches from your hands and blindfold yourself. The group leader guides you to a chair so that you do not know the identity of the person sitting across from you.

As you face your partner, put all of your energy into your hands. Become your hands, and as your hands, reach out and *get acquainted with* the person across from you through her hands. Remember, do not talk. Touch only hands and get to know the person opposite you (three minutes). Now that you have become acquainted, *have a fight* with your hands.

Fight your partner, hands to hands! (Three minutes.) That's good. The fight is over. Now *make up* with your partner through your hands (three minutes). And, now, in your own time, *say goodbye* to your partner with your hands and take off your blindfold (three minutes).

Now share your experience with each other for a few minutes. Then put the blindfold back on and prepare to be moved to a new location.

It is important that the leader give members a chance to face and interact with both sexes. After a few rounds the group as a whole needs the opportunity to exchange thoughts and feelings. This discussion often touches on misperceptions concerning other members, anxieties about touching, fears about fighting, and feelings of warmth and sensuousness. Leaders, through their observations of the activity, can also share their impressions.

Listening

Purpose: This exercise provides members with the opportunity to become more intimately acquainted by sharing themselves with the group. It also provides practice in empathic listening skills and leads to strong intragroup feelings and cohesiveness.

Time required: 1½ hours.

Materials: None.

Preparation: The leader should be experienced in leading groups.

Procedure: Divide into groups of six to eight people of the same sex. The rules are very simple: One person at a time sits in the center of the group and is the focus of the group for ten minutes. When you are in the center, share what it is like for you to be "a man among men and among women" in the world, or "a woman among women and among men." The other group members are there to listen and give you total attention without talking or interrupting in any way. Speak as long as possible. If you do not wish to use up the whole ten minutes, continue to sit in the center silently for the remaining time. When your ten minutes is up, return to the circle. In this manner, each group member takes a turn in the middle of the group.

This exercise is very powerful. For one thing, it is very rare for any of us to have the total, uninterrupted attention of others for ten minutes at a time. With this attention we can safely go deeper into our feelings. The topic of being a man or a woman and relating to others is relevant and meaningful for almost everyone. With time, members will often discover and share hidden parts of themselves. The topic can also generate strong feelings of solidarity among men and among women that may have to be resolved in the total group. In mature groups, the exercise can be conducted so that the men and women take turns, while the other sex silently observes them. The listening exercise can be conducted on a host of other topics too.

GESTALT GROUPS

Much of the personal work in the Gestalt group is done in the hot seat. Other experiments and exercises involve other group members. If there is an experienced Gestalt group leader present, the powerful techniques of dream work, empty-chair dialogues, and exploring resistances can be experimented with safely. Otherwise, the following exercises can provide the entire group with a taste of the Gestalt process.

Zones of awareness

Purpose: This exercise provides basic training in awareness. It is very appropriate early in the life of a Gestalt group.

Time required: 45 minutes.

Materials: None.

Preparation: No special training is required other than the leader's sensitivity to the three zones of awareness.

Procedure: Your experience can be divided into three zones of awareness: the external world, the internal world of your body, and the mental world of your thoughts and fantasies. Choose a partner, sit comfortably facing each other and relax. Begin by taking turns sharing your awareness of the outside world. Say out loud "Now I am aware of . . .," and finish the sentence with your immediate awareness of sensory input from objects and events outside of you: the hum of an air conditioner, the smell of perfume, the shape of your partner's nose. Try to avoid interpreting, judging, or fixating on any one awareness. Complete the sentence as many times as you can for one or two minutes as you try to stay solely in contact with your awareness of the outside world. Now switch and listen to your partner report her awareness. If you find that your partner has slipped into the middle zone and is interpreting or judging, provide feedback and help her return to the outer zone.

Next attend to the stimuli inside of you. Say out loud "Now I am aware of . . .," and finish the sentence with your internal sensations: tightness in your stomach, dryness in your mouth, pressure where your buttocks meet the floor, an itch on your arm. Repeat the statement and stay with your awareness of your inner zone of experience for about a minute. Now switch while your partner shares her awareness of the inner zone.

The third kind of awareness includes mental activity apart from ongoing experience, such as memories, plans, thoughts, hunches, and fantasies. Fritz Perls called this the fantasy zone. First bring the concerns of this zone into awareness by finishing the statement "Now I am aware of . . .," for one minute. You may be aware of wondering about the time, worrying about the exam you just wrote, or guessing the content of your partner's thoughts. Now switch so your partner has an opportunity to focus her middle-zone awareness.

After you have identified and practiced the three zones of awareness separately, observe where your awareness takes you without focusing on any one zone. Say aloud "Now I am aware of . . . ," and finish the sentence with whatever you are aware of at the moment, whether it is in the outer, inner, or middle zone. You may find that most of your awareness belongs to the middle zone. You may also discover connections among the three zones. For instance, you may become aware of a noise in the room (outer), imagine someone watching you (middle), and experience a shortness of breath and tightness in your mouth (inner).

Once you have experienced each zone fully and had the opportunity to observe where your awareness takes you, you are ready to hone your powers of concentration. You can expand your range of awareness and ability to discriminate by shuttling among the three zones. First, shuttle between the inner and outer zones. Complete the sentence "Now I am aware of...," with a report from the outer zone, then with information from the inner zone. Continue to alternate between the two for one minute. Next, listen as your partner completes the shuttling exercise.

Another common confusion is between outer- and middle-zone processes. This confusion occurs whenever you mistake your raw sensory impressions of an event for your intuitive belief, judgment, or hunch about it. Your partner can help you learn to differentiate between these two zones.

Look at your partner and complete the sentence "Now I am aware of . . . ," to describe your partner. Next, complete the sentence "And I imagine that . . ." with whatever fantasy impression or belief you have about your partner. For example, you may be aware of your partner sitting with arms folded and imagine that he or she is feeling cold. Continue reporting your awarenesses and fantasies for about two minutes, then listen to your partner's feedback about the accuracy of your judgments.

Switch and give your partner time to repeat the exercise, then offer feedback. Finally, discuss your experiences with the rest of the group.

Exaggeration or reversal

Purpose: This exercise gives you the opportunity to try out some enactments. An enactment is a role-playing technique in which group members act out some aspect of themselves that they are unaware of or that they are troubled by. Enactments are used to increase awareness of a behavior as a step toward potentially modifying it.

Time required: 1 hour or more.

Materials: None.

Preparation: It is helpful if the leader is experienced in Gestalt and group processes.

Procedure: Let each person in the group choose an unwanted personal behavior or have the group collaborate to select a behavior that the person is not aware of but that is obvious to others. Some examples are a tendency to apologize excessively, to avert eye contact and talk in a whisper, or to be impatient and judgmental.

If the group member is unaware of the identified behavior, he or she should exaggerate it. If the behavior is one that the group member is aware of and finds distasteful, he or she should try a reversal. The apologizer, for example, probably apologizes automatically, without thinking about it. An appropriate exaggeration is to go around the group, speaking to each member in turn, and prefacing each statement with the words "I apologize..." to heighten the member's awareness of the behavior. The shy whisperer, on the other hand, is probably well aware of his or her mild-mannered passivity, and has probably cursed himself or herself at times when it would have been useful to be assertive or demanding. An appropriate reversal for the shy group member is to force eye contact and boast to each group member in a strong, authoritative voice. This exercise helps such participants contact the parts of themselves that are shadowed by timidity.

Allow at least five minutes for each person to fully experience his or her enactment. Leave time at the end for feedback and for sharing feelings with the group.

Polarities: The topdog-underdog conflict

Purpose: This exercise is an introduction to the common topdog-underdog polarity. It provides insight into conflicting aspects of the personality and practice in actively engaging someone else.

Time required: 45 minutes.

Materials: None.

Preparation: Familiarity with the concept of polarities. Experience by the leader in Gestalt therapy is helpful.

Procedure: Sit facing your partner and decide which of you will play the topdog and which will play the underdog. Then engage each other in a dialogue. Stay firmly in your position and try not to give in. If you are the topdog, tell your partner how she should behave or what she should do or accomplish. Bully and criticize from your obviously superior and self-righteous position. If you are the underdog, excuse yourself constantly and whine convincingly. Tell your partner how hard you try, how much you want to please, and how events get in the way of satisfying her demands. Try to get the full experience of the position by taking five to ten minutes to complete this part of the exercise.

Now reverse roles. If you were the underdog, adopt the topdog role. Allow yourself to experience fully the power and authority of the topdog, or the manipulative passivity of the underdog. After five or ten minutes, stop the exercise. Return to the group and share your experiences with each other. (Some group members may report that they felt exhilarated when they enacted the topdog's role. Others will report feeling at home with the underdog position.) Compare the roles that you played with the way you cope in real life. Also discuss the way you felt in the interaction. Did you feel angry or humiliated in the role of underdog? Did you feel guilty and punitive as the topdog? Exploring your reactions to the exercise can provide you with information about these fragmented parts of your personality.

Abandoned store

Purpose: There are a number of fantasy exercises in Gestalt that illustrate the process of projection and help participants identify and perhaps reclaim fragmented aspects of their personalities. The "abandoned store" and other exercises have been described by John Stevens (1971). The value of these fantasy exercises is that people can contact personal attributes of which they have never been fully aware.

Time required: 1 hour.

Materials: A comfortable, dimly lit room.

Preparation: An experienced leader capable of dealing with strong feelings.

Procedure: Lie down on the floor, close your eyes, and relax. Imagine that you are walking down a street in a city late at night. Walk along the street for awhile and explore the city. What do you see? hear? smell? How do you feel? As you walk, you notice a small side street. Turn down this street. As you continue along, you see an old, abandoned store. The windows are dirty, but if you look through them closely you can see something in the window that has been left behind. Examine this object carefully. Now leave the abandoned shop. Walk along the side street until you are back in the city. Now return to the group.

Back in the group, you can find a partner, break into groups of four or five, or give each member five to ten minutes of the group's time. Describe the object you discovered in the window of the abandoned store. Now become this object, describing it in the first person. Try to experience what it is like to be this abandoned object. How do you feel? Why were you left in the store window? What is your existence like as the object? After a few minutes, become yourself again and observe the object in the window once more. Do you see anything new about it? Is there anything you would like to say to it? (Continue around the group so that all members have the opportunity to identify with their abandoned objects.)

There are many alternatives to the abandoned-store fantasy. For example, individuals can imagine that they are entering an old mansion and that when they leave they take with them some object of value or interest. Or they can imagine that they are flowers and describe their color and shape, their blossoms, the soil they are in, the way the sun, rain, and wind feel, and what they can see from where they are planted.

By identifying with an object, we project aspects of ourselves onto it. This exercise is a powerful technique that can take us deep within ourselves very quickly. Make sure that all group members feel they have finished their work so they do not carry around any unfinished emotional business.

The power of language

Purpose: Not only is language a powerful tool for communicating, it is also a potent organizer of our world views. Quite often we are what we are because we identify ourselves or speak about ourselves in that way. A common technique in Gestalt is to help group members change the structure of their language from a powerless or victimized one to one that lets them realize their power.

Time required: 30 minutes.

Materials: None.

Preparation: No special training is required.

Procedure: Sit facing a partner and while maintaining eye contact, speak directly to him or her. Make three statements to your partner, each beginning with the words "I have to...." Without providing you with feedback, your partner offers three sentences beginning with the words "I have to...." Now go back to your original sentences and replace "I have to" with the words "I choose to," keeping the rest of the sentence intact. Be aware of your feelings as you say these new sentences. Now listen while your partner changes his or her sentences to "I choose to...." Take a moment to share your experiences. Try to become aware of any new power or potential within yourself.

Next, take turns with your partner saying three sentences beginning with the words "I can't...." Listen while your partner shares three things he or she can't do. Now go back to your sentences and replace "I can't" with "I won't," leaving the rest of the sentence unchanged. Listen again to your partner's sentences with the new words "I won't...." Share your experience and see if you can become aware of your power to refuse, rather than your incompetence or inability.

Now take turns each completing three sentences beginning with "I need...." Return to the sentences and change "I need" to "I want." Again, share your experiences and check to see if changing a need to a want results in a sense of freedom or unburdening. Ask yourself if this is something you really need for your survival or if it is something you would prefer but can live without.

Finally, share three sentences beginning with the words "I'm afraid to...." Repeat the sentences, changing "I'm afraid to" to "I'd like to," leaving the rest of the sentence the same. Share your experiences with your partner. Ask yourself if your fear is standing in the way of you reaching important goals and interesting experiences.

The words "I have to," "I can't," "I need," and "I'm afraid to" deny your power to be capable, strong, and responsible. There are real alternatives for getting along in the world and enriching your life, and only a belief in your incapability may be standing in your way. By changing your language, you can take a big step in becoming more responsible for your own thoughts, feelings, and actions.

PSYCHODRAMA

The following exercises are not intended to supplant the kind of spontaneous psychodrama that can be conducted in a group setting by a competent director. They do, however, illustrate the basic concepts of the psychodramatic process.

Role-playing

Purpose: This exercise provides a relatively playful method of loosening up a group and practicing the skill of role-playing. It would be appropriate toward the beginning of a group studying psychodrama.

Time required: 30 minutes.

Materials: None.

Preparation: No special training is required.

Procedure: Divide the group in half by forming two circles, one inside the other. On a cue from the group leader, the members in the outer circle move clockwise and those in the inner circle move counterclockwise. On a second cue from the leader, the members stop and face a corresponding person in the other circle. Those in the outer circle are now assigned the role of police giving traffic citations to their partners on the inside, who play the roles of motorists. The members proceed with the role-playing as spontaneously as possible for about three minutes. On a cue from the leader, members stop the role-playing and share their thoughts and feelings about the experience with their partners for a couple of minutes.

On a new cue from the leader, the group repeats the initial process of choosing partners. This time the people on the inside are salespeople trying to sell to prospective customers in the outer circle. After three minutes, participants stop and share impressions.

Additional roles that can be chosen in this exercise include:

- relatives who haven't seen each other in a long time meeting at a family reunion
- a man or woman telling an unsuspecting friend about the recent death of his or her spouse
- children discovering a new toy with which to play
- a young person disclosing his or her homosexuality to a parent

At the conclusion of the exercise, leave time for the group to share feelings and reactions to the various roles. Some roles are apt to have powerful emotional significance for certain participants.

Soliloquy with doubling

Purpose: This exercise is intended to help group members develop spontaneity and practice the skill of doubling. Doubling is excellent for fostering empathy and the soliloquy itself can help the participant gain some objectivity over disturbing emotional issues. It may also provide material for a psychodramatic enactment.

Time required: 30 minutes.

Materials: None.

Preparation: The leader should be experienced in psychodrama techniques.

Procedure: One person begins by standing in the center of the group. If you are that person, begin speaking aloud to yourself about anything on your mind. A soliloquy is a sort of free association in front of the group on any thoughts you are currently having. You might, for example, start by sharing how conspicuous or anxious you feel. Don't make a speech, but simply recite your thoughts out loud. Feel free to move around the room. One way to start is to pretend you are alone in your own room or in the shower.

After a few minutes a second group member volunteers to come up and stand behind the soliloquist, assuming his or her body position and movements without interrupting the action. Try to tune in on the soliloquist's hidden thoughts and, as a double, share them out loud. Don't interfere with the soliloquist's stream of talk. You might begin by repeating each phrase immediately after you've heard it and then gradually intuiting as many unstated thoughts and feelings as you can. Be sure to copy the soliloquist's nonverbal behavior as well. After a few minutes, have another person replace you on the stage. (Each group member should have the opportunity to double at least once.)

Fantasy sociogram

Purpose: This exercise explores the relationships between group members and provides them feedback regarding their perceived role in the group. It also offers practice in psychodramatic enactments and demonstrates the relationship between role-playing a "part" and revealing aspects of oneself. The information derived from the fantasy sociogram can serve as the basis for psychodramas at a later time.

Time required: 1 hour.

Materials: None.

Preparation: Group members must be familiar with one another.

Procedure: A sociogram is a visual representation of a person's relationship to a group, where distance usually represents how close the person feels to other group members. Although there may be consensus about some relationships, with perhaps the most popular person in the group being placed in the center of all the sociograms, each participant's sociogram will be a little different, because it is based on that member's unique perceptions of relationships in the group. In psychodrama the sociogram takes place on the stage by positioning group members in a way that denotes the strength and meaning of relationships. When movement is added to the placement of participants, the technique is called an *action sociogram*. By adding elements of group members' imaginations and fantasies, a *fantasy sociogram* is derived.

One group member volunteers to set the scene. If you are that person, you are the director. Physically position the other group members, using a theme, such as a "Western Movie" or a "Journey in Space." Assign group members roles that best fit your impression of them. For instance, in a Western scene, one person might be the saloon keeper and another might be the villain. As you assign roles, position the characters as in a tableau. To enrich characterizations, give each person a line of dialogue that seems appropriate to the person and the role. For instance, a "gunfighter" might say "I'm the toughest hombre west of the Pecos," with his thumbs wedged into his front pockets. Your assignment of roles and lines is feedback to other group members regarding your perception of them individually and as a group.

The final phase of the exercise is to allow your characters, once the scene is set, to stay in their roles and to interact with each other spontaneously. As director, of course, you can stop the action at any time. After the scene winds to a close, discuss your reactions as a group, sharing how you felt in your assigned role, how you felt about the roles and behavior of the other participants, and how you felt as the director.

Family sculpting

Purpose: Family sculpting is used in family-therapy sessions as well as psychodrama groups to gain insight into family relationships. Therapeutically, the technique can be used to illustrate and deal with difficulties among family members. The family sculpting exercise also provides useful material for later psychodrama sessions.

Time required: 30 minutes–3 hours.

Materials: None.

Preparation: The leader should be experienced in psychodrama, family therapy, or related techniques.

Procedure: Participants volunteer to sculpt or create a living picture of their families.

If you volunteer, choose members who most clearly resemble your family members to portray those people. Include in your family all those who lived in your household while you were growing up. When you have assembled a family, place its members in characteristic positions. Sculpt a scene that reveals something about how your family relates or related. For example, you might position your family around the dinner table. Or you might recall a particular incident significant to you and position family members appropriately. Think of the other members as putty to mold. Give them a little information about each family member to help them in their portrayals. Also use distance to represent their relationships with one another. Be sure to include yourself in the scene as part of the family. You might ask someone else to stand in for you while you arrange the scene.

When the scene is fixed, give each person a sentence to say that would be characteristic of that family member. Allow your new family a few minutes to experience their roles, then ask its members to share their feelings with the group. The group can also give their observations of what life might be like in the family you have sculpted. Be sure to share any new insights you have gained from the experience.

BODY-THERAPY GROUPS

Warm-up

Purpose: Breathing exercises are excellent warm-ups for bioenergetic group sessions. They are useful at the beginning of the group to energize participants and increase body awareness.

Time required: 15 minutes.

Materials: None.

Preparation: No special training is required.

Procedure: Group breathing exercises are done in unison, with vigor and enthusiasm. Here is one approach.

To begin, stand and form a circle. Place your feet about eight inches apart with your weight on the balls of the feet. Keep your knees slightly bent and allow your body to relax and your pelvis to hang loosely. Place a hand on your belly and make eye contact with someone across from you. In unison inhale deeply through your mouth, drawing oxygen all the way down to your abdomen. Exhale together and allow a sound to escape. Keep the sound going as long as you can without forcing it. Then inhale again, gently. Repeat for 16 deep breaths, inhaling and exhaling slowly and deeply. Don't rush or you will probably hyperventilate and feel dizzy. Don't inhibit any sound you may want to make, and maintain eye contact throughout. Be aware of any blocks in your breathing pattern. Note any feelings that develop as you breathe all the way down to your belly and keep your body limp and relaxed.

When you have finished the exercise of breathing together, shake your whole body by keeping your arms hanging loosely at your sides and bending and straightening your knees. Next jump up and down a few times to further energize your body. Jump slowly and barely lift your feet off the floor. Keep going until you are tired. Then rest with your knees slightly bent, your weight forward, and your back straight.

Stress positions

Purpose: Stress positions are fundamental to bioenergetic therapy. They can help increase body awareness and release tension through tremor and involuntary movement.

Time required: 30 minutes.

Materials: A comfortable working area.

Preparation: The leader should have experience in bioenergetics in order to assess positions accurately. Group members should be sure not to overextend themselves, especially if they have physical problems.

Procedure: A skilled bioenergetic therapist may prescribe a given position depending upon the particular stress pattern a person exhibits. Below are some Lowenian stress positions to try as a group.

Lowen bow.   (This position was illustrated in Figure 6-2.) Stand with your feet approximately 18 inches apart, toes turned slightly inward and knees bent as much as possible, while keeping your heels on the floor. Place your fists in the small of your back and arch backward over your fists. Breathe abdominally and maintain the position for about a minute. Note areas of tension in your body. The tension may be in the lower back or the front of the thighs. The group leader or someone else can help you identify where you have difficulty in forming the arch, perhaps in being overly rigid or too loose. If you maintain a perfect arch, keep breathing, and stay relaxed, your legs should start to vibrate.

Lowen curl.   It is a good idea to follow exercises in which the body bends in one direction with a position that requires the body to bend in the opposite direction.

To do the curl, place your feet about ten inches apart, turn your toes inward slightly, and bend forward at the waist. Keep your knees bent and allow your fingers to touch the floor. Keep all your weight on the balls of your feet. Remember to keep breathing deeply through your mouth. Straighten your knees slowly but don't lock them. Hold the position for about a minute. Your legs will start to vibrate as you continue deep breathing. The vibration is the body's natural reaction to stress. The curl position is excellent for increasing "grounding," that is, the feeling contact between the feet and the ground. To stop the exercise, come up *very* slowly, allowing your body to unbend one vertebra at a time.

Pelvic arch.   This position develops feeling in the lower body. Lie on your back on a mat or soft rug. Bend your knees and keep your feet about 12 inches apart. Arch your back by grabbing your ankles with your hands and pulling forward. Your head should fall back so that only the top of the head, the shoulders, and feet touch the floor. Now place your fists under your heels and push your knees forward. Thrust your pelvis out and breathe deeply. You will feel the stretching in your thigh muscles. Try to keep your buttocks loose. By keeping your pelvis loose you can feel it vibrate. To enhance the feeling, try bouncing your pelvis up and down a few times.

These and all other bioenergetic stress positions should not be performed as mechanical exercises. Use them to identify areas of tension and to generate feeling in the body through movement and vibration. You should focus on the sensations you experience rather than on the length of time you can endure a position. Pain comes from tension; pleasure comes from releasing tension. When a position becomes too uncomfortable or painful, terminate it.

Active exercises

Purpose: Active bioenergetic exercises are used to stimulate and express feelings directly through physical release. They provide an opportunity to explore feelings openly in a controlled setting. They are excellent for releasing tension and increasing blood and oxygen circulation.

Time required: 45 minutes.

Materials: A foam bat and a mattress or foam mat.

Preparation: These exercises require trust in the group and the leader. The leader should be experienced and have clinical skills. No one should be coerced to participate in active bioenergetic exercises, and someone should supervise to prevent injury.

Procedure: The following exercises can be done together by the group or by one person at a time.

Anger release.   Use a foam bat, tennis racket, or your fists for this exercise. Stand with your feet about 18 inches apart and your knees slightly bent facing a bed, padded chair, or collection of pillows. Pull your arms back over your head and repeatedly strike the target in a powerful yet relaxed way. Get your whole body into the action. Keep your mouth open, breathe deeply, and let out sounds as you hit. Use any words that express a feeling of anger, such as "No!" or "Damn you!" You may find it helpful to imagine a particular person with whom you have unfinished emotional business. Remember, there is a tremendous difference between hitting a person and hitting the lifeless symbol of a person.

Sometimes group members resist this exercise, claiming they are not angry at the moment, but most people have something to be angry about, and this response is usually a fear about expressing anger. Most individuals can temporarily identify with an aggressive response and resume control over themselves immediately afterwards. In addition, the exercise is excellent for releasing shoulder tension.

Kicking.   Kicking helps to recapture the infant's ability to let go emotionally. Lie on your back on a bed, mattress, or foam mat. With your legs loosely outstretched, slowly begin kicking, with the entire leg making contact with the bed. Alternate legs and raise them high. Gradually increase the speed and strength of your kicks. Loudly say "No!" with each kick as you build intensity.

A more dramatic version of the kicking exercise is a temper tantrum. Do this with supervision because it can lead to dizziness if you are overly controlled. While lying on the mattress, bend your knees so that your feet lie flat. As you begin kicking your legs, flail your arms and pound your fists into the mattress at your sides. Let your head turn back and forth with the movement of your body. As you increase the intensity of the tantrum, scream "No!" or "I won't!" repeatedly.

Most people have something to protest or throw fits about. Kicking helps to promote circulation and relaxes the lower body. According to Lowen, this helps us become less inhibited and more spontaneous in our sexual relations.

Intensive

Purpose: The intensive is a way of allowing group members to reach deep feeling levels with a helper's guidance. This exercise is a sample of the intensive body work that might take place in a bioenergetic group. It would be used after cohesiveness and trust are sufficiently established.

Time required: 1–2 hours.

Materials: Towels, mattresses, floor mats, or a soft rug.

Preparation: The leader needs to be experienced and qualified to deal with strong feeling reactions.

Procedure: To begin, choose a partner. One person agrees to work and the other to help. If you are going to work, lie on your back on a mattress, mat, or soft rug. Lying down encourages a return to an infantile body attitude that facilitates the process of giving up control. The room should be dimly lit. Lie with your knees bent and your feet flat on the floor about 18 inches apart. Keep your eyes closed and concentrate on breathing deeply from the abdomen. Keep breathing deeply and gently for about a minute.

As you lie still with your eyes closed, imagine one of the following incidents from your childhood: (1) a time when you reached out or cried and wanted to be held; (2) a time when you wanted to explore something and were restrained or discouraged; (3) a time when you were angry because a parent wanted you to do something and you refused; or (4) a time when you took another child's toy and your parent was there to react. Visualize the scene in as much detail as you can, and imagine your mother or father's reaction. Express your feelings in that situation to your parent. Talk or cry or yell or do whatever seems appropriate. Don't hold back any sounds. Even if you sigh, make it audible. If you begin a movement, such as hitting, kicking, or reaching, continue with it. Try to get your emotions into your expressions, both verbally and nonverbally. When you feel finished or after five or ten minutes, lie quietly with your eyes closed.

Now for some more body work to open up your feelings and allow for creative, new responses. Breathe deeply from the belly several times, allowing a sound to emerge each time you exhale. After five or six breaths, open your eyes wide as in fright and spread your fingers and toes as wide as you can. Continue for two or three minutes. Next, take the towel and place it as far back in your mouth as possible. Bite down and pull the towel as hard as you can, making a sound as you try to pull the towel out of your mouth. Pulling the towel will help reduce tension in your jaw. You can bite down on the towel very hard indeed if it is placed back where your strong jaw muscles are. After four or five minutes, remove the towel from your mouth, take it in both hands, and aggressively twist it as hard as you can. Make a noise as you twist the towel. Finally, relax and breathe deeply again.

Now close your eyes and refantasize the scene with your parents. This time imagine making a new and different response to them. Share this response with them aloud. After a few minutes open your eyes, breathe gently, and look at your helper. When you are finished, reverse places.

The helper's role is to facilitate the worker and serve as a reassuring presence. As helper, frequently remind your partner to keep breathing deeply and to make sounds. Helpers experienced in bioenergetics may know more active, verbal ways to facilitate expressions of feelings. Be gentle, though, and not provocative. If you notice tightness in a muscle or difficulty in breathing, you may, *with permission,* massage your partner's neck muscles or jaw muscles to loosen the tension. When your partner is finished, encourage him or her to relax and breathe deeply. Then ask how he or she feels and if there is anything else you can do.

Members should respect the limits of their partners and their own limits in determining the depth of exploration. It is also advisable to rely on the guidance of a qualified and competent leader.

DANCE-THERAPY GROUPS

Mirroring

Purpose: Mirroring is an excellent exercise for encouraging body awareness, creative movement, and interpersonal empathy. It offers the experience of both guiding and following someone else.

Time required: 15 minutes.

Materials: None.

Preparation: No special training is required.

Procedure: Divide the group into pairs. Within each pair, one person plays the role of leader while the other follows.

Stand facing each other, and make eye contact. If you are the leader, begin by making some slow, graceful movements with your arms, legs, head, or torso. Be aware of your body and your feelings as you move. Trust yourself to follow how your body wants to move. Throughout the exercise maintain eye contact and awareness of your partner.

As the follower, reflect your partner's movements, making the same movements *at the same time*—as if you are the mirror image of him or her. For example, if your partner reaches out with the right arm, reach out with your left arm. Let your partner guide where and how you move. Don't think about it too much: let your body lead you in experiencing how it feels to follow someone else. After about five minutes, reverse roles. After another five minutes, spend a few minutes sharing your feelings during the exercise.

Animals

Purpose: This exercise allows for symbolic role-playing and creative interaction with other group members.

Time required: 30 minutes.

Materials: None.

Preparation: No special training is required.

Procedure: Choose an animal for any reason at all. You may choose a mammal, reptile, or bird. For the next 20 minutes you are to become that animal, adopting its form, movements, and sounds. The room will serve as your territory and the territory of every other animal chosen by the group members. Most likely more than one person will choose the same animal. You don't have to announce your selection, just move around the room as if you are an animal and interact spontaneously with others. You may have to crawl, leap, hop, or fly. Be creative and try to express parts of yourself that may not be so easy to express in your usual form. Make noises appropriate to your animal. Be aware of feelings you have as you see and meet your world, whether you feel afraid, angry, or loving. Afterwards, spend a few minutes sharing your impressions with the rest of the group.

Follow the leader

Purpose: This exercise provides the opportunity of being both a leader and a follower in a small group engaged in creative movement.

Time required: 30 minutes.

Materials: None.

Preparation: No special training is required.

Procedure: Divide a large group into smaller groups of four or five. Each group forms a line. The person on one end of the line is the leader.

As the leader, move spontaneously and creatively around the room. Experiment with improvised movements of your body. It is up to other group members to follow you in your movements and stay in line. After a few minutes, drop to the back of your small group so that the next person in line becomes the leader. Proceed in this way until each person has had the opportunity to lead at least once and can invest the group with his or her particular style and movements. This exercise can be exerting and very enjoyable, especially if your group moves through and around the other groups in the room.

Free dance

Purpose: This exercise gives each person in the group the opportunity to experiment with dance movements in front of others. It is a fitting finale to a demonstration of dance therapy.

Time required: 30 minutes.

Materials: This exercise is best with accompanying music.

Preparation: No person should be coerced to participate.

Procedure: Sit as a group in a circle. One person begins by getting in the center of the circle and dancing. Don't worry about being a "good" dancer. Move freely and spontaneously and follow your body. You are not competing with the others. After a couple of minutes sit down and invite someone else to replace you. Keep going in this way until everyone who is willing has had a chance to be in the center for a minute or two. The exercise can conclude with the entire group joining together in a free-form dance around the room to the music. Enjoy yourselves!

ART-THERAPY GROUPS

Individual drawing

Purpose: This exercise is excellent for beginning an art-therapy experience. It stimulates creativity and awareness to feelings and helps group members become better acquainted.

Time required: 1 hour.

Materials: Paper and crayons, chalk, paint, or clay.

Preparation: None.

Procedure: Each person in the group should have plenty of paper and crayons available. Find a place where you can be alone with your thoughts. Take a couple of minutes to become aware of your sensations and feelings. Forget about art and being artistic. Just pick up a crayon and begin to make some marks on the page. Use the colors to draw lines and forms that indicate how you are feeling. Try to symbolically capture your present state, whether you feel on top of the world or in a stew. Don't force yourself to draw something organized or of quality. Draw whatever springs to mind. When everyone is finished, the group may share impressions of each drawing without evaluating any of the work. Perhaps you can say something about how your drawing reflects your feelings.

As an alternative, try some other medium, such as paint, chalk, or clay. In any case, trust your inner awareness and try to discover a message to yourself in your work. Use this exercise to stimulate your imagination and to reflect about what's on your mind.

Drawing in pairs

Purpose: This exercise is excellent for exploring interpersonal relationships and dealing with conflict.

Time required: 30 minutes–1 hour.

Materials: Paper and colored chalk or crayons.

Preparation: No special training is required, but experience in art therapy by the leader is helpful.

Procedure: Choose as a partner someone you would like to get to know better or someone with whom you have unfinished business. You should have a large piece of paper between you and a number of colored chalks each. The paper serves as a common environment. Begin by making eye contact with your partner. Now draw spontaneously on the paper without talking. Express your feelings through your artwork. If you wish to communicate to your partner, do so with the lines, shapes, and colors you choose.

When you are finished drawing, discuss the experience between you. Talk about any emotional reactions you have to your partner's drawing. See if you can determine parallels between the way you draw and your functioning in the group. Try to learn something about your partner.

Group drawing

Purpose: This exercise allows the entire group to contribute. It is excellent for looking at role relationships in the group and the influence of others on individual experience (Rhyne, 1973).

Time required: 1 hour.

Materials: Paper and colored pens or crayons.

Preparation: Experience in art therapy and group dynamics by the leader are helpful.

Procedure: Each person begins with a piece of paper and colored pens or crayons. Sit in a circle as a group. Begin drawing something important to you. At a signal from the group leader, pass your paper to the left and receive the beginning of a drawing from the person on your right. Work on this drawing as if it were your own, changing and adding to it as you wish. At the next signal, pass this drawing to your left and add to the one you receive. Keep going until you receive the drawing you initiated. Be aware of your feelings on seeing the expressions others have made on your page. Feel free to keep or change as much of their influence as you wish. Finally, discuss your reactions with the group.

An alternative to this exercise is for one group member at a time to contribute something to a common group drawing or mural, adding something to the composite that expresses a present mood and communicates it to the group. Conclude any group project by allowing members to be alone to draw or paint their private feelings about the group experience, and follow with a group discussion.

Making a clay world

Purpose: This exercise, as with all art therapy, stimulates creativity. It also explores value orientations. It can generate strong feelings of cooperation and competition among group members.

Time required: 1–2 hours.

Materials: Clay or plasticene.

Preparation: The leader should have experience in understanding and dealing with group dynamics.

Procedure: Each group member is given large lumps of clay (Rhyne, 1973). Divide the group into smaller groups of about five to eight people. Consider playing some pleasant flute or harpsichord music to instill a relaxed and mellow atmosphere.

You are one of five or eight people designing a world. Close your eyes and imagine that the clay is the raw material for making whatever you would want to see in the world. With your eyes closed, work with the clay and allow your fingers to express your thoughts and feelings. When you are done with your sculpture, place it on a table together with those of the rest of your group. With the other members of your small group, work with your eyes open to structure a whole world from the respective parts. If you develop feelings about other group members during the exercise, talk them over or express them with the clay. When you are finished constructing your world, share it with the other small groups.

THEME-CENTERED INTERACTION

Selecting themes

Purpose: A TCI group requires an agreed-upon theme to proceed. This is its most unique quality. Once the theme has been selected, any number of experiential exercises drawn from other group approaches may be used to further the group process and maintain the dynamic balancing characteristic of TCI groups.

Time required: 5 minutes or longer.

Materials: None.

Preparation: An effective TCI group requires a trained and experienced leader. Any experiential group can, of course, choose to focus on a selected theme.

Procedure: Themes can be organized according to their relative focus on the I, We, and It points of the TCI triangle. Throughout the group experience, you will, of course, attempt to keep these points in dynamic balance. Here are a number of sample themes for TCI groups that a group or leader may select (Challis, 1974):

It

Being a Woman/Being a Man
Dealing with Negative Feelings
Being a Leader
Responsibility: Having It, Taking It, Shirking It
Holding On/Letting Go
Experiencing and Observing Group Dynamics
Taking Risks
Owning My Disowned Parts

I

Expanding My Consciousness
Being Myself in This Group
Identifying and Expanding My Resources
Finding My Theme with This Group
Setting My Course
Opening Myself to Play
Creative Use of Myself in My Work
Expanding My Power to Be Heard
Clearing the Way for My Sexual Self

We

Appreciating Differences
Accepting and Balancing My Need for Closeness and Distance
Building My Support Systems
Being Alone/Being with Others
Expressing My Wants/Responding to Others'
Becoming a Group
Listening/Being Heard
Getting to Know You/Letting You Know Me

Select a theme. Then use the triple-silence technique to begin the group work.

Triple silence

Purpose: The triple-silence technique (Cohn, 1972) is a favorite opening exercise for a TCI group. It can help establish a constructive group climate and orient members to the group and the theme.

Time required: 15–30 minutes.

Materials: None.

Preparation: No special training is required.

Procedure: Assume that the theme for the workshop is "Getting to Know You, Letting You Know Me." The triple-silence technique consists of three steps.

First, close your eyes, sit quietly, and think about the meaning of the theme for you. Second, after a few minutes of quiet reflection on the theme, open your eyes, return to the group, and become aware of your feelings about being in the group right now.

The third period of silence involves a task to unite the I, We, and It dimensions. For this theme, remain silent and choose someone in the group, an interesting-looking man, perhaps, you would like to get to know. Imagine asking him something about himself. Then imagine sharing something about yourself with him.

After the last period of silence, feel free to communicate to the group whatever you wish regarding the theme, your experiences, thoughts, and feelings. Remember that you are your own chairperson and responsible for giving to and getting from the group whatever you wish.

Two-step silence

Purpose: This exercise is adapted from Bradford Wilson (1969). It illustrates the creative use of silence in a group for reflection and growth.

Time required: 5 minutes.

Materials: None.

Preparation: No special training is required.

Procedure: This exercise is very brief and can be introduced at any point during the group experience. It is most useful when an ongoing group is struggling to personalize a topic, when group members are not spontaneously reacting to the topic but do not appear to be emotionally finished with it:

In the first step sit silently in the group and contact your thoughts and feelings about the topic that has come to the group's attention. After a couple of minutes continue to sit silently and think about what you can now *do* with regard to the topic, based on the thoughts and feelings you have just contacted.

This exercise has wide use in freezing the group process and asking members to touch base with their own roles and responsibilities to the group theme, whether the theme is implicit or explicit.

TRANSACTIONAL-ANALYSIS GROUPS

Ego-state awareness

Purpose: This exercise provides practice in the diagnosis of ego states and an introduction to transactions between different ego states.

Time required: 45 minutes.

Materials: None.

Preparation: The leader should recognize and be familiar with ego-state functioning.

Procedure: The exercise begins with three volunteers sitting in chairs in front of the group. Each volunteer chooses or is assigned the role of Parent, Adult, or Child.

Each of the three ego states represents part of the same person. If you have volunteered, remain in your chosen role throughout the exercise.

Imagine that you are taking a walk through the woods. What do you experience? If you are the Parent you may be concerned about possible dangers or what you should accomplish on the walk. Remember that the Parent often offers value judgments and uses words like "disgusting" and "ridiculous." If you are the Adult you may note the types of birds and trees around you as you process incoming information. The Adult vocabulary consists of words like "constructive," "practical," and "desirable." If you are the Child, you may feel exuberant or bored, warm or cold, and use expletives in your speech. Stay in your role verbally and nonverbally, and share your impressions with the entire group.

At this time the leader can ask for three more volunteers to join the person in front of the group. They are to be another Parent, Adult, and Child of a person of the opposite sex.

To warm up the new volunteers in playing their ego states, invent a new fantasy situation, such as going to a movie. What did you see? How was the show? Perhaps other group members will ask you questions about the experience.

Now arrange the chairs so that the two sets of ego states are facing each other, Parent opposite Parent, Adult opposite Adult, Child opposite Child.

Imagine that you are a married couple experiencing difficulties. Have a conversation. You can talk to the other person or to one of your other ego states. Make sure to direct your comments to a specific ego state, however. You will soon see how even simple messages can mean different things depending upon where they are coming from and where they are going. Stop after five minutes and discuss the experience among yourselves and with the rest of the group. Then either switch to new ego states or invite others from the group to come up and replace you. Keep structuring interactions until everyone has had at least one opportunity to role-play an ego state.

If your group feels particularly adventurous, use all five functional ego states of the person: Critical Parent, Nurturant Parent, Adult, Adapted Child, and Free Child.

Drivers

Purpose: This exercise familiarizes group members with the socially acceptable messages their parents gave them as ways of obtaining strokes.

Time required: 30 minutes.

Materials: Paper and pencils.

Preparation: No special training is required.

Procedure: On a piece of paper list the following five "drivers" or script directives: Be Strong, Be Perfect, Try Hard, Hurry Up, and Please Me (or Please Others). Consider these drivers and see whether any of them conform to early parental messages you heard or experienced. If they do, try to identify their relevance for you. Originally, they were probably things that you did to make your parents proud of or pleased with you. You may still believe that you are OK as long as you comply with them. Rank the drivers in order from those that most influence your life to those that are least applicable.

When all group members have completed their rankings, share with the group the top one or two drivers you listed. Discuss the feelings you get from trying to live up to these slogans. Are there ways in which you sabotage them? As long as your efforts fall short of your drivers, you will not feel OK about yourself.

Family stroking patterns

Purpose: This exercise is derived from the work of the Gouldings (Goulding & Goulding, 1979). It is used to increase an awareness of how family stroking patterns reinforce states of happiness or unhappiness.

Time required: 45 minutes.

Materials: None.

Preparation: The leader should be experienced since the exercise may generate strong feeling reactions.

Procedure: Assume a comfortable position and close your eyes. Imagine standing outside the house you lived in when you were a young child. Picture your family inside the house as they were then. Now imagine that you have just fallen down and skinned your knee. You run into the house sobbing with a little drop of blood running down your leg. Look at the expressions on the faces of your family members. What do they say? What are they feeling? What are they going to do?

Repeat the fantasy exercise for the following situations:

- You run into the house angry and shouting because an older child took your toy.
- You run into the house very afraid because you saw a big animal.
- You run into the house laughing and happy because you won a prize at school.
- You come into the house feeling very ashamed because you wet your pants and some big kids laughed at you.

At the conclusion of the exercise, open your eyes and divide into pairs. Share your experiences. Are there feelings that were unacceptable in your home that you are now reluctant to acknowledge? Are there other feelings that were rewarded that you now use to manipulate others to get what you want?

Script identification

Purpose: This exercise is an introduction to life scripts and helps group members identify ongoing patterns of behavior they may wish to change.

Time required: 1 hour.

Materials: None.

Preparation: The leader should be experienced since the exercise can generate strong feeling reactions.

Procedure: Divide into smaller groups of four or five persons each. Within the smaller groups think about your responses to the following questions [James, 1977]:

- What happens to people like me?
- If I go on as I am now, what will be the logical outcome?
- What will other people say about me when it's all over?

Go around the small group and share as much of your responses to the questions as you wish. These responses may have their source in decisions about your life that you made long ago. You may wish to reexamine these decisions at this time.

The following questions are also useful in identifying life scripts and may be added to the exercise:

- What was your favorite childhood story or fairy tale?
- What is the family story about your birth?
- How were you named?
- What might it say on your tombstone to capsulize your life?

TA contracting

Purpose: This exercise is an introduction to contracting and an invitation to make specific changes in the direction of growth and autonomy.

Time required: 1 hour or more.

Materials: Paper and pencil.

Preparation: The leader should be familiar with the process of contracting.

Procedure: Write your personal answers to the following questions on paper:

- What, specifically, would you like for yourself to enhance your life?
- What needs to be done to make it happen?
- What are you willing to do?
- How will you and others know that you've gotten it?
- How are you likely to sabotage yourself?

These are the steps involved in drawing a good TA contract for change. When everyone has completed their answers to the questions, spend the remaining group time sharing and clarifying your contracts with other group members.

SKILL-TRAINING GROUPS (ASSERTIVENESS TRAINING)

Assertive, nonassertive, and aggressive responses

Purpose: Prior to learning and rehearsing assertive skills, it is necessary to have a conceptual understanding of an assertive response. This exercise will help group members distinguish assertiveness from aggression and nonassertiveness.

Time required: 1 hour.

Materials: None.

Preparation: None.

Procedure: Each group member is asked to demonstrate a nonassertive response, an aggressive response, and an assertive response to a given hypothetical situation. For example, imagine that a friend has "forgotten" to return some money he borrowed from you. With an aggressive response you might say "Damn it! I knew I couldn't trust you to pay me back when you said you would. I want my money!" Nonassertively, you could say "I know I'm bugging you, but do you think maybe you could try to bring the money sometime soon?" An assertive response might be "I thought we agreed that you would pay me back today. I would appreciate you bringing the money by Friday at the latest."

Try to involve everyone, even if it means that each member only offers one of the three responses. Use one situation per person. In role-playing a response, it may help you to identify with the most aggressive, assertive or nonassertive person you know. Remember that your nonverbal behavior tells as much as your verbal behavior, so try to keep your tone of voice and body position congruent with your words. Using the situations listed below, ask for volunteers or go around the group. Following a participant's turn, solicit feedback from the group about the assertive or aggressive qualities of the response. Remember that there are no correct answers and that a good discussion can be very informative.

The leader or the group may wish to generate additional situations like the ones below:

- A friend keeps engaging you in conversation and you want to leave. You say....
- You are in a restaurant and your rare steak arrives at the table well done. You tell the waiter....
- Your bill for automobile repairs is $25 higher than the estimate. You tell the service manager....
- You catch the eye of an attractive person of the opposite sex and know that he or she might be interested in you. You walk over and say....
- Your neighbor's dog has been using your front lawn as a sandbox. You approach your neighbor and say....
- Your roommate has fixed you up with a blind date without consulting you. You tell him or her....
- The people behind you in the movie theatre are disturbing you with their loud conversation. You say to them....
- You've been seated at a fancy restaurant and decide that you don't like the table you were given. You tell the host or hostess....
- A man (woman) you know asks you out and you're not particularly interested in going out with him (her). You say....
- A friend asks you to borrow your car and you don't trust his driving. You say to him....
- A friend keeps embarrassing you in public by telling stories about you. You say....

Conversational skill training

Purpose: Nonassertive persons are often deficient in basic communication skills. This exercise, adapted from Kelley (1978), can reduce anxiety about engaging in social conversation and can allow for practice in communication skills.

Time required: 30 minutes.

Materials: None.

Preparation: No special training is required.

Procedure: Divide the group randomly into pairs. In the first stage, one person in each pair is only allowed to ask *open-ended questions*. Open-ended questions allow your partner to respond more fully (for example, "Do you live on campus?" is a closed question; "Where are you living?" is more open ended). The other person in each pair responds to each question by self-disclosing *free information,* that is, information about the self that is not solicited and goes beyond strictly answering the question (for example, "I live on campus" is not very informative; "I live on campus in one of those new coed dormitories and share a room with two other women" provides a lot of free information about the person). Stay in role for about five minutes, then reverse roles for five more minutes, so that both partners can practice asking open-ended questions and offering free information.

In the second stage of the exercise, one member of each pair begins by volunteering free information or describing a personal experience. The second person attempts to prolong the conversation either by *asking for clarification* or *paraphrasing.* In other words, you put the free information in your own words to show that you are listening (for example, the first member may offer "I took a walk around campus last night to areas I hadn't seen before." The partner might respond "You mean you were surprised how large the campus is?"). After five minutes of dialogue, reverse roles.

In between the two stages of the exercise allow time for the pairs to share their experiences and difficulties. As you become more able and willing to self-disclose, ask questions that allow for a broad range of responses. By using active-listening techniques, you will master the art of conversation.

Relaxation training

Purpose: Relaxation training is probably the most universally used behavioral skill. It can be used as part of an assertiveness-training program, to reduce inhibitions, or to combat specific fears or anxiety in general.

Time required: 30 minutes or more.

Materials: Relaxation tapes or a trained leader.

Preparation: If tapes are not used, the leader should be experienced in relaxation training.

Procedure: Commercial relaxation tapes are readily available, or the group leader can use the following instructions to guide the members. Leaders should use a calm, relaxed tone of voice and stress the ebbing away of tension throughout the exercise.

Sit in a comfortable chair with your arms at your sides, your hands on your lap, and your feet on the floor. Alternatively, lie on your back on the floor. Keep your eyes closed. Take two or three slow, deep breaths, noticing the passage of air into and out of your lungs and diaphragm. Now hold out your right arm and make a tight fist with your right hand. Notice the tension in your fist as you tighten it. After 5–10 seconds of concentrating on the tension, relax your hand. Undo the fist and notice how the tension recedes and sensations of relaxation and comfort take its place. Focus on the difference between the tension and the relaxation. After about 15–20 seconds, make a fist of your right hand again, study the tension for 5–10 seconds and relax. Feel the relaxation and warmth. After 15–20 seconds, repeat the procedure with your left hand. Be sure to focus only on the muscle group you're tensing and relaxing and try not to tense the rest of your body at the same time.

Take your time and use the same tension/relaxation cycle to relax the following muscle groups:

- your arms, by bending each arm to stretch the bicep muscle
- your arms, by straightening each arm to stretch the tricep muscle
- your shoulders, by hunching them
- your neck, by bringing your head forward and digging your chin into your chest
- your mouth, by opening it as wide as possible
- your tongue, by pushing it against the roof of your mouth
- your eyes, by closing them tightly
- your forehead, by raising your eyebrows as high as possible
- your back, by arching it and pushing your chest forward (careful if you have back problems!)
- your buttocks, by contracting the muscles
- your stomach, by sucking it in toward your backbone
- your thighs, by extending your legs and raising them a few inches off the floor
- your calves, by pushing your toes against the top of your shoes

In each case, be sure to relax fully by letting go of all tension in each muscle grouping. Complete the exercise by taking two or three deep breaths and feeling the relaxation flow through your body from your arms to your shoulders to your chest to your midsection and through your legs. When you feel ready to open your eyes, count backwards slowly from 10 to 1. With each number, feel yourself becoming more and more refreshed and alert.

The tension/relaxation cycle can also be practiced at home. As you become better at it, you can speed up the procedure by relaxing, without first tensing, all the different parts of the body.

Behavioral contracts

Purpose: This exercise exemplifies the behavioral goal setting that is characteristic of skill-training groups. It encourages the description of problems in specific, observable terms and offers practice in shaping and reinforcement.

Time required: 1 hour or more.

Materials: None.

Preparation: It is helpful if the leader has experience in behavior therapy.

Procedure: Group members choose specific behaviors that they wish to change *within* the group.

Choose a behavior that is apt to occur frequently as part of the group's natural process. The behavior may, but need not be, an assertiveness skill.

Common examples include speaking up, interrupting, making eye contact, criticizing, smiling inappropriately, nail biting, and so on. Choose a behavior that is easily observable, concrete, and not too complex. Try to state your goal in positive terms rather than in terms of what you want to stop doing. For instance, listening more is a positive way to say talking less. Also tell group members exactly how you would like them to provide feedback. Perhaps you want the feedback to come from specific group members, or at a particular time, or in a particular way.

You will probably need at least an hour of group time to decide on individual behavioral targets. Feedback on the behaviors can be given spontaneously during subsequent group sessions, or time can be set aside explicitly for feedback. It is important for the group to acknowledge and positively reinforce any improvement in the behavior the person has chosen.

Behavior-rehearsal exercises

Purpose: Behavior rehearsal constitutes the core of assertiveness training. This exercise, patterned in part on Lange and Jakubowski (1976), offers a good introduction to the behavior rehearsal procedure. It paves the way to more complex and realistic rehearsals later in the group.

Time required: 1½–2 hours.

Materials: Paper and pencils.

Preparation: It is helpful if the leader is experienced in behavior rehearsal and assertiveness training.

Procedure: Think of a hypothetical situation you would like to master assertively and write it down. You may wish to spend a few minutes brainstorming as a group to come up with ideas, though the situation chosen by each person should be personally meaningful. Most likely the situations will include aspects of making or refusing requests, handling criticism, or communicating positive or negative feelings. Next, divide the group into subgroups of five or six persons each. People in each subgroup volunteer to begin by very briefly describing a stressful situation they have identified, such as approaching roommates about picking up their clothes.

Structure the situation by choosing a member of your small group to role-play the other person (roommate) in the interaction. If you are the volunteer, communicate your message as assertively as possible. After a couple of minutes, pause and allow the other members of your subgroup to offer specific, positive, behavioral feedback on your performance. Then state what you yourself liked about your performance and specify any changes or additions you would like to make. If you are stuck, listen to suggestions from the others. Next, another group member assumes the roommate role, and work on the interaction continues. After a couple of minutes rehearsing with this partner, allow time again for positive feedback and suggestions. Keep going so that you give each person in your group a chance to role-play the other person in the interaction. As you improve and begin to master the situation, the other person escalates the stressfulness of the encounter by being more persistent or antagonistic. It is important, however, to allow the asserter to win each encounter and enjoy a positive experience.

REFERENCES

Bednar, R. L., & Melnick, J. Risk, responsibility and structure: A conceptual framework for initiating group counseling and psychotherapy. *Journal of Counseling Psychology*, 1974, *21*, 31–37.

Challis, E. *Freedom is a constant struggle: Moving from stereotype to personhood in a male-female consciousness-raising workshop*. Unpublished doctoral dissertation, Union Graduate School, 1974.

Cohn, R. C. Style and spirit of the theme-centered interactional method. In C. J. Sager & H. S. Kaplan (Eds.), *Progress in group and family therapy*. New York: Brunner/Mazel, 1972. .

Goulding, M. M., & Goulding, R. L. *Changing lives through redecision therapy*. New York: Brunner/Mazel, 1979.

James, M. *Techniques in transactional analysis*. Reading, Mass.: Addison-Wesley, 1977.

Kelley, C. *Assertion training*. La Jolla, Calif.: University Associates, 1978.

Lange, A. J., & Jakubowski, P. *Responsible assertive behavior*. Champaign, Ill.: Research Press, 1976.

Morris, K. T., & Cinnamon, K. M. (Eds.), *Controversial issues in human relations training groups*. Springfield, Ill.: Charles C Thomas, 1976.

Pfeiffer, J. W., & Jones, J. E. (Eds.), *The 1975 annual handbook for group facilitators*. San Diego, Calif.: University Associates, 1975.

Rhyne, J. *The Gestalt art experience*. Monterey, Calif.: Brooks/Cole, 1973.

Satir, V. *Peoplemaking*. Palo Alto, Calif.: Science & Behavior Books, 1972.

Schutz, W. *Here comes everybody: Bodymind and encounter culture*. New York: Harper & Row, 1971.

Stevens, J. O. *Awareness: Exploring, experimenting, experiencing*. Lafayette, Calif.: Real People Press, 1971.

Wilson, B. J. The creative person's group. In H. Ruitenbeck (Ed.), *Group therapy today*. New York: Atherton, 1969.

13

Summary
and Perspectives

A Sufi story tells of three blind men who encounter a huge elephant and attempt to determine the form, shape, and true character of the animal by touching and exploring it with their hands. The first blind man feels an ear and reports that the elephant is a large, rough thing, wide and broad, like a rug. The second man gropes along the trunk and insists the elephant is formed like a straight and hollow pipe. The third man explores the feet and legs and determines that the elephant is mighty and firm like a pillar. Of course, no single description of the elephant is the definitive one; each blind man is equally correct and equally wrong in his judgment. Similarly, we have examined ten distinct models of the experiential group. Each of these models describes the use of small groups for interpersonal exploration and behavior change. In theory and approach, each reaches slightly different conclusions about the nature of the beast. This chapter presents a brief summary of the defining characteristics of ten approaches to the experiential group, followed by some dimensions for comparison and a statement about the current status of the field.

SUMMARY OF GROUP MODELS

T-groups were among the first deliberately constituted groups meeting for a limited period with a designated leader for self-inquiry and interpersonal learning and growth. T-groups grew out of the Lewinian tradition of action research and experience-based learning, whereby group members could experiment with new behaviors and receive immediate feedback from fellow participants. Fundamental T-group concepts include the notions of a *learning laboratory* and *learning how to learn*, and the principles of *presentation of self, feedback, experimentation*, and the *here-and-now*. The trainer of the traditional T-group plays an indirect leadership role so that the group members democratically share responsibility for the progress of the group in meeting its task goals. These goals have generally included interpersonal skill development and the study of small group processes. The latter goal is especially prominent in Tavistock groups, the British cousin to the T-group, in which the leader is more of an aloof, psychoanalytically trained observer of the group than a role model of openness, trust, and affective involvement. Later on, the sensitivity-group wing of the T-group movement courted the total enhancement of the individual participant. One contribution of T-groups is its promotion of understanding of psychological processes among a large segment of society.

Encounter groups emerged on the frontier of T-groups, sparked by the dynamic leadership of individuals such as William Schutz and Carl Rogers. Encounter groups generated more of a public stir than other experiential groups because they dealt with controversial, seemingly revolutionary ideas such as the display of strong emotions in public and the search for immediate intimacy. They were heavily promoted at a time (the late 1960s) when a counterculture cried out for a sense of community and an antidote to feelings of estrangement and alienation from society at large. Encounter groups aim for authenticity in relationships and the total enhancement of the individual. Central concepts in this experiential adventure include *self-disclosure, self-awareness*, including body awareness, a strong emphasis on *individual responsibility, attention to feelings*, and a commitment to focusing on the *here-and-now*. The format of the encounter group is often shaped by the leader's personality. Some leaders, such as Rogers, are relatively gentle and accepting, whereas others are more probing and confronting. Encounter groups have broadened the concept of psychotherapy from a strictly healing model to include awareness and improved communication. The active risk taking encouraged in encounter has led to greater experimentation in subsequent group approaches.

The Gestalt group has been closely identified with its founder, Fritz Perls. The Gestalt group was one of the first approaches to make no distinction between growth and psychotherapy. The goal in either case is to reawaken the organismic process within the group member: awareness shall set the person free to find new and more fulfilling behavioral alternatives. The underlying concepts of Gestalt include *figure and ground, awareness* and *present-centeredness, polarities, safety functions*, and *maturity*. Basically, individuals are thought to use safety functions such as introjection, projection, and retroflection to block awareness of anxiety-arousing dimensions of themselves. Gestalt therapists use a number of awareness experiments to awaken the group member to undiscovered potentials and hidden aspects of the self. Gestalt therapy in groups was originally conducted as individual work within a group setting. Contemporary Gestalt leaders are becoming more oriented to making active use of the group process and Gestalt remains a popular and influential approach.

Psychodrama has a lengthy history emanating from the specific contributions of Jacob Moreno, who is sometimes credited with being the founder of group psychotherapy. Psychodrama may have been the first group approach to move beyond the purely verbal mode since its roots are in the theater. Basic concepts include *role-playing, spontaneity, tele, catharsis*, and *insight*. The group member is encouraged to have an emotional experience leading to insight and behavior change by reliving or extending an important personal or interpersonal issue in dramatic form. The action techniques originated by Moreno to facilitate this process are now found in many experiential groups.

The body therapies consist of a heterogeneous collection of group methods that have a common commitment to studying the intricate relationship between psychological and physical process, such as how individuals move and hold their muscles. The popularity of body therapies emerged in a reaction to the limitations of purely verbal and cerebral therapies. The body therapies include the seminal contributions of Wilhelm Reich, the bioenergetic approach of Alexander Lowen, primal therapy, the Alexander technique, structural integration (Rolfing), and the Feldenkrais method. Many of the individual contributors were not originally psychologists or psychotherapists at all, but trained in fields having to do with the body and physical processes. The basic concepts that tie their work together include *energy, muscular armoring*, and *grounding*. The notion of catharsis also plays an important role in body therapies since attention to the body and manipulating it is thought to release feelings and insights that encourage behavior change. Techniques contributed by body therapists during the past two decades are frequently used in conjunction with verbal group approaches.

Dance therapy and art therapy are specialized group approaches that require training in particular artistic disciplines. Both methods grew out of a psychoanalytic tradition and were primarily used adjunctively to verbal psychotherapy. They supply a nonverbal way of skirting deficiencies in verbal skills and cutting through the defensiveness of patients. In recent years both the theory base and the client base have been extended considerably to make dance therapy and art therapy more clearly experiential group approaches that offer growth opportunities in their own rights. Humanistic leaders have taken the disciplines beyond their psychoanalytic roots, and application of art and dance therapy methods has spread from hospitals and institutions to other educational and therapeutic settings.

Basic to dance therapy is the study of *body/mind* and the use of *spontaneous movement* to facilitate change. The group leader encourages movement, which, in turn, leads to heightened body awareness, contact with emotions, social skill development, and feelings of greater self-worth.

In art therapy, a focus on *spontaneous painting and modeling* is fundamentally important, as is the psychoanalytic concept of *sublimation*. Art has been used in groups as an outlet for catharsis, as a vehicle for diagnosis and interpretation, as a means to establish a therapeutic relationship, and as a method to increase body awareness and improved self-image.

The theme-centered interaction (TCI) group was the contribution of Ruth Cohn, and is another experiential and humanistic approach with some debt to psychodynamic thinking. The basic concepts of TCI groups are the ideas of *living/learning, transference, countertransference, theme,* and *dynamic balancing.* The leader in the TCI group is very much a participant/leader who serves as a guardian of the method to keep the group members invested in both the theme and each other. The Gestalt sense of personal responsibility is evident in TCI groups through communication guidelines advanced by the leader, such as being one's own chairperson and speaking for oneself. The interdependence of the participants is acknowledged through the process of sharing themselves around a stated theme. TCI groups are not as well known as other experiential groups in North America but they have an extremely broad range of application.

Transactional analysis was Eric Berne's creation, growing out of his disillusionment with the efficacy of traditional psychoanalytic group therapy. TA is a popular, pragmatic, and optimistic group method. Basic concepts include *ego states* (structural analysis), *transactions, games,* and *scripts.* TA leaders negotiate contracts with individual group members to select target goals for change and steps to take to achieve the goals. The group leader gives participants permission to experiment with new behaviors, provides protection and support to members when they experience excessive discomfort, and draws upon a variety of potent, active techniques to further therapeutic progress. Today TA practitioners have branched into many different offshoots of the original method and incorporated techniques found in other experiential groups into what was initially a cognitive approach.

Finally, skill-training groups represent a behavioral orientation that highlights the study of observable behaviors and deemphasizes the exploration and awareness of strong feelings. Skill-training groups carry as basic concepts the idea of an *educational model* (as opposed to a medical or therapeutic model), *measurement and evaluation,* and *goal setting.* Skill-training groups can be viewed as experiential in that behaviors are relived and practiced within the here-and-now setting of the group, and members are encouraged to give their reactions to one another. Assertiveness training is a good example of the skill-training group. Structured techniques are used to assess and encourage appropriate assertive behavior, leading to a greater sense of personal responsibility and behavior potential. The actual techniques used in the group may include methods shared with other approaches, such as the role-playing of psychodrama and the relaxation training of body-therapy groups. The rationale for using these methods may be different, however. For example, role-playing in psychodrama is done less for behavioral practice than to release feelings associated with disturbing past events. There is reason to believe that the structured format of the skill-training groups is gaining in popularity.

The basic concepts characteristic of each type of experiential group are summarized in Table 13-1.

TABLE 13–1.   Basic concepts of experiential groups

Groups	Basic concepts
T-groups	learning laboratory learning how to learn presentation of self feedback experimentation here-and-now
Encounter	self-disclosure self-awareness individual responsibility attention to feelings here-and-now
Gestalt	figure and ground awareness present centeredness polarities safety functions maturity
Psychodrama	role-playing spontaneity tele catharsis insight
Body therapies	energy muscular armoring grounding
Dance therapy	body-mind spontaneous movement
Art therapy	spontaneous painting and modeling sublimation
Theme-centered interaction	living-learning transference and counter transference theme dynamic balancing
Transactional analysis	ego states transactions games scripts
Skill training	educational model measurement and evaluation goal-setting

COMPARISONS AMONG GROUP MODELS

Comparing experiential groups is made difficult because there is frequently as much diversity within a given approach as there is between any two approaches. Therefore, any reasonable comparison among the approaches assumes a "pure" form of each type, uncontaminated by exposure to the influence of other types and unadvanced by more progressive practitioners representing the type.

In the introductory chapter, experiential groups were compared along the dimensions of rational thinking/affective spontaneity and leader-centered/member-centered. It was mentioned that experiential groups also differ along lines of goal orientation (information versus insight, for example), structure, duration, and clientele (Cohen & Smith, 1976). The great majority of groups described in this book are person- or insight-oriented as opposed to information- or task-oriented. The most obvious example of a task-oriented group might be a T-group designed for organizational development and problem solving. Some skill-training groups also concentrate on disseminating information about certain behavioral deficits, such as groups for acquiring dating skills or managing stress.

Each type of group can be either short-term or ongoing, depending upon the needs of the participants and the reality constraints imposed upon them and the leader. Encounter groups, in particular, are often single-shot weekend affairs. Theme-centered interaction groups frequently employ a single session of a few hours. T-groups have historically been part of a residential setting, lasting a week or more. The other experiential groups can be offered in single sessions but more commonly are organized on at least a weekly basis and last many weeks. Some, such as a skill-training group or a primal-therapy group, may offer a fixed course extending a few weeks or months. When an experiential group constitutes all or part of a training program or a psychotherapy process with individuals suffering significant emotional problems, it can be extended indefinitely as some members leave and new members join. Toward the end of his life, Fritz Perls was urging that Gestalt therapy be part of a total community experience in which members would live together as well as participate in growth groups together.

It has been pointed out that the distinction between healthy and disturbed participants has become increasingly blurred, as has the distinction between growth and therapy. A recent study by Morton Lieberman (1977) found that individuals entering experiential groups are higher than the normative population on stress and psychological symptoms. The majority of members of encounter groups and the other new group forms attend, in part, for assistance with personal problems. For them the human-potential movement offers help with life problems. T-groups, by definition, are reserved for nonclinical populations. The other experiential groups may address either type of audience and tailor group goals and methods accordingly. For example, teaching assertiveness skills to college students is different from teaching job-hunting skills to former mental patients, though the basic strategies and underlying concepts are the same. Likewise, the games and scripts that characterize a university population may be somewhat less self-destructive than those that pertain to a seriously pathological group, but the principles of TA are equally relevant. A humanistic approach to art therapy may easily stimulate creativity, self-exploration and interpersonal communication in a community group; analytically based art therapy can similarly be used to diagnose or encourage verbalizations in hospitalized patients. In TCI groups the theme for a group of teachers (such as "Finding New Ways of Contacting My Students") would most likely be different from a theme selected for outpatients (for example, "Dealing With Anger"), though the strategy of running the group would be similar. In either case dynamic balancing would preclude intensive psychotherapeutic work with one individual.

In psychodrama, university students and mental patients might both enact childhood situations of neglect and abuse, though one might expect the intensity and effect of the abuse to be greater in the clinical group. In Gestalt groups the type and depth of feelings that are defended against and the mechanisms used to deny them might vary, but the techniques for fostering awareness and resolving interpersonal conflicts are the same. In body-therapy groups, armoring might hide different levels of psychic pain, though the methods for releasing energy and insight are similar. In dance therapy the level of body awareness and the inhibition of spontaneous movement would differ depending upon the client population, so that the pace of promoting awareness and encouraging movement would also differ. In encounter groups, distinctions among participants are too often neglected, though the conscientious leader would push the disturbed member less, offer more support, and remain sensitive to the time limitations of the group experience. Of course, competent leaders of all experiential groups will declare some potential members as inappropriate because of their own lack of clinical experience or skill, the group's membership or structure, or the individual's need for individual attention or a different approach.

The amount of structure found in an experiential group depends to some extent upon the type of group and is also instructive of a possible trend in the practice of small groups. Structure refers to the extent to which goals and an agenda are clarified prior to and during the group experience. Structure is not necessarily related to the level of activity or input of the leader. A Gestalt leader, for example, is generally very direct and active, but the flow of the group depends very much upon the immediate phenomenological awareness and concerns of the members and cannot be specified beforehand. A traditional Rolfing experience, on the other hand, is composed of ten separate sessions focusing on a distinct segment of the body and gives a definite structure to the group experience. Primal therapy groups may vary greatly in structure (Freundlich, 1979). In transactional analysis, participants typically work on specific contracts and report their progress in a session, again giving the group a framework within which many unpredictable experiences may occur for a given individual and among the participants. Psychodrama leaders may also choose to move systematically through the membership in initiating role-playing situations or may be free flowing and loose in format.

Skill-training groups are certainly the most structured groups. Each skill-training session might have a particular focus stated in advance. T-groups have historically been an unstructured part of a larger, structured-learning laboratory in the sense that members have been free to develop their own agendas and procedures while the leader offers some support and guidance but little direction. It has been shown, however, that even the most unstructured groups typically move through a predictable sequence of stages as they define themselves and the relationships among members. T-groups now conducted in organizations and in the community are more focused and structured. Specific experiential-learning exercises are often selected by the leader, sometimes in conjunction with the members, to allow them to tackle particular issues and reach definable goals.

In some ways, then, the chapters in this book come full circle and the structure found in behavioral skill-training groups forms a bridge to research-based but more humanistic T-groups. One of the reasons for the increasing popularity of some behavioral procedures within humanistic groups is the realization that to have a permanent effect on members, the group must help the participant behave differently in the real world. Specific action programs to promote change beyond the group experience are welcome additions to the interpersonal growth process of many experiential groups (Egan, 1975).

FUTURE CONSIDERATIONS

Therapists operating from very different theoretical orientations have historically been blind to one another's contributions and reluctant to acknowledge the potential benefits to be gained from cross-fertilization of their views. This myopic attitude has been very evident in the lingering clash between behavioral and humanistic therapy models in psychology. It has also been apparent in the reluctance of traditional, psychodynamic group therapy to greet and acknowledge the presence of the newer group therapies described in this book. In spite of persistent efforts by many veteran representatives of the mental health professions to denigrate their legitimacy, experiential groups cannot easily be distinguished from traditional group therapy on the basis of their clientele or their practitioners' credentials (Lieberman, 1977).

Most recent innovations in group practice tend to derive from the newer, experiential group forms. Gradually some of these innovations percolate down to the more formal types of group psychotherapy, where their impact is widespread. An excellent example is the increased transparency and involvement of the group leader today (Lubin, Lubin & Taylor,

1978). The newer groups have lessened the distance between group members and the leader through mechanisms such as informal settings and increases in therapists' self-disclosure, participation, and physical contact. Consequently, graduates of these groups are no longer receptive to remote and rigid group leaders. The experiential group movement has also generated an explosion in self-help groups—for example, attacking the common concerns of students or family members of alcoholics.

It has recently been suggested that though it may be difficult, if not impossible, to reconcile some theoretical differences among orientations, it may be time to seek a rapprochement at the level of strategies or principles of change (Goldfried, 1980). Two strategies cited by Marvin Goldfried as possibly common to all psychotherapy schools are (1) providing the client with new, corrective experiences, and (2) offering the client direct feedback. I believe that these two features are particularly common to experiential groups. It is a central characteristic of these groups that participants engage in novel, corrective experiences. Group members are forever encouraged to explore behavioral options and risk trying something new, whether it be movement in a dance-therapy group, disclosing hidden parts of themselves in an encounter or T-group, or attempting an assertive response in a skill-training group. Even in contemporary Gestalt groups awareness is not enough. The group member is given "the opportunity for relevant practice in behaviors he may be avoiding. Through his own discoveries in trying out these behaviors, he will uncover aspects of himself which in their turn will generate further self-discovery" (Polster & Polster, 1973, p. 252).

Second, experiential groups give participants direct feedback to promote a greater awareness of current thoughts, feelings, and actions and to offer the opportunity for change. The availability of feedback from a variety of other individuals is, of course, one of the unique advantages of the group format and one of the key reasons for its proliferation. In behavioral groups, the feedback may be meticulously precise and based on specific record keeping. In other groups the feedback may range from the direct confrontation of some encounter groups to the more nondirective reflection of feelings in a Rogerian group. Both the group leader and the other members are there to provide ongoing feedback, and developing the skill to do so constructively is sometimes an explicit group goal.

The power of the group to influence individual behavior through the process of feedback can be a disadvantage of the group format, in that the individual is potentially vulnerable to group pressure (Shaffer & Galinsky, 1974). Experiential groups have various mechanisms for safeguarding participants from the intrusive influence of the group: encounter group leaders offer warnings about personal responsibility to resist unwanted pressure; TCI group leaders use periods of silence and reflection; transactional-analysis and skill-training group leaders employ individual contracts and goal setting; some Gestalt and body-therapy leaders discourage group interruptions as they work with individual members; T-group leaders provide concrete guidelines for giving and receiving feedback. Most of all, experiential groups work toward the development of independent thinking integrated with interpersonal cooperation and intimacy.

There is always the temptation to conclude a survey of different models of a phenomenon such as the experiential group by naming one as the best approach. Rather than fall into that trap, it is wise to remember that at this stage of development, the conduct of a group is as much art as science. In this light, the art of group therapy can be compared to the art of composing and performing music (Frank, 1979). To ask whether psychodrama or Gestalt is better is as futile as asking the same about Beethoven and Bach. We can always rate the composers on the specifics of volume and rhythm and harmony, but in the end it is the listeners who must say if they have been well served.

REFERENCES

Cohen, A. M., & Smith, R. D. *The critical incident in growth groups: Theory and technique.* La Jolla, Calif.: University Associates, 1976.

Egan, G. *The skilled helper.* Monterey, Calif.: Brooks/Cole, 1975.

Fiedler, F. E. A comparison of therapeutic relationships in psychoanalytic, nondirective and Adlerian therapy. *Journal of Consulting Psychology,* 1950, *14,* 436–445.

Frank, J. D. Thirty years of group therapy: A personal perspective. *International Journal of Group Psychotherapy,* 1979, *29,* 439–452.

Freundlich, D. Primal experience groups: A flexible structure. *International Journal of Group Psychotherapy,* 1979, *29,* 29–38.

Goldfried, M. Toward the delineation of therapeutic change principles. *American Psychologist,* 1980, *35,* 991–999.

Lieberman, M. A. Problems in integrating traditional group therapies with new group forms. *International Journal of Group Psychotherapy,* 1977, *27,* 19–32.

Lubin, B., Lubin, A. W., & Taylor, A. The group psychotherapy literature: 1978. *International Journal of Group Psychotherapy,* 1978, *28,* 523–576.

Polster, E., & Polster, M. *Gestalt therapy integrated.* New York: Brunner/Mazel, 1973.

Shaffer, J. B. P., & Galinsky, M. D. *Models of group therapy and sensitivity training.* New York: Prentice-Hall, 1974.

Appendix

Lost at Sea Answer and Rationale Sheet

According to the "experts," the basic supplies needed when a person is stranded in mid ocean are articles to attract attention and articles to aid survival until rescuers arrive. Articles for navigation are of little importance: Even if a small life raft were capable of reaching land, it would be impossible to store enough food and water to subsist during that period of time. Therefore, of primary importance are the shaving mirror and the two-gallon can of oil-gas mixture. These items could be used for signaling air-sea rescue. Of secondary importance are items such as water and food—e.g., the case of Army C-rations.

A brief rationale is provided for the ranking of each item. These brief explanations obviously do not represent all of the potential uses for the specified items but, rather, the primary importance of each.

1. Shaving mirror
   Critical for signaling air-sea rescue.
2. Two-gallon can of oil-gas mixture
   Critical for signaling—the oil-gas mixture will float on the water and could be ignited with a dollar bill and a match (obviously, outside the raft).
3. Five-gallon can of water
   Necessary to replenish loss of fluid through perspiration, etc.

Reprinted from: J. E. Jones and J. W. Pfeiffer (Eds.), *The 1975 Annual Handbook for Group Facilitators*. San Diego, CA: University Associates, 1975. Used with permission.

4. One case of U.S. Army C rations
   Provides basic food intake.
5. Twenty square feet of opaque plastic
   Utilized to collect rain water, provide shelter from the elements.
6. Two boxes of chocolate bars
   A reserve food supply.
7. Fishing kit
   Ranked lower than the candy bars because "one bird in the hand is worth two in the bush." There is no assurance that you will catch any fish.
8. Fifteen feet of nylon rope
   May be used to lash equipment together to prevent it from falling overboard.
9. Floating seat cushion.
   If someone fell overboard, it could function as a life preserver.
10. Shark repellent
    Obvious.
11. One quart of 160-proof Puerto Rican rum
    Contains 80 percent alcohol—enough to use as a potential antiseptic for any injuries incurred; of little value otherwise; will cause dehydration if ingested.
12. Small transistor radio
    Of little value since there is no transmitter (unfortunately, you are out of range of your favorite AM radio stations).
13. Maps of the Pacific Ocean
    Worthless without additional navigational equipment—it does not really matter where you are but where the rescuers are.
14. Mosquito netting
    There are no mosquitoes in the mid Pacific.
15. Sextant
    Without tables and a chronometer, relatively useless.

The basic rationale for ranking signaling devices above life-sustaining items (food and water) is that without signaling devices there is almost no chance of being spotted and rescued. Furthermore, most rescues occur during the first thirty-six hours, and one can survive without food and water during this period.

Name Index

Subject Index